Beyond Theory

ALSO BY BENJAMIN BENNETT

Beyond Theory

Eighteenth-Century German Literature and the Poetics of Irony

BENJAMIN BENNETT

Cornell University Press · Ithaca and London

First published 1993 by Cornell University Press.

International Standard Book Number 0-8014-2841-6
Library of Congress Catalog Card Number 92-46530

Printed in the United States of America

Librarians: Library of Congress cataloging information appears on the last page of the book.

⊗ The paper in this book meets the minimum requirements of the American National Standard for Information Sciences—Permanence of Paper for Printed Library Materials, ANSI Z39.48-1984.

This book is dedicated to two men, Walter H. Sokel and Frank G. Ryder, who have in common a quality for which etymology suggests the term "prophetic." They speak not only with their own voices but with voices that in each "speak for" a preterpersonal spirit, a whole world of literary sensibility.

In Walter, it is that European spirit which is utterly at home in the literary universe, that sensibility for which, in the whole range of actual or conceivable writing, "nihil alienum est." It is knowledge in a form both self-evident and constantly self-astonishing, as if the pre-understanding posited by hermeneutic theory had somehow found its way into articulable experience, a knowledge that enjoys its formulations but is not addicted to them, and enjoys its texts in the manner I think Longinus means when he speaks of reading "as if we ourselves were the creators of what we hear."

In Frank, by contrast, the spirit that speaks is peculiarly American, a sensibility that treats literary phenomena as if it had found them washed up on the beach, as if the Constitution of literary studies were yet to be devised. No doubt there are silent depths of artifice in this attitude. But its results, when it is maintained at the level I call prophetic—such as the first substantial advance since antiquity in the understanding of poetic metrics, an analysis of our critical palate for verse—make us all into neophytes.

In any event, I have spent most of my working life, so to speak, between these men, and I trust them to understand me *exactly* when I sign myself,

Das Weltkind in der Mitten

Contents

Acknowledgments

I am deeply indebted to the people who have read drafts of chapters: Jane Brown, Volker Kaiser, Robert Leventhal, and Helmut Schneider, as well as a large number of graduate students at the University of Virginia. And I am grateful to the University of Virginia itself for giving me some time off after my years of drudgery as department chair. Parts of the book were developed from lectures and papers I read: on Goethe at Harvard in 1983, at Michigan in 1985, at Duke in 1986; on theater of the mind at Chicago in 1986; on irony at the M/MLA in 1989; on Herder for the International Herder Society in 1990; on Lenz at the AATG in 1991. I am grateful to the organizers of these events and to all who participated in the discussions. As usual, I am indebted to Bernhard Kendler and his colleagues at Cornell University Press, as well as to the anonymous consultants who read the manuscript. The consultants, whose suggestions were unusually probing and detailed, will find that in many cases I have altered the text to avoid raising the questions they pointed out, in order to hold the book down to a manageable length. I do not claim to have left those questions behind. There will be more books.

All translations are my own unless otherwise noted. The work of Peter J. Burgard, whose dissertation I refer to in footnotes, appeared in revised form, after the closing of my manuscript, as a book, *Idioms of Uncertainty: Goethe and the Essay* (University Park, Pa., 1992).

B. B.

Abbreviations

A&P	Ronald Taylor, ed. *Aesthetics and Politics*. London, 1977.
AR	Wolfgang Iser. *The Act of Reading: A Theory of Aesthetic Response*. Baltimore, 1978.
AW	Friedrich Gottlieb Klopstock. *Ausgewählte Werke*. Munich, 1962.
DF	Thomas Mann. *Doktor Faustus*. Frankfurt am Main, 1956.
DVLG	*Deutsche Vierteljahrsschrift für Literaturwissenschaft und Geistesgeschichte*
EG	Eric A. Blackall. *The Emergence of German as a Literary Language: 1700–1775*. 2d ed. Ithaca, 1978.
FA	Friedrich Hölderlin. *Sämtliche Werke*. Frankfurter Ausgabe. Edited by D. E. Sattler. Frankfurt am Main, 1975–.
FS	Friedrich Schlegel. *Charakteristiken und Kritiken I (1796–1801)*. Edited by Hans Eichner. Paderborn, 1967. = Volume 2 of the *Kritische Friedrich-Schlegel-Ausgabe*. Edited by Ernst Behler. 1958–.
GQ	*German Quarterly*
GSA	Friedrich Hölderlin. *Sämtliche Werke*. Große Stuttgarter Ausgabe. Edited by Friedrich Beißner. Stuttgart, 1943–.
H/A	Max Horkheimer and Theodor W. Adorno. *Dialektik der Aufklärung: Philosophische Fragmente*. 1947. Frankfurt am Main, 1969.
HS	*Die Hauptschriften zum Pantheismusstreit zwischen Jacobi und Mendelssohn*. Edited by Heinrich Scholz. Berlin, 1916.

HvK   Heinrich von Kleist. *Sämtliche Werke und Briefe*. Edited by Helmut Sembdner. 2 vols. 5th ed. Munich, 1970.

IR   Wolfgang Iser. *The Implied Reader: Patterns of Communication in Prose Fiction from Bunyan to Beckett*. Baltimore, 1974.

JJR   Jean-Jacques Rousseau. *Oeuvres complètes*. Edited by Bernard Gagnebin and Marcel Raymond. 4 vols. Paris, 1959–69.

JPS   J. P. Stern. *Hitler: The Führer and the People*. Berkeley and Los Angeles, 1975.

KuG   Theodor W. Adorno. "Kulturkritik und Gesellschaft." In his *Prismen*. Frankfurt am Main, 1976.

KW   *Kants Werke*. Akademie-Textausgabe. 9 vols. 1902ff. Reprint, Berlin, 1968.

L-M   *Gotthold Ephraim Lessings sämtliche Schriften*. Edited by Karl Lachmann and Franz Muncker. 23 vols. 3d ed. Stuttgart, 1886–1924.

LW   Jakob Michael Reinhold Lenz. *Werke und Briefe in drei Bänden*. Edited by Sigrid Damm. Munich, 1987.

LY   *Lessing Yearbook*

MdM   Michel de Montaigne. *Oeuvres complètes*. Edited by Albert Thibaudet and Maurice Rat. Paris, 1962.

MiN   Johann Georg Hamann. *Sämtliche Werke*. Edited by Josef Nadler. 6 vols. Vienna, 1949–57. ("Magus in Norden.")

MLN   *Modern Language Notes*

MM   Moses Mendelssohn. *Gesammelte Schriften*. Jubiläumsausgabe. 17 vols. 1929ff. Reprint, Berlin, 1971–.

NLH   *New Literary History*

NW   Friedrich Nietzsche. *Werke: Kritische Gesamtausgabe*. Edited by Giorgio Colli and Mazzino Montinari. Part 3, vol. 1. Berlin, 1972.

PdM   Paul de Man. *The Rhetoric of Romanticism*. New York, 1984.

PMLA   *Publications of the Modern Language Association*

SA   *Schillers Sämtliche Werke*. Säkular-Ausgabe. 16 vols. Stuttgart and Berlin, 1904.

SW   *Herders Sämmtliche Werke*. Edited by Bernhard Suphan. 33 vols. Berlin, 1877–1913.

WA   *Goethes Werke*. "Weimarer Ausgabe." 143 vols. Weimar, 1887–1918.

WMW   *Wilhelm Meisters Wanderjahre.* In Johann Wolfgang Goethe, *Sämt-liche Werke, Briefe, Tagebücher und Gespräche.* 40 (planned) vols. Deutscher Klassiker Verlag. Part 1, vol. 10. Frankfurt am Main, 1989.

Beyond Theory

Introduction:
The New and the Original
Eighteenth Century

Constellations are curious things. They have no being except in our naming of them, and yet they are among the most persistent identities in our cultural experience. Do those twisted celestial circuitboards never evoke *new* resonances, say in the postmodern mind? Is there no comfortable little cluster somewhere for us to name "Knowledge," vis-à-vis the bold asymmetrical scatter of "Information"? Are there no Paul Klee versions of Narrativity, Performativity, and Legitimation waiting to be discovered?

The constellations of history, the large chronological or conceptual structures by which we locate particular "events," have something of the same character. We know them to be arbitrarily redefinable, but we forget about actually redefining them, even where change is obviously called for, and even in the face of examples, such as the nineteenth-century invention of the Renaissance, that show how useful occasionally shifting the furniture can be. In fact, the arbitrariness of our articulation of history *impedes* change. How, if the structure is arbitrary to begin with, can we say that a particular change is "called for"? I try to answer this question with respect to a limited historical moment by interpreting in detail a number of poetic and parapoetic texts, mainly from late eighteenth-century Germany, and by showing that the interpretations require a revision of larger historical conceptions. This method is not unassailable, since interpretation itself is always historically conditioned. But I try to minimize the element of theoretical uncertainty by encircling my conclusions with a number of different arguments from different kinds of evidence.

Germany and the Eighteenth Century

I contend that we need a new eighteenth century: "need" in the sense that its lack creates unnecessary difficulties in our own literary thought, "new" in the sense that it has yet to be invented. But it must also be—we cannot get around this—the original eighteenth century, the way things actually were. However deeply we understand the rhetorical and historical conditioning of historical writing, we can never incorporate that understanding *into* our writing at a depth that actually silences or neutralizes the idea of objective accuracy. I claim, then, that the specific quality of writing and of intellectual culture in the eighteenth century is badly misunderstood and that the detailed examination of a number of (especially German) texts and intertexts provides a perspective from which this misunderstanding can be reduced.

A good deal of the work of discovering or inventing a new eighteenth century has already been done. A book of essays, mainly on British literature, bears the idea in its title: *The New Eighteenth Century: Theory, Politics, and English Literature*, edited by Felicity Nussbaum and Laura Brown.[1] And Suzanne Gearhart's *Open Boundary of History and Fiction*, by staging something like an actual debate between figures of the French Enlightenment and such modern thinkers as Michel Foucault, Hayden White, and Louis Althusser, uncovers an important part of the mechanism by which the eighteenth century has been forgotten.[2] Although I too locate my arguments historically by including a number of texts from outside the eighteenth century, I do not try to match Gearhart's methodological strength and directness. I do not think I need to, since the new

[1]Felicity Nussbaum and Laura Brown, eds.,*The New Eighteenth Century: Theory, Politics, English Literature* (New York, 1987). I think I am using the idea of a "new" eighteenth century in a somewhat more focused—not to say contentious—manner. Nussbaum and Brown still speak, for example, of a "dominant culture" and a "periphery" (p. 3). My point, concerning mainly German literature, is that our customary manner of gauging cultural dominance is questionable, that the eighteenth-century culture of irony was a good deal more deeply rooted and powerful than we are ordinarily willing to recognize.

[2]Suzanne Gearhart, *The Open Boundary of History and Fiction: A Critical Approach to the French Enlightenment* (Princeton, 1984).

eighteenth century (or the need for it) lies much closer to the surface in the mainly German texts I concentrate on.

It is, in any case, the eighteenth century in Germany that occupies me in this book, especially the emergence, late in the century, of a specifically German poetics of radical irony. But "specifically German" does not refer to the idea of a quasi-organic national culture. In fact, the idea of national cultures, from the early nineteenth century on, has been a major factor in obscuring the German eighteenth century. My point is that a number of historical accidents combine to produce a set of communicative conditions that favors the growth of the poetics I describe. It is clear pretty much on the face of it that the literary situation in late eighteenth-century Germany is more than just the German manifestation of broad tendencies in European culture. In my *Modern Drama and German Classicism*, for example, I argued that the development of the genre of drama in German Classicism had no parallel elsewhere in the Europe of its time.[3] My concern now is to unfold that German literary situation in more depth and detail.

Kant, Foucault, and the Articulation of Intellectual History

Let us begin by looking at how our historical view has become distorted. The eighteenth century, we are told, is the age of Enlightenment or Reason, the *Aufklärung* or *Siècle des lumières* (which all mean slightly different things). It includes the Restoration and Augustan periods in Britain, the different and differently situated European neoclassicisms. It is marked by the ascendancy of the novel, by "bourgeois" dramatic forms, by interest in folk poetry and balladry, by "aesthetic" theory. It exhibits a culture of sentiment, of philosophical narrative, of the letter, of "Privateness Oriented to an Audience,"[4] of *Sturm und Drang*, of pre-Romanticism, and so on. This profusion of attempts to characterize the century, it seems to me, is the symptom of a typical *structural* condition in intellectual histo-

---

[3]I refer to my *Modern Drama and German Classicism: Renaissance from Lessing to Brecht* (Ithaca, 1979).

[4]Jürgen Habermas, *The Structural Transformation of the Public Sphere: An Inquiry into a Category of Bourgeois Society*, trans. Thomas Burger and Frederick Lawrence (Cambridge, Mass., 1989; orig. 1962), p. 43.

riography, present with special clarity in Michel Foucault's *Order of Things*.

Despite the variety of texts, and of interesting juxtapositions of texts, used in his argument, and despite his focus on a notion of "representation" that is meant to grapple those texts at a point entirely beyond the reach of their own systematic insights and pretensions, the "Classical Age," for Foucault, is still anchored firmly at both ends, thus in effect defined, by the claims of epoch-making systematicity made by René Descartes and Immanuel Kant. For all his insistence that the epistemic shift from "Classical" to "modern" is a "profound breach," which, "though it must be analysed . . . cannot be 'explained,'"[5] Foucault still articulates intellectual history at exactly those points where it does appear to "explain" itself with the greatest systematic clarity. The advent of the modern *episteme*, as Foucault locates it, *can* in fact be "summed up," if not "in a single word," at least in a single phrase: the innovation in philosophical systematics made by Kant's *Critiques*.

Kant's position, in Foucault, seems ambiguous at first. On one hand, "The Kantian critique marks the threshold of our modernity. . . . [I]t sanctions for the first time that event in European culture which coincides with the end of the eighteenth century: the withdrawal of knowledge and thought outside the space of representation" (Foucault, p. 242). But on the other hand, Kant is relegated to the "first phase" of the modern turn, in which "words, classes, and wealth" do not yet "acquire a mode of being no longer compatible with representation" (p. 221), to that phase in which the problem of "a discourse whose tension would keep separate the empirical and the transcendental, while being directed at both" (p. 320), is not yet established. Kant does not yet operate in the presence of "that *not-known* from which man is perpetually summoned towards self-knowledge" (p. 323); he is still fascinated by "the transcendental motif that [he] had derived from Hume's critique" (p. 325). To an extent, by insisting in a particular way on the question "*Was ist der Mensch?*" Kant is even to blame for the besetting fault of modern thinking, "the sleep . . . of Anthropology" (p. 341).

Thus Kant is repeatedly shouldered out of the center of Foucault's historical plot—precisely because he *is* its center. Foucault's main methodological move, which is apparent on every page, is to restrict

[5]Michel Foucault, *The Order of Things* (New York, 1973; orig. French, 1966), p. 217.

himself scrupulously to what is *recorded* in the texts he deals with. When he quotes, he quotes in passing; he never remains with a single text long enough to become trapped in what it does *not* say. He always reaches the opposite shore on a skip, so to speak, and never needs to be fished up from the slimy bottom. He permits illustrative texts to protrude into his own discourse only to the extent that they make themselves heard, and in turn make that discourse itself heard, in moments where it threatens to slip out of earshot. An approach of this type must inevitably segment history wherever the loudest and most systematically self-assured voice emerges *within* history (a voice like Kant's), to proclaim its division. But that same voice, that same pretended historical punctuation, once its purpose has been served, must also be suppressed and decentered, lest its very audibility bridge the unbridgeable gulf we imagine it has created. Hence the strain in Foucault's relation to Kant. The Red Sea closes behind us; and our foreign leader, our Moses, is duly murdered, that the "profound breach" be closed behind us yet again, behind what *we* now are, and separating us by engulfment from the captive people that we, nevertheless, still *are*.

The present or post-Kantian age, for Foucault, is therefore discussible only in terms of negativities, but negativities that constantly look over their own shoulders at the idea of an inevitable (thus positive) negativity that is needed to mark its object as what we are still in the midst of being. Negativities, therefore, that are never negative enough. "The unthought," for example, is a crucial category in *The Order of Things* (pp. 322–28), but only as a general category, as it were skimmed from the boiling mixture, only (paradoxically) where it makes itself heard. Not the unthought in the sense of the *unrecorded*; not in the sense that we discover it only by fastening on a single text, which we pick apart doggedly until we reach its most resolute silence; not the unthought of *radical irony*, insisted on by an unthinking that does *not* make itself heard. And it is this irony— which appears only under cross-examination—that I trace in eighteenth-century poetic theory and discourse, especially that of the late eighteenth century in Germany, in a discourse that does not pretend to conquer new territory, like Kant's, but pretends *not* to conquer new territory, a discourse whose apparently conservative turn, upon cross-examination, is revealed as a mere rhetorical pose, significant both for what it conceals and for the act of concealing.

I use Foucault as a convenient example (and in subtlety, complexity and erudition, a culmination) of the understandable academic tendency to articulate intellectual history at those points (such as Kant) where it stands back and records its own progress in the form of a *critical system*—as if what is thus recorded had not long been existent and operative (and prevented from becoming a system precisely *by* its operancy) in the unrecorded interstices of particular textual weaves. And in the case of Kant, the effect of this typical academic move is to present the eighteenth century as the *descending half* of a trajectory that mounts aloft with Descartes. The profusion of ideas used to characterize the eighteenth century thus appears to offer no problem. The age itself, after all—in the Foucauldian view—was coming apart at the seams, ripe for replacement by a new synthesis.

But there are passages in Foucault himself, referring to the post-Kantian age, that with minor modifications well summarize what were in fact already pre-Kantian conditions. The idea of "the unthought" is an instance I have already mentioned. "The Return of Language"—in the question, "What is language, how can we find a way round it in order to make it appear in itself, in all its plenitude?" (Foucault, pp. 303, 306)—is actually the return of what I later call Herder's "body," a body that is in a sense borrowed, at yet a further remove, from Montaigne. And in the section "The Retreat and Return of the Origin," we read that

> in this infinite task of conceiving the origin in what is nearest to it and what is furthest from it, thought reveals that man is not contemporaneous with what makes him be—or with that upon the basis of which he is; but that he is within a power that disperses him, draws him far away from his own origin, but promises it to him in an imminence that will perhaps be forever snatched from him; now, this power is not foreign to him; it does not reside outside him in the serenity of eternal and ceaselessly recommenced origins, for then the origin would be effectively posited; this power is that of his own being. [Pp. 334–35]

The only conceptual difficulty in this passage (if we imagine it to refer to the pre-Kantian eighteenth century) is the very idea of "conceiving," which in truth has nothing to do with the "origin." The origin, in crucial texts from the later eighteenth century, becomes an object of *enactment*, of a form of enactment that manifests exactly the "power" Foucault is speaking of, and has the effect, in one and the same move, of both *being* its object and displacing that object into the realm of the strictly inconceivable.

Interpretation, Poetics, and History

Enactment of origins, then, is an important interpretive idea in this book. It is related to the idea of irony by the consideration that irony, when practiced in the uncompromising manner that we can learn from the eighteenth century, *enacts the origin of language*, the unfolding of language across the face of the strictly inarticulate, its birth in the bosom of the radically silent, of that which is not (or interminably not *yet*) language. As a concept, enactment of origins is not hard to lay hold of, either abstractly or historically. It appears in the wake of various Renaissance notions of originality and is articulated in the eighteenth century, for example, in the analogy between poetic creation and divine world-creation that we associate mainly with Shaftesbury, but which is developed, especially in Germany, well beyond Shaftesbury's actual formulation. But when we attempt to exploit it interpretively, enactment of origins creates difficulties, given a basic Cartesian context in which, in the first instance, writers and readers are imagined as determined individuals, by nature excluded from any but a passive relation to the strictly original. And my contention is that in the texts I examine, these difficulties lead to the recognition that the very idea of the determined individual, especially *the individual reader*, is untenable, whence the complex of poetic thought arises that I attempt to capture in the phrase "the community as a reader." It is possible, by lumping together disparate types of text and rigidly standardizing the depth at which one reads them, to argue that "relations between author, work and public" in the eighteenth century are characterizable as "intimate mutual relationships between privatized individuals" (Habermas, p. 50). But cross-examining texts, or attending to how eighteenth-century texts cross-examine one another, quickly brings to light the limitations of such an argument.

These are the main ideas I work with: *radical irony*, an irony that definitely conceals, but does not admit the existence of any articulable relation whatever to its concealed content; *enactment of origins*, as the description of how a poetic text operates in its communicative environment; and the *reading function*, considered as an experimental device by which to undermine and resituate the experience of individuality, hence to open the problems of subjectivity and community. To the extent that central or typical texts from Foucault's "Classical Age" are subject to valid interpretation in terms of these ideas, the whole conception of a "Classical Age" of representation becomes suspect, and the possibility of a new eighteenth century emerges. We will in a sense have begun to modernize the eighteenth century, to recognize in it, from another angle, the same sort of paradoxical contemporaneity, with our own pressing theoretical and poetic concerns, that Gearhart's study suggests.

In other words, I want to do more than offer alternative readings of eighteenth-century texts. I want to lay hold of the *poetics* that operates in late eighteenth-century Germany, the implied governing framework for poetic communication, the method by which poetic endeavors are originated, developed, and understood. Special problems are created by the idea of a poetics of irony, which by nature resists the type of theoretical summary or closure that any critical discussion of it, by nature, projects as a goal. Such a poetics is, in this sense, beyond theory. But I think these problems remain manageable if we bear in mind that although the guiding interpretive ideas I have listed must be authorized by the poetics they are aimed at, they do not *constitute* that poetics. This distinction is also important for maintaining the boundary with Freudian and Lacanian theory that is created by my use, later, of the concepts of subject and ego. I am not attempting to develop a poetic theory that is in any sense *based* on any theory of subjectivity. The notion of subjectivity with which I operate is itself derived *from* the idea of a poetics of radical irony, which is tenable, in turn, only to the extent that its historical and interpretive specificity is conscientiously observed.

The Notion of a Poetics of Irony

Irony is always a move of concealment. At the simplest, thought A is expressed in order to conceal, however transparently, thought B, which is the real force behind the utterance. By radical irony, however, I mean an irony whose resolution (into the "real" thought B) is strictly impossible, an irony whose concealed object lies entirely outside the range of articulation and so, for the purpose of explaining the ironic utterance, in effect does not exist. This concept, although not difficult to understand, is troublesome to develop. If there is any relation whatever between language and the strictly inarticulable, does it not follow that the inarticulable is necessarily concealed (or repressed) by *every* utterance, by the very act of utterance? And how, then, can irony be said to distinguish one particular utterance from another?

This difficulty does not invalidate the concept of a *poetics* of radical irony. It is not hard to imagine a literary culture in which the basis for communication—the shared prior knowledge that is brought into play by both writer and reader whenever an utterance is recognized as poetic—is constituted by a particular idea of the inarticulable. The problem here arises when we try to *describe* the poetics of such a culture. How can the relation of poetic writing and reading to a communicative basis be exposed, except by articulating that basis, or by finding it articulated, however indirectly, in the documents that make up our evidence?

I hope to get around this problem by changing the question. I ask not *what* the concealed basis for communication in late eighteenth-century German poetics is, but *where* it is. I ask not *what* is thought beneath the surface of radical irony, but *where* the thinking of that thought takes place. I ask after *the locus of irony* in German pre-Classical and Classical literature, and arrive at an answer in the form of a diagram by which irony is located in a pattern of semiotic relations (relations of signification and reference, strictly differentiated) among concepts derived from interpretation. Again, the boundary with psychoanalytic theory is important. Julia Kristeva's notion of the semiotic, for instance, carries a universalizing force that is inappropriate to this book, whose larger ambition, to revise the manner in which European intellectual history is given structure, demands historical specificity in its argument.

I in fact associate with the locus of irony at least two entirely concrete historical entities, the theater and the Jews. The argument on this point, in Chapter 6, builds on Peirce's insight into the irreducible triple structure of semiosis and refers back to my own *Modern Drama and German Classicism*. But it is worth remarking here that if the Jews, as I maintain, occupy a crucial *positive* place in the structure of eighteenth-century German poetic thought, then the consequences for an understanding of the unfolding of German anti-Semitism in the nineteenth and twentieth centuries are considerable. The "roots" of the Nazi movement, as these are usually imagined, turn out not to be roots at all, in the sense of an uninterrupted quasi-organic process traceable as far back in history as documents permit.

On the contrary, Nazism, considered as a phase of German culture, has at least in one aspect the character of a violent and arbitrary *severing* of historical continuity. I go into this matter at the end of the book.

In any event, I do not appeal to the cases of superficial philo-Semitism that can be found in eighteenth-century literary circles. My argument on the Jews is basically *structural*: that the situation of what we once learned from Erich Heller to think of as a "disinherited" literary language, in the larger fabric of eighteenth-century German politics and culture, resonates significantly with the situation of the Yiddish-speaker among German-speakers. As far as I know, only two literary figures of the time, Lessing and Goethe, actually thought through their situation to the point of grasping this resonance. I claim, however, that the paucity of textual evidence does not invalidate my marking the Jews as an aspect of the locus of irony, which brings me to a final, more general remark.

A poetics of radical irony cannot possibly consist of a set of ideas that is known to govern poetic communication because it is known to have been shared by all the members of the literary culture under discussion. Irony depends on a relation to what is not "known" at all, to the unthought, the unrecorded, the inarticulable. And the poetics I am aiming at, accordingly, consists of a diagram by which the locus of irony is more or less fixed in a structure of conceptual relations; it assigns a conceptual *position* to that locus, but not a conceptual content or identity. The concepts with which the diagram is constructed must be justified by interpretation. But not every concept must be rejustified for every text; and especially the concepts that name real aspects of the locus of irony itself (the theater, the Jews)—aspects, so to speak, of the repressed—will not be demonstrable in much textual material. What counts is the pattern of conceptual relations, and the question of whether a sufficiently large and cohesive body of poetic communication, of text and intertext, aligns itself with that pattern, to enable us to speak of an ironic literary culture.

Beyond Theory

"Literary theory," as we call it, is riddled with paradoxes, and as a rule is willing enough to admit it. For if "theory" is associated with a form of awed or rapt *seeing*, and if its object is therefore imagined as quasi-visible, hence quasi-spatial, hence (transposed into the realm of concepts) as having the character of a relatively settled system, then what we practice is clearly a striving *beyond* theory. Its favored tactic is to undermine; it is especially sensitive, in itself and its objects, to the quality of the subversive; and practically any instance of conceptual stability is suspected of depending on an essentializing move.

But this striving beyond theory is still theory. Its procedure in detail is recognizably similar to that of, say, Aristotle or Thomas Aquinas, involving a largely abstract vocabulary and a logic of argument that creates the expectation of conclusions from premises. It is thus an attempt to make theory itself move beyond theory, to create by discovering or discover by creating a flaw, a fissure, an opening in the history of theory, through which a type of thinking no longer entangled in the ocular metaphor might emerge, a type of thinking more thoroughly and responsibly intertissued, as thinking, with its own historical and social activeness. It therefore attaches itself not to intellectual traditions that appear gradual or cumulative in structure, but to those that include the deepest possible controversy, especially to the multiple tradition of dialectics from Hegel, and to psychoanalysis.

This general form of theory, then, lives by criticism—and dies by co-option, by being used as what it after all still is, as theory. The scrupulousness, for instance, with which Jacques Derrida avoids the pretense of occupying a position somehow uncontaminated by the logocentric history he exposes, is a principal source of the strength of both his criticism of metaphysics (the move beyond theory) and his reading of texts, including the reading of Rousseau that figures in my argument later. But precisely this scrupulousness makes Derrida's technical vocabulary available for use as a theory of self-reflexive rhetoricity, which happens in Paul de Man's reading of Rousseau and entails a deep confusion of semiotic concepts. Or to take a diametrically opposed example, the strength of the feminist position is that it finds itself beyond theory *from the outset*, since the gender difference that grounds it is strictly untheorizable, being a different difference, involving indeed a different conception of difference—a different range of possibilities or issues—depending on the side it is viewed from. The problem here is not how to sever or loosen a connection with the history of theory, but how to create a connection, for the sake of intelligibility and effectiveness; and the co-optive move is thus anticipated in the basic act of articulation.[6]

The threat of co-option goes a certain way toward explaining why *irony* does not appear to operate centrally in our theoretical striving beyond theory. At first glance, irony would seem to be called for, as a way of using the conventions of theoretical discourse to mask communication on an entirely different plane. And the relations among the concepts of irony, individuality, and community, which I discuss in detail, suggest at least a possibility of bridging the gulf between an individual's grasp of social rationality and the same rationality in a communal form capable of translating itself into action—that gulf which is kept open by the very *genre* of earnest theoretical discourse that is practiced by Jürgen Habermas, for example.

But the trouble with irony—or ironic theory, if there is such a thing—is that it seems uniquely exposed to co-option. One need only take the ironic discourse at its word in order to co-opt it. And co-option is in fact part of the historical process that has obscured the eighteenth century for us. Ironic discourse *in its entirety*, to be sure, is in a sense immune to co-option, since the relation of its inarticulability to its surface remains substantially the same, however badly the surface is misused. It is to this quality of irony that we owe what I contend is the *retrievability* of the eighteenth-century thought I discuss. But in an intellectual climate where co-option is recognized as a major threat, it still appears safer to articulate one's position as completely as possible than to entrust one's communicative destiny to historical accidents.

A more important source of our apparent discomfort with irony, however, is the attachment of modern theory, as a genre, to the tradition of the history of consciousness, in which Hegel's *Phenomenology of Mind* is the classical instance. Theorizing beyond theory seems not only paradoxical but pointless without the assurance that there is such a thing as consciousness, sufficiently substantial and structurable to have a history, and the assurance that history in this sense is made by the critical folding of consciousness on itself, a process in which theoretical reflection plays a significant and indeed glamorous part. Theorizing beyond theory, in its maximized self-reflection, does not see itself as a passenger in history; it receives from history of consciousness a license to imagine itself in the driver's

[6]On Luce Irigaray and the establishment of a connection with intellectual tradition via Nietzsche, see my "Bridge: Against Nothing," in *Nietzsche and the Feminine*, ed. Peter J. Burgard (Charlottesville, forthcoming).

seat. And irony, in anything approaching a radical sense, is strictly excluded by this idea of a history in which no potential content of consciousness can be permanently silent, in which the very possibility of a content of consciousness is equivalent to the possibility of its becoming an articulable object of consciousness.

Hence our tendency to suppress the eighteenth century, to dismiss it as a relatively unreflected phase of history. But in response to this tendency, I do not stop at the assertion that the history of consciousness, as we habitually practice it, thus fails to do justice to the eighteenth century. I contend, further, that in late eighteenth-century Germany, the very idea of history of consciousness is subjected to a strong positive critique. The reappraisal or reinvention of the eighteenth century is therefore useful not only because it changes the subject (calling upstairs to the philosopher in his study that it is time to move some furniture), and not only because it unmasks those bad habits that have produced what I hope to show are obvious if common misreadings of eighteenth-century texts, but also because, by making available an eighteenth-century critique of the history of consciousness, it suggests exactly the type of deep-cutting self-critical move, beyond theory, by which theory itself is now constituted.

Again, therefore, I hope to uncover, for us, a form of significant contemporaneity in the eighteenth century, in a complex of poetic thought that is itself concerned with the move beyond theory. And it is important, in consequence, that the argument make no claim whatever to speculative or conceptual innovation. We are, I think, *ready* for a new eighteenth century. Not much more is needed than unswerving attention to textual detail, especially to those texts and those details that call our customary view of literary and intellectual history into question.

CHAPTER ONE

The New Holy Scripture of Humanity: The Reader of the Novel and the Mission of the Genre in *Wilhelm Meisters Wanderjahre*

This book is about the eighteenth century; but I open with the discussion of a nineteenth-century novel, *Wilhelm Meisters Wanderjahre*. For Goethe's book is itself mainly a reinterpretation of the history of eighteenth-century ironic narrative (Fielding, Sterne, Voltaire, Diderot, Wieland, Goethe himself), and thence by implication a reassessment of the whole epoch, especially in Germany, in a sense that validates the idea of *enactment of origins* as a primary interpretive category. Interpretive authority is a crucial question in my arguments. What authority have we for reading a particular text in a particular way? And I begin by invoking the at least relatively clear authority of a reader who is reading, among other things, himself.

How Do We Read?

To what extent is it permissible to speak of the reader of fiction as an *active* participant in the constitution of the text's meaning, while at the same time conceding that this activity must also be subject to the text's "guidance"? This general manner of thinking, which we associate with Wolfgang Iser[1]—but which is already developed by Henry

[1] I refer to Wolfgang Iser, *The Implied Reader: Patterns of Communication in Prose Fiction from Bunyan to Beckett* and *The Act of Reading: A Theory of Aesthetic Response* as *IR* and *AR*. For the idea of the reader's activity in "meaning production," see *IR*, pp. xi, 30; for the idea of textual "guidance," *IR*, p. 47; for the resulting synthetic notions of

James, and already derivable (as Iser shows) from Henry Fielding's addresses to his reader—appears to be dictated by the simplest possible reasoning. The idea of a reader's "response" (assuming there is such a thing) and the idea of "the text" itself are categorically disjoint on a level that excludes any relation by which either one might be imagined as determining the other; but at the same time, interpretation seems to become nonsense if we assert that the reader is perfectly free, that any response is adequate to any text. Therefore Iser (and others) spend much effort on establishing exactly how the reader is active, and exactly how he or she is guided by the text, in different cases. "The reader"—considered as the vessel of "response"—is in effect *defined* as a kind of middle ground between free imaginative activity and textual guidance or structure. It seems to me that the existence of such a middle ground is questionable. Even if the text suggests a "range" of possibilities within which the reader may make "decisions" (AR, p. 85), does that range not still set a crippling limit to our "activity"? And even if the supposed middle ground of reading exists, how can *we* ever be confident (as readers) that it has not already been overstepped in one direction or the other, that we are not already either violating the text's complexity (by "deciding" too firmly) or else simply permitting ourselves to be controlled by it?[2]

"configurative meaning" and "gestalt," IR, p. 42, and AR, p. 127. IR, AR, and all other works designated by abbreviations in the text are cited in full in the front matter to this book.

[2]It seems to me that there is cause for political concern in Iser's insistence on combining the ideas of "activity" and "guidance"—which mean freedom and control. If the novel really creates the illusion that freedom and control can be *combined*, then it becomes a potential instrument of propaganda advocating the *acceptance* of control. For example, Iser (IR, p. 30) quotes Northrop Frye's elaboration upon the idea that "all works of literary art without exception" can be described as "a picnic to which the author brings the words and the reader the meaning" (*Fearful Symmetry: A Study of William Blake* [Boston, 1962; orig. 1947], pp. 427–28). But Frye's argument has a strongly *liberal* tendency. In order to grasp adequately even one word in literature, he suggests, we must always conduct a critical reexamination of literature as a whole; the "meaning" we bring to the present text is not merely a "response" to that text, and is certainly not a response that is "prestructured" by the text (IR, p. 32), but is an implacable *questioning* of response in all its possibilities. Iser, on the other hand, speaks of "participation" in the text, which always hovers on the brink of meaning a *submission* of the reader to whatever he is "*made* to feel for himself" (IR, p. 30, my emphasis). I do not think I am using Iser merely as a straw man, despite Stanley Fish's explanation of "Why No One's Afraid of Wolfgang Iser," *Diacritics* 11, no. 1 (Spring 1981), 2–13. For even the act of dismissing Iser can find itself implicated—as Fish finds himself implicated—in what is most wrong about Iser. Fish is correct that the theory of AR "falls apart because the distinction on which it finally depends—the distinction between the determinate and the indeterminate—will not hold"

"Experience" provides no positive evidence here. No raw form of experience—especially of our experience as readers—is available to us as a basis for argument. Theories of reading are always, so to speak, readings *of* our experience, not results derived *from* it. But the evidence with which Iser supports his argument is of a different sort. He speaks, in his first title, of the "implied" reader; and his contention is that in many fictional texts, especially Fielding's, a more or less direct appeal is made to exactly the sort of reader, the sort of middle ground, he postulates. The trouble with this evidence is that it cuts both ways. The very directness of a text's appeal to a particular reader or reading process, the clarity with which reader X is thus *profiled* in the text, creates a distance of objectivity between reader X and whoever (or whatever) the "actual" reader is. When Fielding, in *Tom Jones*, suggests that the reader must make "his own conjectures" about certain parts of the story, does he expect the actual reader to accept that suggestion, simply to *be* the reader he is addressing? Iser apparently thinks so—despite the jocular context in *Tom Jones*, in which the word "blanks" suggests something quite different from what it does in his own Englished argument.[3] Fielding in fact *thematizes* the reader he apparently addresses, who is now as much a fictional personage as the characters in the story; and the extent and manner of identification between that personage and the person who is actually reading the book are, at the very least, debatable. But Iser's notion of the "implied" reader slurs over the difference between the implying of a "character" by a text and the taking of texts as evidence implying an actual state of affairs.

Exactly what existential status must one grant "the reader"? Experience (whether or not I think my reading is like what Iser describes)

(Fish, p. 6). But Fish himself cannot avoid operating with this distinction. And in order to show that his version of it is not "absolute" (p. 12), he entangles himself in the question of the shaky distinguishability of literary fiction from "the world itself" (p. 8), which keeps open the possibility of equating reading with "experience" (p. 2), and so still sanctions the general Iserian approach, which I call the theory of "romance reading," a theory that manages to suggest—even if Iser, positioned "on both sides of almost every issue" (p. 12), denies it—that the subjection to "control" of even our subjective experience, although perhaps not a "task" (p. 11), is still a legitimate object of desire. My point, in this and the following two chapters, is that the German eighteenth century already fears this possibility, and deals with it by relocating the whole idea of experience.

[3]See *IR*, p. 51, referring to Henry Fielding, *Tom Jones*, ed. Sheridan Baker (New York, 1973), p. 88, in bk. 3, chap. 1. For Fielding's use of the term "blanks" in the sense of lottery blanks, which have *no* value, see *Tom Jones*, bk. 2, chap. 1, p. 59. For Iser's sense of "blanks" as the locus of *all* literary value, see *IR*, p. 113, and *AR*, p. 9 and passim.

provides no positive evidence. But experience can provide negative evidence, especially concerning the notion, prevalent at least since Henry James, that the business of the novel is to enable us to live "another life" (AR, p. 127), and that the verbal strategies of fiction therefore aim at transforming the process of reading (for us) into an experience of intense engagement not only with the text, but with the fictional world (which thus becomes "life"), an experience sufficiently absorbed and nontheoretical to produce genuine personal "discoveries" about ourselves. What disturbs me here is that the people who articulate such theories do not *themselves* read in the way their theories require. When I read a novel, I can gauge the depth to which it has interested me by the amount of scribbling in the margins; and I think the same could be said, safely enough, of Percy Lubbock, of Georges Poulet, of Wolfgang Iser, and (shall I say "you"?) of the reader of the present argument. "Reading" for me—for us—is *writing* in an entirely concrete sense. It is a constant developing of our own externally conceived theories about the work, theories about the author, theories about the genre, general theories of narration or style or literary history, and of course theories of "the reader." We do not submerge *ourselves* in the world of the fiction, but rather we submerge in it, as it were, a baited intellectual hook ("the reader") by which we seek to tempt forth the insights, arguments, and quotations that sustain us in the world of professional literary study. Is "the reader" we speak of really anything more than a condescending glance at what we suppose are the primitive mental processes of people who have not yet taken our courses?

Plurality of Reading in Goethe's *Wanderjahre*

Perhaps this appeal to the habits of professional readers will be considered out of place. Shouldn't a distinction be made between the actual players in the game of reading and the referees? I will attempt to deal with this objection not on general grounds, but by a consideration of *Wilhelm Meisters Wanderjahre*, especially of the question: Why does Goethe include in the book two very large and diffuse collections of aphorisms? Or, having decided to include them, why does he not make more of an effort to integrate them into the fabric of fictional description and action—an effort that is at least gestured at in *Die Wahlverwandtschaften*? Or yet again, if the aphorisms are

18   Beyond Theory

supposed to be a detachable commentary, why are they printed so
that at least one collection (in the original plan, both) *interrupts* the
narrative?[4] At least one answer to this question suggests itself immediately. The contrast, the rupture, between two different types of
text in the *Wanderjahre*, is meant to make us conscious of *the contrast between two entirely different types of reading*.

Goethe, no less than Fielding, thematizes and repeatedly appeals
to the experiencing, conjecturing, participating reader. Even though
the flow of the story, such as it is, is constantly interrupted in the
Wanderjahre by letters and other documents, by complicated shifts
in point of view, leaps backward and forward in time, expository di-
gressions, addresses to the reader, glaring anomalies in the articulation of chapters and sub-chapters, and so on—not to mention the
collections of aphorisms—we are still invited to think of our reading
as a steady motion in one direction only, from the beginning of the
text toward its end. I say that we are invited to *think of* our reading
in a particular way, as if it were a progressive accumulation of the
text's content in our mind. This process, if it really happened, would
imitate our sense of time as the accumulation of experience and enable us to experience the fiction (following Iser) as a matrix of significant self-discovery. Thus I accept Iser's view to the extent that it
describes how we are sometimes invited to *think of* our reading. The
author does not address me, as I really am; but he does sometimes
address a fictional personage who represents me, as a kind of projection, and who is strictly located (by being addressed on page *x*,
line *y*) at a particular point in the supposedly linear unfolding of the
fictional account. Thus I am invited to think of *myself* as always located at some particular point in the text, by analogy with my sense
of myself as always located at some particular point in time, the present. I am invited to accept the metaphor of a textual present, a
place in the text from which the pages already read and the pages
still supposedly unread represent a kind of past and future for me.

But when we are offered a collection of aphorisms and quotations,

[4]Eckermann (*Gespräche mit Goethe*, 15 May 1831) insists that the inclusion of the collections of aphorisms had been an emergency step taken by Goethe to fill out the skimpy
second and third volumes of the novel's original printing; and he claims that Goethe authorized the elimination of the aphorisms in future editions. Actually, Goethe had wanted
"Aus Makariens Archiv" at the end of the novel's *first* volume (letters to Wilhelm Reichel,
4 and 19 March 1829). And there is ample evidence that the inclusion of substantial
amounts of aphoristic material had been intended well before the novel's completion. See,
for example, WA, 25/2:58–62, 114–15.

the process of reading is entirely different. We are no longer asked to locate ourselves in the text. We are no longer asked to think of our reading as moving straight ahead. Instead, we are invited to skip around, to pick and choose, to concentrate on particular statements that catch our interest and leave the rest for another time when our mood or circumstances may suit them better. For the purposes of my argument now, it does not matter whether this approach to the reader reflects more accurately what "actually" happens when we read. Nor does it matter especially whether there are perhaps more than just two types of reading suggested. What is important is the radical *difference* between the two (or more) types of reading that the various types of text in the *Wanderjahre* require. For this difference brings to our attention the fact that there is no such thing as *the* way we read, that reading is necessarily always the combination and collision of radically different "acts," a dynamics of difference which is only confused by any attempt we might make to subject it to a single coherent description.

The manner in which this dynamics operates is exposed very clearly in the *Wanderjahre*. It has often been remarked in commentary and criticism that the individual aphorisms in the "Betrachtungen im Sinne der Wanderer" and "Aus Makariens Archiv" show strong connections with particular figures or events in the narrative fiction, connections we must perceive and think about. Goethe in fact instructs his publisher not to allow any of the aphorisms to be printed anywhere but with the novel, since in any other context they would lose their meaning and perhaps even become offensive (letter to Reichel, 2 May 1829). *How* we must think about the connections between aphorisms and narrative, moreover, is suggested strongly on two occasions in book 1: in the discussion of the aphoristic inscriptions with which the "Oheim" decorates his house, where the reader is called upon to supply imaginary intellectual contexts in which the given statement becomes true;[5] and in the description of Makarie's "archives" as composed of "results, conclusions, which, if we do not know the cause that led to them, appear paradoxical, but which therefore compel us to go backward, by a process of discovery and invention in reverse, and as far as possible to imagine the filiation of such thoughts, from their earliest and deepest beginnings" (*WMW*,

[5] *WMW*, pp. 328–30. I avoid the Weimar edition here because of its failure to print the aphorisms with the text of the novel.

p. 389). In order to understand the aphorisms adequately, we require intellectual contexts and experiential matrices or filiations; and we are meant (indeed we are told) to find these aids to understanding in the novel's fictional world. Therefore the process of reading now entails our *dipping back into the fiction* at various points for the intellectual, emotional, and historical information we need in order to complete the sense (to establish the validating context) of the cryptic fragments before us. Or more precisely, we find ourselves dipping back into *a different type of reading*, into a more or less Iserian reading of the fiction as quasi-experience.

We are thus invited to carry out our reading as a constant *rereading* of the text in exactly the professional or scholarly manner I described above, a constant judicious dipping into the fiction for insight, for evidence, for material by which to develop our thought. In the *Wanderjahre* our marginal scribbles are as it were printed for us in the collections of aphorisms; what we have to do is find the places in the narrative where they belong. Nor does this process automatically exclude the idea of quasi-experiential or participatory reading, reading in the sense of James, Lubbock, Poulet, or Iser. On the contrary, Iserian reading is presupposed here, as a device we require for luring our slippery intellectual quarry into the light of verbal formulation, as the needful vehicle by which parts of the text take on, for us, the type of reality that enables them to substantiate or contextualize or validate this or that aphorism. And conversely, it does *not* follow from the present argument that reading by skipping around may *not* be, on some level, an enactment of "experience" considered as the possibility of self-discovery. What must be questioned is the status or range of the idea of reading Iser proposes: whether "reading"—in the sense of the whole of what happens in our dealing with a fictional text—is really the object of his argument to begin with; whether, indeed, "reading" *can* be the object of any such argument. And it seems to me that the idea of reading suggested by the structure of *Wilhelm Meisters Wanderjahre*, along with certain discrepancies between theories of reading and how the authors of those theories actually use texts, provides a start for such questioning.

The Convention of Romance Reading

The general theory of reading that I am questioning—mainly on the grounds that it attempts the coherent "phenomenological" descrip-

tion of a process that is in principle not subject to such description—
is composed of at least three related elements: (1) the idea of a balance or middle ground between activity and guidance in the reader's
relation to the text; (2) the idea that this middle ground is normally
fertile with a "configurative meaning" or "gestalt" (see, e.g., *IR*, p.
42; *AR*, p. 127) which, for the reader, has the quality of "another" life
or "another" world or "another" personal identity, thus creating new
possibilities of self-exploration or self-discovery; and (3) the idea that
the reader of fiction, as part of his or her contribution to this process,
normally acquiesces in the pretense that reading is a constant progress through the text, comparable to the direct experience of time. I
use the term "romance reading" to refer to any theory of reading of
this general type, any theory that depends on the possibility of a
reproduction or appropriation or generation of fictional experience,
or of fictional or textual time, in the reader's own more or less direct
experience of self.

What is the status of such theories? On the one hand, it is clear
that romance reading is not a satisfactory account of how we "actually" read fiction, nor even an adequate description of how we generally imagine that actuality, except when we more or less deliberately
set out to position ourselves as romance readers. But on the other
hand, romance reading cannot be dismissed as a falsehood or a delusion. It is too well entrenched not only in the tradition of critical
thought, but also in the tradition of the novel itself, in texts in which
the romance reader is clearly "implied." What we are talking about,
in other words, is a *convention*, which is unquestionably a factor in
our literary experience and activity, but not in the sense that it de-
termines our behavior or defines any literary entity on the level
where we might speak, for instance, of "genre."

The trouble with the concept of "convention" is that it always
comes to mean "*mere* convention." Our ability to understand a convention, to describe how it operates in particular cases, how it affects
the behavior of people or some recognizable quality of works, always
implies a detachment on our part, hence that our own thought or
behavior is *not* determined by the convention we mean. But it is still
possible, in certain cases, to argue that a convention can be well
understood yet continue to operate as a governing convention *for us*.
Important for our purposes is the idea—which I think stands behind
any discussion of an "implied" reader, a reader constructed from text
interpretations—that the absence or nonrecognition of the convention in question would produce interpretive chaos. Even if romance

reading cannot be demonstrated in reality (the argument might go), still the idea or posture of romance reading remains indispensable for the discussion of interpretive formulations concerning the novel. If we do not adopt this posture, we cannot communicate about novels.

There are cases in which an argument of this type appears valid. Without the conventional analogy between textual sequence and temporal sequence, for example—considered merely as a device for describing texts, not as a description of reading experience—it would be impossible to speak of a "dramatic" quality in texts, of "climaxes" or "reversals" or "development"; it would even be difficult to speak of a poet's "saying" something. And yet that analogy *is* a convention, a "mere" convention. It is not a property of the real experience of the interpreter; it is overturned or dispensed with in actual literary texts, in loose-leaf novels, for instance, or in poems such as Stéphane Mallarmé's "Un coup de dés"; and it is routinely called into question even in the course of interpretive endeavors that explicitly employ it, when the argument aims at showing a text's "architecture," or its "circularity," or its "materiality." Or to take another example, from the theoretical perspective of intertextuality, rigorously understood, the whole idea of *a* particular text is revealed as mere convention, but is still a convention that cannot be dispensed with even in rigorous theoretical discussions of the intertextual; for we cannot avoid naming, at least to ourselves, the particular texts whose substantiality we are denying.

Does the convention of romance reading have the same standing as that of the analogy between the text and time, or that of the idea of "a" text? Would eliminating that convention from critical discourse threaten the same sort of apparently pointless disruption? I maintain, on the contrary, that superseding the convention of romance reading—or relegating the romance reader to the rôle of a character in certain types of fictional structure—*opens* interpretive possibilities that are by no means chaotic, by no means eccentric, by no means ahistorical. I maintain that the convention of romance reading—or the assumption that that convention is interpretively indispensable— has contributed to a profound interpretive blindness with respect to eighteenth-century literature, especially in Germany. The idea of enactment of origins is crucial in approaching eighteenth-century texts; and a categorical insistence on the convention of romance reading tends to obscure this idea. Goethe, in any event, suggests a cogent interpretive approach to eighteenth-century narrative which *opposes* romance reading to the actual historical business of the texts.

But the historical situation and significance of romance reading are still important factors in the argument. And it will help our understanding if we divide the notion of romance reading into two components: (1) the idea of reading as a constant forward motion through the text, an accumulation of the fictional content, an analogue to our direct experience of time, including the pretense of a textual present, a *point* where we now find ourselves in our reading, and (2) the idea of reading as a meeting or confrontation or interaction between a written text and a relatively isolable individual personal *self* (the "reader"), which is the vessel of its own experience, the place where experience happens, where character is formed, and where character can be modified by the absorption and processing of external influences (such as the text).

We have already seen how the first of these components is exposed and undermined in Goethe's *Wanderjahre*. And once we have stopped regarding that temporal self-positioning as something like a natural quality of the reading experience, the historical provenance of the idea becomes clear. The forward-striving reader—who, from some particular point in the text, recalls what is past and more or less uncertainly anticipates what is to come—is the developed version of a typical figure *in* fiction, namely the hero of the medieval quest-romance that traces its lineage to the *Aeneid*. Like the quester-hero, the romance reader (my christening of whom is thus explained) experiences *as if* it were the uncertainty of time, a structure that, from another perspective, has much more the character of *space*: in the quest-romance, it is the figural structure of history, history viewed from the vantage point of eternity; for the romance reader, it is the structured material object, the printed book. The relation between the quester-hero and the reader becomes especially plain in the German Bildungsroman, which shares with the quest-romance a pattern of analogies that relates textual linearity, the time of immediate experience, and large-scale biographical time; for in two seminal instances of the German genre, Goethe's *Wilhelm Meisters Lehrjahre* and Novalis's *Heinrich von Ofterdingen*, the hero does actually become the reader of a text practically identical to the text we are reading. Not that these novels thus actually presuppose romance reading; on the contrary, they thematize it and so distinguish it from whatever our actual reading process might be.

The second component of the idea of romance reading, reading considered as the more or less isolated interaction of a self and a text, is more difficult to deny as an element of actual experience than the first. Surely in the age of printed books, where a small amount of money or a library card enables us to become readers of practically anything we wish, where neither our general social condition nor our particular social contacts determine our reading except in ways we consider ourselves able to change at will, surely now reading *is* a direct and at least pragmatically isolable contact between my self and a text. But I maintain that Goethe, especially in the *Wanderjahre*, in effect does deny this reasoning with respect to an important segment of eighteenth-century narrative fiction, which includes his own work. For Goethe, the individual reader is merely a convention, a pose; reading does not actually happen except on the level of the community; reading is not only a social act *of* the individual, but more fundamentally an act of the community *through* the individual.

This point will take some effort to establish. But if we inquire into the historical provenance of the idea of a self's meeting a text, we discover that the question is difficult not because the necessary arguments are elusive or subtle, but because they are all too common, because practically any theory of the history of consciousness, of individuality, or of individualism implies a genealogy of the supposedly solitary readerly experience. One especially interesting instance is Harold Bloom's satanizing of Descartes, his location of the "anxiety of influence" primarily in the ages after "the Cartesian engulfment, the flooding-out of a greater mode of consciousness."[6] For what is anxiety of influence, in all its forms, if not the experience of a fundamental incommensurability between the *conditions* of ephebe and established precursor, that is, the incommensurability of a self and a text in their collision—"text" being the condition in which our precursors appear to us—a type of collision that presumably did not occur in the same way in "the giant age before the flood"? (Bloom, p. 11). And when seen from this perspective, the theory of romance reading, in which the self is supposedly activated and fructified in its collision with a text, appears merely an optimistic or eudaemonic avoidance of Bloom's gloomy vision, thus itself perhaps precisely the symptom of a more general literary anxiety.

[6]Harold Bloom, *The Anxiety of Influence: A Theory of Poetry* (Oxford, 1973), p. 72.

Bloom's own idea of reading is different: "The anxiety of influence is an anxiety in expectation of *being flooded.* . . . The ephebe who fears his precursors as he might fear a flood is taking a vital part for a whole, the whole being everything that constitutes his creative anxiety, the spectral blocking agent in every poet. Yet this metonymy is hardly to be avoided; every good reader properly *desires* to drown, but if the poet drowns, he will become *only a reader"* (p. 57). The reader is here characterized by a *lack* of activity—which is a more honest inference than romance reading from any theory of the history of consciousness that arrives at an idea of alienated subjectivity. Reading is rescued only by being categorically distinguished from writing. But in Goethe, I contend, the question of the reader's activity or inactivity does not arise in this form. Theories of the history of consciousness necessarily include a self-consciously mythological element; the simpler, as it were prelapsarian age that precedes ours, since we cannot know it from experience, takes on the quality of a myth when contrasted with our own all too ascertainable reality of corruption or alienation. But Goethe did not merely *believe* himself "incapable of creative anxiety" (Bloom, p. 51). For Goethe, the categories of myth and reality are simply reversed. It is the *post*-lapsarian age that has the quality of myth; and precisely our development of this myth, our otherwise clearly pointless and morbid attachment to the story of our own corruption, marks us as a myth-making people, a people of the origin, a people that reads actively *as a community.* Schiller attempts to make sense of this view when he presents the "naïve" as an actual poetic possibility in the present. Lessing anticipates it in what I contend is his cyclical version of the history of consciousness.[7] I attempt to get at it by interpreting eighteenth-century literature not as a nostalgic reenactment, but as an *enactment* of origins.

Reflections of Reading in the *Wanderjahre*

Let us examine specific references to the process of reading in Goethe's novel, for example the opening sentence: "Im Schatten

[7]See my "Reason, Error, and the Shape of History: Lessing's Nathan and Lessing's God," *LY* 9 (1977), 60–80.

eines mächtigen Felsen saß Wilhelm an grauser, bedeutender Stelle, wo sich der steile Gebirgsweg um eine Ecke herum schnell nach der Tiefe wendete" (*WMW*, p. 263; In the shadow of a huge boulder, Wilhelm sat at a terrifying, significant point, where the steep mountain path quickly took a sharp turn downward). We are struck here by a very curious combination of adjectives; Wilhelm is sitting at a "terrifying (comma) significant" place. The first adjective suggests a helpless abandonment to experience, whereas the second suggests cool detachment; and when we learn in the next few sentences that Wilhelm is entering his observations in his notebook, we tend to regard the disproportion between those adjectives as a gentle mockery of this overearnest young seeker after education. In a situation that might properly overwhelm him with emotion, Wilhelm is captivated by significance ("Bedeutung"), and scribbles, as it were, his marginal notes. Or perhaps, for all we know, "terrifying" implies an attempt on Wilhelm's part to *read* emotional significance *into* his situation.

But the joke is also on us. For although the text posits as its object an immediate human experience (undergone by Wilhelm), still, precisely as a text, it can never actually contain *for us* anything other than the recordable or writable "significance" of that experience; any experienced immediacy, on our part, must be forcibly read into our situation. We as readers, like Wilhelm, find ourselves already (always already) having taken a conscious step backward out of an experience that by convention (the convention of romance reading) we might be tempted to imagine ourselves somehow in the midst of; our recognition of that disproportion between adjectives already constitutes such a step backward. Wilhelm, as we first see him, is thus an image of ourselves, a reflection of the process of reading not as vicarious experience, but as that detached cataloguing of significance which, for us, it inescapably is.

A dialectically minded reader might object here that when we recognize ourselves in Wilhelm, we—in a manner of speaking—identify with him, and thus enter the fictional experience after all. It seems to me, on the contrary, that this "identification" detaches the figure of Wilhelm from *his* supposedly real circumstances, and thus disrupts precisely the integrity of that reality as a possible scene of experience for the reader. (We think of conventions of the time in portrait painting—Tischbein's "Goethe in der Campagna"—in which an evidently significant landscape fragment is used as background, but without actually containing the posed subject.) And this focus upon our quality as the text's permanent reader, not its temporary (or imaginary) experiencing reader, is developed by the adverb "schnell"; the mountain path *quickly* turns a corner and proceeds downward, as if it were in motion. We recall *Laokoon*, in which Lessing argues that a verbal text is always an action in progress through time, so that even a static object, in being described, must be resolved into action. The question, however, is whether we, the readers, keep pace with the dynamic text in the action of reading, or whether, rather, the text as action and experience does not (so to speak) pass us by ungrasped, as the mountain path plunges past Wilhelm.

And this theoretical allegory is then elaborated by the descent of "St. Joseph" and his family along that path, a sudden, fleeting apparition that "tears" Wilhelm away from his "observations" (*WMW*, p. 265). Thus stirred up, Wilhelm is now determined to become as it were a participating reader by getting up and himself following the path downward, by matching action to action in order to prolong and deepen the momentary promise of a symbolically pregnant experience he has just received. It is, after all, always the symbolic dimension of a text (what else?) that seduces the permanent reader, especially the literary scholar, into adopting the stance of the romance reader. And just as we, the permanent readers, then find ourselves, willy-nilly, thinking and talking in professional, artistic categories, so Wilhelm discovers not a profound symbol, not a mysterious echo in present reality of the legend of the Holy Family, but rather a case of deliberate imitation of paintings of the Holy Family. Again, precisely by knowing about the supposed obligation of the reader to develop the fiction as experience, even by accepting that obligation and stepping actively onto the path laid out for us, we find ourselves at an insurmountable conscious remove from the experience we have anticipated. Our identification with Wilhelm, such as it is, changes nothing. The convention of romance reading, for us, is strictly historical, in both senses of the word. It belongs, if anywhere, to the historical past and no longer actually shapes our relation to the text. And it belongs to the story, the fiction; it is entirely thematized or allegorized, and offered us as an object of detached critical scrutiny.

Throughout the *Wanderjahre* we are reminded repeatedly of our situation as thinking and commenting readers, and not only by such expectable devices as the frequent remarks that some particular event, presumed in the fiction to be real, is "romanhaft" or novel-like. At the house of the "Oheim," for example, we encounter a whole family of fiction readers, who are precisely not romance readers in the sense of people who substantially expand their range of quasi-immediate experience by reading. Rather, they are all *specialists* in reading (*WMW*, p. 309). Each one develops and reinforces his or her own characteristic manner of experiencing by seeking out a particular kind of literary fiction that answers or flatters it. Any broadening of the self's possibilities, any learning, happens only in social contact *among* these individuals. It is at this house that Wilhelm is given a manuscript in which he reads, "Wer ist denn so begabt, daß er vielseitig genießen könne?" (p. 346; Who is so gifted as to be capable of many-sided enjoyment?). This question suggests a negative answer. "Enjoyment" of a fictional text, or of any work of art—in the sense of an interaction between work and recipient that operates, for the latter, as something close to intense immediate experience—is not simply a cultural fact; it is not automatically available to any human individual whose reception of the work is sufficiently governed by a convention like that of romance reading. Enjoyment, rather, in this sense—assuming that it ever occurs, which is not strictly verifiable—is a matter of specialization, conditioned by the inevitable one-sidedness of the recipient.[8] And it follows that our personal profit from most texts or works, or our personal involvement with them, is engendered only indirectly, by contact, conversation, sympathy, and, perhaps especially, disagreement ("Widerspruchsgeist" [*WMW*, p. 309]) with people who specialize in them. Precisely those works that *can* significantly increase our range of experience or produce genuine self-discovery on our part affect us only by way of someone else's commentary on them. Thus, incidentally, the whole idea of the "work" as a vessel for anything we might call meaning or experience is called into question.

This aspect of the idea of reading in the *Wanderjahre* is especially prominent in the Italian interlude in book 2, in which frame story and inner story melt into one another, and in which the presence of a major character, the painter, can only be accounted for by his being the reader of an actual published book, *Wilhelm Meisters Lehrjahre*. That we ourselves, here and now, are reading the same book's sequel

---

[8]This idea takes issue with Kant's insistence on the absence of *interest* in aesthetic enjoyment. On how Goethe does take issue with Kant here, see my *Goethe's Theory of Poetry: "Faust" and the Regeneration of Language* (Ithaca, 1986), pp. 240–44.

clearly marks the painter as our projection or representative inside the fiction. And the first thing we hear about this character—after the ironic remark assigning him to "that sort, of whom lots wander around like familiar spirits in the wide world, and even more in novels and plays"—is that he is "an excellent artist who knows how to decorate watercolor landscapes with ingenious and well-drawn and developed staffage [German "Staffage," the accessories, especially human figures, added in order to make a landscape interesting]" (WMW, p. 496–97). His "passionate" interest in Mignon, in other words, is also a *professional* interest—Mignon is the theme, the justification, the token of artistic control, in his landscapes—whence it is suggested that we too, when we appear to become passionately involved in a literary fiction, are in truth only collecting "staffage," making reflective judgments in the development of our own imaginative concerns.

Then, however, in the very next sentence, we hear of Mignon's "image, which lives in all sensitive hearts"—an idea that suggests not only the possibility but the general efficacy of romance reading after all. And then, perversely, a paragraph further on, we hear of several watercolors in which Mignon is captured "to a T" ("wie sie leibte und lebte"), not owing to the artist's imaginative submergence in the novel but because "Wilhelm managed to help along his friend's happy imagination with exact description, thus to contain his generalizing thought within the narrower limits of personality" (WMW, p. 497). Romance reading turns out not to be enough. Our imagination is too "general"; literary fiction takes on the intense particularity of an experience we can learn from only if we can be instructed miraculously by an actual inhabitant of the fictional world. And then the pendulum swings back yet again, toward the idea of romance reading, when we hear, next, that the picture that captures Mignon best of all had been done *before* the artist's meeting with Wilhelm (p. 498).

This whole section, I contend, thus reduces to the absurd, or to the ridiculous, the idea of romance reading. If we take seriously the possibility of entering into a literary fiction and undergoing it as experience (as an experience characterized by tension or balance between the text's relatively objective authority and the relative subjective freedom of our imagination), then we find that we are imagining something uncomfortably similar to the story of Wilhelm Meister's artist friend. Namely, we project ourselves into the fiction as a kind of participating character who is also, however, not really a character but a member of the reading public. And this character/reader then sets himself or herself the task of making real (making physical, making available to "the sense of sight" [*WMW*, p. 497]) another character (Mignon) who unquestionably belongs to the fiction (precisely in this passage, which speaks of her) and yet, precisely for the purpose of being made real, of being represented, is also absent from the fiction. And in order to carry out this supposed task, we of course seek objective authority within the fiction (as the artist does from Wilhelm—and also from the Italian landscape, which, however, is not "within the fiction" in the same sense), but only in order to discover (or pretend to discover), precisely in the passage that does authoritatively reestablish Mignon as a present fictional figure ("with all her character traits" [p. 498]), that that authority had never been needed after all. I leave it to the reader to separate, enumerate, and perhaps even (if he or she wishes) experience the tangle of contradictions here.

Finally, still in the same fictional connection, there is a passage that raises even deeper theoretical doubts. After describing the praise lavished on the painter's work by other characters, the narrator continues: "But in order to avoid the suspicion that we are merely using vague phrases to foist off on the gullible reader works of art that we are not in a position actually to show, there follows the opinion of a connoisseur who, several years afterward, dwelt admiringly on the works we have been speaking of, as well as on other similar works of the same artist" (*WMW*, p. 506). Then comes, in quotation marks, a full page and a half of very detailed, professional-looking description and criticism. Of course this is a put-up job, a friendly joke between author and reader, for we know perfectly well that both the paintings themselves and the supposedly authenticating quotation are fiction.[9] But it is also more than a joke, for it raises not only the question of whether a work's fiction or content can assume the quality of experience for us but also the question of the status of the work itself as experience in the context of our larger real experi-

---

[9]It is possible, indeed even likely, that Goethe has actual works of art in mind, perhaps the watercolors of Georg Melchior Kraus or the copperplates of the younger Gabriel Lory. And it is possible that the commentary of the "connoisseur" was actually written by Goethe's friend Heinrich Meyer, who also provided Goethe with much technical and anecdotal material on the weaving industry. But the fiction is still a fiction. No one claims to have found an artist who actually chronicled Mignon, or a demonstrable direct reference in the commentary. See the notes in *WMW*, pp. 1127–31.

ence—the question, we might say, of whether Walter Benjamin's term "aura" names any actual thing or happening—the question of whether we ever really find ourselves in the presence of the *work*, let alone in interaction with its fiction.

Are the nonexistent watercolors of Wilhelm's friend any less real for me than paintings I have actually seen? Do the works I have actually seen (experienced "directly") exist for me, when I think about it, in a form at all different from the form of that fictional "authentication"? At least if I try to retrieve my "direct" experience from memory and communicate it, such a supposedly firsthand *verbal* commentary is inevitably the form it will assume. At least the effective cultural or historical existence of a painting is therefore not clearly distinguishable, in my experience, from the existence of a convincing description. The existence of the work as an object is perhaps ascertainable; like Dr. Johnson, I can kick it if need be. But I cannot kick the work *as a work*, as an intentional object, as a vessel of significance or experience, as an element in the structure of culture or history.

And if such questions can arise with respect to paintings, which are material objects, then how much more so with respect to works of literature, such as the work we are now reading, where memory has a constitutive rôle even in our supposedly immediate experiencing of the narration. It may happen that while turning the pages of a novel we undergo an intense experience of self-discovery; but these two events cannot simply be lumped together and characterized as "reading," certainly not as a reading of *the work*, in the sense that such an entity exists in culture. As readers of the work, we are always essentially commentators. From where, if not from some form of commentary, does the work receive that measure of ontological closure, of identifiability, which enables us to speak of "the work" to begin with? Even in the extreme case of painting, our immediate experience of the work—our standing in its "aura"—can never be ascertained; the very act of ascertaining distances it, makes it inaccessible. What we have of the work—of that original authority which is a necessary component of romance reading—is in truth never anything more than memory or recollection, essentially a commentary that, when analyzed with respect to its object, turns out only to reconstruct or develop prior commentaries (actual or implied) and can never arrive at the presumed original entity.

Goethe's Narrative Irony and Reading as a
Social Act

It is clear, then, that in Goethe's view, the idea or convention of romance reading plays a part in the structure and cultural operation of narrative, but is not "implied" by narrative texts in the way Iser wants it to be. The corresponding positive point, however, is less easily grasped. How can the *community* be implied as a reader, or indeed be a reader? This point can be approached by an account of Goethe's narrative career.

Werther is a relatively simple case. Throughout most of its main epistolary section, the reader is maneuvered very neatly into a position of seeming to participate in the fiction. We are given only Werther's letters; but in order to understand their context, we are obliged to supply at least the gist of Wilhelm's letters from our imagination, thus as it were to compose them. We find ourselves therefore *playing the rôle* of Werther's correspondent. This form of participation in the fictional world unravels a bit when letters not addressed to Wilhelm are introduced, and especially when the "editor" takes over; but as long as at least the editorial pose stands up, we are still able to imagine a place for ourselves in the same world that is inhabited by Werther and by the other characters and the writer of the words we are reading. The fiction is still "naturalized"; the pieces of paper before us (i.e., the book *Werther*) still correspond to pieces of paper *in* the fictional world.

The trouble is that the editorial pose does not stand up; for it becomes clear toward the end that the "editor" is in truth an omniscient narrator, able to relate what Werther does and thinks when alone, and in possession of details, especially about Werther and Lotte's last meeting, that no one could conceivably have told him. Of course romance reading requires no particular narrative technique; there is no reason to exclude the omniscient narrator from the number of acceptable conventions by which a reader's participatory response may be elicited. But in *Werther* a basic narrative rule, a limit on how far and in what ways the point of view may wander, is first established firmly and then *changed* abruptly in mid-text; not only the particular form of "passive synthesis" (*AR*, pp. 135–59) by which we are involved as individuals with the text but the whole idea of such syntheses, in their relation to narrative techniques, is thus dragged into the light and made an object of scrutiny.

I must now *reflect* on my reading, and especially on the fact that if my reading were really completed within my individual consciousness, it would become difficult to differentiate my own consciousness from Werther's. The two crucial characteristics of Werther's consciousness are a lack of immediate social openness (which we share, if we really read in solitude), and a special attentiveness (which we share if we read attentively) to certain simple truths about the human condition that make death desirable. If I read in this manner, therefore, as an isolated individual consciousness in contact with the text, then it appears to follow—at least if I reflect on the matter (uncontrolled reflectiveness being yet another property of Wertherian consciousness)—that I must make a choice between either committing suicide myself or else concluding that suicide is not, after all, a plausible consequence of Werther's conscious state in the fiction. And conversely, assuming that we are *not* faced with this choice, that we do find Werther a plausible character, it follows that our sense of the process of reading as individual quasi-experience has been replaced by a sense of that process as an essentially social game of manipulable conventions in our own real world. The reading of the novel becomes for us a kind of admonitory training for life in society.[10]

If this reasoning seems strained, at least it is reasoning, and is a good deal less strained than the claim made in practically all theories of romance reading that the reading process, *as* individual experience, somehow miraculously suspends that subject-object opposition on which the whole idea of individual experience depends to begin with. But the reading of *Werther* I suggest implies only the necessity of the *idea* of reading as a social act. It does not establish anything resembling a fact. And this problem leads in the direction of Goethe's *Unterhaltungen deutscher Ausgewanderten*, in which the much more explicit insistence on the idea of the social, on matters of propriety and decorum, and on the question of how the stories we read serve the immediate communal interest of the group in which they are told is such that I think we cannot but become confused about our situation as individual readers of a book. Actually, the original readers were readers not of a book but of installments in Schiller's *Die Horen*; and perhaps we may surmise that delivery in installments was meant to have the effect of *socializing* the text, of

[10]See my "Goethe's *Werther*: Double Perspective and the Game of Life," *GQ* 53 (1980), 64–81, and "Werther and Montaigne: The Romantic Renaissance," *Goethe Yearbook* 3 (1986), 1–20.

integrating it into the weave of a larger segment of our existence than is usually occupied by one literary work, of giving it almost the character of an actual social circle in our world to which we return from time to time in the course of our other affairs.

But even if this is the case, the result is to make us still more aware of our situation as individual silent *readers*, and uncomfortable with that situation, by contrast with the suggested but (for us) nonexistent face-to-face social reality that the text seems to insist on. There is a constant tension and interplay between our situation as readers and the imagined possibility or desirability of our direct participation in the social dynamics depicted. When the Baroness, for example, claims the right to expect in her circle that people express opinions only to those who already agree with them ("indem der eine dasjenige sagt, was der andere schon denkt" [WA, 18:114]), we perhaps wonder whether this condition can or even should be satisfied. But in consequence of the reflection upon reading that the text suggests, it must also occur to us that *as readers* we in a sense do fulfill the Baroness's condition, at least in its passive aspect. By doing our part in constituting the text's meaning, in filling its Iserian "blanks"— although I am now thinking more along the line established by Poulet—we ourselves *do* "already think" the thought of an "other," of the character or attitude articulated by the text we are reading; and we do so even when that thought is new to us, indeed even if the thought as such offends us. The thought would not be there for us in the first place, and so could not offend us, if we did not do our part in thinking it, in constituting it, in "supplying" it, as Goethe says.[11] In fact, given the attitude we adopt when reading, especially when reading fiction, the offensive thought will probably not offend us anyway in the way that it would if it were flung at us in an actual conversation such as that between Karl and the Geheimerath. Therefore, if we could adopt and maintain that readerly attitude in actual society, the Baroness's requirement would be met—and without detriment to the honesty, radicality, or variety of opinions expressed, since it would be met in the act of listening, not of speaking. The same applies to the old pastor's bitter remark that nothing is more of a nuisance in society than an invitation to serious thought and insight (WA, 18:121). Again, if we could bring our readerly open-minded-

[11]See, for example, WA, pt. 2, 3:118, and the conversation with Riemer from late 1831 in H. G. Gräf, *Goethe über seine Dichtungen*, pt. 2, vol. 2 (Frankfurt am Main, 1904), p. 601.

ness along with us into society, the cause of the pastor's complaint would disappear.

But it is clear that "the reader" and "readerly," in this context, refer to the romance reader, whose consciousness is expanded by participation in the text's unfolding. Does this mean that Goethe, in the *Unterhaltungen*, accepts the convention of romance reading after all? The same problem arises from the *Wanderjahre* discussion earlier. How can we concede that the idea of romance reading operates in shaping the text's meaning for us, but without being an operative literary convention? What is suggested in the *Unterhaltungen* in response to this problem is that romance reading was never a strictly *literary* convention to begin with, but rather a *social* convention. The self-expansive conscious exercise of romance reading becomes useful and fruitful if carried out in the dialogic actuality of society, whereas (already in *Werther*) it becomes futile, contradictory, clearly ungenuine, when insisted upon in the solitude of silent reading. Somehow we have managed to import into our readerly solitude a behavioral convention that belongs properly to our direct relations with other people. Or perhaps this importation is itself a mere illusion. Perhaps the act of reading has never really been a solitary act after all; perhaps reading is always a strictly social act, every bit as social as actual conversation ("Unterhaltung")—by which I mean conversation with other real people, not an abstract, Gadamerian "hermeneutic conversation." Perhaps the supposed mental solitude of the silent reader is never anything but a perverse denial of simple fact. I recall, in this connection, my earlier invocation of professional scholarly reading; for those scribbles we make in the margins *are* strictly conversation, fragments of an actual debate with other real commentators.

Certain features of the *Unterhaltungen* bear directly upon this problematic notion of reading as a strictly social act, especially the uncomfortable open form of the work, the prominence in both the inner stories and the frame story of frustratingly unanswerable questions. We think especially of the character Friedrich, who promises to develop his idea for an explanation of the story of the singer Antonelli, but never says another word on the subject (WA, 18:144), and who later tantalizingly mentions a mysterious "talisman" in his family (18:157–58), which we also never hear of again. These are not "blanks" for the reader to deal with, in Iser's or in Roman Ingarden's sense; they are more like slaps in the reader's face, clear narrative signals of a coming development that never occurs. By raising such specific expectations and then failing to satisfy them, Goethe draws our attention *to the expectations themselves*, hence to a special character of our situation as readers—since the same expectations, although they might arise in actual social intercourse, would also quickly fade, as they apparently do for the personages in the frame narrative. Why do we have such expectations of *closure* in reading? What is our insistence upon a particular kind of closure in literary narrative, if not the attempt to experience a corresponding closure or self-wholeness in the supposedly individual self who is reading? And if this move to achieve individual closure now becomes the *content* of our reflection (in the markedly unclosed *Unterhaltungen*), does it not follow that we have already acknowledged the strictly social quality of the act of reading—even if we cannot say exactly how our reading has this quality? In any case, the questioning of closed individuality is clearly suggested as an interpretive possibility in "Das Märchen," the closing section of the *Unterhaltungen*.

Reading and the Truth of Science

Another question suggested by the *Unterhaltungen* is the question of *truth*. "A story," we read, "must be true if it is to be interesting" (WA, 18:143). Our first inclination is to interpret this statement as simply as possible: an interesting story must refer to an actual event. But a few pages later the idea recurs in a context that suggests the epistemological complications of natural science and historiography: "It seems to me, said Karl, that every phenomenon, and every fact, in itself, is what is actually interesting. The person who explains it, or correlates it with other instances, is usually at bottom only having his own joke and putting it over on us, I mean the natural scientist, or the historian. An individual action or incident, however, is interesting not because it is explainable or probable, but because it is true" (18:150–51). We might dismiss this speech as an insistence on the strictly local character of what we claim to recognize as truth, if it were not for the parallel meditations on theory and theorizing in the foreword to the *Farbenlehre* (WA, pt. 2, 1:xii)—meditations, incidentally, that are picked up and developed in several aphorisms in the *Wanderjahre*. As soon as we open our eyes and look at the world, says Goethe, we have already begun to form explanatory theories, whether we admit it or not, theories which interfere with our relation to "Erfahrungen," "experiences," in the sense that these latter would otherwise simply be *there* for us. Does the word "truth" (as Karl uses it, referring to strictly "individual" objects) not evidently mean that quality of simple there-ness which, paradoxically—because of our theoretical mode of perception—is also always just beyond our reach? Is this not also what is meant by "Das alte Wahre" in the poem "Vermächtnis," which is also a part of the *Wanderjahre* (*WMW*, p. 585)? The possible etymological relation between the German "wahr" (true) and the notion of perceptual immediacy ("gewahr," "wahrnehmen," English "aware") perhaps operates here for Goethe as it does later for Heidegger.

But in the *Farbenlehre* Goethe does not conclude that immediate contact with the simple thereness of phenomena or "experiences" is strictly out of the question. In order to achieve a scientific grasp of the true in this sense, he says, we *must* theorize (since we cannot avoid it); but, "to use a daring expression," we must theorize with *irony*. Somehow we must set up an ironic relation to our own theorizing in order to cancel our *dependence* on theory and open our eyes to the true, to what is simply there. And in the *Unterhaltungen*, which were written alongside the work leading up to the *Farbenlehre*, this thought is employed to focus our attention on the situation of the reader. The trouble with Karl's speech quoted earlier is that it does not fit the circumstances in which it is spoken. Everyone present, including Karl himself, is in the process of suggesting theories about the bursting desk top, correlations of events that might account for it. The lesson of the bursting desk top is thus precisely that in the real world there is no such thing as Karl's "true" phenomenon, unobscured by our theorizing drive, our need to make sense of reality. But what about the bursting desk top *from the point of view of the reader*? The reader's attention, our attention, in that passage is focused not on the various explanations themselves, but on what they reveal about the characters who suggest them. We are not ourselves worried about explaining the phenomenon. We accept it as a textual given; it is *simply there* for us. The relation between the bursting desk top and the mind of the reader as reader is therefore analogous to the relation between what Karl calls a "true" phenomenon and the hypothetical pure mind that encounters it as such. Karl's words, by *not* strictly applying to himself, suggest this application to *us*.

Or perhaps we do wonder, after all, about how the bursting desk top might be explained. But at least we do not take our wondering seriously; we recognize it as part of an interpretive game that we have allowed ourselves to be engaged in with the text. If we theorize, that is, then we do so only "with irony," with a perspective on our theorizing, thus again carrying out an action analogous to the adequate perception of the true. I do not mean that the bursting desk top *is* a "true" phenomenon as we receive it. In our real world, it is not a "phenomenon" at all. I mean that by reading we find ourselves approximating *the type of mental activity* necessary to achieve perception of the true. If *Werther* is training for life in society, then the *Unterhaltungen* are training in irony, in the scientific approach to truth.

On one hand, the *Unterhaltungen* bring home to us that our situation as readers verges problematically on the social; on the other hand, the work provides training in irony. And these two characteristics are related by the consideration that irony itself is a strictly *social* phenomenon. One cannot be ironic with oneself, or ironic in solitude, since irony requires an irreducible measure of uncertainty about what is meant by the presumed ironic utterance. If theorizing "with irony" means nothing but *my* adoption of a detached or questioning perspective on *my* theorizing, then my supposed irony merely belongs to the original theorizing as a qualification, a limitation on its range or probable accuracy, hence an increase in its precision, which tends to *fortify* it (for me) as theory, not to induce that self-questioning of theory as such which might disclose the true. Irony means nothing except in a social or intersubjective space. Nor does this recognition necessarily imply that the idea of an *ironic text* is without meaning. It implies, rather, that that idea, which we use routinely, like the whole idea of romance reading, is an importation of social conditions into what we imagine as the solitary reading process; or more precisely, it implies that the notion of an ironic text is a silent acknowledgment that reading is never truly solitary after all, but always—even when we imagine ourselves alone with the text—a social act.

The statement that reading is a social act is still counterintuitive, but it is clear that our reading of the *Unterhaltungen* at least *verges*, perhaps uncomfortably, on the social. The both untenable and unavoidable idea of the strictly individual reader, in any case, is a theoretical embarrassment. Iser, for instance, dissociates himself repeatedly from what he calls Poulet's "substantialist" notion of the reading "consciousness" (*IR*, p. 293; *AR*, p. 155);[12] but the dynamic or multiple entity he puts in its place, the "contrapuntally structured personality" of reading (*AR*, p. 156), is still too single, too individual, too solitary, not multiple enough, to accommodate the irony gestured at by Goethe's text. Poulet, in fact, may come closer to a social conception of reading (and to Goethe's thinking) when he insists on the author as the vessel of a *second* personality involved in the process of reading. There is an interesting quotation in "Aus Makariens Archiv" (Goethe mistakenly attributes it to Laurence Sterne), which insists on the author of the text as an actual person for the reader, whether or not identifiable with some particular historical person (*WMW*, p. 767).[13] But this aphorism does not imply that the closeted intercourse of author and reader, as Poulet imagines it, establishes the social quality of reading in the sense that Goethe requires.

The connections among scientific truth, irony, and the social are by no means absent in Goethe's explicit view of natural science. The perception of the "true"—I am still borrowing this term from the *Unterhaltungen*—in the sense of a somehow not-yet-theorized experience or phenomenon is clearly the only form of perception that can be fully shared by individuals who are otherwise shut off from one another within the less-than-true conceptions that are produced by each ego's particular theorizing. Indeed, the ability to be shared is the only conceivable *test* of the true in this sense of the word—as is suggested by the *Wanderjahre* aphorism that reads, "In natural science a categorical imperative is as necessary as in morals" (p. 578). Goethe does not actually state this new categorical imperative. But it is fairly clear that Kant's "act as if . . ." will be replaced by "perceive nature as if . . ."—it being understood (1) that perception is not a simple given in experience, but is always already corrupted by theorizing; (2) that our theorizing, however, and hence also the perception with which it is entangled, is subject to our "ironic" control, that even the "truth" of sense perception (as the poem "Vermächtnis" suggests) depends on clarity of "understanding"; and (3) that irony in

[12]Iser quotes mainly from Georges Poulet, "Phenomenology of Reading," *NLH* 1 (1969), 53–68. See also Poulet's article "Criticism and the Experience of Interiority," in *The Structuralist Controversy: The Languages of Criticism and the Sciences of Man*, ed. Richard Macksey and Eugenio Donato (Baltimore, 1972), pp. 56–72, and his book *Entre moi et moi: Essais critiques sur la conscience de soi* (Paris, 1977).

[13]Goethe is quoting Richard Griffith, *The Posthumous Works of a Late Celebrated Genius, Deceased*, 2 vols. (New York, 1974; facs. of 1770 ed.), 2:195. Griffith was confused with Sterne even in the 1813–14 edition of Sterne's works.

turn is not just a solitary mental exercise, that irony in science, on the contrary, can be realized only in our actual relations with *other* theorizers and perceivers.

Therefore the same aphorism continues, "But it must be borne in mind that with such an imperative one has arrived only at the beginning, not at the end." For science at this level is no longer the business of an individual thinking mind vis-à-vis nature, of a mind that might be satisfied with its conclusions; science now involves the social dynamics of a constantly changing community of thinkers. The idea of this social dynamics is already developed in the essay "Der Versuch als Vermittler von Object und Subject," and is then picked up in the *Wanderjahre* and in the vision of an "edle Geisterschaft" in the poem "Vermächtnis," where it appears that only radical change and competition among theories can produce the atmosphere in which any particular theory becomes ironic. "Nothing," says another *Wanderjahre* aphorism, "is more offensive than the majority" (*WMW*, p. 582); to accept a widely held theory is to strengthen that theory's claim to objective validity, hence to protect theory in general *against* irony, thus to violate perceptual truth. Therefore, "Geselle dich zur kleinsten Schar" (p. 586), which I take to mean: make a point of joining precisely the smallest of the competing theoretical armies, in order to promote the profoundest questioning of theory, hence the propagation of irony, hence the closest possible approximation to a universal perception of the true. "Geselle dich zur kleinsten Schar" is perhaps itself a cryptic version of the new categorical imperative.

It may be, in fact, that the relation between reading as a social act and reading as an individual act is exactly parallel to the relation between perceptual truth and theory in Goethe's view of science. It may be that there is no way to *say* adequately that reading is a social act, even though—precisely *in* our reading, and in the reflection on reading suggested by the "ironic" quality of certain texts—we are confronted repeatedly by anomalies that require the operation of the social for their resolution, by the recognition that a strictly individual or private relation to the text of *Werther* would face us with a choice that, in fact, we do not worry about, by the suggestion in the *Unterhaltungen* that what we think of as literary conventions are better understood as social conventions, and by the concept of the "ironic" itself, which we routinely apply to texts considered as objects of individual scrutiny, but which assumes meaning only in relation to a realization of the social that is perhaps modeled, but certainly not accomplished, in the supposed intercourse between author and reader. Reading is unquestionably an experience; and in fact, in relation to the reflection on it suggested by the texts we have looked at, it is exactly the experience we are engaged in while reflecting. But it appears that the very act of calling it "reading," of distinguishing it *as* an experience, necessarily produces a theory of the individual or private reader—in the manner of the tradition from James to Iser—which turns out to be flawed. This paradox corresponds exactly to our relation with the true, which is always there, always present in our experience of nature, yet also always necessarily corrupted by theory as soon as we distinguish or identify it *as* an experience. As truth is our basic perceptual relation to nature, we might say, so reading is our basic perceptual relation to text, or to the linguistic in general, considered as text. And yet, both truth and reading, in this sense, are beyond theory, immune to any conceivable form of general definition.

Fate and Irony in Goethe's *Lehrjahre*

In Goethe's *Wilhelm Meisters Lehrjahre*, which for a time was in progress side by side with the *Unterhaltungen*, the theme of the opposition between fate and chance ("Schicksal" and "Zufall") is insisted upon so obviously that it stands close to the center of practically every interpretation. It is generally recognized, with variations in detail, that the revelation of the rôle of the secret Tower Society at the novel's end strongly discredits the idea of fate; what had appeared to be fate now turns out to have been chance or error or the calculation of fallible mortals. But if the reader of the novel is fully engaged as an individual in the process of constituting the fiction, if his or her situation is in truth as Iser describes it at the end of *The Implied Reader*, then that reader has become thereby, in spite of the plot, a *believer in fate*. For the "virtual" persistence of our own self (*IR*, p. 293)—even while, as an "alien" self (p. 293), we experience the "unfolding of the text as a living event" (p. 290)—must include the knowledge that the text pre-exists as a concrete object and cannot be changed; and to experience as a "living event" something that is determined in advance is, quite simply, to believe in fate. The novel's content, its establishment and demolition of the idea of fate, thus clashes directly with the posture of romance reading, which is structurally equivalent to a belief in fate.

Wilhelm's behavior early in the novel repeatedly parodies the behavior of a hypothetical naïve reader. He begins to respond emotionally to some experience or other; he then speculates elaborately on the place of that experience in a larger, fatal (or we might say, fictional) order of things, on its rôle in his destiny; and this speculation magnifies dangerously his initial emotional investment, which in turn makes it more pressing for him to believe in fate. The revelation about "fate" at the end, or about Wilhelm's self-indulgently self-blinding confusion of concrete response and abstract speculation, is therefore also a revelation about ourselves as readers. Wilhelm himself has argued that fate is more at home in the drama than in the novel (WA, 22:178); and we, as readers of this novel, are reminded accordingly that *we* do not really believe in fate. Not that we somehow suddenly become a different type of reader in the last two books. We are reminded, rather, that we have *never* really been romance readers in the manner that is parodied by Wilhelm's immature behavior.

The *Lehrjahre*, like *Werther* and the *Unterhaltungen*, thus insists that we reflect upon our reading and that this reflection take account of itself in a manner that not only recognizes but also constantly regenerates the quality of *irony*, the inevitability of a social or intersubjective component in our situation as readers. It is the second main aspect of the theory of romance reading that is rejected here, or at least challenged: the idea of the *solitary* reader, of reading as the encounter or collision between a self and a text, the impression we have of being *alone* with the text, no matter how much our readerly state may reflect social or cultural conditions.

Like Lucidor in the novella "Wer ist der Verräter?" the reader, in what he or she imagines as an intense emotional privacy, is in truth *never alone*—never really in a position to experience the fictional world, even temporarily, as a strictly private world. Reading, rather, must be imagined as one of those patterns of relation among widely separated individuals that are the principal theme of the *Wanderjahre*, one of those "noble threads" (*WMW*, p. 405) which in defiance of time and distance bind us to others. (We think again of "Vermächtnis" and its "edle Geisterschaft.") The "world" or "experience" of the fiction may seem to be entirely proportional to our individual needs while we are reading; but like the main figure in "Die neue

Melusine," we not only live in that world, we also *see* ourselves living in it, and so cannot really live in it after all. (The "artificial division of our personality" that Iser speaks of [*IR*, p. 293; *AR*, p. 155] itself becomes an object of our critical scrutiny.) And this allegory, like that of "Wer ist der Verräter?" suggests that the idea of solitary reading, for practical purposes, contains a contradiction. *As* an idea, namely, as an account we give of our reading, if only to ourselves, it is involved in communicative relations that disintegrate its own supposed solitary object.

As readers who are conscious of being such, we live primarily in a world of *other readers*, which truth is borne in on us in the *Wanderjahre* by the constant focusing of our attention on the process of reading. The ultimately alienating gymnastics performed with narrative point of view and chapter divisions serve this end, as do the aphorisms, and in them the extended homage to Laurence Sterne, in whose case, says Goethe, we are "reminded that of everything, or at least of most of what delights us in him, we are meant to absorb no part into ourselves" (*WMW*, p. 771). And we recall the frequent, more or less obvious *images* of reading, or of readers, in the *Wanderjahre*, the catalogue of which can be augmented by what turn out, in the final published version, to be the text's last words, the poem "Im ernsten Beinhaus war's . . ."

The figure in this poem of the speaker contemplating a skull suggests not only *Hamlet*—specifically Yorick, and therefore, again, Laurence Sterne—but also, very precisely, our situation as we read. For we too, with the *text* in our hand, are holding an object that is now dead, but bears in its form the divine trace, "Die gottgedachte Spur," of past intellectual vitality. (A living person once produced that text.) This parallel between the text and the skull is hinted at broadly in the verb "beschauen"; in the latent image of books on a shelf, "in Reih' geklemmt," with perhaps even a direct allusion (the idea of "hate") to Jonathan Swift's *Battle of the Books*; in the words "Entrenkte Schulterblätter" (wrenched-out shoulder blades), in which we also hear the concept of "leaves" or pages; and especially in the concepts of "shell," "kernel," "sense," with respect to a "script" ("Schale," "Kern," "Sinn," "Schrift"). We, the readers, like the speaker of the poem, are thus obliged to initiate and experience a reanimation of the dead object before us; we must constitute the text's meaning (in Goethe's term, "supply" it), and in doing so we presumably discover, like the speaker, important truths about ourselves and the world. In other words, the whole structure of romance reading is present in the poem, and present in our reading of the poem. But at the same time, our reading of the poem in precisely this sense is also revealed to us as a *gesture* we make, indeed an explicitly *theatrical* gesture, like Hamlet's, or like the actor's in playing Hamlet, which presupposes a communal situation, an audience. Even to the extent that we *are* solitary readers, therefore, this condition is not one by which we are governed, but is a conscious gesture on our part, an act, somehow, of communication.

And yet, no sooner do we think about reading, no sooner do we attempt to give an account of it, than we find ourselves using the model of the solitary reader. Even the question of reading as a social act inevitably becomes the question: in what sense can, or must, *the* reader be regarded as performing an act in society? The difficulty here lies in the basic theoretical move that replaces every particular reader (me, for example, with my own name and family and social conditions) by a construct called "the" reader, who *is* strictly solitary (as I myself, in reality, never am) precisely, and exclusively, in the sense of having been isolated *by* that theoretical move. Is it possible to escape this bind? Is it possible, in this connection, to move beyond theory?

The Institution of the Solitary Reader and Its History

It seems to me that a logical or theoretical escape becomes unnecessary as soon as we recognize the historical contingency of the solitary reader considered as an institution. For in order to be strictly solitary, the reader must become (or be imaginable as becoming) *anonymous*; we must be in a position to imagine that in reading we somehow temporarily shuck our name, our specific identity, all the confining social determinations of our existence, and become simply *the* reader.[14] And such an idea of reading, in order to assume even a minimal appearance of validity—without which it could not operate as an institution and so could not support the convention of romance reading—requires as a precondition not only the genre of fictional

[14]On the institution of the anonymous reader, and its relation to the ontological status of the text and to the organic metaphor for poetic integrity, see my *Theater As Problem: Modern Drama and Its Place in Literature* (Ithaca, 1990), pp. 63–64, 130–32.

romance, in which a "world" must be realized in the recipient's imagination, but also the technology of printing and the practice of offering printed books for sale to the public. There are plenty of cases, before the age of mass bibliopoly, where romances and other early fictional forms, especially those in prose, were received by a reader, not a listener. But in those cases the production and distribution of written texts was cumbersome enough to permit (or compel) every reader to retain the awareness of a direct *social* relation, if not with the author, then at least with other readers: the awareness that if I were not the particular person I actually happen to be, in particular social or family circumstances, I could not have become the reader of this particular text in the first place. The situation generally presupposed by the idea of solitary reading, where the reader can be imagined as anonymous, where the reader can be *anyone at all* and can therefore be strictly alone with the text, does not arise to any considerable extent until printed books are offered in exchange for sums of money (itself an anonymous substance) that practically anyone might possess.

Even as early as Plato, however, in the discussion of the art of writing in the *Phaedrus* (274b–278c), the possibility of the solitary reader is anticipated, and is regarded as a danger, since the resulting minimum of external control (by operative social circumstances) on the relation between discourse and its recipient will allow the illusion of wisdom to arise in practically any mind, hence the very idea of wisdom to become diffuse and perverted. And the notion of a wholesome external control exercised upon the individual by a community of thought and debate is by no means missing in Christian Europe, where the solitary reader comes to be represented by the figure of the magician closeted with his forbidden books—for example, by Faustus—whose freedom from such control is at least problematic. "Mich plagen keine Skrupel noch Zweifel" (I am plagued by no scruples or doubts), boasts Goethe's version of the midnight reader. Goethe thus operates within a traditional complex that includes a deeply critical attitude toward the solitary reader; and this historical situation forms a background to my argument on the development of Goethe's narratives.

But none of the works from *Werther* to the *Wanderjahre* is aimed at overthrowing the institution of the solitary reader. Such an aim, if it were necessary, if the institution were established with sufficient permanence to require overthrowing, would obviously be futile. My point is that Goethe's narratives are meant to focus a consciousness (in his time) of having *already*, in the development of the European novel, superseded the idea of solitary reading that accompanies the ascendancy of the genre of prose romance and the widespread sale of books. Even in the late twentieth century the pure prose romance is alive and well and enjoyed in often furtive solitude by millions; but Goethe, especially in the *Wanderjahre*, calls attention to what I contend he sees (in his time) as the opposing development of the *ironic novel*—especially in Sterne, also at least in Wieland and Diderot— where the figure of the solitary reader is thematized, reduced to an object, permitted to display its inconsistency as an idea and its illusoriness as an experience, where it is used, in other words, primarily as a foil for reasserting and bringing to light the undeniable (if also untheorizable) *communal* quality of reading. The historical contingency of solitary reading, hence of the convention of romance reading, is crucial. I maintain that for Goethe this contingency is still sufficiently obvious, that the habit of regarding the solitary reader not as a simple theoretical given but as an object of suspicion and scrutiny, is still sufficiently alive, to permit him to recognize (or believe he recognizes) the *end* of the historical phase dominated by the illusion of romance reading—in a manner which we, from a twentieth-century perspective, must make a special effort to reproduce.

The Community of Readers and the Bible

But precisely what kind of community must reassert itself in the ruins of romance reading? The idea of responding to the presence of the author as a separate person, or of responding to the thematized image of the reader by reading with an eye to other readers, still presupposes solitary reading on our part. And my initial suggestion concerning the practice of modern professional literary scholars refers to a community that did not exist in Goethe's time. For Goethe, the literary scholar is the "philologist," who is treated equitably but is not flattered in the *Wanderjahre* aphorisms (*WMW*, pp. 568, 768). What, then, does Goethe envisage? In order to make reasonable sense of our hypotheses, we require a model, an example from Goethe's experience, of a group of texts and a group of readers such that the texts are essentially fictional, but the readers take them not in the spirit of romance, but in the constant knowledge of drawing upon and contributing to a community of understanding and debate. The text I have in mind is the Bible. Goethe's was a time of radical Bible criticism—the names most familiar to literary scholars are Reimarus, Lessing, Herder, even Goethe himself[15]—which subjected the text to cross-examination especially on its historical accuracy and its narrative structure and significance, and thus tended to transform the Bible into a kind of fiction. But reading the Bible, for both believers and critics, is still always a community-oriented action. One is never alone with the text in the sense that one is supposedly alone with a prose romance, which one is free to elaborate as far as imagination will permit. The discoveries that even the passionate believer makes about himself in reading are not self-discovery in the sense of romance reading, but always *generic* in character, concerning the sinner, the faithful servant, the soul in a state of grace, and so on.

There is, then, at least a possible model for the type of reading Goethe thinks is demanded by the developing ironic novel of his age; but it is a problematic model. In "Aus Makariens Archiv" we read: "I am convinced that the Bible becomes all the more beautiful, the more it is understood, the more we comprehend and perceive that every word—which we interpret generally and apply to ourselves in particular—once had its own special, immediately individual reference to specific circumstances, specific conditions in time and place" (*WMW*, p. 755). The word "beautiful" is significant, for this concept is carefully distinguished in the *Wanderjahre* from that of the *true*. Does the Bible also become *truer* for being subjected to critical scrutiny? Does it become more of a binding force in the community of its readers? Does Bible criticism strengthen that fundamental religious feeling, "daß man in Leben und Tod zusammen gehöre" (p. 344; that in life and death we belong together)? I think the answer is clearly no. The controversy of opinions raised by Bible criticism tends to divide, not to unite; it becomes necessary, as we hear in a late conversation with J.P. Eckermann, that we pass beyond our "Christianity of word and belief" to a "Christianity of sentiment and deed" (11 March 1832). And if the old "word" (the Bible) is no longer sufficient, then what word, what text, *will* accompany this renewal of our religion? Even Lessing, in *Die Erziehung des Menschengeschlechts*, acknowledges that a new gospel, a new form of holy scripture, is

[15]For Goethe's more or less serious experiments in this field, see, for example, "Israel in der Wüste" (WA, 7:156–82), as well as the early sketch "Zwo . . . biblische Fragen" (WA, 37:175–90).

historically necessary; and a similar recognition is evident in writings of Blake and Hölderlin and some German Romantics. But in Goethe's view, that new holy scripture does not have to be desperately or acidly or volcanically created in something like Blake's prophecies or Hölderlin's "hymns," because it is already evolving naturally, as it were pelagically, in the history of the ironic novel. Like the Bible itself, our new scripture arises in a gradual accumulation of texts, texts that repeatedly break down the illusion of romance reading and establish for themselves, over time, the habit of being read *by* the community *as* a community.

The *Wanderjahre* are full of suggestions of a future religion that will include and supersede Christianity: in the pedagogical province, in the circle surrounding (or emanating from) Makarie, in the Abbé's idea of "Weltfrömmigkeit" (*WMW*, p. 514; secular [or universal, or ecumenical] piety). And if we agree that the far-flung society of "Renunciants," along with its various offshoots and affiliates, is an image of the invisible community of the novel's readers, then the connection between that future religion and the literary tradition of the novel is fairly clear. Goethe's notion of "Weltliteratur" also suggests this connection. "World literature" for us is a commonplace; we teach it all the time. But for Goethe its coming represents an "epoch" in cultural history, a new form of human belonging-together ("zusammen gehören"), hence a phenomenon bordering on the religious.[16] Nor does it matter that this view neglects the status of the novel as an aesthetic object, since for Goethe the novel is not an aesthetic object to begin with. In "Aus Makariens Archiv," in another quotation Goethe believed to be from Sterne, the status of *any* poetry as "art" is denied: "Poetry . . . was breathed into the soul, when it first quickened, and should neither be stiled art or science, but *genius*" (*WMW*, p. 769).[17] Accordingly, in the pedagogical province, there is no preserve for poetry, which I take to mean literature in general; poetry, rather, is permitted to arise naturally from the study of music and the visual arts. The work of literature is not something a human being makes or contemplates, but rather part of what humankind, from the soul's first quickening, *is*.

[16]See, for example, Eckermann, 31 January and 18 July 1827; and Fritz Strich, *Goethe und die Weltliteratur*, 2d ed. (Bern, 1957), who lists (pp. 369–72) all the occurrences of the word "Weltliteratur" in Goethe.
[17]I quote the original English from Griffith, 2:182. On poetry as neither "speech" nor "art," compare WA, 7:115–16.

And the novel in particular, I contend, is seen by Goethe not as an aesthetic object, but as a locus of social existence, a vehicle of the truth that we are *never alone*. The history of the ironic novel, which rescues us from the historically threatening condition of the solitary reader, is the growth of a new holy scripture of humanity: "Even at the present moment, every educated person ought to take up Sterne's works again, so that even the nineteenth century might learn how we are indebted to him, and understand how we can become further indebted to him" (*WMW*, p. 769). The ironic novel, our main debt to Sterne, is a kind of pre-criticized scripture, immune to the divisive effects of something like Bible criticism because it is known from the outset to be fiction. And precisely because it is fiction, it is in a position to mobilize our "secular piety," our "Weltfrömmigkeit," by focusing our consciousness not on a sacred content or message about which we might disagree, but on the community of wisdom and truth that arises in the act of reading it, in *nothing but* the act. As in the poem "Im ernsten Beinhaus war's . . ." the gesture of reading is itself the whole fundamental content of reading.

The Secular Religion of Literature

We are left with the question of the substance of the new "religion" we are talking about. I think we have already in effect answered this question, in a manner consistent, for example, with the aphorism that suggests the need for a new word, "Volkheit" ("peoplehood"), that would be related to the concept of "people" as "childhood" is to "child" (*WMW*, p. 756). Just as the ironic form of the novel counteracts the threatening ascendancy of the solitary reader, so the religion of the novel opposes philosophically the establishment of the *individual* as the accepted atom of human existence. The currency of social-contract theory in the eighteenth century—along with the theory of natural law, or natural rights, which is understood (except perhaps in Rousseau) to be necessary as the contract's sanction—represents the development of an atomistic view of society as an association of at least originally or essentially free individuals. And the novel, for Goethe, in the dynamics of our reading it, opposes this tendency by promoting the recognition that we are *never alone*—never even in a position to evince either Thomas Hobbes's original egoism or Hugo

Grotius's social need—a recognition that the individual simply does not happen in the form suggested by the pose of solitary reading, that the individual has no existence whatever prior to his or her dialectical relation with society. There is no state of nature, either in the form of innocence or in that of the war of all against all. Or more precisely—to recall my formulation of Goethe's position on the history of consciousness—our present condition, including our mythologizing of it as the result of a fall or rupture, *is* the state of nature. Our alienated individuality is never in truth anything other than a particular form of belonging to society, of being contained and determined by the community.

Accordingly, the idea of the individual not as a primary but as a *secondary* manifestation of the human, as a function of the community, is prominent in the thought of such figures as Montan and the Abbé; even the idea of the individual as an organ of the species, as an experimental "apparatus" (*WMW*, p. 760) for establishing contacts with nature, is suggested in Makarie, in the sensitive discovered by Montan, in the aphorisms, and in the poem "Vermächtnis." The trouble with these quasi-religious ideas, however, is that when expressed as doctrine or theory, they automatically become confused; for doctrine as such presupposes the possibility of disagreement, hence the independence and primacy of the individual, the individual's right to stand where he pleases in relation to others. It is this difficulty that frustrates Herder, for example, and produces the ugly character of his campaign against Kant. His quarrel is at bottom with Kant's taking of the individual mind as a primal model for human reason, with Kant's failure to acknowledge the priority of the strictly communal entity represented especially by language. But precisely this quarrel, *as* a theoretical quarrel (regardless of its content), reinforces the Kantian position. Hence the usefulness, and the historical significance, for Goethe, of the ironic form of the novel. For in the novel, which is recognized from the outset as fiction, the truth of communal priority cannot take the form of doctrine, but rather, by way of our experience of community even in the apparent anonymous privacy of our armchairs, is inscribed indelibly *in the gesture of reading*.

That this type of philosophical truth is inaccessible to theory makes it unavailable, as well, to the interpretation of any given text. But once we have begun thinking on this line, we suddenly find it very easy to deal with a number of otherwise intractable problems in interpretation of the *Wanderjahre*. In particular, a parallel is drawn between the three gestures of salutation in the pedagogical province—the first expressing reverence for what is higher, the second for what is lower, the third for what is level with ourselves—and three fundamental types of religion, the ethnic, the Christian, and the philosophical. But the historical and natural order of the religions appears to differ from that of the corresponding gestures; Christianity, embodying reverence for what is below, is the culminating stage in religion (*WMW*, p. 429), whereas philosophical religion corresponds to the culminating gesture of communal solidarity. Moreover, in two of the parallel triads that are spoken of, the triad of gestures and the analogy of the Trinity, the emphasis at the philosophical stage is on community, on an "inspired community . . . of those who are good and wise in the highest degree" (p. 423), whereas in the abstract and concrete versions of the historical triad, the emphasis in philosophical religion (which includes Christ's activity as a sage and a maker of parables) is on a "teaching for individuals" (p. 427), on the wise man's living "in a cosmic sense alone in the truth" (p. 422). And precisely the ambiguity in the last quotation, which could be read to mean that "only" the wise man lives in truth—without being, in other respects, "alone"—acknowledges the problem in the structure of concepts.

In order to untangle these triads, I propose first to relate the three gestures of greeting to the gestural process of reading a novel. The initial gesture, of reverence for what is higher, represents the situation of the experiencing or participating reader of romance, whose attitude, at least in its structure—as we saw in connection with the *Lehrjahre*—is necessarily that of a believer in fate. The second gesture represents the stage at which, in responding to narrative irony, I find myself excluded from the firmly destined or ordered world of the fiction, suddenly in my own "real" world, which—precisely by contrast with the reliable fictional order—takes on the character of a dangerous and unaccountable world of chance. In reading a novel, however (and by analogy, in a properly conceived education), we encounter this world of chance not as a simple objective reality—as if there were such a thing—but as a contrast, as itself in effect an aspect of that fiction whose strictly fictional (hence human-fashioned, affirmable) character the same narrative irony has insisted we acknowledge. That is, even the dangerous world of chance (and suffering and sin and evil) has been realized as a manifestation of human

formative activity—we recall Schiller's idea of transforming death itself into a human act—thus a possible object of affirmation or, in the
image, of "reverence."

This argument depends on the assumption, which I think I have
justified, that the principal content of the *Wanderjahre* for a
reader—like the content of the poem "Im ernsten Beinhaus war's
. . ."—is the act (and the question of the act) of reading, in at least as
strong a sense as a similar statement might be made of *Tristram
Shandy* or *Jacques le fataliste*. Once this assumption is made, a great
many things fall into place. We may now ask, once more, *why* the
convention of romance reading (the first gesture of reverence) is invoked in texts whose reading is not meant to be governed by it. That
convention opens for us the prospect not only of living "another life,"
but of living life *in another way*, a better way, a way somehow ex-
empt from "the subject-object division" (*AR*, p. 155), a life in which
the foreground is occupied not by uncertainty, suffering, evil, but by
what ordinarily occupies only the dim background: destiny, "Bildung," totality, the object of the first gesture. But the convention of
romance reading is *only* a convention. Actually, we neither read nor
live in the realm that the first gesture of reverence envisages. What
that gesture accomplishes, in fact, is to *profile*, to bring into focus, to
establish as an intense foreground, precisely what it denies: the subject-object division considered as the root and vessel of our helpless
subjection to chance, suffering, evil, mortality. And yet, this profil-
ing also presents us with its object as an artistic shape, a fiction, a
myth, a human act, hence itself a possible object of affirmation or
reverence. And the act of revering it, the second gesture of reverence, when we carry it out, immediately becomes a reverence for
what is "below." For that act itself *lifts us up* out of the condition it
reveres; it is precisely *not* an act of helpless submission. The convention of romance reading thus operates as a lever by which we are
enabled to assert the fictionality not of the novel's ostensible content,
but of our *real* existence, in a sense of "real" that otherwise suggests
only suffering and despair; it is employed to assert and reveal the
mythical quality of our actual, supposedly "fallen" condition.

And then there is the question, which we have not yet touched on,
of the *transition* from the gesture of romance reading to the actuality
of communal reading. Again the second gesture of reverence is significant. For with that second (intermediate, temporary) gesture of
affirmation—the corresponding stage of abandonment to chance is

kept "as short as possible" in education (*WMW*, p. 421)—the transition to the final stage of solidarity is *already* effected, since that second gesture *cannot be made on behalf of the individual alone*, who in relation to the world of chance is by definition (in that narrow, contingent particularity which *is* the individual) merely its victim, not in a position to view it as his or her own act or object of reverence. The second gesture of reverence in a sense originates with the individual (the romance reader), but at the same time is always *already* made on behalf of the community; or more exactly, it is made *by* the community *through* the individual, and so reveals a primally communal quality even in the gesture that had preceded it. And then the gesture that follows, the final gesture of reverence for what is on a level with us, the gesture that explicitly signals communal solidarity, turns out to suggest not social intercourse among individuals, but community in a more tenuous sense. The boys stand in a line, all with their eyes to the right (p. 415), so that each watches the next watching the next, and so on, in a pattern that corresponds exactly to the situation of the reader of a novel in which the reader is fully thematized, the situation of a reader who does not read except, so to speak, over the shoulder of other readers. We must imagine a community not only *of* gesture, but *in* gesture, whose very substance is the gesture that characterizes it. This community, again, is not subject to doctrinal formulation, since doctrine as such presupposes the free individual. It is a community of "renunciation"—renunciation, ultimately, of the very idea of atomistic individuality—and is there for us only *in* the gestural quality of the act of reading by which we affirm it.

The interpretive difficulty with which we started, the apparent inconsistencies among triadic structures in the pedagogical province, can now be dealt with if we consider the three painting galleries as *models for interpretation* of the experience represented by the three gestures. For the ethical climax of the novel as a genre—and by analogy, the climax of education—is the acknowledgment in practice that our exposed condition as mortal individuals is not a simple fact, not an external condition, but a fiction, a myth, a freely made gesture, a Christ-like sacrifice that is dialectically required for the grounding of our actual communal nature—in the same way that variety is dialectically necessary for the realization of unity, or Becoming for Being, in Neoplatonic thought. If we once achieve this interpretation of the act of reading—corresponding to the gallery of Christ's suffering, the gallery that neither we nor Wilhelm actually see—if we once succeed in "recognizing humility and poverty, mockery and contempt, disgrace and misery, suffering and death as divine," if we succeed in "revering even sin and transgession not as hindrances but as furtherances of the holy, and so come to love them" (*WMW*, pp. 422–23), then it does not matter particularly how deep a philosophical understanding we have of the community to which we now belong. Understanding, after all—in the sense of a theoretical grounding—is not only unnecessary, but a positive danger, since it automatically threatens to become doctrine. Therefore, of the three picture galleries, only one is not visited at some time by all the province's pupils: the second, corresponding to philosophical religion—the gallery of Christ as *teacher*—which is opened only to those pupils who "grow up with a certain depth of thoughtfulness" (p. 430).

Philosophical religion is the theoretical culmination of both history and human growth. But for practical purposes, the culmination is Christianity considered as a religion of suffering and sacrifice, the sanctum that is opened only once a year in a ceremony for the province's departing graduates (*WMW*, p. 430), since this religion—in combination with the idea of a chosen people, the "ethnic" religion of the first gallery—already implies the social and ethical aspect of philosophical religion in the same way that the second gesture of reverence already implies the third. Or in terms of the literary analogy, even an entirely naïve view, an "ethnic" interpretation of the community of readers as a kind of chosen people, is sufficient to support the requisite interpretive conclusion concerning the ultimately communal value of our insistence on endangered, mortal individuality as an act of sacrifice.

It is of crucial significance, however, that just as one of the three galleries is not opened to all of the pupils, so also another one of the three, the gallery of sufferings, is not opened to us, to the reader. For the content of that gallery is already present to us *in the act of reading*. It is the secret content of the act of reading considered as an affirmative, sacrificial gesture; and it becomes that secret content only by *not* being part of the actual text, only by contrast, only by being "real," only by being utterly *other* than the controlled, fate-like structure of the fiction. The discrepancy between historical views of the triad of religions, therefore, is nothing but a reflection of the difference between the condition of being a character in the fiction (a pupil for whom education culminates in the vision of suffering) and the condition of being a reader.

Not that this difference is absolute. Among the pupils there are a few specially "thoughtful" ones who cannot stop short of theory, but must be conducted beyond theory, and are therefore admitted to the philosophical gallery, the gallery of Christ as parabolic teacher. And we, by being readers, by insisting, inevitably, on an interpretation of the text, also automatically belong to that group, which requires the full philosophical vision of its community as virtually all humanity, and of the dialectical relation between individuality and totality (hence the two else puzzlingly opposed emphases in connection with philosophical religion) that opens that community to the truth. "Geselle dich zur kleinsten Schar" (Join yourself to the smallest company). Perhaps the "kleinste Schar," the smallest group, is just the individual alone; perhaps the combination of this idea with that of the social ("Geselle dich") suggests the idea of asserting individuality *as* a social act, as an act (apparently "my" act) on behalf of the community, which, however, by being carried out, is revealed as the community's act *through* the individual, indeed as the very genesis of individuality, as a gestural enactment of the origin of an individuality that is in turn itself nothing but the community's own self-developing gesture. "Geselle dich zur kleinsten Schar." This is perhaps not only the scientific categorical imperative, but also a basic religious tenet, meaning, Join the virtually universal human community by associating yourself voluntarily with its smallest, but still fundamentally communal, unit, which you might otherwise have experienced as your "own" individual being.

Irony, Community, and the Subversive

But we must not lose sight of the fact that, for all its philosophical pretensions, the idea of community in the *Wanderjahre* is not merely a utopian poetic vision. It refers, in Goethe's view, to an entirely concrete development in the history of reading, a development that can be located with respect to such historical facts as the significance of the form of the ironic novel, especially as practiced by Sterne, Diderot, and Goethe himself, in the eighteenth century; the larger history of the prose romance; the improving technology of printing; and social and economic conditions favoring the widespread sale of fiction in book form. In its structure and operation, moreover, the *Wanderjahre* community shows strong similarities to a community whose existence in Goethe's time can be demonstrated on relatively objective grounds, the community of readers of a criticized Bible. And it is possible to show parallels with what we might reasonably call the community of literary study in our own day. We do, we students of literature, read as a community in something very like the manner required, and we do so with a maximum of self-consciousness. We *are* not "the reader" when we read, but rather our reading is always an asking about "the reader" and can often become specifically a debate about "the reader." "The reader," that is, is not a real individual, but an individualizing *gesture* that operates as a definition of the individual in its relation to a text or to texts in general. And it is in effect a gesture made by and for the community as a whole, as a means of articulating its communicative operation.

The question of the social or political or religious function of the *Wanderjahre* community, or of its *justification* in these realms, is therefore not an idle one. This community is not a visionary alternative to actual structures in society; on the contrary, it must, assuming it exists, play a historical rôle in relation to those structures. But the question of that rôle is at least as difficult as the corresponding question with respect to the community of literary study. For it is a theoretical question and can be posed reasonably only within the framework of what I call, in broad terms, the Enlightenment discussion of individual and society, which proceeds from mainly speculative origins in the historical "Enlightenment," by way of nineteenth-century social theory, especially Marx, down to such thinkers as Horkheimer, Adorno, Marcuse, and Habermas: a discussion that presupposes the individual and is focused on the problem of understanding, locating, configuring, and maintaining individual *autonomy* as a social fact. From this perspective, what conceivable justification can be given for a community in which the individual does not exist except as a gestural enactment of the origin of individuality? "Communicative action" in Habermas's sense, to be sure, may have a certain gestural quality. But it is an action that *arrives at* understanding, at a necessarily articulable or theorizable consensus among individuals, whereas the communicative action of reading in the *Wanderjahre* is strictly ironic, the realization of what one might call a *prior* "consensus" that defies theorizing.

The community of reading, or the community as a reader, thus needs to *be* justified politically or socially; it does not make sense even as an idea if it cannot be assigned a real historical rôle. But it is not *justifiable*, not able to receive any theoretically grounded justification, because of the situation of the individual relative to theoretical discussion as such (as I argued above), and because of the character of the specific Enlightenment discussion in which such justification would have to be embedded. The condition of being justified but not justifiable, however, assuming it holds, implies that in the political realm, the community as a reader, or by analogy the community of literary study, or by extension literature itself (in Goethe's view), is *radically subversive*, subversive with respect to *any* established political or quasi-political order—given that every established order is associated with a system or doctrine that presents a target for the subversive. It follows, in fact, that literature as practice subverts any possible determination of its own content, which is practically a definition of irony. (Here in general, incidentally, as within Goethe's writings in particular, the analogy with natural science suggests itself. For science as the vessel of *any* particular content is what Kuhn calls "normal" science, with respect to which science as a repeatedly revolutionary practice is radically subversive, attacking that content by way of the very idea of world that supports it.[18])

This reasoning may perhaps be regarded as a short path to Theodor Adorno's idea of "The dual essence of art: social fact and autonomy," the idea that art "is social primarily because it stands opposed to society."[19] For Goethe—as for Adorno, *mutatis mutandis*—the question is not the articulable "political stance" of reading, but rather "an immanent dynamic in opposition to society"; and the paradox of a

[18]See Thomas S. Kuhn, *The Structure of Scientific Revolutions*, 2d ed. (Chicago, 1972), esp. chap. 10, "Revolutions as Changes of World View"; also the "anarchic" view of Paul Feyerabend, *Against Method*, rev. ed. (London, 1988). Kuhn, for all the justified praise his work has received, still insists on a facile distinction between "interpretation" and "illumination" (pp. 122–23), still genuflects before "modern psychological experimentation" (p. 126), and still imagines "the world" that "has not changed" (p. 150), all of which throttles the subversive tendency of his own thought. Feyerabend, even while genuflecting to Kuhn (pp. 229–30), is more consistent. A measure of the difference between the two—and a comment on Goethe and irony—is that only Feyerabend's more frankly political and subversive thought could be taken to authorize Goethe's apparently amateurish and reactionary (anti-Newtonian) science, his attempt, for instance, to integrate a "theory" of colors with a history of theories generally regarded as obsolete. In any case, Goethe's idea of "community" (and "categorical imperative") *excludes* precisely the "community" Kuhn associates with a "paradigm" (pp. 176–91). The shared paradigm—Goethe would think of the Newtonians—doctrinalizes and de-ironizes the communal.

[19]Theodor W. Adorno, *Aesthetic Theory*, trans. C. Lenhardt (London, 1984), pp. 320, 321.

justified but unjustifiable community corresponds to Adorno's idea of the "social function" of art as "the function to have no function" (p. 322). But Adorno's thought also shows exactly the theoretical character that Goethe's procedure is designed to avoid. Adorno himself, in his precarious conceptual balancing with respect to the idea of the "fetish character" of art (pp. 323–26), shows himself nervous about the inherent tendency of systematic theory to make fetishes of its governing concepts. Perhaps, therefore, Adorno's thought is useful for understanding Goethe's insistence on simply removing the novel, considered as a focus of opposition or subversivity, from the domain of aesthetic theory and on associating it instead with problems of community and irony. In any case, we will return later to the larger problem of the subversive in literature.

The Relativity of Social Doctrine in the *Wanderjahre*

The question of content, and of "political stance," brings us back to the *Wanderjahre*, whose final book contains a vision of reformed human community and a defense of that vision by arguments that appear to be entirely serious and practical in intent, if perhaps not workable in reality. What is the status of this vision, of these arguments? To what extent is the society organized around Lenardo, Friedrich, Wilhelm, Montan, and the already absent Lothario meant to represent *our* community, the community as a reader? In what manner are that society's doctrines related to the novel's character as a focus of reading? Must we infer, in particular, that Jews are excluded from the community as a reader (*WMW*, pp. 668, 687)?

The doctrine and structure of the great community at the novel's end, in any case, are not presented at all coherently—by contrast, say, with the doctrine and structure of the pedagogical province earlier. Plot complications, crossing narrative strands, and new characters constantly get in the way. Lenardo's diary and his finding of the "nut brown maid" (we keep hearing *Tristram Shandy*)[20], Hersilie's letters and Felix's mysterious casket and Felix himself, Montan and

---

[20]The "nut brown maid" occurs at the end of vol. 7 of *Tristram Shandy*. See Laurence Sterne, *Tristram Shandy*, ed. Howard Anderson (New York, 1980), p. 378. There is also, incidentally, an interesting (and of course indecent) parallel to the three gestures of the pedagogical province, in vol. 2, chap. 7, pp. 72–73.

his sensitive, a walking garment manufactory in the persons of Lydie and Philine, a spiraling quasi-planet in the person of Makarie—all these make demands on our attention, not to mention the two very curious novellas that punctuate the actual founding ceremonies of the new society. The second of these novellas, in fact, the one from the life of Odoard, mimics in miniature the growing structural disorder of the novel as a whole. The point of view in that novella changes bumblingly, constantly trying to provide an adequate background for what has already been narrated; Odoard's story quickly becomes at least three different stories, each of which is necessary for the others but also gets in the others' way; and no attempt is made (any more than in the whole novel) to gather these narrative strands into an ending. This novella, the last one in the novel, is entitled "Nicht zu weit" (Not too far), which (given the overall focus on the relation of text to reader) I think can be read as an admonition to both reader and author of the novel in general not to go "too far" in pretending to create reality or experience via the text. The result will be precisely that disorder and confusion which does in general characterize reality for us. And it follows, further, that we must not go "too far" in imagining we can apply the doctrines of the novel's new community to our own real situation.

To read a novel, in other words, is to make a "dangerous wager." Like St. Christopher in the novella of that title, "Die gefährliche Wette," we find ourselves somehow inside the novel with no ladder by which to escape (*WMW*, p. 664), no scale or gradation of inferences by which to relate the world of the fiction to our actual reality. But it is not that the dangerous world of the novel now *contains* us. On the contrary, we have always *already* escaped from it, even while standing pensively ("in Gedanken" [*WMW*, pp. 664]) in its midst; and like St. Christopher, we cannot, or do not, give an account of how we manage this escape. The theory of romance reading, in any case, would not be a satisfactory account; even the idea of a "division, within the reader himself" (*AR*, p. 155), contains a ladder of thought or personality by which that division is bridged. The only satisfactory account of both our presence in the novel and our escape from it is an account that cannot be given, an account of the community as a reader, in terms of which precisely the individual reader (who would have to give the account) is "the actual criminal" ("der eigentliche Verbrecher"), the cause (*by* being an individual) of his own unaccountable situation.

There is yet another dimension to the confusion or disorder by which we are endangered as individuals (readers or writers) in respect to the novel, an intertextual dimension. "Die gefährliche Wette," namely, is about a man's large nose; and even in the absence of the slightest explicit reference, there is no denying that the mere existence of *Tristram Shandy* therefore puts Goethe's text in danger of becoming at least mildly indecent—with perhaps even a suggestion of the homoerotic. The point is that what we mean by a text, or understand from it, as individuals, is without consequence in the intertextual space where the text actually develops its signification. And if we agree that "reading," at the very least, is a name for the operation of texts among people, in society or in history, then it follows that we, as individuals, are not agents in that process, that the "acts of constitution" in reading (*AR*, pp. 180–231) are entirely beyond the purview of the individual. Or to put it differently, reading, for the individual, is characterized by radical irony, which is illustrated with special clarity in the present example. For Tristram can say as much as he pleases that "by the word *Nose*, throughout all this long chapter of noses, and in every other part of my work, where the word *Nose* occurs—I declare, by that word I mean a Nose, and nothing more, or less."[21] We are still in the position of *knowing* that what he asserts is not the case, but of having no clear grounds upon which to *say* what we know—how can a word "mean" what its author denies it means?—any more than we can say exactly how Goethe's story is infected.

Beyond Theory: Readers and Jews

Thus the context of the programmatic statements that mark the founding of the fictional new society is clearly subversive with respect to any interpretation whatever of those statements' content. This subversive movement is in fact also enacted, or foreshadowed, *within* the fiction, in the bleeding off of a large portion of the new community into the two projects initiated by Odoard and by the senior official ("Amtmann") of the castle where all of book 3 is set. In chapter 1 there are already some signs of dissolution ("The very strange repetitions, the constant resurgence of a song threatening to

[21]*Tristram Shandy*, vol. 3, chap. 31, p. 159.

fade out, seemed to constitute a danger for the company itself"
[*WMW*, p. 595]), although the large band of mainly skilled craftsmen
still seem unanimous and enthusiastic about their coming migration.
After Lenardo's speech in chapter 9, however, it turns out that many
have decided not to emigrate; and Odoard recruits these men with
ideas of communal existence which on some points are directly opposed to Lenardo's. Lenardo insists, for example, that cities and
towns must take shape of their own accord (p. 689), whereas in the
district administered by Odoard, everything has been surveyed and
planned in advance (p. 693). And in the song he has them sing from a
printed sheet, Odoard unobtrusively reminds his recruits that they
will still have the taverns that are to be denied the emigrants (pp.
696, 690). This much might perhaps be understood as a natural division in a corporate body still firmly focused on radical social renewal.
But the motif of subversion is clearly established at the next stage, in
which the castle official, characterized as an "Egoist" (p. 739), plans
to exploit the attractions of the local girls in order to drain off some of
the assembled talent (including some emigrants) for his planned furniture factory. The plot of the novella "Nicht zu weit," in which not-
quite-infidelity (i.e., subversion) is multiplied by not-quite-infidelity,
is perhaps an exaggerated allegory of this situation, but an allegory
nonetheless.

I contend, in fact, that the lengthy programmatic discussion of a
renewed social order functions mainly to create a target for the text's
own inexorable subversiveness, to bring that subversiveness into
focus, thus to create a text that is *nothing but subversive* with respect
to anything that might be claimed as its content. But at the same
time, I have argued that the *Wanderjahre* focuses on the problem of
reading, and that the actual agent of reading in this novel must be
understood as a radically subversive community, a community that
cannot *continue* in existence without becoming the target of its own
subversiveness, a community, therefore, that must be constantly renewed, whose existence is thinkable only as an unceasing enactment
of its own origin. And if this is the case, how can the renewed, self-
originating community in the last book *not* be an image of the community as a reader?

Clearly the program of the emigrant community must in some
sense be applicable to our community as readers. But clearly its *positive* content cannot be directly applicable here. I contend that this
contradiction is resolved by the recognition that Lenardo's program

must refer to our situation as readers by what it *denies*, by what it itself fears as a subversive influence, which brings us to the Jews. I have already argued that Goethe sees the community of novel-reading as a kind of new Israel in its accumulation of texts toward a new holy scripture. And the argument I now propose—that a subversive reading (i.e., a correct or adequate reading) of Lenardo's program arrives at an identification of the readers as a new Jewry, an identification that the text means, but cannot say without exposing it to the same subversiveness that produces it—is supported by the strong element of illogic in Lenardo's presentation. The Jews, "that people which has appropriated, before all others, the blessing of eternal wandering" (*WMW*, p. 668), represent the logical result, which Lenardo backs away from, of his own praise of movement and movability. And the rejection of the Jews because of their rejection of the supposedly Christian origin of certain religious principles— principles which, as they are stated in the text, can actually all be read out of Ecclesiastes (*WMW*, pp. 686–87)[22]—is equally transparent in its logical failure. Such, in any case, is the operation of ironic subversiveness, that *only* the Jews—precisely in being unequivocally (and arbitrarily) rejected—can operate as a sign for the actual reading community.

Complications of this sort, complications that have to do with the radically twinned concepts of community and irony, are unavoidable in a serious attempt to come to grips with the idea of reading. For community—in any sense of the word that is not restricted to naming the observable behavior of individuals—requires a common basis (not necessarily an unchanging basis) that is *known*, but is beyond the range of what can be *said* coherently, since what can be said is already in principle, and in reality, an object of dispute. And irony in turn, as I have argued, has no meaning that justifies its existence as a distinguishable concept (as the concept it after all is, for instance, in literary study) except where it operates in a strictly intersubjective realm. The two concepts are thus indissolubly coordinated; in fact, if

[22]Especially the idea of the uses of *time* recalls Eccles. 3. And the idea of existence as a "valuable gift," to be made most of even in the face of undeserved suffering, is the burden of Eccles. 9. Nor can consistency be imposed on the *Wanderjahre* at this point by recalling the rôle of Christianity in the pedagogical province. Lenardo speaks of Jesus only as the preacher of philosophical religion, not as the focus of a "reverence for what is beneath us." The allusions to Ecclesiastes, in fact, remind us that even that supposedly Christian "reverence" (if we think back to the pedagogical province, and think of Ecclesiastes as a whole) can be derived from *Jewish* writings.

we admit the existence of irony in the fully developed sense of the word, then the existence of community, in a sense sufficiently non-empirical to support the idea of the community of novel-readers, follows as a consequence.

Nor is this idea of community without its parallels in intellectual tradition. Rousseau's version of the social contract, for example—if we are correct in understanding it as a contract without any prior sanction in natural law—results necessarily in a community that exists only by constantly enacting its own origin, which is practically what Rousseau says in his argument on the Assembly of the People.[23] Or we might return to the example of the more or less contractually constituted community of literary study, a community which is radically subversive at least in the sense that it is occupied ceaselessly with shaking its own foundations. As I have suggested, what we really mean by "theory" in a "literary" context is a constant critique and clash and competition of theoretical initiatives that adds up, in effect, to a move against or beyond theory.

[23]See JJR, 3:425–28. There is plenty of debate in detail about Goethe's knowledge of the *Social Contract*; but I think we can disregard it. (See, for example, Carl Hammer, Jr., *Goethe and Rousseau: Resonances of Mind* [Lexington, Ky., 1973], esp. chap. 7.) Lenardo's movable seat of government (*WMW*, p. 689) is certainly an echo of Rousseau (3:427). And if the allusion to the *Social Contract* is as obvious as I think it is, then Lenardo's insistence on Christianity (and on excluding Jews) is strongly ironized by our recollection of Rousseau's final chapter on civil religion (3:465–67).

CHAPTER TWO

Hölderlin's "An die Parzen": Poetry as a Game in Society

In order to test Goethe's idea of the significance of the eighteenth-century novel, it is not sufficient to interpret eighteenth-century novels. For if we begin by admitting even merely that it is *reasonable* to approach, say, *Tristram Shandy* or *Jacques le fataliste* in the same way we approached *Wilhelm Meisters Wanderjahre*, the result will not actually be a test of anything at all. We need to take a broader view, including the whole idea of poetic or literary language, and of language in general, at least in eighteenth-century Germany. This chapter, in any case, is the closest approach to a rigorous demonstration that I have to offer. And its subject matter is not merely one poem, and not merely Hölderlin's personal view of poetic language. It is Hölderlin's sense of the relatively *normal* operation of poetic language, in a text in which he has not yet broken with eighteenth-century German poetic style, especially the Hellenizing style developed mainly by Klopstock.

Analysis and Understanding

The particular poem I have in mind, the short Alcaic ode "An die Parzen" (To the Fates), has the advantage of dealing explicitly with the question of the nature of poetry. The complete text is as follows:

> Nur Einen Sommer gönnt, ihr Gewaltigen!
> Und einen Herbst zu reifem Gesange mir,

Daß williger mein Herz, vom süßen
Spiele gesättiget, dann mir sterbe.

Die Seele, der im Leben ihr göttlich Recht
Nicht ward, sie ruht auch drunten im Orkus nicht;
Doch ist mir einst das Heil'ge, das am
Herzen mir liegt, das Gedicht gelungen,

Willkommen dann, o Stille der Schattenwelt!
Zufrieden bin ich, wenn auch mein Saitenspiel
Mich nicht hinab geleitet; Einmal
Lebt' ich, wie Götter, und mehr bedarfs nicht.

[FA, 5:541]

[Only One summer grant, you mighty ones, and an autumn to me for
mature song, that more willingly my heart, sated with the sweet play,
might then die. That soul, to which in life its godlike right was not
granted, finds no repose even down in Orcus; still, if once that sacred
thing which is of great concern to me, the poem, is accomplished,
welcome then, o silence of the world of shades. I am content even if
my string music does not accompany me on the way down; Once I
lived like the gods, and more is not needed.]

The main point I intend to make about this poem is that precisely
as a *written* text—by way of the reader's awareness of its writtenness, not by way of some imagined hearing of the speaker's personal
voice—it effects an unveiling of the fundamentally intersubjective or
communicative quality of its language, an unveiling of exactly that
quality of language which Adorno, for example, even in insisting on
an indissoluble relation between "Lyric Poetry and Society," excludes categorically from the range of valid poetic expression.[1] My
argument makes use of and develops the idea from Chapter 1 of a
strict coordination between the notions of irony and community.
Like the solitude of the novel-reader for Goethe, the supposed solitude of the lyrical utterance is stripped by Hölderlin of all but a
thoroughly relativized function.

I will not begin, however, by laying down a conceptual basis for
this point, but rather conduct a word-by-word analysis of the text,
using at the outset only relatively obvious concepts, and adding new
conceptual material only when the analysis arrives at apparent contradictions that make it necessary. In this manner the argument will

[1]Theodor W. Adorno, "Rede über Lyrik und Gesellschaft," in his *Noten zur Literatur*,
ed. Rolf Tiedemann (Frankfurt am Main, 1974), pp. 49–68, esp. p. 57 on the "contradiction between poetic and communicative language."

progress, so to speak, outward by concentric stages, which I name Exegesis, Interpretation, Poetics, and Communication, until it rejoins, and, I hope, reinforces, the argument on Goethe given earlier.

It seems to me that part of what is important about lyric poetry— especially short, highly organized pieces such as "An die Parzen"—is precisely its amenability to this sort of detailed formal and semantic analysis. For the analytic procedure exerts maximum stress upon the interpretive and historical presuppositions we impose on the text and brings to light the anomalies and aporias in those presuppositions. To take Adorno as an example again, what is wrong with his essay on poetry and society, and still more wrong with his long piece on Hölderlin's parataxis,[2] is the absence of patient and painstaking analysis, the stance of the aesthetically experienced connoisseur, the insistence on a personal "affinity" with the poetry, which he boasts of indirectly by expressing astonishment that no one else seems to be bothered by Heidegger's lack of it (Adorno, "Parataxis," p. 452), and which of course excuses him from the drudgery of analysis. The result, in Adorno on Hölderlin, for all his railing against Heidegger, is not much more than Heidegger all over again, a social-historical-philosophical rhapsody that justifies its own terminology by connecting it syntactically with bits of Hölderlin—including part of lines 5 and 6 of "An die Parzen" (p. 463)—which are used like musical quotations, a procedure that is cryptically justified, in its turn, by the argument that Hölderlin himself uses language as if it were music (p. 471). There may be points on which we agree with Adorno. The notion of dialectic (pp. 477, 485, passim) figures strongly in the analysis below; and I treat the question of language and music later, in connection with Herder. But for the sake of coming to grips with our own critical presuppositions, our procedure is as important as our conclusions.

There is one further reason for the procedure I have adopted. As I have said, I do not think our relation to the eighteenth century, or to the view of the eighteenth century I am trying to sketch, is one of strict ignorance. Our knowledge of the eighteenth century, rather, is *obscured*, not only by a historical distance that we might otherwise allow for, but also by several specific theoretical moves that we ourselves make more or less deliberately: the acceptance of the conven-

[2]Theodor W. Adorno, "Parataxis: Zur späten Lyrik Hölderlins," in *Noten zur Literatur*, pp. 447–91.

tion of romance reading as indispensable to interpretation; the Foucauldian setting of an epistemic break in the vicinity of Kant; and, we might add, the element of posturing, of a parodied *fin de siècle*, in today's discussion of modernity and the postmodern. What we need, I claim, is therefore not so much to learn about the eighteenth century as to awaken our own self-obscured familiarity with it. And in the present chapter, accordingly, I want to convince the reader not merely that my conclusion about Hölderlin is valid, but that he or she in effect already knows this, that the reading I propose is accessible by an unbroken and relatively straightforward analytic path, requiring no radical conceptual or perspectival leaps.

Exegesis I: The Game of Ambiguities

A distinction is made at the outset of the poem, via the metaphor of autumn and summer, between the writing of poetry (autumn) and, we must infer, the single intense summer-like surge of emotion or vitality ("Einen," capitalized for emphasis) from which the process of poetic creation takes its origin. The distinction, in other words, is between experience or inspiration itself, in its perfect singular immediacy, and the extended conscious reflection upon experience by which the discursive structure of a poem is developed. But the exact relation between inspiration and reflection becomes ambiguous in the metaphorical vehicle. The implied image of growth, and the word "reif," suggest that experience develops naturally or organically into an artistic expression of itself; but the force of the preposition "zu" (for the purpose of), as well as the difference between the emphasized "Einen" and the same word unemphasized in connection with autumn, suggests that art is fundamentally different from what it expresses, that a poem is a harvesting, a purposeful exploitation of what nature has provided. And the question of the status of *this* poem in relation to its own idea of poetry is also a problem. For the speaker does not himself appear to be recollecting a climax of intense feeling; he speaks of the unique moment of inspiration as if it were yet to come. Is "An die Parzen" itself, the text before us, not yet a true poem? Can it qualify as poetry without satisfying the criteria suggested by its own opening metaphor?

These are not the only problems. The first word, "Nur," already opens onto a plurality of meanings. If the whole poem expresses the

speaker's desire for sufficient time to achieve poetic maturity—
"When I have fears that I may cease to be"—then the opening lines
appear to mean, "Grant me *at least* one full summer and autumn, let
me live long enough for my poetry to become a natural, rounded
whole." But the literal meaning of "Nur," especially in view of the
emphasized "Einen," suggests, "Grant me *not more than* one summer, and then an autumn to complement it." This second possibility
helps explain the relation of the poem to its own idea of poetry, for it
enables us to imagine the "*one* summer" as past, not in the future;
the speaker, in this case, would be hoping that the intense feeling he
has already experienced might exhaust itself in a single revelatory
burst, rather than recur in different forms, that it might thus provide
both a powerful impetus and a well-defined subject matter for poetry.

This ambiguity is quickly developed by another one. Does the
clause "Daß williger mein Herz . . ." attach itself to the whole of the
clause preceding or only to the part about autumn? Is the speaker
saying that summer and autumn are both required, so that we have a
sense of our life's completeness and become reconciled to death? Or
is he saying that at the climax of summer, the point of maximum
vitality, death is simply inconceivable, and that therefore an autumn
of gradually subsiding vital intensity is needed to prepare us for
death? This question has a bearing on whether "summer" is past or
yet to come. If summer is still in the future, then the poet is reflecting upon his present unwillingness to die and hoping for a combination of intense feeling and controlled poetic order that will make his
life an achieved totality. If summer is past, or in progress, then the
poet is hoping primarily for an autumn of calm productivity that will
let him down by easy degrees from his apparently unquenchable vitality.

Does the poem say, "Grant me one summer and one autumn, that
my life achieve organic completeness"? Or does it say, "Having
granted me *one* surge of intensely fulfilled existence, grant me in
addition an autumn that will make it easier for me to accept death"?
This ambiguity is never resolved, but persists as an element of the
poem's structure. The very last words, "Einmal / Lebt' ich, wie Götter, und mehr bedarfs nicht," suggest that the speaker will be satisfied by his one summer of fulfillment; the emphasized "Einmal" recalls the emphasized "Einen," which refers to summer only, and the
verb "leben," in a context colored by the distinction between imme-

diacy and reflection, associates itself more readily with the former. But the end of the second strophe appears to state that the finishing of the poetic task ("ist . . . gelungen"), the metaphorical autumn, is the most important matter in life.

And what of the adverb "williger"? The comparative degree appears to fit best with the idea of poetry as a gradual descent from the intensity of immediate experience; little by little, in our productive autumn, we become "more willing," or "more nearly willing," to accept death. But in the second and third strophes, there is no question of degrees. Once the poetic mission has been fulfilled, the poet is not "more satisfied" but simply "satisfied," and death is "welcome." And what is the "sweet game" (or "beguiling game") by which the poet's heart will be "satiated"? The occurrence of the same word, "Spiel," further on, in the compound "Saitenspiel," which refers to poetry, suggests one answer to this question. But how does the idea of a game fit with the idea of "mature song" or of poetry as a sacred duty? Perhaps the "game" refers to life, not to poetry—compare "the sweet games of life" in the poem "Die Muße" (FA, 3:94)—and perhaps the speaker therefore desires not an order or a limit to life, but simply more life, at least one more occurrence of summer and autumn, so that he may die "more willingly," more nearly sated. Such a desire would be natural in a poem to the Fates, but still conflicts with the exact meaning of the poem's opening words. Thus yet another reading is both supported and resisted by the text as a whole.

One point can be made, however. Given the association of the "game" with poetic creation, and given that the poem raises questions about its own nature as poetry, it is clear that we must look for a connection between the idea of "beguiling play" and the actual structure of the text before us; this text *is* a game of ambiguities (perhaps a "Seiten-spiel," a game of multiple sides or aspects or perspectives), which have to do mainly with the distinction of immediacy and reflection. The idea of poetry as an ingenious playing with meanings is not surprising in Hölderlin. To take examples only from the immediate vicinity of "An die Parzen": we think of the poet's fondness for the Heraclitean pun on βίος (life), and βιός (bow), in "Lebenslauf"; of "Menschenbeifall," in which the word "leerer" (emptier) is a pun on "Lehrer" (teacher); of the verb "dämmern" in "Der gute Glaube" and "Sonnenuntergang," which refers to either increasing or decreasing light; of the etymological play on "danken" and "gedenken" in "Die scheinheiligen Dichter." The notion that art is play, moreover, and that its function is to close the gap between immediacy and reflection, is central in Schiller's *Über die ästhetische Erziehung des Menschen*, a work Hölderlin had thought about deeply (letter to Niethammer, 24 February 1796) long before "An die Parzen." The direction we must take in interpreting therefore seems clear. We must seek the exact sense in which the poem's pattern of ambiguities may be regarded as a sweet or beguiling game, and the exact sense in which such a game satisfies the idea of poetry's sacredness.

Exegesis II: Reflection as a Type of Death

There are more ambiguities, even in the first strophe. Consider the apparent double possessive in the clause, "Daß williger mein Herz . . . dann mir sterbe." The use of the dative, "mir," to indicate possession, is common in German and analogous to usages in Latin and Greek. To express the idea, "so that I [taking 'my heart' as synecdoche] might then die more willingly," which is what we expect in a poem to the Parcae, only "Daß williger *das* Herz . . . dann mir sterbe" would be required. The possessive "mein" thus usurps the possessive function of the "mir," and suggests that perhaps the "mir" has a distinct function of its own, as it does for example in "Mnemosyne": "Am Feigenbaum ist mein / Achilles mir gestorben" (GSA, 2/1:198). Perhaps, therefore, in "An die Parzen," we must translate, "so that my heart [not my whole person] might then more willingly die in relation to me," or "die, leaving me behind," or in colloquial English, "die on me." This possibility is not incompatible with the larger pattern of meanings. The transition from immediate experience to conscious reflection, the supervention of reflective awareness, casting a pall over our intense feeling, could easily be what is meant by the death of the heart as distinct from the death of the whole person.

"To be One with the All, with all things, that is life for the deity, that is heaven for man" (FA, 11:585), says Hölderlin's Hyperion; and the connection with the idea, "Once I lived like gods," hence also with the *one* summer at the beginning of "An die Parzen," seems clear. But Hyperion continues: "I often stand on this lofty perch, my Bellarmin! But a moment of reflection throws me down. I ruminate and find myself as I had been before, alone, with all the pains of mortality, and the asylum of my heart, the eternally unified world, is gone; nature closes her arms, and I stand like a stranger before her and do not understand her" (11:585–86). Intense feeling is quickly followed by an experience of reflection and disillusion and alienation that Hyperion calls "my paralyzed heart" (11:590) and a "long death" (11:628) of waiting for renewed feeling. Reflectiveness is also death for those overeducated, overdisciplined "barbarians, who imagine they are wise because they no longer have a heart" (11:590). And in another passage from *Hyperion* we read, "The wave of the heart would not spume so beautifully upwards and become spirit, if that old mute rock of fate did not stand against it. But its impetus nevertheless dies in our bosom, and with it our gods die and their heaven" (11:626). The death of inspiration and feeling is more death than death itself. "O, man is a god when he dreams, a beggar when he reflects" (11:586). And we are led from this quotation back to our own text when we recall the end of "Mein Eigentum," where the idea of life as an enthusiastic, unreflecting dream occurs in connection with the image of the Fates: "and that the Parca not too quickly terminate this dream" (5:619).

The idea of poetry as a beguiling game by which the heart's death (as distinct from the person's death) becomes easier to bear makes better sense the deeper we go into it. Our heart, one way or the other, will die in us; the freshness of experience will be supplanted by reflection and disillusion. In fact this process, this death, is only hastened if we resist it, if we attempt to actualize our youthful dream in a permanent form; for precisely such conscious manipulation of the heart's divine energy *is* its death and leaves us beggars. The members of the society of Nemesis had started out with a dream similar to Hyperion's; but their attempt to develop that dream into a political and social program has burned them out, left them negative, cynical, heartless. Hence the importance of poetry. We must affirm (in the manner suggested by Schiller) our otherwise inevitable fate; we must enact it as a game that we play deliberately, as if it were our original desire. "Mature" poetry is not an outburst born directly of feeling, but a "willing" enactment of the process by which feeling dies, a process we have to undergo anyway.

And by transforming conscious detachment into a game, we also transform the object of consciousness, the immediacy of experience itself, which now takes its place as an element of the game. Thus continuity is established, after all, between immediacy and reflection as stages in the game of life, which is now not different from the game of poetry. Hence the ambiguity in the images of summer and autumn in "An die Parzen." Poetry as a beguiling game is still a harvest, an exploitation of what nature has provided; but it is also a season, the natural continuation of summer, since immediate experience has now also put on the aspect of a game. "Why are we excluded from the lovely circular path of nature?" asks Hyperion, but then continues, "Or does it include us as well?" (FA, 11:596). Or if we recall Hyperion's idea of world unity as "the asylum of my heart," and if we associate this idea with the image of summer in "An die Parzen," then a corresponding passage in "Mein Eigentum" suggests that the character of autumn (or song) is not different:

> Und daß auch mir zu retten mein sterblich Herz
> Wie andern eine bleibende Stätte sei
> Und heimathlos die Seele mir nicht
> Über das Leben hinweg sich sehne
>
> Sei du, Gesang, mein freundlich Asyl!
> [5:619]

[And in order that for me too, to preserve my mortal heart, as for others, there be a permanent place, and that my homeless soul not long for somewhere beyond life, you, poetic song, must be my congenial asylum.]

Poetry, as a reflective playing by which even immediate experience is made to assume the character of a game, has the effect of protecting our heart, our sensitivity to life, that we may enjoy our fill of it.

The triad of Christian salvation narrative, starting from innocence or integration with nature, passing through alienation, and culminating in the reattainment of unity on a higher plane, operates in Hölderlin's theory of "excursion and return to the self" (FA, 11:622), or of the "two ideals of our existence," the state of natural simplicity and the state of highest conscious cultivation by which nature is reattained (10:47). In "An die Parzen," however, the vehicle by which we complete our "circuitous journey,"[3] by which we are enabled to reenter the "lovely cycle of nature" from which consciousness had excluded us, is named "play," as in Schiller's *Über die ästhetische Erziehung des Menschen*, where "play" is the third term of a triad

---

[3]This term is borrowed from M. H. Abrams, *Natural Supernaturalism: Tradition and Revolution in Romantic Literature* (New York, 1971), esp. chaps. 3–5.

and the restoration of "totality" in our human being.[4] But does the notion of play in "An die Parzen" have the same philosophical weight as it does for Schiller?

Exegesis III: The Godlike Right of the Soul

Assuming the normal meaning of the German word "göttlich," the "godlike right" ("göttlich Recht") of the soul, in "An die Parzen," is not a "god-given" right, but a right shared with God or with the gods. Thus the text appears to say that only the soul whose godlike-ness is achieved can find the repose of death; the more godlike we are, paradoxically, the more conclusively we die. If we take death to mean the death of the "heart," then perhaps the eternally restless soul is the person who, rather than willingly play the game of reflection, attempts to preserve the instant of intense feeling as perfect immediacy and is doomed to unfulfillment by the inevitable conscious self-detachment *in* such an attempt. But does this idea explain how poetry is a "right"?

It is not even certain that the "right" spoken of here refers exclusively to poetic production. The clause, "Zufrieden bin ich, wenn auch mein Saitenspiel / Mich nicht hinab geleitet," suggests that poetry, once achieved, becomes *nonessential*. ("Saite," again, suggests "Seite" and such compounds as "Seitenweg.") Poetry is perhaps the particular vehicle by which the present speaker fulfills his godlike destiny. But the suggestion that that destiny itself, or his right to it, is something more general, is strongly reinforced by the poem's last words. Surely we associate the idea of once having "lived like gods" with the soul's "godlike right"; but then the verb "leben" and the emphasized "Einmal" suggest not the autumn of poetry so much as the summer of intense feeling.

The idea that intense feeling is the principal human manifestation of the "godlike" is common enough in German literature of the Classical-Romantic period. "Am I a god?" cries Faust when he is overwhelmed by the vision of the Macrocosm. And in *Hyperion*, especially in connection with the first summer (compare "An die Parzen")

[4]My own essay "Trinitarische Humanität: Dichtung und Geschichte bei Schiller," in *Friedrich Schiller: Kunst, Humanität und Politik in der späten Aufklärung*, ed. Wolfgang Wittkowski (Tübingen, 1982), pp. 164–77, takes issue with this view as an *interpretation* of Schiller. But the ideas are still usable in describing the resonance between Schiller and Hölderlin.

during which the hero knows and loves Diotima, we find such passages as the following: "We are like fire sleeping in dry wood or a pebble; we struggle and seek in every moment the end of our narrow confinement. But they come, they are worth eons of struggle, those instants of liberation where the Godlike bursts its dungeon, where the flame frees itself from the wood and billows up victoriously over the ashes, ha! where it seems to us that our unshackled spirit, its suffering and bondage forgotten, returns in triumph to the halls of the sun" (FA, 11:643). There is a "god in us" (the Ovidian phrase occurs repeatedly in *Hyperion*) struggling to be free, and that god is liberated in moments of overwhelming enthusiasm, when time stops and all nature rings with our own feeling.

That Hölderlin, in "An die Parzen" as well, has in mind something like the Diotima experience, is clear from any number of parallels in *Hyperion*: the idea that every person has the "right" to be godlike, that "man is a god as soon as he is man" (FA, 11:678); the repeated use of capitalization to emphasize forms of the word "Ein"; and passages such as the one in which Hyperion justifies the lengthy narrative of the growth of his relation to Diotima: "I am building a grave for my heart, that it might rest; I spin myself into a cocoon because winter is everywhere; I wrap myself up in blissful memories as protection against the storm" (11:657). By remembering, by reflecting upon our supreme experience, our summer, we build a grave that makes it easier for the heart to die—and to die a death from which, as from the death of emotion in self-consciousness, an eventual reawakening is perhaps possible. Moreover, the idea of play is combined explicitly with the image of the Parcae in Hyperion's account of his first meeting with Diotima: "Untroubled in mind and soul, strong and cheerful, with smiling earnest, I play in spirit with fate and with those three sisters, the holy Parcae" (11:638).

If, therefore, we regard "An die Parzen" and *Hyperion* as versions of the same basic text, then "godlike," in that text, appears to refer to the moment of immediate feeling. "Once I lived like the gods, *and more is not needed*." Hyperion's creed, "that it is better to die because one lived than to survive because one has never lived" (FA, 11:624), which anticipates lines 5–6 of "An die Parzen," does not specifically require the poetic mastery of experience. The function of poetry appears to be ancillary: to make our self-consciousness a game, thus to lend a play character to all our existence, and so to preserve our godlike experience of immediacy by assimilating it to reflection.

But this does not settle the matter. The "poem," after all, is still spoken of as "sacred"; and its "achievement" ("ist . . . gelungen") is still apparently the key to the speaker's being "satisfied" in the underworld, which parallels it with the "godlike right" of the soul. Moreover, the phrase, "das Heil'ge, das am / Herzen mir liegt, das Gedicht," *subordinates* the word "Herz" (heart)—which in strophe 1 had been pregnant with ambiguity—by reducing it to its mere function (with no independent semantic identity) in a common idiom. The "poem," it appears, now overpowers, or supersedes, the "heart" in the sense of immediacy of feeling. "Herz," incidentally, is in yet another way a key word, for it helps define a perfectly symmetrical pattern of concepts in the poem. Exactly one word for poetry occurs in each strophe ("Gesang", "Gedicht," "Saitenspiel"), and the three possible pairings of the strophes are suggested by three other concepts; strophes 1 and 3 have the idea of "Spiel" in common, strophes 2 and 3 the idea of godlikeness ("göttlich," "wie Götter"), and "Herz" completes the pattern by linking strophes 1 and 2. Can we read over this word in lines 7 and 8 without worrying about its idiomatic subordination?

The reading of the poem that takes the soul's "godlike right" and living "like gods" to refer to poetic production, thus invoking the eighteenth-century commonplace (Shaftesbury, Lessing, Herder, etc.) that compares the creating poet to the creating God, is supported even by the lines, "Zufrieden bin ich, wenn auch mein Saitenspiel / Mich nicht hinab geleitet," which seem to suggest the non-essential quality of poetry. For these lines have an exact parallel, in the ode "An Eduard," which tends in the opposite direction. The poet asks what he can offer his friend in return for all he has received from him, and answers:

> Und diß, so ers geböte, diß Eine noch,
> Mein Saitenspiel, ich wagt' es, wohin er wollt'
> Und mit Gesange folgt' ich, selbst ins
> Ende der Tapfern hinab dem Theuern.
> [FA, 5:675]

[And this, if he commanded, this in addition, my string music, I would venture it wherever he wished, and with song, even to the end of brave men, I would follow my dear friend.]

The whole meaning here is quite complex, but a principal suggestion is clearly that the poet's song would accompany his friend to the underworld, in the sense that it would celebrate him after his death. (Compare also the first stanza of "Dem Genius der Kühnheit.") Applied to "An die Parzen," this idea suggests that the lines we are concerned with may be read, "I will be satisfied even if, when I die, my song does not serve as *a celebration of myself*, even if it does not perpetuate the memory of me as a particular individual." The poetry as such, in other words, and for the poet the act of creation, is what matters, *not* the person, the "heart," the particular feelings that had made up his life. Thus the importance of poetry and the importance of experienced immediacy appear not merely to complement, but to *contradict* each other.

Interpretation I: The Poem as a Process, Grammar as Drama

The possibility of contradiction in this structure of ambiguities raises the question of whether we are approaching the text from the right direction. Certain types of weaving, if we look at the wrong side of the material, make no sense; with study, we can perhaps deduce the pattern, but it is easier simply to turn the fabric over. In particular, I maintain that a poem for Hölderlin does not trace the given shape of a thought or mood or feeling, but rather is *a temporally extended process in which thoughts appear and disappear and evolve in accordance with an inexorable mechanics of self-reflection.* When the poem arrives at thought A, we must not ask what thought follows as the next step in presenting some object or idea or experience; we must ask, rather, what thought arises *necessarily* in a mind that thinks A and also knows that it has thought A. The poem has the character of a dialectical system, as is suggested in the sketch "Wechsel der Töne." The "tone," says Hölderlin, changes in the course of a poem; and it changes, as far as we can judge from the sketch, by a process of inevitable reflective detachment from the tone or mood preceding.[5]

What we have in "An die Parzen" is not contradiction but dialectic. Poetic reflection (autumn) is presented as a natural development of direct experience (summer), but then reveals itself as contrary in na-

---

[5]"Wechsel der Töne" is the title under which the material in FA, 14:340–42, has been known. See also Lawrence Ryan, *Hölderlins Lehre vom Wechsel der Töne* (Stuttgart, 1960).

ture to its origin, a dialectical antithesis. The "sweet game" suggests mutual assimilation of thesis and antithesis; but the inevitable question of "right" raises the issue of primacy and so reinstitutes separation and tension. The idea of reflection as a kind of death implies that consciousness incessantly produces *radical change* in its own object; and this idea is supported by the image of the nether regions ("Orkus," "Schattenwelt"), which suggests a whole world of diminished experiential intensity when the immediacy of the divine has been smothered by consciousness. (Compare the use of the underworld as a metaphor in "Brod und Wein," where the poet insists—in exactly the terminology of "An die Parzen"—that ours is an overreflective, uninspired age, "for we are heartless, shades" [FA, 6: 252].)

But the clearest instance in "An die Parzen" of how meanings change radically as they develop is what we might call a moment of grammatical drama between strophes 2 and 3. The word "doch," in normal German, sometimes acts as a conjunction in the sense of "but"; and like the German conjunction "aber," it is then followed by normal rather than inverted word order. But strictly speaking, "doch" is an adverb; and when it introduces a simple declarative clause, therefore, it can be immediately followed by the verb, as it is in the sequence, "Doch ist mir einst das Heil'ge . . . gelungen."[6] These words, however, then turn out in the poem *not* to be a declarative clause; for if we take strophe 3 into account, it is evident that the inversion, the position of "ist," must be understood as transforming the clause into a condition, supplying the function of an "if." And this recognition, that the "Doch . . ." clause expresses only a condition, not a fact, comes as a kind of dramatic surprise; for if we read the end of strophe 2 *in isolation*, it is perfectly natural to translate, "but I *have already* once accomplished that sacred task, the poem, which is dear to my heart." The possibility of this reading is increased by the strophe break—the words do, to an extent, stand in isolation—and also by its relation to questions already present in our mind: How does the poem reflect upon itself as poetry? Is the poetic achievement in the past or in the future?

The development from strophe 2 to strophe 3, however, represents a *change* of meaning, not merely the discovery that our initial

---

[6]Hölderlin's willingness to use "doch" *both* ways around the time of "An die Parzen" can be seen in the short odes "Diotima," "Der gute Glaube," "Das Unverzeihliche," and "Dem Sonnengott."

understanding of the clause with "Doch" had been a mistake. For *it is not really a mistake* to read that clause as a direct statement. The declarative meaning is *preserved*, as it were beneath the surface, by a subtle manipulation of verb tenses. If it were not for the word "dann" ("then," carrying the force, "then I will say"), the opening of strophe 3 could be spoken by one who is *already actually arriving* in the underworld, his poetic achievement satisfactorily behind him— which makes excellent sense if we take the underworld to mean a world of diminished experiential intensity. And this possibility is sustained in the clauses, "Zufrieden bin ich, wenn auch mein Saitenspiel / Mich nicht hinab geleitet." On the surface, both present indicative verbs refer, in normal German fashion, to the future: "I will be satisfied even if my music does not accompany me." But it is not grammatically necessary that the verb "bin" refer to the future; and "geleitet" is also the past participle of "geleiten," so that, assuming a normal omission of the auxiliary "hat" (and making allowances for the "wenn auch," to which "obwohl" would usually be preferred in speaking of the past), the sentence could be taken to mean: "I *am* satisfied even though my music *did not* accompany me down here." Moreover, the use of the past tense to abbreviate a future perfect—if "Einmal / Lebt' ich, wie Götter" is taken to mean "Once I will have lived like gods"—is much less common than the use of a present for a future; and the feeling, by consequence, that the verb "lebte" might actually refer to the past is strengthened by the possibility that living "like gods" refers to experience, not poetry, to an experience that could be in the past even if the poetic task were not yet accomplished. Once we are prepared to regard "lebte" as a true preterite, however, we are reminded that it is possible to imagine the speaker as already having fulfilled his destiny and arrived in the underworld—which notion, again, is not even fanciful if we relate it to the idea of death as an image of conscious reflection.

The poem is thus a process in time; its meanings are susceptible to *real change*. The last clause in strophe 2 is not ambiguous in the sense that it hovers quasi-spatially between a declarative and a conditional meaning, but rather it is *first* declarative and *then* conditional, without ceasing to *have been* declarative. This opposition, between extension in time and unchanging spatial structure, is also part of the poem's thematic material, as appears from one further ambiguity in the last strophe. Do the words "Einmal / Lebt' ich, wie Götter" mean "at one period in time I [will have] lived a life like that of the gods"?

Or do they mean, in view of the emphasized "Einmal" and the not strictly necessary comma, "I [will have] lived my life just Once, in the same way that the gods live just Once"? The latter possibility fits easily with the general pattern of questions in the poem. That the gods live "Once" would mean that their life is eternal form or structure, without extension in time, hence without change. If our own life can be given the sort of permanent shape and simplicity that the speaker appears to desire in strophe 1, then in a sense we too live the life of gods. And the opposite condition, of living as it were more than Once, is exemplified by Hyperion, whose life alternates between reflective despair and reawakenings of intense feeling, with Adamas, with Alabanda, with Diotima, at war—and apparently, in memory and self-knowledge, at the end of the novel.

This ambiguity, however, at last brings us directly up against the problem of reading. Does the superseded declarative meaning of lines 7–8 persist for us, as we read, or does it not? Is the linearity of the text, in our experience of reading, a sufficiently complete analogue of time to permit us to say that those lines "did" mean, but no longer mean, that the poet has achieved his task? Or shall we say that those lines "Once" had that meaning—in the sense of a "Once" so perfectly unified that it is not even subject to time in the first place, like the life of the gods? After all, if we ask ourselves *when* those lines were not yet part of a conditional sentence, we should have to answer, strictly speaking: never. And yet, the lines do still make an unconditional assertion, an assertion, in fact, which we—as witnesses to the existence of *this* completed poem, "An die Parzen"—are tempted simply to acknowledge as valid. What is actually going on when we read? Do we have here, as in the *Wanderjahre*, a reduction to the absurd of the whole idea of the individual (i.e., ourselves) as a reader?

Interpretation II: The Inseparability of Feeling and Reflection

For the time being, let us concentrate on the speaker, whose sense of himself is first suggested by the concept "Gewalt" ("ihr Gewaltigen"), which implies arbitrary power, ungoverned by reason or justice. The speaker presents himself as subject to death, which may take him, for no reason, whenever it pleases; and this stance clashes with the idea of the soul's "godlike right" in the next strophe. How does the speaker pass from the one attitude to the other, from an acceptance of helpless mortality to the assertion of a right ("Recht," in German practically the opposite of "Gewalt") that prevails even against death, in that its fulfillment is a condition of the soul's finding repose? We must not argue around this difficulty. We must ask *how*, in dialectical time, the speaker gets from one idea to the other.

Hence the importance of the concept of play, which evidently operates in the development from the attitude of strophe 1 to that of strophe 2, and which is illuminated by a passage from Schiller, at the intellectual climax of *Über die ästhetische Erziehung des Menschen*:

> Let us say it straight out: man plays only where he is human in the full meaning of the word, and *he is wholly human only where he plays*. This proposition, which at this point perhaps appears paradoxical, will receive great and deep significance when we have arrived at the point of applying it to the double earnestness of duty and fate. . . . Only the scholarly mind is really surprised by this proposition, which was already vitally present, ages ago, in art and in the feeling of those preëminent artistic masters, the Greeks; the Greeks, however, transferred to Olympus their vision of what ought to be realized on earth. Guided by the truth of the proposition I have stated, they eliminated from the image of the blessed gods all that labor and earnest which wrinkles the mortal brow, as well as the trivial cheerfulness which relieves us. [SA, 12:59]

We may gauge the importance of this passage for Hölderlin by comparing a passage in *Hyperion* that we have already mentioned:

> But man is a god as soon as he is human. And once he is a god, he is beautiful. . . . In this sense the Athenian was human, I continued, and necessarily became so. Beautiful he emerged from the hands of nature, beautiful in body and soul, as we say.
>
> The first child of human beauty, of divine beauty, is art. In art, godlike man rejuvenates and recapitulates himself. He wishes to experience himself; over against himself, therefore, he sets his beauty. Thus man provided himself with gods. For in the beginning man and his gods were One, in the age of an eternal beauty unknown to itself. —I am speaking mysteries, but I speak of what is. — . . . The second daughter of beauty is religion. Religion is the love of beauty. The wise man loves beauty itself, the infinite, the all-encompassing; the people love beauty's children, the gods. [FA, 11:678]

In each case, the phenomenon of art is presented as both a symptom and a representation of the true and full realization of human being. Schiller does not say that man is a god; but he does say that the Greeks, in their gods, imagined no more than the hypothetical completion of their own humanity. Hölderlin does not employ the concept of play; but the concept of beauty establishes the connection. That beauty exists, for Schiller, is logically equivalent to the existence of completed humanity, hence empirical proof of the effectiveness of the play-drive. "Experience can teach us *whether* beauty exists, and as soon as it has instructed us, we shall know whether humanity exists"; but beauty is "the common object of both drives [form-drive and matter-drive], that is, the object of the play-drive" (SA, 12:56–57).

The passage quoted above from *Hyperion* thus opens a new dimension in the concepts of feeling, reflection, and play in "An die Parzen." Reflection is not only the death of feeling but also its genesis. "In the beginning," humankind and the gods were the undifferentiated aspects of an "eternal beauty" that had no knowledge of itself; and in order that this utterly unified but insensate Being be realized in the mirror of perception and feeling, it was necessary that a division take place, comparable to the inward division in human self-consciousness. It was necessary that beauty (as human) set beauty (as gods) "over against itself." Practically the same idea occurs in a passage from "Der Rhein," in which we read that "because perfectly blissful beings [i.e., gods] feel nothing of themselves," suffering mortal man is necessary as a mediator (GSA, 2/1:145).

But I have argued, apropos the first strophe of "An die Parzen," that by making a game out of reflection, we transform even feeling into an element of the game, and so prolong it in our playing. The idea of self-division as the origin of feeling develops this thought. Reflection, by detaching us from the feeling of divine unity with all things, is a kind of death; but our reflective consciousness, if we practice it with an attitude of affirmation, itself turns out to be as much an intimation of divinity as the original feeling, since it is *an enactment of the origin*, of that original self-division by which eternal Beauty is realized as experienced beauty in a world of humans and gods. If we could preserve our feeling of immortality by resisting self-consciousness, then we would in fact violate our divine heritage by refusing to carry out as humans the painful but necessary act of self-division by which the very possibility of a "feeling" of the divine originates. Even on purely psychological grounds, we might ask whether feeling exists without reflection. Can we feel something if we do not know that we feel it? Reflection is still feeling's death; but by a paradox both metaphysical and psychological, it is also feeling's origin, and must be affirmed in our awareness of our divine being.

The passage in *Hyperion* that occasions these thoughts, however, bears a clear relation to the passage in the aesthetic letters in which Schiller triumphantly justifies the concept of "play"; and this relation shows the "sweet game," in "An die Parzen," to be more than merely an easing of the pain of reflective self-division. In particular, our subjection to the arbitrary power ("Gewalt") of fate (1) calls forth, when we reflect on it, the conception of what we truly possess, and what is therefore principally threatened by that arbitrary power, namely our occasional inspired feeling of divine wholeness (2). Precisely this *act* of reflection (3), however, upon further reflection, is recognized as the death of inspiration, of the "heart," hence an anticipation of fate, an *appropriation* of the power that threatens us. And with this affirmative reflective move, reflection has become a "game" (4), by which—it turns out—we enact not only the demise, but also the origin of our divine being, so that those moments of inspiration (even in their absence) now belong to us (to the consciousness that generates them) as a kind of "right" (5). There are complications here. The very concept of a "right," for example, performs the staking of a claim, which presents arbitrary fate with a new target. But the five steps—from subjection to dominion—still show one route that links the concepts of "Gewalt" and "Recht" in dialectical time.

Interpretation III: The Word "Spiel" as a Dialectical Climax

Schiller relates his assertion concerning play to the "twofold *seriousness*" of life, consisting of "duty and fate," or internal and external compulsion. When we succeed in asserting our total humanity by way of the play-drive, both internal and external compulsion vanish; fate becomes "small" (insignificant, negligible), duty "easy" (SA, 12:57), which seems to be exactly what happens in Hölderlin's poem. The idea of fate as a frighteningly unpredictable power ("ihr Gewaltigen") yields to a mood of untroubled acceptance; and the sense of duty suggested by the word "sacred" ("das Heil'ge") receives an emotional investment ("das am / Herzen mir liegt") that dissolves the quality of compulsion.

The poem's dialectic, by which this movement is effected, starts out from a *tension* between human desire and the arbitrariness of fate, a tension, however, that exists in its original or pure form only (so to speak) in the moment of silence before the poem opens. For the speaking, as soon as it actually begins, is *already* modified by a reflective distance from itself, which can be measured by the importance in the poem of a word that never occurs, the word "noch." "Nur einen Sommer noch" (Only [at least] one *more* summer)—with the verb still in abeyance and *no* ambiguity in the "Nur"—would have captured entirely the tension between desire and fate. But these words inevitably presuppose a *reflection* that at once both contains and performs the recognition that our "summer" of intense feeling is not, after all, merely a fact that can be prolonged or repeated ("noch"). Feeling simply does not happen without the movement of reflection that sullies it. In mid-sentence, therefore, the word "noch" is dropped, and the speaker now desires "Nur Einen Sommer," with emphasized "One," a single *limited* unity of thought and feeling, instead of the endless self-dissatisfaction his unspoken "noch" would have implied.

Even this new unity, however, is valueless, in effect nonexistent, if it is not known, if there is not a space or time from which it can be reflected on, which the speaker now specifically desires in the words "Und einen Herbst zu reifem Gesange noch" (and in addition ["noch"] an autumn for mature song). But again the word "noch" is superseded in mid-sentence. For in the reflection upon reflection that is now taking place, it becomes clear that any reflective awareness of the unity of feeling and reflection must itself *belong* to that unity, hence that there is no "noch," no "in addition." The implications of the word "reif" (which suggests "Reif," "closed circle") thus begin to operate in the instant of its speaking. And the implications of the word "Gesang" operate as well. For "Gesang" can refer to the physical activity of singing, but can also refer, with no sense of special metaphorical extension, to a poem in its linguistic and intellectual aspect. It thus forms a *synthesis* of the suggestions in the other two words by which "An die Parzen" refers to poetry: "Gedicht," namely, means the poem as an intellectual or formal entity, with no suggestion of any physical object or activity; and "Saitenspiel" ambiguously names both a physical object and an activity, the stringed instrument and the playing of it, but without a formal or intellectual dimension. "Gesang" thus means a totality—by which the split between immediacy and reflection, between object and subject, between the physical and the intellectual, might be repaired—and the concept "noch" is no longer applicable.

But now the word "noch" is no longer merely omitted. It is *replaced* by the word "mir"; for the envisaged circular or seasonal totality of feeling and reflection is now recognized, upon reflection, as the supposed wholeness of personal identity. And no sooner is this word spoken—no sooner do "I" say "me," and so set myself over against myself as an object—than precisely that identity, along with the totality it represents, is called into question, which is what happens in the words "daß williger mein Herz . . ." The words "my heart" (in the sense of "my immediate emotional self") carry out an *analysis* of the identical self along precisely the division between reflection and feeling that had apparently been transcended; and the comparative degree of the adverb "williger," accordingly, *reinstitutes the erased concept "noch,"* the idea of a situation in which doing "more," or doing something "in addition," makes a difference. In the moment of silence before the poem opens—if it is permitted to imagine that moment—the moment in which the poem as reflection does not yet exist, the unspoken word "noch," the desire for nothing but extension of the moment of our existence and exposure to fate, is still operative; the poem itself is added ("noch") to that primal moment of nothing but feeling. But as soon as the mechanism of reflection, the poem, begins to unfold, the concept "noch" is superseded, since the object of desire turns out to be a unity admitting no supplement or addition. And yet now, in line 3, the force of the "noch," though without the exact word, returns. Why?

(Let us stop here to recognize that this method of interpretation, by way of a word that *does not occur* in the text, is in the particular case not at all farfetched. For the treatment of the word "noch," in the poem, is exactly analogous to the treatment of the declarative meaning of lines 7–8. Like that declarative meaning, the word "noch" is in the condition of: [1] not, in the strict sense, being there; [2] *having* been there, however, at some earlier point in dialectical time; and [3] being preserved, under the surface, by verbal subtleties such as the comparative adverb "williger." And if the idea of the moment of silence before the poem opens is objected to, I respond that precisely the absent word "noch" *stands for* that absent moment and calls it to our attention.)[7]

To recapitulate: The poem's dialectic, in lines 2–3, turns on the idea of personal identity. This idea, when it occurs, raises the question of the speaker's own situation with respect to the content of his utterance, which is inescapably a situation *inside* life and hence lacks both the perspective and the authority to speak of life as that closed totality which can be inferred, in the abstract, from the inseparability of thought and feeling. Precisely the consideration that had made necessary the second erasure of "noch," the consideration that life never presents itself as a closed object to which, for instance, a perspective for "Gesang" might be added, now compels the speaker to acknowledge that *for him* life is after all characterized by *incompleteness* and must therefore be thought of in terms of adding to what is there, in terms of becoming "more willing," in terms of a still unrepaired division between thought and feeling, in terms summarizable by the concept "noch." In fact, even the absent concept "noch" has now undergone a change of meaning and become ambiguous. For it now turns out that in spite of our reflection upon reflection, and our recognition of the necessary unity of thought and feeling, we are *still* ("noch") thinking of life as incomplete, as a progress into uncertainty.

And yet, there is also a difference. In the moment of silence before the poem opens, when no specific possibilities are yet articulated, there *can* be no desire but "noch," the desire for mere continuance or addition; but now, in line 3, the same desire represents the willing (or "more willing") acknowledgment of a result of reflective thought. (Thus thought and feeling meet again at the ends of a returning circle.) What had once been mere mute necessity is now *acted out as a dialectical game*; and it is at exactly this point, accordingly, that the climax of the strophe arrives, in the word "Spiel," which is modified by the adjective "süß" (sweet), which suggests, ambiguously, *both* the fulfillment *and* the origin of desire. At this point the dialectic achieves temporary *repose*, since the reflection upon "Spiel" *is* still precisely what the word "Spiel" refers to. Reflection now, for a moment, no longer enforces a dialectical separation from its own object, but rather, as "play," is identical with its object.

[7]See Gerald L. Bruns, *Modern Poetry and the Idea of Language: A Critical Study* (New Haven, 1974), esp. pp. 189–205, "Negative Discourse and the Moment before Speech: A Metaphysics of Literary Language."

The movement envisaged by Schiller is thus completed; and the idea of "play" is now seen to be applicable not only to the point where the word occurs, but to the whole of the strophe, beginning at the latest with the words "ihr Gewaltigen." For as far as we can tell, the speaker starts out from an unarticulated awareness of the arbitrary power of fate. But as soon as he begins to speak, it follows from the nature of what he is doing that the object of his awareness has changed; the act of speaking presupposes, over against oneself, not an amorphous power, but a person or persons capable of understanding—here the Fates, and in a plural form that mirrors their quality as the result of articulation. Thus the simple urge to live becomes, in its articulated form, a detailed, complicated, ambiguous request; indeed, it is hardly even a request, hardly a prayer any longer, but has become, rather, a game, a kind of adventure, in the intricacies of the speaker's own intellectual and psychological situation. (Hyperion introduces the account of his relation with Diotima by announcing that he now feels strong enough to "play with fate"—which means to articulate the external and internal details of his encounter with fate.) Or to put it more generally, *desire itself*, along with the reflective mechanism that both creates (by articulating) and defers or frustrates desire, has become a kind of game.

Thus the word "Spiel" summarizes the whole strophe and reinterprets it as a *solution* to the initial problem, not merely an expression of it. German syntax here collaborates with Hölderlin by permitting the words "gesättiget" and "dann mir sterbe" to follow the climax rather than precede it. The idea of satiety is (1) a cryptic acknowledgment of the state of satisfied repose at which the poem has arrived with the word "Spiel." But the rules of precisely this dialectical "game" require that we also acknowledge the uncompletedness of our condition in life, hence that satiety still be, for us, (2) a state hoped for in the future. Furthermore, the words "dann mir sterbe" at last bring to light the ambiguity of the word "Herz"—as representing either the whole person or just the state of unreflected feeling— and so establish (1) the idea of self-consciousness as a type of death, an incorporation of death itself into the "game" of life, hence more a completion than a disruption of our nature. But the same words also *name* for the first time, as "death," the object of that dread from which the poem begins, and name it in a tentative manner (with the subjunctive), which, in the very process of "playing," also acknowledges (2) the original nameless menace *as* a menace.

After the climax at the word "Spiel," however, these ambiguities operate no longer as dialectic, but as *irony*, in a strict sense of the word. Obviously it would be wrong to decide that one of the two contradictory suggestions in the idea of satiety, or one of the two contradictory responses to the naming of death, is what the words "really" mean. But it is equally wrong, in either case, to say that *both* responses are meant. For although it is possible in the abstract to occupy an intellectual point of view from which two contradictory meanings are both equally present in the same utterance, still, in the present case, such a point of view is excluded, is made illegitimate, by precisely the concept of "game" or "play" without which there would be no meaning in the first place. If I claim to know that the human condition (hence, in particular, my condition, what is given to me, "mir") is unified and *completed*, paradoxically, by my willing acknowledgment of its *un*completedness, then precisely that claim violates my supposed willing acknowledgment. We thus find ourselves in a position where we understand an utterance, the poem's first strophe, yet are also prevented from saying, or claiming to know, what we understand. We cannot decide in favor of one meaning over the other; but we can also not insist on both meanings together without excluding *ourselves* from the range of the utterance and so denying its meaning. That this situation belongs to the domain of irony, as discussed in the preceding chapter, is evident, as is also its relation to the question of where we stand, as readers, with respect to the poem's dialectical "time."

Poetics I: The Resurrection of Mortality, the Poem as Life Itself

The first strophe of "An die Parzen," then, is very nearly a poem in its own right, a complete system of meaning, a dialectical cycle that creates and resolves a single problem. This feeling of cyclical wholeness suggests an almost factual corroboration of the speaker's apparent assertion, in the last two lines of the second strophe, that he has already, once, *accomplished* the sacred task of poetry. But precisely the completeness of the first strophe also initiates a continued dialectical movement in the second. *Within* the system of the first strophe, the utterance "Spiel" produces a moment of repose or stability. But that moment then itself constitutes a perspective from which the whole of the first strophe is viewed as an object; and the instability of this new viewing, the initiation of yet another dialectical movement, is a result of *the nonsustainability of irony for the solitary individual*, which we discussed in Chapter 1. The trap into which we fall when we claim or pretend to know that both of the contradictory meanings at the end of the first strophe are equally present and valid is a trap that *cannot be avoided* by either the solitary reader or the solitary meditative speaker. Irony—as the condition of understanding an utterance, yet not knowing, not being able to say, what is understood—can happen only in a social or strictly intersubjective space. But the reader or the speaker, as an individual, *cannot* be in the condition of not knowing what the first strophe of "An die Parzen" means. The reader, like the speaker, cannot avoid *taking seriously* the concept of play, which violates precisely the envisaged resolution of human nature in the form of a game.

We now find ourselves thinking of that game, perversely, as a "godlike right," as our right to experience what Schiller calls the "aesthetic state," in which we know ourselves free from all compulsion and—in the sense of Schiller's description of the Olympians— "live like gods." Hölderlin here touches a crucial difficulty in his own and Schiller's thought. Once we have understood the potential divinity in human being, the end of the journey from nature through alienation to higher nature, how shall we speak of it without speaking nonsense? Can we say seriously that we are gods, or even potentially gods, without violating the very conditions under which this statement has meaning—not to mention certain obvious perceptions of fact in human life? This, for Hölderlin, is the problem of Empedocles, the man who calls himself a god, and with solid philosophical justification, yet becomes all the more an abjectly suffering human for it.

In any case, our possession of a "right" is potential, not actual, not like the presence of godlike playfulness *in* the speaking of the first strophe; our relation to a right is mediated by the implied necessity of demonstrating our entitlement to it. In the first strophe the speaker had arrived dramatically at a sense of divine completeness in his existence; now he reflects on this sense, discovers it is grounded in human nature, and concludes that it is a state to which all humans are entitled, although experience appears to teach that not all humans achieve it. The divine is now a "right," and it occurs to the speaker, as it must, that the accidents of existence can deprive us of the enjoyment of it. Hence the image of the unfulfilled soul in the underworld. In this way the dread, arbitrary power of fate, which had apparently been overcome at the very beginning, is resurrected in a more terrible form. The word "Recht" expresses a defensiveness, which acknowledges the power against which we must defend ourselves; the precise balance of strophe 1, between consciousness as self-completion and as confused self-division, between knowledge of life and immersion in life, now becomes a tension between the rights of the individual and the unbending laws of reality. Tension, conflict, dread, suffering mortality—all reappear and are now the sharper for our knowing that they are not only unpleasant but also unjust, against "right."

Hence the possibility of reading the end of the second strophe ("Doch . . .") as a direct statement, not a condition. Indeed, the poem in its entirety would make good sense if that statement were *not* dramatically transformed into a condition. For in strophe 2, in which the speaker is confronted again with the dread power of fate, he is also able to *remember* (as a completed unity) the dialectical achievement of strophe 1, "once I accomplished the sacred task of poetry"; and although that achievement is no longer immediately present to him, as "Gesang," but has become merely an intellectual possession in memory, a "Gedicht," still the knowledge that it did once exist as experience is a source of comfort, like Hyperion's comfort in remembering Diotima. Even if he must die in his present condition, even if his "Saitenspiel," the immediacy of godlike playfulness suffusing even our sensual existence, may not accompany him in death, still the intellectual aspect of his achievement, his knowledge, cannot be taken from him. "Once"—namely in the first strophe—he had lived like gods, "and more is not needed."

Thus we arrive at a complete reading of the poem as *monodrama*, in which what the speaker talks about is exactly what happens to him *in the course of his speaking*. He achieves a moment of inspired philosophical insight, upon which he then looks back with elegiac resignation. We have seen, moreover, that the verb forms in the final strophe are adjusted to sustain the possibility of this reading beneath the surface of the language, untroubled by the apparent transformation of lines 7–8 into a mere condition. Or perhaps, since this reading focuses on the inevitable decay of "Gesang" into "Gedicht," we should call it a reading of the poem not as monodrama but as the emptied vessel of monodrama—comparable to the skull, the emptied vessel, which is contemplated in (and also *is*) Goethe's poem "Im ernsten Beinhaus war's . . ." For our distance, as readers, from the presumed experience of the speaker, is at least as great as the speaker's own developing distance from the inspired insight of strophe 1.

But this reading of the poem is still not valid. The clause in lines 7–8 is, after all, a condition; its quality as a condition is inevitable, even *within* strophe 2, as we can see from the relation between the concepts "göttlich" (godlike) and "heilig" (sacred). The difference between these concepts is a difference in point of view; the godlike is the divine as a god knows it, the sacred is the divine as a mortal knows it. But in speaking of the divine as our "godlike right"—in thus taking seriously (as a "right") the inspired game of strophe 1, which remains godlike only as long as it *is* still a game—the speaker has *already* reduced the godlike to the sacred; he has himself adopted the standpoint of helpless mortality, viewing the divine from below. From the point of view of godlike humanity, in the throes of realizing the whole divine potential of human being, as from the point of view of the gods themselves, it is literally true that nothing is sacred, that everything is the object of exuberant play. But in strophe 2, once the words "göttlich Recht" have been pronounced, it follows that "the poem," "das Gedicht"—whether this word refers to strophe 1 itself, or only to the idea of poetry it represents—is "sacred" after all, is "das Heil'ge," not "das Göttliche." And if the poem, now recognized as "sacred," is also regarded as a *task*, then it follows further that the task not only has not been accomplished but *cannot* be accomplished. The word "sacred," again, implies a point of view from which the complete divine object to which it refers is strictly out of reach. The clause "Doch ist mir einst das Heil'ge . . ." is therefore *necessarily* a condition, and in fact an *impossible* condition.

Thus we find we have embarked on an entirely different reading of "An die Parzen," which hinges on the idea of "the poem" as a task. We are now thinking in terms not of monodrama but (again) of dialectic, in which details of word order become crucial. For the idea of a task does not really arise until the word "gelungen" occurs. By "das Heil'ge," otherwise, the speaker could easily mean a sacred piece of knowledge or a sacred memory. Any number of verbs could reasonably complete the clause "Doch ist mir einst das Heil'ge . . ." The speaker could be leading up to "erteilt worden" (was bestowed on me) or "zur Gewißheit geworden" (became a certainty to me); or he could intend simply "geworden," in the same unusual sense as that of "ward" in the line preceding. Thus the word "gelungen" (the idea of the task to be accomplished) carries a certain dramatic force when it arrives.

In line 7 ("Doch ist mir einst . . .")—if we read word by word, registering the suggestions of each word before passing on to the next—the speaker apparently first derives comfort from a "sacred" memory; he clutches to his "heart," as a vestige of the divine, the "poem," the intellectual precipitate of his "song." But the word "Gedicht" also replaces the vague suggestion of a sacred memory with the more specific idea of a personal *achievement*; and the strong temporal separation indicated by the perfect "ist . . . gelungen" (taking lines 7–8 as a direct statement), along with the distinction between "Gedicht" and "Gesang," then brings to light the contradiction inherent in the notion of a *past* achievement. Achievement, after all, exists *as* achievement only in the achieving of it; and the poem, accordingly, is truly a "poem," an adequate representation of "song," only by *not* being finished. Thus the sacred knowledge becomes a sacred task—and as such an impossible task. Precisely in taking it as a statement referring to the past, we discover that the clause at the end of strophe 2 necessarily becomes a condition referring to the future, as it were pivoting on the ambiguous adverb "einst."

A crucial feature of this dialectical reading of "An die Parzen," as opposed to the reading as elegiac monodrama, is the manner in which it involves us, the reader, in its structure. For the speaker himself, in thinking of his "poem" as a past achievement, adopts *the position of a reader* with respect to it, not that of its singer. And when the statement of lines 7–8 then transforms itself into a condition, it is clearly suggested, by analogy, that we too must transform our relation to the poem we are reading, that the poem must somehow become an uncompleted task for us, a task we still find ourselves in the midst of. But this means that our situation as readers becomes as impossible, as hopeless, as the speaker's situation. We are asked to regard the text we are reading as a special kind of text, which, if we succeed in making it our own task, our own creative endeavor, will reveal the divine component of our being ("Einmal / Lebt' ich, wie Götter") and reconcile us with death. We are asked, that is, to regard this text as *a sacred task*, which—given the distinction between "heilig" and "göttlich"—implies its impossibility as a task, for us no less than for the speaker.

This reading of "An die Parzen," then, produces for both speaker and reader a dialectical plunge into the impossible. (We recall the impossible situation of the reader with respect to the question of *when* lines 7–8 are declarative, or *when* the initial moment of silence occurs.) And how shall we now account for the mood of the final strophe, its reconciled affirmation? We can perhaps deal with this problem by beginning with the word "Herz," which, laden with meaning from the first strophe, invites us in the second (see "Exegesis III") to discover the suggestion that intense feeling is valuable not in itself, but mainly for the sake of "the poem." When we arrive at the word "gelungen," the opposition of feeling to reflection, including the idea (from "Herz" in the first strophe) of reflection as the "death" of feeling, is in the process of receiving some emphasis.

It must now occur to us, therefore, that the achievement of strophe 1, our certainty of the god in us, after reaching its completion ("ist . . . gelungen"), has died in exactly the same way that our feelings die. And the opening of strophe 3 is then an affirmation of *this* death, this smothering by reflection of our playful, godlike sovereignty in existence, the sovereignty which, in strophe 1, had itself been constituted by reflection. Thus the dialectic of the poem as a whole *repeats* the dialectic of strophe 1. The achievement of strophe 1, its completed dialectic, turns out, in strophes 2 and 3, to be available to us neither as a sacred memory (since the clause "Doch ist mir einst . . ." inevitably becomes a future condition) nor as an immediate act of achieving (since that condition is impossible). The "poem" of strophe 1 is now as thoroughly dead, as perfectly *not there* for us as the pure surge of feeling that had presumably obtained in the silence before the speaking begins. But if we now affirm the death of the "poem," as the death of the "heart" had been affirmed in strophe 1, if we *make an act* of that death, in the same way that the words "Willkommen dann . . ." actively carry out the already inevitable transformation of the preceding clause into a condition, then perhaps the dialectical achievement of strophe 1 is repeated, thus retrieved, after all. Our very failure to recover the "poem," in the sense of "song," does after all recapture the movement of failure and affirmation which *is* "the poem" in strophe 1. And the mark of this reachieved dialectical game in strophe 3, curiously enough, is the word "Einmal," which, precisely by stressing the *un*repeatability of "the poem," carries out the movement of acceptance and affirmation (of its loss) which *does* repeat it.

But this repetition contains a crucial element of difference. The paradoxical association between godlikeness and mortality—that achieving repose in Orcus depends on our receiving our "godlike right," that it is godlike to have *only* "One summer"—is referred in strophe 1 to the moment of silence before the poem opens. Only that moment can contain perfect unreflected feeling, if such a thing exists; and only in that moment does the fear of death, the confrontation with arbitrary fate, operate in all its primal power, not yet softened by self-conscious strategies like the dialogizing address "ihr Gewaltigen," or like the ambiguity in the poem's first word, "Nur," which costumes death as a possible object of desire. But in the dialectic of "An die Parzen" as a whole, the unrepeatable unity of non-reflection is represented by the unrepeatable dialectical closure of strophe 1; and the fear of death is now located exactly by the word "sterbe" at that resurrection of stark mortality to which the playful dialectical achievement of strophe 1—precisely *because* we value it as an intimation of our total being—exposes us. The double starting point of the dialectic—unreflecting experience, unmitigated fear of death—which in strophe 1 had been purely hypothetical, strictly extratextual and extralinguistic, has now become *a textual or linguistic event* woven into the poem's language. Indeed, that event—since the dialectic of strophes 2 and 3 operates *for the reader*—is woven into the poem's language considered even as "Gedicht." It no longer matters whether or not "Saitenspiel" (the quasi-physical immediacy of the poem as speaking) accompanies our reading of the text. The confrontation with death, at its most direct, is now built into the situation of even a mere reader.

Again, godlikeness and mortality are equivalent. Precisely the "aesthetic state," the experience of our total being, exposes us totally to death, exposes (so to speak) *more* of our self to death than does any relatively determined and fragmented conscious state. And it is mortality in this extreme form that we must affirm as an object of play in order to achieve the totality of our being after all. But in strophes 2 and 3, this affirmation, "Willkommen dann, o Stille der Schattenwelt!" is more than merely a gesture; for death itself *has* been made an object of play by being woven into the dialectical play of the language. We are now playing, at the extreme of paradox, even with the inevitable death *of our playfulness*, even with our detached situation as *readers* relative to the inspired closure of strophe 1. And the concept of play as it occurs in strophe 3,

"Saitenspiel," is now part of what we claim we are prepared to do without.

The repetition of the dialectical movement in "An die Parzen" therefore includes a development from the hypothetical (the moment of silence) to the actual (the structure of the text, as writing), by which the poem becomes, even for the reader, *an enactment of life itself.* The feeling of mortal helplessness at the beginning, from which we infer that the poem takes its origin, is not really part of the poem; it is already dispelled by the onset of the speaking. The achievement of the first strophe is thus hypothetical, a demonstration of how one *might* cope with the precariousness of the human condition. But the resurgent mortality of the second strophe is woven into the stuff of the language; it exists in the form of dynamic relations among the concepts of "Spiel," "Recht," "Herz," "göttlich," "heilig." It is an actual event, here and now, as we read; and its overcoming by affirmation, in the third strophe, is an actual achievement. The poem is now not merely a detached comment on life; it is life itself.

Poetics II: The Separation between
Thought and Language

Obviously this argument goes too far. In order to make it, we have to retain the idea of the *mere* reader, the detached interpreting reader of a "Gedicht," who is defined by the difference between his attitude and that of the involved, experiencing quasi-hearer of "Gesang." And then we have to insist that this very difference is somehow nullified or reversed in the case of "An die Parzen." Who—we are obliged to ask—what particular real person, actually undergoes the confrontation with death that is structured into the poem's language? And yet, on the other hand, given the complexity of the game of ambiguities from which we began, it is hard to see how an argument at least as precarious as that of the preceding section can be avoided. I used the metaphor of weaving earlier; and it appears now that if "An die Parzen" is really characterized by a single clear pattern, then we are still looking at the wrong side of the fabric. The question is one of poetics. How do we look at a poem in the first place?

Let us begin by recalling that the argument of the preceding section is based on two distinct readings of the poem, which I called the monodramatic and the dialectical. The former takes lines 7–8 as a direct statement and reads strophe 3 as the speaker's monologue expressing elegiac resignation. The latter acknowledges that lines 7–8 become a conditional clause and insists that the impossibility of the condition they express involves the reader directly in the unfolding of meaning. Now it is clear that neither of these two readings can be accepted as the single valid reading, since each implies the other in a kind of circle—perhaps a seasonal circle, a "year of our soul" as in "Menons Klagen um Diotima" (FA, 6:173). Precisely the assumption that "the poem" of strophe 1 is a completed whole (monodramatic reading) implies in strophe 2, with the word "gelungen," the contradictory idea of past achievement, which makes lines 7–8 a future condition and produces the dialectical reading. And the dialectical reading, in turn, is held together only by the implied claim that death is resurrected, that the whole shock of mortality is present, *in the language of the text as "Gedicht,"* which means that at least the whole text of "An die Parzen" satisfies the idea of achievement in lines 7–8. But from this new perspective, which depends on our recognizing that the dialectic of the whole poem repeats the dialectic of strophe 1, we cannot avoid acknowledging the completedness of strophe 1 after all, at least from the speaker's point of view, whereupon we reenter the monodramatic reading.

It appears, therefore, that we are obliged to accept both readings as valid, which must (I think) lead to formulations at least as extravagant as those in the preceding section. In any case, plenty of interpretations of poems exist that are more extravagant and (I think) less well founded than that argument. And there are plenty of ways in which the argument might be developed. We might suggest, for instance, that the circle of mutual implication between the two main readings produces a condition of *both* achievement (since it is closed, a "Reif") *and* nonachievement (since the circular motion never arrives at repose). But still the formulations are unsatisfactory, in the sense of being infinitely self-complicating. We are still looking at the wrong side of the fabric.

The right way of looking at the pattern, it seems to me, is suggested by the concept of irony. As in the case of the ideas of satiety and death in strophe 1 (see "Interpretation III"), we find ourselves committed to two different readings of the poem, each of which is valid, yet neither of which—because of the difference between them—can be *said* to be valid. And as in the case of strophe 1, the argument that ensues when we attempt to assert that both readings are simultaneously valid turns out to be unreasonable, if not strictly contradictory. Once again, we are in the situation of understanding the text, yet also being prevented from saying, or claiming to know, what we understand—which is the condition of irony.

We must therefore be willing to think in terms of a separation between thought and language, even though this approach contradicts our accustomed idea of lyrical structure. Or rather, we must acknowledge that we have *already* separated thought from language by distinguishing between a monodramatic reading (of the poem as an individual's thought) and a dialectical reading (which represents experiences by linguistic events). We have noted that the idea of a separation between thought and language is present in vocabulary, in the division of the concept "Gesang" into its intellectual and physical components, "Gedicht" and "Saitenspiel," into the theoretical intention (thought) and its actualization in practice (comparable to language as distinct from thought). And the speaker suggests directly that his thinking mind, his memories of "Once," must now part company with his "music" or "instrument." And we recall that that same word "Einmal" (Once), can be understood fully only if we think, in its place, the concept "Twice," the *repetition* of the poem's dialectic. (See "Poetics I".)

Especially important in this connection is the notion of play, about which our interpretive argument has run roughly as follows. In strophe 1 the concept of play is the dialectical climax and makes possible, temporarily, an immediate grasp of the godlike in human existence. In strophe 2 the speaker loses hold of this idea by taking it seriously, but then recognizes that precisely by doing this, by losing his grasp of the truth, he is putting into practice yet again that idea of play which had made possible his knowledge of truth in the first place. And in strophe 3, accordingly, he intentionally continues the act of playing in which he had caught himself unawares, so to speak, in strophe 2. He no longer attempts to retain a direct grasp of the truth but rather keeps an ironic distance. He now deliberately renounces his recovery of truth by saying, "Once I lived like gods," as if he were speaking of a unique past experience, the mere shadow of which he retains in memory. And by carrying out this renunciation, he does reachieve the original victory; for the godlike in us is not, after all, a feeling, but an act, the free acceptance and affirmation and assertion, as play, of our self-conscious condition.

One of the questions raised by this argument has to do with what we mean by thought or knowledge. When we say that the speaker loses and then recovers his grasp of truth, are we talking about a kind of oscillation within the thinking mind? And are we to infer that we, the readers, undergo the same sort of oscillation, that we first know, then fail to know, and then, by failing to know, know again? Obviously this is not what we mean. When—as in the questions, when does the poem stop being silent? when is the word "noch" still there? when are lines 7–8 still declarative?—when do we fail to know what we after all claim to know precisely in this interpretive argument? The oscillation or dialectic we are speaking of can happen only in the space opened up by a *difference* between thought and language, a difference both required and created by the concept of play. The oscillation in question is a repeated approach and separation between language and thought, which brings us back to the question of irony and the social. For in the mental world of the solitary individual there is no space of difference between language and thought that can accommodate the dialectic of approach and separation. From the point of view of the thinking individual, if a thought is formulable, then it is in effect already formulated. Only in the domain of the social or intersubjective can the nonstatement of a thought make a substantial difference in its quality as thought or knowledge. Only thought in the sense of *common* knowledge (whether or not ascertainable as such), or in the sense of understanding or agreement or perhaps sympathy, can *actually* carry out a movement of approach and separation with respect to language. Precisely our interpreting the poem as if it were the musings of a solitary mind thus leads to the recognition that we are in fact treating it as an utterance in society.

This line of inference is already dictated by the operation of ambiguity in the poem. The words "Einmal / Lebt' ich, wie Götter," for instance—if we take them to mean "I will have lived just Once, in the same way that the gods live just Once"—contain the poem's whole dialectical meaning: that our apparently disruptive self-consciousness, if we affirm it as "play," always leads back in a circle to our existence as unity, as a "Once" in which time, Plato's "moving image of eternity" (*Timaeus*, 37d), is merely the game by which we carry out our godlike function as the origin of "feeling." But this meaning still requires for its validation the presence of *different* meanings in the same words, a meaning referring to the past ("Once I did live like gods") and the meaning of what might be said in the future ("when my condition is met, I shall be able to say, 'once I lived like gods'"). And *for whom* does the utterance possess these subsidiary but necessary meanings? Either they are swallowed up in the main philosophical meaning (our meaning, and the speaker's), whereupon they are not "felt," and so *fail* to perform their validating function. Or else we must imagine an intersubjective space in which the ultimate meaning of the verbal figure (which we ourselves do know) is not fully ascertainable, a space in which there can be other subjects for whom other meanings are really meant.

I am not suggesting that Hölderlin's text magically creates an intersubjective space for itself. I mean, as in the case of *Wilhelm Meisters Wanderjahre*, that the text operates to bring into focus the *existing* social dimension of its genre. The relation between immediacy of experience, or pure feeling, and the complexity of conscious reflection is not only a main focus in "An die Parzen" but also a typical feature of poems of the period, and tends to mark the lyric as a *meditative* genre, representing the thought of an individual in solitude. Nor is this tendency affected by the subversion of the distinction between feeling and reflection in "An die Parzen." We have traced the interpretive significance of the argument that in "An die Parzen," the relation of priority between feeling and reflection becomes reversible ("Interpretation II"). We have seen that this reversibility informs the uncertainty about whether "*one* summer" or "*the* poem" is the actual object of desire. And we have argued that the dialectic of the poem as a whole repeats exactly the dialectic of strophe 1, even though the one dialectical pulse springs from an extratextual moment of silence, whereas the other originates in the text's reflection upon itself. But a focus on the *question* of feeling and reflection, in all of these instances, still apparently marks the discourse as meditative.

The trouble is that precisely this radical criticism of the idea of an experience prior to reflection cannot take place except in a discourse that understands consciousness as "consciousness of," requiring an object distinct from and prior to itself, so that reflective consciousness, our consciousness of our own being and doing, requires the idea of a prior unreflective something in us, a primitive and unified level of inner life, which we name feeling or experience or immediacy. Schiller remarks that feeling and self-consciousness are the two irreducible elements of our mental life, in the sense that we cannot think coherently without making the distinction (SA, 12:74–

75). And the speaker of "An die Parzen" repeats the idea of "One summer" by remembering (or anticipating that he will remember) a *prior* time "Once," when he had lived like gods—even though the very act of repetition establishes that time as a textual *present*.

Meditative discourse itself, therefore, as Hölderlin uses it, turns out to be strictly (intersubjectively) ironic, in the sense of being conditioned by a separation between thought and language, by our speaking in a manner we "know" to be grossly inadequate, with a knowledge that cannot be separated from discourse except in the form of *common* knowledge. Again, "An die Parzen" does not *create* a social or communal space for itself, but rather it brings to light the social dimension of the meditative lyrical discourse in which it participates. Like *Wilhelm Meisters Wanderjahre*, it implies a historical commentary on its genre with respect to the idea of the social.

Poetics III: Lyric Poetry and the Social

Compared to "An die Parzen," Goethe's *Wanderjahre* is easy to deal with. For the idea of the community as a reader is at least clearly *modeled* there, not only within the fiction but in the real world as well, in the community of critical Bible readers or the community of literary study or, cryptically, the community of the Jews. Even without such models, the "social dimension" of the novel is a concept we are relatively comfortable with. But how do we read lyric poetry? With poems from the general area of the Romantic period, we tend to regard the utterance as meditation, an operation performed by the speaker's self upon itself, a fine tuning of the mechanism of self-consciousness. And how shall we read except by carrying out the same operation on ourselves in sympathy with (or imitation of) the poet? Unlike other forms of verbal expression, poetry (we assume) is not meant to shape or affect relations among different individuals. It is, rather, a therapeutic exercise every individual carries out alone. We the readers, all of us presumably grown flabby in the inward part of our existence, are hardly even aware of the others lined up alongside us. Our attention is riveted on the trim figure of our verbal calisthenician, whom we imitate lumberingly, movement by half-comprehended movement. Even the poet, therefore, from whom our gaze does not waver, is not really a distinct individual for us, but rather an ideal image of ourselves, a leotard-size into which each of us, alone, hopes eventually to cram the uncomfortable folds and bulges of the spirit.

It is important that this view be stated in a drastic form, for it represents the strict logical consequence of a very common approach to poetry, especially to the work of individuals like Hölderlin, whose eventual madness appears to justify our thinking of him as trapped in a private world where metaphysical speculation and common sense have changed places. If we assume that the poet is meditating in solitude, I do not see how we can avoid the idea of the reader as equally self-preoccupied. Why else do we read? Is the poet an interesting psychological case? So (let it be admitted) are many of our colleagues. Are we interested in the poet's ideas as ideas? Then the poem is superseded by its interpretation. Are we interested mainly in the development of the human spirit or of a particular culture, for which the poem serves as evidence? Then, given our original assumption, there must at some time have been an audience of individuals willing, each in private, to stretch their mental muscles in imitation; otherwise the poem would not be historically important.

On two occasions in his *Anatomy of Criticism*, Northrop Frye quotes John Stuart Mill to the effect that the artist, in particular the poet, is not heard but overheard; and precisely the lyric, he elaborates, is "preeminently the utterance that is overheard."[8] Frye does a disservice to his own thought by insisting on Mill's formula, which is as wrongheaded as it is brilliant. It is Victorian in spirit, and Victorian in a sad sense, despairing of direct human contact, redolent of strained parlor-encounters with tiny veterans of the *méthode drastique*. We think of the importance of eavesdropping (deliberate or otherwise) in Victorian literature—often with less dramatic justification than, say, Jim Hawkins's apple barrel—and of the set of absolute disjunctions thus implied among various areas of human intercourse, with self, servants, family, business associates, school chums, and so on. Overhearing, under these conditions, is the only way of even approaching a complete idea of the human world one lives in; and in the case of poetry it is the only possible guarantee of sincerity. If the speaker were aware of us, our presence would have a determining

[8]Northrop Frye, *Anatomy of Criticism: Four Essays* (New York, 1966; orig. 1957), p. 249, also p. 5.

effect on his utterance, which would then take its place in whatever class compartment we ourselves hold a ticket for, and so deny us even a passing glance beyond the normal run of our life.

Frye requires no assistance from Mill. His own formulation, if less pithy, is much more accurate: "The lyric poet normally pretends to be talking to himself or to someone else: a spirit of nature, a Muse . . . a personal friend, a lover, a god, a personified abstraction, or a natural object" (Frye, p. 249). The important word is "pretends," which applies to the reader as well. The idea that in responding to poetry we somehow *actually* put off our social being, in order to become either keyhole-watchers or (in the mind's gymnasium) weight-watchers, is absurd. In reading poems of a certain type—though by no means all recognizably "lyric" poems—the reader's contribution to the communicative process includes treating the utterance as if it were overheard; but if something of importance does not happen on a level of consciousness at which poet and readers form a community in the acknowledgment that they are only pretending, then the exercise has been wasted.

And the question of why such a pretense is necessary, I think, has already been answered. For Hölderlin, again, the level of consciousness at which we speak the truth, or speak about the truth, may not be arbitrarily chosen; a particular ironic attitude is required to validate the truth, to stabilize our relation to it. If a discourse is to be built, for instance, on the truth that feeling and reflection constitute a single, indispensable structural articulation in existence itself, by which their own operation and difference are theoretically superseded, then precisely that discourse may not itself pretend to supersede the discourse *of* feeling and reflection (in that order of operative priority) without violating its own assertion of their indispensability. And this or a similar principle seems to me necessary in the conception of all imaginative literature. We the readers, even if we happen to be alone at home, participate in a complex social ritual that provides the only possible ground for a meaning that starts out (as poetry) by dissociating itself from any (rationally or empirically) "objective" ground.

Poetry is not "overheard"; and Frye himself suggests an argument to this effect that is stronger and more general than mine. If the idea of the "anagogic," as understood in the *Anatomy of Criticism*, and the idea of a "literary universe" that inevitably expands "into a verbal universe" are taken at all seriously (Frye, pp. 122, 350), then they imply, by a visionary but binding logic, a world in which the fabric of verbal relations among people is indistinguishable from the substance of the individual self, or contains the self as a woven image. And the compartmentalization of discourse that makes overhearing necessary has no place in such a world. Even if our situation as eavesdroppers implies our identification with the speaker of a poetic utterance, still precisely that identification circumvents the complex of *communicative* relations by which language must carry out the world-shaping and world-building function Frye assigns it.

Communication I: The Unveiling of the Social

That the language of "An die Parzen" *possesses* a social dimension, then, is clear. My point, however, is that this particular text contrives to *unveil* its social dimension dramatically, in the passage from strophe 2 to strophe 3, where the grammar branches off abruptly and creates (1) the impossible question of *when* the end of strophe 2 had been declarative, hence a disruption of chronological linearity, which means time as experienced *by the individual* (especially the solitary reader), and (2) a break between thought and language in the form of two readings of the poem, the monodramatic reading (thought divorced from language, persisting only behind it) and the dialectical reading (sheer language, dynamics of ambiguity and word order, which makes both feeling and reflection into textual events, equally present for both reader and speaker). The suddenness with which this break is opened, I contend, produces a sense of *irony* sufficiently radical to enforce our recognition of that concept's social implications.

But what precisely is unveiled? Another of Hölderlin's essay sketches, given by some editors the title, "Über die Verfahrungsweise des poetischen Geistes," opens with a practically endless conditional sentence in which the basic requirements for practicing poetry are outlined; and the first requirement, presumably the most basic, is: "When the poet has once mastered the spirit, when he has felt and appropriated to himself that communal soul which belongs to all in common and to each individually, when he has held it fast and made himself sure of it . . ." (FA, 14:303). The idea of a single human soul that is somehow *both* common *and* individual property is also suggested in "Brod und Wein," where we are told that true human community cannot arise "until our Father Aether has recognized each one and belongs to all" (FA, 6:252).

On the basis of what I have said about "An die Parzen," we can understand this idea at least in part. The aim of the poem, considered as meditation, is apparently to stabilize the condition and consciousness of the individual soul represented by its speaker. This holds for the monodramatic reading (psychological stability, resignation) and for the dialectical reading (metaphysical stability, unity of feeling and reflection, in language). But it turns out that this aim can be achieved only by the operation of *both* readings together, hence only by irony in the strict sense, hence only in society, in the medium of language as communication among *different* individuals. As long as we merely think in solitude, the individual self cannot be stabilized and in a strong sense does not exist. *Cogito ergo absum*, we might say; but correspondingly, *conloquimur ergo sumus*—which is suggested by Hölderlin's "Seit ein Gespräch wir sind" (GSA, 3:536; since we have been a conversation). Only by way of language as a communal event do we receive an enduring conception of the individual self, which means we must acknowledge that self (*my* self, for example) as community property. Once we make this acknowledgment, however, as the speaker does in the break that opens strophe 3, the self thereby becomes our own personal property after all, our true individual self, and is revealed as having an eternal or divine dimension even in the present. "There was once a time when I lived like gods," we say to each other; but by our participation in the social or ironic complexities of this utterance, each of us does live like gods here and now.

Nor is this type of thinking by any means historically isolated. In early post-Kantian thought, in Schiller's complicated notion of "Person," in Fichte's inflation of the notion of "Ich" (I) to the point where it no longer has meaning but only gives meaning, in Hegel's insistence on "Geist," the concept of the *individual* has already practically ceased to operate as a credible basic unit for describing human existence. In poetry we think of Blake, of the transient "Individual" as opposed to the eternal "State." And when Hölderlin speaks of "the communal soul" that must be mastered by the poet, "die gemeinschaftliche Seele," he is therefore being as clear as he needs to be. The idea of communal "spirit" ("Geist") is, and was, a normal way of speaking. But "Seele" usually refers to what the individual has in common with no one else, the source of his deepest feelings, the vessel of his deepest experience, shared only with God. And it is this level of individuality that Hölderlin insists is a social or colloquial phenomenon.

> Viel hat von Morgen an,
> Seit ein Gespräch wir sind und hören voneinander,
> Erfahren der Mensch; bald sind wir aber Gesang.
> [GSA, 3:536][9]

[Much—from morning onward, since we have been a conversation and hear of each other—has man learned; but soon we shall be song.]

We are not first individuals, who then converse with each other about the content of our individuality, about what we have "learned" or experienced ("erfahren"). We are, rather, first a "conversation" in which our hearing of each other only then produces the experiencing individual. And individuality, once established, is not even permanent; for it is our destiny to become "song," a raising of voices that no longer defines us severally but unites us as elements of a single greater harmony.

Or to look at the matter differently, the repeatability of the dialectic in "An die Parzen" suggests that the individual self does exist as the source and object of a recurrent divine self-certainty. But the existence of this self, and of this feeling, is perhaps more a curse than a blessing; perhaps it would be better if we did not exist. (The opening of the μὴ φῦναι strophe in *Oedipus at Colonus* is used as the epigraph of volume 2 of *Hyperion*.) For the very exactness and undeniability of our knowledge of the self produce an attitude of earnest reflective awareness (not "play") that alienates us from our knowledge and casts us back into doubt, into an uncertainty that is all the more tormenting because we had already achieved an apparent intellectual conquest of it. The problem posed is not merely to know the self but to know the self in such a way that this knowledge is humanly toler-

---

[9]These words have received much commentary, most of it going back to Martin Heidegger, "Hölderlin und das Wesen der Dichtung" (orig. 1937), in his *Erläuterungen zu Hölderlins Dichtung*, 2d ed. (Frankfurt am Main, 1951), pp. 31–45. (The version I quote from was discovered only in 1954. Heidegger quotes from Hellingrath's edition: "Viel erfahren hat der Mensch. / Der Himmlischen viele genannt, / Seit ein Gespräch wir sind / Und hören können voneinander." Compare GSA, 2/1:137.) Heidegger, as we might have expected, stresses the idea of *language* and the idea of the *one* conversation (pp. 36–38). What seems to me strangest and most interesting, in both versions of the passage, is the word "*voneinander*." We do not "hear each other" in language; we hear "*of* each other."

able—as it proves in the end intolerable for Goethe's introspective Werther.

Therefore, to return to Hölderlin's reading of Schiller, we must affirm our self-awareness as a *game*—but not, we must now add, as a kind of solitaire. It is a game we play with others in the social medium of language. The picture of the Greeks in "Brod und Wein" is relevant here:

> Vater Aether! so riefs und flog von Zunge zu Zunge
> Tausendfach, es ertrug keiner das Leben allein;
> Ausgetheilet erfreut solch Gut und getauschet, mit Fremden,
> Wirds ein Jubel, es wächst schlafend des Wortes Gewalt
> Vater! heiter! und hallt, so weit es gehet, das uralt
> Zeichen, von Eltern geerbt, treffend und schaffend hinab.
> [FA, 6:249]

[Father Aether! was the cry that flew from tongue to tongue thousandfold, no one endured life in solitude; when distributed this wealth brings happiness and when traded, with foreigners, it becomes jubilation, sleeping the word's power grows, father! serene! and echoes, as far as it goes, the ancient sign, inherited from forebears, accurately and creatingly on down.]

The idea of the growth of "the word's power" while it is "sleeping" is crucial. That the true power of a particular utterance is "asleep" suggests that it resides in a hidden meaning of the utterance, which does not participate in the immediate signification of the words. That this power should "grow" while sleeping, therefore, is understandable from the irony of "An die Parzen," especially in connection with the idea of an utterance used for communication and exchange with "foreigners," individuals distinctly different from ourselves. Precisely what is not spoken out in communal language, the *present* relation of the self to the divine (which is concealed by such statements as "*Once* I lived like gods"), becomes by its silence (its sleep) an ever more permanent and powerful truth. Or in view of the allusions to Christ in "Brod und Wein," the concept of the "word" in the above passage can be taken to refer to the λόγος of John the Evangelist, the meaning being that concealed or as yet unrealized (asleep), but still powerfully present in the Greeks' entirely *communal* conception of gods, there lay a deeper idea, the unspoken idea of a god who is also human, hence the idea of the godlike quality of the individual human self.

Communication II: The Meditative and the Communicative

But again, *what* is unveiled in strophe 3 of "An die Parzen"? We are evidently meant to learn that language as a social medium provides a salutary escape from the constantly re-poisoned atmosphere of the self-investigating self; and this lesson must be applicable to our relation, via language, with the poem we are now reading. The question is *how*, since we are dealing with a printed text, not a real person; we do not after all, as readers, find ourselves in a real social situation. How is the social constituted, here and now, for us as readers?

If we take the poem as the record of an individual's thoughts, then the ambiguities that make up its structure can be interpreted dynamically, as transitions and climactic syntheses in a dialectical process. But dynamic interpretation—which takes the poem as meditative language (including both the monodramatic and the dialectical)—is what *resolves* the ambiguities and *explains* how the multiple meanings fit together, while at the same time (I have argued) still requiring that each such meaning actually be meant in order that the rules of the "game" be satisfied. And the question is still: *for whom* are those subordinated meanings meant? For whom does "Einmal / Lebt' ich, wie Götter" mean "Once, in the past, I did live like gods"? In order to understand the text completely, we find ourselves needing to posit the existence of readers different from ourselves, readers unconstrained by a knowledge (like ours) of the dialectical resolution of ambiguity. Indeed, to the extent that those other readers really exist, we ourselves then join their number, since in an *intersubjective* space our private knowledge of the subordination of meaning to resolution no longer affects the operation of the utterance. (If "I" know something, then I know that I know. But it is possible that "we" know something without knowing that *we* know, without knowing that the knowledge is shared, without being able to locate the knowledge in other subjects.) It is true that in an actual social situation, language is always ambiguous in this manner, because we are always in the position of needing to work out different possible receptive attitudes toward an utterance directed at us. But just this observation makes clear the social nature of the ambiguities we encounter in "An die Parzen," which focus our awareness of the social aspect of language in general.

The change from meditative to ironic or communicative language in the last strophe of "An die Parzen" is therefore really only a development of emphasis, the unveiling of something that had been there unobtrusively from the beginning. If we listen carefully, we hear, as it were, two separate voices throughout the poem, one thinking as if in solitude and one speaking to us as if in a social situation. And these two voices, though separate, are *related by mutual necessity*. From a meditative point of view, communicative language is an ironic device that proves necessary precisely in order for the speaker or protagonist to achieve metaphysical self-possession in the idea of game or play. And just as the poem's whole meditative content is *expressible* only by devices that belong strictly to social language, so also, correspondingly, the irony, the communicative aspect of the utterance, is *explicable* only by reference to a meditative process in the speaker. Thus we are brought back to the question of how the poem can itself be poetry yet also express the yearning for poetry as a distant goal, which the paradox of mutual implication between meditative and communicative speaking answers very simply. As meditative speaking, the text can never arrive at its goal, never be fully a poem, since the idea of the divine self can never be stabilized except in the extra-meditative atmosphere of irony and ambiguity. As communicative speaking, however, and for the same reason, the text can and does attain its goal, but only by irony, only by acting as if it were a brooding in solitude. Without this meditative pose, no sense of goal-directedness could arise in the first place; the text (if we could imagine its even existing) would be *nothing but* social language, an evanescent conversation, not an unveiling of that quasi-divine personal self which arises by way of the recognition of the self's communal ground.

But more still needs to be said about this "unveiling." On a sufficiently deep level, it is true that reading *always* happens in the presence of other readers, as a social act. And on a sufficiently superficial level, it is true that no amount of mutual implication between meditative and communicative language makes any difference in my needing to come to grips with the text for myself, in solitude. What then is actually accomplished by the special combination of subtleties we observe in "An die Parzen"?

Communication III: Reading as a Social Act

How does the text of "An die Parzen" actually operate as an event in human society? We have established that the poem is *hypothetically* an event in society; but if the development from the hypothetical to the actual—which we followed earlier on the level of meditative language ("Poetics I," the actuality of death in the written text)—is not repeated on the level of communicative language, the achievement is incomplete. A hypothetically communicative language is not yet sufficiently separate from the meditative to produce the paradox on which the poem's meaning depends; the recluse's hypothetical understanding of the necessity of the social does not in itself make him or her any less a recluse. The meaning of "An die Parzen," that is, is fully realized only when its language *actually* becomes communicative—not in the sense of conveying exactly the writer's thought or feeling, but in the sense that we experience it as a medium shared by individual minds radically different from our own, yet without the pretense of identification or overhearing.

Let us approach this matter by recalling the distinctions among "Gesang" (song), "Gedicht" (poem), and "Saitenspiel" (string music). At the end of "An die Parzen," the speaker declares himself willing to do without the "music" of his utterance if he is but granted the completion of the "poem"; and for us, as readers, the difference here is clearly the difference between the imaginable experience of being swept up in the work's powerful immediacy (music) and the printed text we actually have before us (poem). (The printing of lyric poetry in lines of course recalls the historical relation of the form to audible music; and the four gradated lines of the Alcaic strophe suggest specifically the four strings of the simplest lyre. Thus, for a reader, exactly the *absence* of music is profiled, brought into focus. The sympathetic vibration of musical strings, in any case, is a common metaphor for the supposed preverbal or preterverbal communication of experienced or emotional immediacy, for that form of communication which "An die Parzen" firmly renounces.[10])

Thus we are reminded of how *little* we actually receive as readers; we are reminded that the revelatory intensity of "song," if it ever existed, is inaccessible to us. For us, the work is entirely a "poem," a structure that has become spatial and permanent, and has thereby lost its presumed original vital immediacy as an experience unfolding in time. But once we have thus been reminded of the *deficiency* in our perception of the poem—where shall we find even the "dialecti-

[10]See, for example, the opening paragraphs of Herder's *Abhandlung über den Ursprung der Sprache*, Goethe's *Faust* (line 28), and Hölderlin's own "Hyperions Schiksaalslied."

cal time" needed for our interpretation?—it also becomes clear that
by analogy with the speaker's renunciation of "music," we are meant
to *accept* that inevitable deficiency, to declare ourselves "satisfied"
with it and affirm it as if it were an act of renunciation on our part. Of
course the printed text, as a condition of communication, is unavoidable. The task here, as in Schiller (e.g., SA, 12:101–3, 266), is to
recognize an *intersection* of the categories of unavoidable condition
and free act.

That we are looking at a piece of writing, then, is not merely one
fact among others; it is an integral part of the poem's meaning, to
which our attention is strongly drawn. And once we have understood
this point, it is clear how the poem functions as social language; for
the parallel act of renunciation, by the speaker at the end of the
poem, is precisely a renunciation of the meditative in favor of the
communicative, an *abandonment* of the attempt to achieve unity between thought and expression, or sympathy between "speaker" and
reader. Our acceptance of the limitations of the printed text becomes
an acceptance of the same essentially social condition of separation
between individuals that the speaker accepts—individuals who only
"hear *of*" each other ("hören *von*einander," in "Friedensfeier"). We
no longer imagine that we overhear the speaker's thoughts; it is no
longer even clear that we are justified in imagining an individual
whom we might name "the speaker." The written text, accepted in
its bare writtenness, can no longer be regarded as the representation
of a voice, but has become something closer to the verbal medium as
such, something closer to that "conversation" in which we are related
to other individuals only by "hearing *of*"—not by "hearing," or "music," which is what has been abandoned (or actually, *prevented*) in
the strict socialness of the medium.[11]

Or let us recall that "Saitenspiel"—the third and final word by
which the poem "An die Parzen" refers to itself—means not only
music for strings, or the playing of such music, but also *the stringed*

---

[11]The use of the term "renunciation" in this argument recalls, uncomfortably, the discussion of Rousseau's conception of writing as renunciation in Jacques Derrida, *Of Grammatology*, trans. Gayatri Chakravorty Spivak (Baltimore, 1976), pp. 142–43, which Paul de
Man interprets as questioning Rousseau's "good faith" (see de Man, "The Rhetoric of
Blindness: Jacques Derrida's Reading of Rousseau," in his *Blindness and Insight: Essays in
the Rhetoric of Contemporary Criticism*, 2d ed. [Minneapolis, 1983], p. 113). But I do not
think the question of good faith arises in Hölderlin or in the present interpretation, which
arrives at a focus on the written *text* as manifesting a social language that is in truth *prior*
to either the writing or the reading subject, hence prior to the gesture of renunciation,
which gesture is thus *ironic*, not merely devious.

instrument, the physical thing, on which music can be played. This twofold meaning suggests an entirely radical separation between thought and language. Even the poem, even language in the form of a specific utterance or "parole," does not contain or express a particular thought, but is merely the instrument on which, so to speak, any number of different thoughts might be performed—thoughts that are all present in the instrument, and all in principle knowable, but knowable only in the sense that the meaning of an ironic utterance is knowable, without the presumption of knowing *that* we know what is meant.

In "An die Parzen," the relation between speaking and writing is thus employed to "strip the veil of familiarity" from social or colloquial language, from the verbal medium in which our entire existence unfolds anyway. As in the *Wanderjahre*, an apparently necessary literary convention involving the idea of presence is invoked—in this case, the idea that lyric poetry requires us to imagine ourselves in the presence of a meditative speaking voice that we hear like eavesdroppers, hear being nothing but itself, thus hear as if it were our own—and is then revealed as a mere pose, not an operative convention after all. What is important about the poem, we discover, is precisely its quality as written, its unveiling of the central void in verbal communication, the irreducible separation between thought and language, or between individuals, which is obscured when we find ourselves apparently in direct contact, speaking and hearing, with others. We do not in truth ever *hear* each other as if the ego were a substantial entity capable of making itself heard. In truth, the ego is a secondary or derivative phenomenon, a product of the "conversation" that we *are*, a fiction that is at best *heard of* in a verbal medium that is therefore less delusively represented by writing than by speaking.

There is, to be sure, a contradiction in this argument. The unveiling of the social is an unveiling or defamiliarizing of the strict writtenness of the text, hence a dramatic unveiling of the impossibility of any such drama—since the needful *time*, in which we first do not know and then do know what is unveiled, is shown to be absent. But this contradiction has already been incorporated into our reading of the poem. Like the moment of silence before the speaking begins, or the operation of the word "noch," or the declarative meaning of lines 7–8, the unveiling of the social cannot happen, but still always already *has* happened. It thus is not only an answer to the question of what happens when we read—by recognizing that it is precisely "we" who read, the community as a reader, never "I"—but also an integral part of the game of ambiguity that raises that question in the first place. The unveiling of the social does happen, but the idea of its happening to "me" produces a contradiction, an absurdity. It happens, in truth, only to "us," and in its happening is precisely an enactment of the *origin* of the individual, of the possibility of saying "me." Thus, from "my" point of view, it is *already* that act of self-undermining which I gesture at making of it.

Hölderlin, so to speak, turns the argument of the *Phaedrus* inside out. It may be true, as Plato suggests, that the form of writing makes available to me, as an individual reader, the harmful illusion of knowing more than I in fact do (by providing me with what I am tempted to regard as my own externalized memory) or of being wiser than I in fact am (by carrying out for me a philosophical argument that I may regard as my own, but without having to test my claim to it in debate).[12] But if the writtenness of the text is made the object of an unveiling in the midst of an ostensibly meditative process, and if my acceptance of the text as writing is figured *in* the text as the act of unveiling—hence ultimately neither "my" act nor a "speaker's," but at most "our" act—then reading itself has become a social act in a sense very close to the sense in which, for Plato, philosophy must be a social or colloquial act. The indispensable ironic or self-questioning component of philosophical thought, for Plato, can be sustained only in actual conversation with others. For Hölderlin, however, as for Goethe—we recall the complaints about social intercourse in the *Unterhaltungen*—actual conversation has degenerated historically and now only flatters the pretense of substantial individuality. The literary has invaded and corrupted the social; and now, therefore, the ironic or self-questioning tendency of an established *literary* genre must be developed to the point where the apparently solitary reader acknowledges—or indeed, experiences—the actual social component, the quality of "conversation," in what he or she is doing.

Religion: Individuality as *Imitatio Christi*

I have used the words "in truth" a number of times; and I claim that this locution does not make my argument inconsistent. The philosophical interpretation of "An die Parzen" with which we began is

---

[12]See the *Phaedrus* 274–77. In his letter to Neuffer of 10 October 1794, Hölderlin mentions the plan for an essay that would imply a "commentary" on the *Phaedrus*.

unquestionably *affected* by our understanding of the poem as an instance of social language; but it is not *obliterated*. The poem's irony, after all—the separation between thought and language, which marks language as social—operates not only to question the truth of the self's nearness to god but also to endow that truth with the quality of sustainable knowledge, to preserve it against the corrosive effects of meditative self-consciousness. And this knowledge, in turn, creates an ironic perspective on the whole social game of language— even while the game, the "conversation," continues to *constitute* that perspective, our individual being, for us—a perspective without which social language could not have the quality of a game to begin with. The conversation or game—which for us in a strong sense simply *is* the written text—enacts the origin of individuality. If, therefore, we claim to understand the text from a perspective *other* than that of our strict individuality—if we reject the concepts of "truth" and "renunciation" as an unwarranted dramatizing of the text—we thereby deny the foundation of our own reasoning.

Irony thus works in both directions throughout the poem—as also, for instance, in the tension and mutual implication that relate the meditative and the communicative. It is the idea of philosophical or religious truth, the content of the meditative utterance, that keeps this tension open and preserves the possibility of an ironic distance relative to social language itself, without which the idea of social language (or the idea of "play") would become the *simple meaning* of the poem and produce a truly destructive contradiction. Social language, again, is what it is only in the practice of irony, the separating of thought and language, which must include an ironic perspective (i.e., a self-conscious and self-asserting individuality) relative to social language itself. The result is an opening of possibilities, like melodies latent in the text's stringed instrument. Once the communicative quality of the language is understood, for example, it becomes possible to regard even the poem's meditative aspect as a communicative device, a communicative pretense of not wishing to communicate, whereupon even *our* individuality loses the quality of necessity and is available to be interpreted as an act, a deliberate social pose, an act paradoxically cognate with the act that renounces our claim to it.

In any case, if we must accept and affirm, as our own act of renunciation, the limitations of what the poem can actually offer us, still we accomplish this only by analogy with our understanding of what transgresses those limits: the poem as meditation, which for all its dismemberment (as monodrama and dialectic) is still operative, like our dismembered individuality, and in which what is renounced, our "godlike right," the divine nature of the self, is established permanently *by* being renounced. There is no denying the operation of a sense of philosophical or religious truth in the poem, a sense that establishes (by being located there) the space separate from language which is required precisely by irony, or by the social. There is of course also no denying the *danger* in this sense, the opening of a place for inevitable "error" and for "the possibility of loss of being" (Heidegger, p. 34); if we clutch the poet's message to our bosom, even to the extent of understanding it, then we inevitably mistake it and lose it. The philosophical or religious truth could be stabilized, once and for all, only by a practically inconceivable bridge of sheer identity between the revelatory writtenness or *stasis* of the poem's language, for us, and the Hellenic or Platonic or perfectly *kinetic* operation of language as a medium of exchange with others, which creates that hidden chamber where the true word or λόγος, by sleeping, gains steadily in power and truthfulness after all.

But we cannot avoid this danger. We cannot deny that we know what the poem means with respect to our dismembered (but undeniable) individuality, which is at once both the vessel of a "godlike right" and a finite (mortal) object that is at best "heard of" in conversation. These two aspects of individuality correspond to two recurrent and undeniable phases in self-consciousness, our feeling of certainty about the self's conquest of fate and our feeling of helpless subjection to fate, phases that are related by a dialectic. When we attempt to lay hold of the individual self as a gateway to the infinite, we immediately find ourselves confronted by and restricted to our finite ego, since only the finite can be laid hold of as an object of consciousness. Only by affirming, as a deliberate act of renunciation, this finitude, which is our individuality in relation to others in society, can we anchor in ourselves as knowledge—if perhaps now not a comforting or advantageous knowledge—the divine or infinite dimension of the self.

However precarious the position in which this theorizing places us, we have no choice but to continue. The "game" imposes it on us. And if, accordingly, we ask *who* carries out the act of sacrifice or renunciation that is required of us and is embedded in the text's ambiguities, then it is clear that the sacrifice in question is not *mine*, as distinct from someone else's, since individuals are distinguishable and comparable only on the level of the finite ego that is that act's product. It is, rather, a sacrifice on the part of the "god in us," the divine spark in human being, which is the individual's property only by first being community property. Or if we say simply, it is a sacrifice, an act of renunciation, on the part of God, then we arrive at the idea of finite or mortal or social human existence as an *imitatio Christi*. In each of us, to the extent that we willingly assume the sufferings of mortal individuality, the godhead is present exactly as it is present in Christ. This idea, however, is nothing but a meta-Christian version of what we spoke of as the "secular religion" of the *Wanderjahre*—the idea of individuality as a communal act (especially in reading)—and in fact a version Goethe himself flirts with in *Faust*.[13] Again, the operative category here, in both Goethe and Hölderlin, the thought that resists both the nature and the structure of the individual mind that is nonetheless needed to think it, the thought beyond theory, is that of irony.

The idea of irony is not the only problematic feature of Hölderlin's poetic thought that has a parallel in Goethe's. Exactly what, we have asked, is unveiled between strophes 2 and 3 of "An die Parzen"? And we have answered: the sheer writtenness of the text. But then what exactly, or where exactly, *is* that sheer writtenness? The very recognition that some physical object is a "text" already renders the object to some degree *transparent*, if not with respect to the kinetic experience of a person's "speaking," or to possibilities for interpretive activity, then at least to a historical dynamics on the level of genre. And where, then, is the *stasis* of the poem on which everything depends, its quality as a practically dead object, like the skull (and the text) in "Im ernsten Beinhaus war's . . ."?[14]

I ask only "where" that stasis is, not "whether" it is. Obviously the text—especially as presented to us in a printed book (a "Seitenspiel"? a game of pages?)—*is* on some level static, never at all different from what it is. My point is that this level, or this quality of stasis, is as difficult and elusive as the quality of irony and may even serve as an allegory of irony—or as an allegory of what I will call the

---

[13]See my *Goethe's Theory of Poetry: "Faust" and the Regeneration of Language* (Ithaca, 1986), pp. 37, 50, 54, 121–22, passim.

[14]For another parallel in Goethe, see the argument in my *Goethe's Theory of Poetry*, chap. 8, esp. pp. 215–31, on the attempt in *Faust* to interfere even with the possibility of the work's *generic* identity, hence to bring to the fore something very like the quality of stasis in Hölderlin.

"locus" of irony, the place where the thinking "behind" irony is thought. Perhaps this stasis and this locus belong to the meaning of "Der veste Buchstab" in "Patmos" (GSA, 2/1:172), or to that of the last line of "Andenken" (2/1:189). And the parallel difficulty in Goethe lies in the idea of the history of the novel as the growth of a new "scripture"—scripture being by definition a body of writing that is canonized and above all *closed*, itself now static and substantial, however various our opinions about it. How dependable is the bridge (in Goethe) between *this* idea and the operation of irony?

The gulf that thus opens, for both Goethe and Hölderlin, between the inaccessibly indeterminate and unstabilized and concealed (irony) and the inaccessibly concrete and static and obvious (the text as "written") is a recognizably late eighteenth-century phenomenon and is interestingly parallel to the inaugural gulf between "transcendental subjectivity and the mode of being of objects" in Foucault's idea of the "modern *episteme*."[15] But I do not mean that this phenomenon thus looks forward into the nineteenth century. On the contrary, I propose to show that it looks backward into the unabandoned and unabandonable problematics of the eighteenth.

[15]Michel Foucault, *The Order of Things* (New York, 1973; orig. French, 1966), pp. 246–47.

CHAPTER THREE

Lessing's *Laokoon*: The Poetics of Experience

The discussion of Hölderlin arrives at strictly contradictory formulations. On one hand, the text must be realized as an act of renunciation by the reader, whereas, on the other hand, reading is really *not* an act of the reader but an act of the community *through* the reader, indeed the origin of the reader, an enactment of the origin of individuality. It is not an accident that this contradiction has a theological flavor. European religious tradition, the religion of Jews and Christians, operates as a central metaphor in the self-understanding of literature in the period we are concerned with—not only in Goethe's narratives and Hölderlin's poetry. But can this contradiction in the idea of reading be resolved or accounted for in the history of poetic theory?

Poetic Theories in Poetic Tradition

An interpretive argument in literature is always felt to be stronger if it is supported by parallels between the poetic text and an expository text either written by or known to have affected the poet. With regard to "An die Parzen," it is useful to recall that Hölderlin knew Schiller's *Über die ästhetische Erziehung des Menschen*. But the difference between a "poetic" and an "expository" text, upon which this critical method depends, also makes it problematic. For one of the characteristics by which we recognize poetry is that the technical means of representation and construction come closer to having a denotative function than in expository writing. In dealing with "An die Parzen," for example, we must ask what ambiguity signifies *as* a technique; there must be an element of meaning that is denoted by the technique and escapes denotation in any other form. Without an understanding of this point we cannot even begin to grasp the social dimension of the idea of play, which in turn has an effect on the meaning of every word in the text.

Philosophical texts whose content can be related to the sense of words or concepts in a poem are therefore not sufficient to validate an interpretation. To be confident about our understanding of the denotative operation of technique, we should require an expository text from which to learn about technical theories of poetry, either the poet's own or those current in the age. (This "text," of course, is normally *constructed* by us from various actual texts that we locate variously on the scale from "poetic" to "expository.") And such a text, to the extent that it is useful, tends also to be illegible. For a technical theory of poetry, like a mathematical theory of light, however lucid on its own terms, is meaningless unless we can relate it to the experience from which it takes its origin—the experience of reading poetry or, by analogy, the experience of seeing. But whereas we normally assume that the experience of seeing is the same for everybody who has eyes, the corresponding proposition is not by any means normally accepted for the experience of reading poetry. We do not pretend to understand how poetry is read in an age or culture different from our own (assuming we even know what we mean by "our own") except *by way* of what seems to us the relevant poetic theory. Thus we enter a circle. In order to read the poetry properly, we must grasp the theory; but in order to grasp the theory (here the analogy with theories of light operates) we must be able to carry out a proper reading of the poetry.

This matter can be approached from different directions. When Northrop Frye points out, for instance, that modern English lacks an adequate *terminology* for literary criticism, he is making a statement that could be made of any language at any time. For part of what we mean by the concept of poetic literature is that poetry is how languages grow. Since Plato, there has been disagreement about the sense in which our language shapes our existence as a whole; but that languages differ substantially, as systems in a complex relation to "world," is fairly clear. And the internal principle of change in each language, by which languages come to differ from each other, is as a rule (especially since the eighteenth century) a main component of what we mean by the poetic. If we are not prepared to argue that a text operates to expand the limits of its language, to conquer new verbal territory, we are not treating that text as poetry.

Poetry is thus a point where our language differs significantly *from itself*, which makes an adequate terminology for literary criticism unattainable. Poetic theory is not impossible; if it were impossible to see beyond the present boundaries of the world as ordered by a particular language, then poetry itself would be impossible. But the terminology of poetic theory never fits its object exactly, is never recognized as *determining* its object in the manner of other technical terminologies. It is related to its object only by a fabric of analogies or metaphors—borrowed from less obviously problematic intellectual disciplines—which we can decipher, again, only by way of a *prior* understanding of the poetic. I do not want to make a mystery of "the poetic"; I am talking about what we *normally mean* by that concept. One could argue in fact that the prominence of the hermeneutic problem-field I have sketched, the insistence with which those problems intrude even into what ought to be the simplest areas of inquiry, is itself in practice a characteristic by which we assure ourselves that what we are talking about is, precisely, "the poetic."

The project of the present chapter, to find a reasonably exact formulation of late eighteenth-century German poetic theory, mainly by way of a reading of Lessing's *Laokoon*, would be doomed from the start without some possibility of circumventing this theoretical impasse. Such a possibility is opened in literary *tradition*—not in the idea of tradition, but in the actual details of the tradition we are talking about and talking within. My main point, again, is that *we* need a new eighteenth century, that political and social and literary discussion in the late twentieth century favors historical suppositions that produce an especially distorted or superficial view of eighteenth-century texts. If we agree, therefore, that there is such a thing as literary tradition, and consequently that there is some form of historical reason for our preferential misreadings of the eighteenth century, then it is reasonable to infer that in analyzing and correcting those misreadings, we find ourselves in contact—for all our theoretical misgivings—with "actual" eighteenth-century poetic thought. And one result of this move, if we carry it out responsibly, is a uniquely useful critical perspective on our own situation, a perspective less subject to the corrosive effects of instant self-reflexivity than the play of perspectives by which recent literary theory attempts to imagine itself as a moving beyond its own positions.

The Significance of Lessing's *Laokoon*

It is not enough, therefore, simply to read theoretical documents contemporary with the literature that interests us. *How* we read them is at issue. Let us begin with some observations about how an unquestionably important document in eighteenth-century poetics, Lessing's *Laokoon*, was read in its own time. Goethe says, in *Dichtung und Wahrheit*: "One has to be young to appreciate what an effect Lessing's *Laokoon* had on us, by lifting us up from the region of miserably limited observation into the wide open spaces of thought. That long misunderstood dictum, *ut pictura poesis*, was instantly dispensed with; the difference between plastic and verbal arts was now clear, their respective pinnacles were now seen to be separate, despite the tendency of their bases to meet" (WA, 27:164). He then mentions Lessing's argument for the admissibility of the ugly in poetry, and continues: "We now considered ourselves liberated from all evil, and reckoned we were in a position to look down with a certain pity upon that once so glorified sixteenth century, where, in German pictures and poems, life could be imagined only in the form of a capped and belled fool, death only in the deformity of a rattling skeleton, and the necessary or accidental evils of the world only in the image of a grotesque devil" (27:165). Whether or not it is literally true that *Laokoon* thus suddenly kindled in Goethe a new idea of poetry, it is important for our purposes that Goethe attempts to give this impression. My aim is not to set Lessing up as the inventor of a *new* poetics, but to show the depth of correspondence between poetic theory in *Laokoon* and the practice of writers like Goethe as evidence of the operation of an inexplicit or *unrecorded* poetics.

It appears frequently, as in *Dichtung und Wahrheit*, that German literary figures of the period see in Lessing's work more than we do, a significance for which no clear terminology was available. Friedrich Schlegel recalls being displeased with *Laokoon* at first because it had appeared to promise an explanation of the difference between painting and poetry in the form of "rock-solid science" and had not kept that promise. But later, says Schlegel, a clearer understanding made Lessing's works into a "labyrinth" for him, easy to get into and extremely difficult to get out of again (FS, p. 111). Thus both Goethe and Schlegel claim to discern in *Laokoon* something more profound than merely a systematic demarcation of the realms of pictorial and verbal art, an extra something that, from our point of view, might account for the excitement and controversy generated by the work.

In any event, the systematic aspect of Lessing's argument, the exact separation between poetry and painting, met with little agreement in its time.[1] It did not in fact deserve to meet with agreement. Its logic is far from sound; the argument on pictorial art in particular is often perfunctory; and we will see that in the work's genesis, the original systematic plan was quickly superseded by deeper poetic considerations that undermine it. Among contemporary commentators, Herder comes closest to understanding this situation when, in the first *Kritisches Wäldchen*, he perceives a specially intimate relation between *Laokoon* and poetry, both in the book's mainly literary orientation and in our sense of the author as a critic who also "feels himself a poet" (SW, 3:10). *Laokoon* is not only a poetics, but a poetics from within; its thought is derived not from a philosophical idea of the poetic but from a flexible and minutely detailed sense for the practical problems faced by poet and reader. It does not stand back from the realm of poetry, to produce a map of it, but gives an immediate account of the ebb and flow of poetic production and communication.

I maintain that the central idea in the book, an idea for which critical terminology as yet had no accepted name, is the idea of *experience*, in more or less the sense of the later term "Erlebnis,"[2] experience in the sense, in English, of "*an* experience," as the occurrence of a particular vital interaction between subject and object. This idea

[1]See, for example, the selection of responses printed in Gotthold Ephraim Lessing, *Werke*, 8 vols. (Munich, 1970–79), 6:870–72. For an extremely detailed discussion of Wilhelm Heinse's response to *Laokoon*, which may be interesting because of Heinse's relation with Hölderlin, see Rita Terras, *Wilhelm Heinses Ästhetik* (Munich, 1972), pp. 45–86.

[2]René Wellek, "Genre Theory, the Lyric, and 'Erlebnis,'" in *Festschrift für Richard Alewyn*, ed. Herbert Singer and Benno von Wiese (Cologne, 1967), pp. 392–412, attacks vehemently the use of the idea of experience (especially in the German form "Erlebnis") as a defining concept for the genre of lyric. In the process, with some assistance from Gadamer, he points out that the *word* "Erlebnis" is a relatively late coinage (pp. 408–9) and does not occur in the writings of such figures as Herder, Goethe, Novalis, or Schleiermacher, whose work it is afterward used to characterize. Only in Wilhelm Dilthey's work, says Wellek, and, as it were, without Dilthey's consent, does "Erlebnis" become "the shibboleth of German poetic theory" (p. 411). This argument does not affect the concept of experience as I develop it. What it does, in fact, is provide an instance of precisely the historical mechanics of poetic theory that is discussed in the preceding section. "Erlebnis," by the time it establishes itself in the domain of terminology, is already a trivialization, a forgetting, of the theoretical and metaphorical event (in the eighteenth century) to which it owes its existence, and which it struggles to pin down.

is what impresses Goethe, the idea that the task of poetry is not to draw conclusions from experience, not to criticize experience in accordance with moral or philosophical prejudices, not to avoid experience by suppressing the subjective and producing a "picture," but rather to re-create and explore experience as such, to articulate its own shape, to reveal experience, or "life," as a basic positive value requiring no extrinsic justification. The accomplishment of this task, however, is more than merely a matter of crying out, "Life, in whatever form, is good" (WA, 4:107). For experience includes reflective consciousness in its subjective aspect, while also offering itself as an object of consciousness, and so brings with it all the problems we have discussed in connection with Hölderlin. In particular, as the intereffectiveness of subject *and* object, experience cannot become wholly an object of detached intellectual inquiry without losing its very nature. Not only the poetry of experience, therefore, but also the discussion of such poetry (e.g., *Laokoon*) must somehow account for *the process of reading*, the version of "experience" that *we* are in the midst of, here and now.[3] Experience must include not merely "the reader," in the sense of a set of particular cultural assumptions, but the *process* of reading, in a form comparable to the dialectical unfolding of "An die Parzen." Complications of this sort are centrally important both in the shaping of Lessing's thought and in the poetry of his period.

The Reading of *Laokoon*

Reading *Laokoon* in terms of the issues that have concerned us raises three questions:

1. *Does the relation between reading and experience not resurrect what I called earlier the theory of "romance reading"?* In the thought of *Laokoon*, as in the rhetoric of the eighteenth-century ironic novel, the idea of romance reading has an important structural value, but

[3]The locution "poetry of experience" recalls Robert Langbaum, *The Poetry of Experience: The Dramatic Monologue in Modern Literary Tradition* (New York, 1963; orig. 1957). The modern or Romantic or post-Enlightenment "doctrine of experience," says Langbaum, asserts "that the imaginative apprehension gained through immediate experience is primary and certain, whereas the analytic reflection that follows is secondary and problematical" (p. 35); but precisely this "disequilibrium between experience and idea" (p. 36) *is* a characteristic experience, an experience that includes the quality of being "deliberate" and so problematizes the whole idea of experience in its turn. I differ from Langbaum mainly in seeing these problems already firmly established in eighteenth-century poetics. On the details and problems of the idea of reading as itself an experience, "an *event*, something

does *not* claim to describe the actual or desired process of the text's own reception. It serves rather to articulate the idea of reading, by contrast or negation, on a level that altogether defies systematic fixing. In Goethe it is the idea of reading itself that is developed to the point where it splits open and produces a discontinuity in the discourse that had engendered it. In Lessing a similar rôle is played by the idea of experience. Experience is the implied ultimate object of imitation or illusion in *Laokoon*; but it turns out to be an object too big for the discourse of imitation (in a sense that includes the idea of romance reading) to swallow.

2. *If our reading of "Laokoon" arrives at a systematic poetics centered on the idea of experience, how shall it avoid attributing this system to the poetic text, which would produce a contradiction by detaching the text's meaning from the process or experience of reading?* The aim of my argument overall, to authorize specific interpretive strategies with respect to texts from the German eighteenth century, cannot be accomplished except in the form of a relatively systematic poetics; and in this chapter I intend to describe such a poetics. Thus the conflict between the idea of system as such and the idea of non-objectifiable experience cannot be avoided. It is not sufficient to point out that the actual completion of the system requires a terminology that was not available to Lessing, that the system was thus not a system *for* Lessing, although it becomes one for us. If, as I have suggested, we must approach the poetics of *Laokoon* by discovering its relation to our own poetic thought, then that relation must still belong, for us, to *poetics*. And the poetic concept of experience cannot be rescued, for us, by deficiencies in the theoretical vocabulary available to Lessing.

This difficulty, however, can be met by asking about the relation between the poetic *system* and the *thought* it makes the gesture of containing or summarizing. In the case of the *Laokoon* poetics, I will argue, the systematic fixing is not the ground upon which the thought rests, or from which it develops, but rather is relativized by its own content into a kind of *metaphor*, a strange flower (strange precisely in its symmetry), which unfolds and displays itself, so to speak, *atop* the working of the nameless dynamisms that it presents

that *happens* to, and with the participation of, the reader," see Stanley Fish, "Literature in the Reader: Affective Stylistics" (orig. 1970), especially its revised version in Fish, *Is There a Text in This Class? The Authority of Interpretive Communities* (Cambridge, Mass., 1980), p. 25.

in the form of concepts, propositions, and references. This idea can be grasped best by recognizing that it implies a particular view of intellectual history as a whole—a view I attribute to Lessing. Do conceptual systems (explicit or potential or inferred) really function as the basic articulations of intellectual history—this being a tacit assumption in most historiographical practice? Or is the appearance of fixable systems not more nearly accidental, indeed parasitic, like mushrooms marking the presence of an old tree root?

If we admit that conceptual systems do not have a simply real or objective historical existence, that system, rather, is the individual mind's organizing of the otherwise intractable material of history, an act by which the mind places "history" and itself vis-à-vis, then it follows that the idea that systems have a primary shaping function in intellectual history depends on the assumption that such history is *made* in (and by, and out of) individuals' readings of it. But I claim that just this assumption is *challenged* by the eighteenth-century German poetics of community-as-reader. I will argue, in fact, that this poetics raises doubts about whether thought can be considered a function of the individual to begin with.

For the time being, I ask the reader to attend to the difference between the present argument and how the systematic aspect of Lessing's thought is treated by such writers as Tzvetan Todorov and David Wellbery. Todorov says that "[Lessing's originality] is the originality of a system. More precisely, Lessing is the first to juxtapose two commonplace observations of the period: that art is imitation, and that the signs of poetry are arbitrary. He is the first, too, to decide that this juxtaposition poses a problem."[4] Todorov does not claim that Lessing produces a complete or valid system. "Lessing's argument is seductive in its rigor," he says; but this rigor obscures "the fact that Lessing used the words ['imitation' and 'resemblance'] in different meanings from one line to the next" (Todorov, p. 145). And yet, a systematic *tendency* in Lessing is presented as justifying the conclusion that "Lessing was the first to integrate the theory of art convincingly into a general reflection on the sign; the first, too, to affirm in an explicit way the grounding of each art in its raw material, thus that of literature in language. And perhaps the soundness of his thinking struck a more serious blow to imitation than any other, at

[4]Tzvetan Todorov, *Theories of the Symbol*, trans. Catherine Porter (Ithaca, 1982; orig. 1977), p. 137.

the very moment when he was trying to protect it: he proved *a contrario* that the reign of imitation over aesthetic thought was approaching its end. Romanticism was ready to be born" (p. 146). Lessing's thought is thus supposedly systematic in spite of itself. In its quality as a system, it closes and terminates historically its own discourse.

Wellbery goes further than Todorov. He attempts to anchor Lessing's thought in *existing* systematics, especially the system of Wolffian epistemology, which he (Wellbery) explicates with exemplary clarity.[5] But the end of his argument is similar to Todorov's in that it attributes to Lessing the perfection of Enlightenment aesthetics. For Lessing, namely, "Poetry . . . regains the experience of presence, the transparency to intuition, which language left behind" (Wellbery, p. 237). Again the systematic tendency in Lessing is regarded as a sign of historical closure and culmination, the sign that a new epoch is about to be born (see Wellbery, p. 238), which presupposes, for Wellbery as for Todorov, that systems are the actual articulations of intellectual history, hence that history is made in the tension between historical material and the individual mind. And my point, by contrast, is that the poetic system derivable from *Laokoon* operates primarily as a metaphor, as one literary manifestation, among others, of a matrix of thought that had only just begun to bear fruit. Were Goethe and Schlegel both blind? Was the significance of *Laokoon* for the future merely that it so securely wrapped up the past?

3. *In view of the complications suggested in the preceding section* ("The Significance of Lessing's *Laokoon*"), *plus the absence of a clear terminology, what kind of evidence can enable us to trace the communication of the ironic "Laokoon" poetics in its own time?* Or, how can it be shown that Lessing's terminologically incomplete poetics was part of the communicated intellectual life of its time? In a sense, Eva Knodt answers this question in her argument on the profound dialogic relation between texts of Lessing and of Herder, which we will look at later.[6] But an element of uncertainty remains nonetheless, since our own reading of the text can never exactly reproduce the contemporary reading we postulate. Our access to the text— given the developments in terminology that make its interpretation both possible and valuable—must always be by a route that is differ-

[5]David E. Wellbery, *Lessing's "Laocoon": Semiotics and Aesthetics in the Age of Reason* (Cambridge, 1984), pp. 9–98.

[6]Eva Knodt, *"Negative Philosophie" und dialogische Kritik: Zur Struktur poetischer Theorie bei Lessing und Herder* (Tübingen, 1988), esp. chap. 2, pp. 33–64.

ent from the route used by contemporary readers, or at least not demonstrably the same.

In particular, the easiest interpretive route for us proceeds by way of a discussion of the *genesis* of Lessing's text. This is the route taken by Knodt (p. 35), by Peter Burgard, by Carol Jacobs[7]—and by me, in the next section. Both Knodt and Jacobs, in fact, suggest that that genesis—which we are able to trace only with the aid of unpublished manuscript material—was sufficiently "transparent" (Knodt, p. 35) to operate as a communicative device in its own right, that it created "a polemical framework that can be immediately recognized as historically fictional" (Jacobs, p. 488). This point is not only dubious; in both Knodt and Jacobs it is also unnecessary. Knodt's discussion, and Burgard's, of the dialogic in *Laokoon* (and in its reception), is supplemented by Jacobs's very strong arguments on the idea of the disgusting (pp. 495–501), on the negative in poetry and the cloud of invisibility (pp. 503–8), on the image of snakes (pp. 510–12), and in general on Lessing's ostensible wandering from his own path, all of which can be translated into arguments on the text's communicative ambitions. The absence of an adequate terminology still denies us complete certainty. But I have pointed out that certainty about this matter would be an argument *against* the operation of Lessing's thought as part of an actual practical poetics in its time.

The Genesis of *Laokoon*

In the foreword to *Laokoon*, Lessing makes a point of referring to his book in the plural, as "Aufsätze" (essays), of which he says: "They came into being accidentally; they were shaped more by the course of my reading than by the methodical development of general principles. They are thus not so much a book as the raw collectanea for a book" (L-M, 9:5). Documents that Lessing did not publish, however, cast doubt on the honesty of this modest pose. One of the earliest sketches for *Laokoon*, probably written no later than 1763, concentrates precisely on the systematic aspect of the thought (14:334–38; includes dating). It contains the crucial distinction between "Körper" (bodies) and "Handlungen" (actions), and develops this distinction in almost exactly the words later used in chapter 16 of the book (14:334–35; cf. 9:94–95); it deals more systematically than the fin-

[7]Peter J. Burgard, "The Serious Game: Essaying Goethe's Essays" (Ph.D. diss., University of Virginia, 1988), pp. 130–31, 228–33; Carol Jacobs, "The Critical Performance of Lessing's *Laokoon*," *MLN* 102 (1987), 483–521.

ished work with the concepts of beauty and ugliness (14:336–37); and it introduces the systematic distinction borrowed from Jean-Baptiste Dubos, which was clearly to have become central in the work's continuation, between "natural signs" and "arbitrary signs" (14:334–36). Then, in July and August 1763, Lessing gives to Mendelssohn and Nicolai, for their comments, an expanded version of this systematic outline on painting and poetry. The skeleton is now fleshed out with specific examples that survive in the published book—Spence, Caylus, passages from Homer. But neither Winckelmann nor the Laocoon sculpture is yet mentioned; the emphasis is still on overall conceptual structure. And the comments of the two friends tend even more strongly toward the systematic; Mendelssohn, especially, suggests a refinement and generalization of the terminology, and an expansion of scope to include music and dance.[8]

The conceptual system, then, was well established prior to being embedded in a series of particular arguments on art, literature, and classical scholarship; but later Lessing *deliberately* seeks to give the impression of a rambling development out of which general ideas only gradually emerge. The earliest sketch in which Winckelmann and the Laocoon sculpture are mentioned was apparently written in part shortly before, and in part after, the appearance of Winckelmann's *Geschichte der Kunst des Altertums* at Christmas 1763. But then, in his next version of the systematic outline, Lessing plans to open the second part of *Laokoon* with the remark that Winckelmann's *Geschichte* has "just" been published (L-M, 14:379), as if the publication of that book had surprised him in the midst of a longstanding meditation. The idea of saying anything at all about Winckelmann probably did not arise until after the forthcoming *Geschichte* had been announced; and although the book, when it appeared, enabled Lessing to modify his judgment in a positive direction, still his overall critique of Winckelmann remains a unified conception (see L-M, 14:377–78). But now he sets out to create the impression that his "essay" in opposition to Winckelmann's earlier note on the Laocoon had been written long before the appearance of the *Geschichte*, the impression that his critique is not a conception at all, but merely a series of reactions, at various times, as Winckelmann's works had become available. And this touch is retained in chapter 26 of the published *Laokoon*.

<hr />

[8]Mendelssohn's and Nicolai's marginal comments appear in the notes to L-M. See, for example, L-M, 14:344–45, 348, 352–53, and 366–71.

In working out his original system, and especially after having weaknesses noted by his friends, Lessing gradually arrives at the decision to *pretend* that his book had arisen as a loose collection of essays and that he had made the connections among them only after the fact. Why? He himself suggests a reason in his foreword, when he criticizes Baumgarten's systematic *Aesthetica* and concludes, "If my reasoning is not as rigorous as Baumgarten's, at least my examples will have a more natural and authentic smack [mehr nach der Quelle schmecken]" (L-M, 9:5). The critic's first task, Lessing implies, is to immerse himself in his real subject matter, his "examples." The conceptual systems of which "we Germans" (9:5) are so fond have the effect of reducing the illustrative examples to mere counters, no longer actual experiences, whereupon there remains no pressing reason to treat them systematically in the first place.

But if we consider the argument of *Laokoon* as a whole, it also emerges that the difference between a systematic work and a work whose structure emerges gradually from particulars is approximately the same as the difference between merely descriptive poetry and poetry that (in Lessing's terms) is truly vivid or graphic. A conceptual system pretends to exist in what we might call abstract *space*, as a type of "body" whose inherently simultaneous elements resist the convention of successiveness in writing and actually prefer to be represented by diagrams. But Lessing attempts to produce in *Laokoon* a critical-philosophical *history*, a temporally successive representation of the temporal growth of its own thought, the representation of thought not as a "body" but as an "action." In Herder's words, "We see his work *becoming*" (SW 3:12). He does not represent the *actual* growth of his thought; he creates, rather, a fictional history for his meditations, and emphasizes its temporality, in the manner of historical novelists, by locating within it an actual event, the publication of Winckelmann's *Geschichte*. But whether or not the implied history is factual does not affect the point that the aesthetic doctrine of *Laokoon* is itself *applied* in the creation of the work's form.

These considerations may seem out of place in a work of the type Lessing is writing; he himself, after all, distinguishes poetry from "speech" in general, or "prose" (L-M, 9:101; 14:429–30), which need not hesitate to represent spatial relations in writing.[9] Indeed, the

[9]Lessing's treatment of his own critical prose as if it were poetry—provided this point holds—is a strong argument against Wellbery's conclusion. For it compromises the status of poetry as a privileged realm—where verbal signs achieve perfect motivated transparency—on which Wellbery's conclusion depends.

authorial stance in *Laokoon* may even be regarded as dishonest. But there is consistency in what Lessing does; for the same basic idea lies behind both his remark about Baumgarten and the poeticizing of his work's own overall shape, the idea of *experience*. If criticism has an obligation to preserve the experience of its subject matter in maximum immediacy ("nach der Quelle"), rather than merely cull illustrations from it, then the accrescent or historical progress of Lessing's book asserts, as the source of this obligation, the quality of critical thought as *itself* an experience, an instance of personal growing, and not merely the registration of judgments. The importance of the idea of experience, in any case, is clear from the tack Lessing takes at the very outset, in his argument concerning the Greeks' ability to undergo the whole range of human emotions with no detriment to their heroic resolve or prowess, whereas we modern barbarians, in order to be heroes, think it necessary to deny ourselves the experience of fear, of weeping, of pain. The Homeric hero and the modern literary critic both appear to embody superhuman claims: the latter, in that his or her critical intellect apparently smothers what might seem to us a natural, nonintellectual response to the *oratio sensitiva* of poetry. In his argument, Lessing shows that the idea of the superhuman Homeric hero is wrong; and the form of his work makes a corresponding suggestion about literary criticism or theory.

There is a further reason for the reluctance to systematize in *Laokoon*. Mendelssohn points out in his comments that the generality of Lessing's basic concepts demands a system of all the arts, not merely a comparison of painting and poetry. And although Lessing did plan to include a discussion of music and dance in the continuation (L-M, 14:383, 431–35), his ideas on these subjects are not at all firm. My point, in fact, is that Lessing, in considering the comments of his friends, discovers that even the pictorial arts are not part of what he is really interested in, that his work is really a poetics, and a poetics of experience. The argument on the relation between poetry and painting is still important, but it now receives a new function, which I will argue is that of *metaphor*.

The Poetic Bias in *Laokoon*

In chapter 16 of *Laokoon*, in which Lessing claims to anchor his observations in an argument "from first principles" (L-M, 9:94), the relation between painting and poetry is presented as symmetrical. For every advantage of the one art, a corresponding quality is found in the other, and this relation is marked by correspondences in syntax and vocabulary among the propositions. But in the rest of the book, such symmetry is absent. Poetry is repeatedly spoken of as the broader art, able to depict and express much more than its sister. We hear of the "narrow limits" of painting and the "capacious sphere" of poetry (9:4); painting is the "smaller" entity of the two, which can be "contained in the larger" (9:45); the poet is "permitted" (9:62) everything that is permitted to the painter and more besides, especially the use of "negative features" (9:65) and of ugliness (9:139, 148) in description.

The argument on poetry is also much more cohesive. Lessing's first main point about the pictorial arts is that their "highest law is beauty" (9:4), and that this law restricts them in their subject matter; Laocoon, in the sculpture, may not scream, because screaming distorts the lines of the face, obscures the ideal that dwells in them (9:13; 14:354–55, 412, 415). Immediately afterwards, however, Lessing advances a completely different argument. Laocoon may not scream because his screaming would not leave enough to our imagination; since painting or sculpture can depict only one instant, the instant chosen must be "fruitful," and "Dasjenige aber nur allein ist fruchtbar, was der Einbildungskraft freyes Spiel läßt" (9:19; Only that is fruitful which leaves free play to the imagination). The trouble is that the concepts of beauty and fruitfulness are not coordinated; and when we arrive at the theoretical high point in chapter 16, the situation becomes yet more confused. Here Lessing compares painting and poetry by way of the general principle that "Zeichen" (signs) in art must have "ein bequemes Verhältniß" (a comfortable relation) to what they signify (9:94), which means that the spatially related signs of painting are suited to depict "bodies," whereas the temporally related signs of poetry are suited to represent "actions." But this argument is not nearly so symmetrical as Lessing pretends. The signs of painting are such that they *can* represent only spatial situations, whereas Lessing concedes in the next chapter that the signs of language, being "arbitrary" (9:101), *can* represent bodies in space, but *ought* not to when used in poetry. The principle of the "comfortable relation" between signifier and signified, therefore, merely reflects an elementary fact about painting but gives rise to a profound and problematic assertion about poetry; and again, this principle does nothing to elucidate the concepts of beauty and fruitfulness from earlier in the argument.

The details of Lessing's thinking about the pictorial arts are no more cogent than the main line of thought. One type of painting he had planned to attack on general principles, for example, is allegory, "Allegoristerey" (L-M, 9:5). But does the allegorical exclude the beautiful? Can the instant depicted in an allegorical painting not be fruitful for our imagination? Does allegory conflict with the nontemporal nature of painting? When Lessing actually comes to deal with allegory, in chapter 10, he points out that personified abstractions are more easily incorporated into poetry; but he does not even try to carry out his promised argument on their positive inappropriateness in painting.

This aspect of *Laokoon*, then, is not at all unified. But if we collect the ideas on poetry that correspond, case by case, to the scattered ideas on painting, we find a consistent pattern. To the law of beauty in painting corresponds not a restriction in poetry but a special freedom, the freedom to employ ugliness judiciously for the purpose of awakening "vermischte Empfindungen" (compound feelings) in the reader (L-M, 9:139, 148). To be sure, there is no obvious reason why ugliness in painting should not also provoke feelings that contain both pleasant and unpleasant components; Mendelssohn, in his comments, suggests at least two possibilities (14:350–51). But Lessing is adamant; in chapter 24 he contends that Mendelssohn's own argument on the phenomenon of disgust also applies to "ugliness in visible forms" (9:143), that such ugliness is repellent even as a subjective idea and therefore cannot excite compound feelings in which an objective unpleasantness is balanced by a pleasant subjective component.[10] Ugliness, he says, is useful in art only when it "so to speak ceases to be ugliness" (9:139), when its "coexistent parts" are disassembled by poetry and made "successive" (9:145). Thus, with respect to *poetry*, the argument on beauty and ugliness is correlated with the

[10]That Lessing's thought on "compound feelings" goes hand in hand with Mendelssohn's is clear from a footnote at L-M, 9:139. See esp. MM, 1:394–402; also 1:570–72, for the 1761 version, which Lessing had while composing *Laokoon*. Mendelssohn's argument on disgust appears in the *Briefe, die Neueste Litteratur betreffend, Vter Theil* (Berlin, 1760), pp. 97–104 (= no. 82), in vol. 1 of the facsimile reprint (Hildesheim, 1974), with original pagination only. Jacobs's argument on the matter of disgust is both ingenious and persuasive, especially the idea of a "new mimesis" whose "formal gestures . . . are at once total identity and total alterity, an obliteration of the difference between sameness and otherness" (p. 501)—with terminological echoes, incidentally, of Foucault on "origin."

argument on spatial and temporal factors; and this correlation relieves us of the need—which is present but unfulfilled in the argument on painting—to find a *definition* of "beauty." The argument on
poetry requires only that we have *an* idea of the beautiful (so that we
can experience its persistence even in its violation), not that we have
a *particular* idea of the beautiful to use as a standard for judging the
appropriateness of artistic subject matter.

The advantage of "compound feelings," according to Mendelssohn,
is that they penetrate and establish themselves more deeply in our
inner life, since their unpleasant component stimulates us and prevents satiety (MM, 1:396–97). In Lessing's terms, compound feelings
are a condition of our being "interested" in something (L-M, 9:140);
and "interest," the engagement of our feelings and sympathies, is a
principal object of poetry. The idea of interest is what justifies
Homer, Sophocles, and Vergil in allowing their heroes to scream
with anguish. If the poet shows a character passing through "all the
possible phases" (9:22) of an action that involves intolerable suffering,
and if the character stoically refuses to complain, then the most we
can feel is "admiration"; "but admiration," says Lessing, "is a cold
affect, an inactive awe that excludes any warmer passion and any
more vivid mental impression" (9:10). Its greater latitude imposes an
obligation on poetry. Poetry must employ the means at its disposal to
"interest" us in actions and characters (9:22); it must awaken an *active*
emotional participation (not "inactive awe") on our part. Hence the
importance of compound feelings and the usefulness of the ugly;
hence the requirement that poetry develop those feelings which in
painting are but potentially present in the "fruitfulness" of the instant; hence the argument that poetry should represent only actions,
that it should not linger, but move forward with a "swiftness" (9:101)
that prevents our thinking about our feelings and so maintains them
in something like a pure state, as if we were reacting directly to
a reality perceived by our senses. In connection with Ewald von
Kleist, Lessing speaks of the properly made poem as actually *consisting*, in the main, of "feelings" (9:106–7).

Both Lessing and Mendelssohn suggest in passing, moreover, that
in reality there is no such thing as a strictly non-compound feeling
(L-M, 9:29; MM, 1:399), which implies that the vivid and developed
compound feelings of poetry are a kind of distillation of our emotional experience in general. In reading poetry, we are invited to
understand and undergo our normal emotional existence in height-

ened form, thus to become more fully ourselves. (Number 78 of the *Hamburgische Dramaturgie* in fact suggests that tragedy provides *training* in a crucial area of our emotional life that involves pity [L-M, 10:117–18].)[11] Unlike the thinking on pictorial art, the poetic thinking in *Laokoon* is thus well focused with respect to the idea of the emotional depth and breadth and continuity of our experience as readers. The "ideal of actions," corresponding to the ideal of beauty in painting, includes "compression of time" and "intensification of motives"; but both of these are important mainly because of their contribution to the third element of the ideal, the "arousal of passions" in us as we read (L-M, 14:381).

Poetry and the Illusion of Experience

These ideas do not yet constitute a poetics; nor do they explain why Lessing develops his ideas on poetry in a comparison with painting. The crucial point is contained in his definition of a "poetic painting":

> Jeder Zug, jede Verbindung mehrerer Züge, durch die uns der Dichter seinen Gegenstand so sinnlich macht, daß wir uns dieses Gegenstandes deutlicher bewußt werden, als seiner Worte, heißt mahlerisch, heißt ein Gemählde, weil es uns dem Grade der Illusion näher bringt, dessen das materielle Gemählde besonders fähig ist, der sich von dem materiellen Gemählde am ersten und am leichtesten abstrahiren lassen. [L-M, 9:92]

> [Every stroke, every combination of strokes, by which the poet renders his object so sensorially vivid to us that we are more conscious of the object than of his words, is called graphic, is called a painting, because it brings us closer to that degree of illusion of which the material painting is especially capable, to that notion of illusion which is primarily and most easily abstractable from the idea of material painting.]

"Illusion," according to Mendelssohn, is the state of being convinced for a moment that we are perceiving the actual object, not merely an

---

[11]On the moral significance of pity, a compound feeling, see also Lessing's letter to C.F. Nicolai of November 1756. On the culture of pity in general, see Hans-Jürgen Schings, *Der mitleidigste Mensch ist der beste Mensch: Poetik des Mitleids von Lessing bis Büchner* (Munich, 1980).

artistic imitation;[12] and this idea, in the tradition of thought from
Dubos, is most naturally associated with painting. What we see in a
painting, after all, are exactly the shapes and colors we would expect
to see in reality.

How shall we apply this to poetry? Lessing insists on the idea that
in reading poetry we cease to be conscious of the words and "believe
that we are experiencing true sensory impressions of the objects presented" (L-M, 9:101). How is this possible? In observing a painting,
we presumably receive the same raw visual stimuli we would if confronted with reality. And with respect to poetry, the analogous situation must be: in reading poetry, the sequence and pace and rhythm
of our *inner* experience, our thoughts and feelings, are exactly the
same as they would be in the presence of the described action itself,
so that for a moment we can believe ourselves affected by what, in
reality, would be the raw sensory causes of such feelings. *The experience of reading the poem must, in its inward aspect, coincide with
the inward aspect of the hypothetical experience depicted or described in the poem.*

This is a radical version of what I called earlier the theory of romance reading; and it is a crucial element in Lessing's poetics. It
explains the usefulness of the ugly and of compound feelings in poetry; for by increasing the range of the reader's emotional response,
poetry expands just that area of the experience of reading which can
be made identical with the experience represented. It explains the
implied requirement that poetry carry out in detail those extreme
actions and feelings which the painter leaves to our imagination;[13]
sequence and rhythm in feeling are what poetry may not leave us to
supply on our own, but must actively shape to coincide with the
corresponding properties of experience inside the fiction. And it ex-

[12]See esp. "Von der Herrschaft über die Neigungen" (MM, 2:147–55). Victor Anthony
Rudowski, *Lessing's "Aesthetica in nuce": An Analysis of the May 26, 1769, Letter to
Nicolai* (Chapel Hill, 1971), pp. 58–59, maintains that for Lessing in 1757 the very "concept of illusion" (as defined by Mendelssohn) was "unnecessary" or "superfluous." This is
not so. In his letter of 2 February 1757, Lessing argues with Mendelssohn about the
particular way in which the latter describes the interaction of rational and sensitive faculties; he does not argue against the concept of illusion. And while it is true that at the end
of the letter to Mendelssohn of 18 December 1756, Lessing points out that the immediate
sensory illusion in drama is a function of the acting, not of the text, this does not mean that
illusion, in a broader sense, is not created by poetry. See also my "Idea of the Audience in
Lessing's Inexplicit Tragic Dramaturgy," *LY* 11 (1979), 59–68.
[13]That this is a requirement, not merely a possibility, comes closer to being spelled out in
the paralipomena; see, for example, L-M, 14:376.

plains, above all, the restriction of poetry to the representation of actions. The experience of reading is assumed to be successive, with no significant spatial dimension; therefore any attempt in poetry to depict a spatial situation directly—rather than merely "by implication" (L-M, 9:95)—must produce a "collision" (9:104) between our experience here and now, in the process of reading, and the fictional experience that ought to merge with it.

We can see the working of Lessing's mind in the growth of the concept of "action." In one of the systematic sketches from 1763, we read already that "Gegenstände . . . die auf einander, oder deren Theile auf einander folgen . . . heißen überhaupt *Handlungen*" (L-M, 14:344; Objects that follow each other, or whose parts follow each other, are called in general *actions*). But Mendelssohn comments correctly that the general term for such objects is "Bewegungen" (motions), not "Handlungen" (14:344); and Lessing, in his next outline, reformulates his argument accordingly: "Poetry depicts motions, and depicts bodies by implication from motions" (14:372; cf. 14:380, 381). An "action" is now defined as "a sequence of motions that are directed at a purpose" (14:372); and this definition corresponds closely to the earlier definition of "action" in "Von dem Wesen der Fabel" (7:429). But in the published version of *Laokoon*, there is no mention of "motions"; and the original formulation, restricting poetry to "actions" (9:94–95), is resurrected without comment or justification.[14] Why does Lessing thus retract his acceptance of Mendelssohn's well-founded objection?

The reason, it seems to me, is that "motion" is an entirely objective (hence virtually *pictorial*) concept; in order to distinguish a motion we need only perceive it, whereas in order to distinguish an action, we must make a *judgment* concerning purpose. The difference between a purposeful and a purposeless motion, from my point of view as an observer (or reader), consists solely in my subjective relating of the motion to its presumed end. But the experience of reading poetry must be made to coincide with the experience represented; therefore the subject matter of poetry not only must possess temporal (rather than spatial) extension but must also have a shape that reflects the normal progress of our thoughts and feelings. What poetry shows must resonate in our subjective experience as we read.[15] It must *make sense* to us; it must admit our attributing something

---

[14]See Burgard, pp. 134–36, who draws conclusions concerning the very idea of system.
[15]"Resonance" is Lessing's own metaphor. See his letter to Mendelssohn of 2 February 1757.

like "purpose" to it. That is, it must be not only a "motion," but also an "action." If it were merely a motion, then it would not yet have the character of mental experience, and there could be no illusion, no merging with the present subjective experience of the reader. If only the temporal successiveness of poetry had been at issue, "motion" would have been sufficient.[16]

Or let us consider Lessing's intention to argue against allegory in painting, which had been part of his earliest thinking on Laokoon (see L-M, 14:344). Evidently the corresponding argument on poetry would have emphasized the admissibility of allegory in the verbal medium; and in a note on Milton, Lessing makes clear the type of poetic allegory he prefers, the unelaborated personification of abstract concepts in the simplest possible actions and attitudes (14:404). In Laokoon itself, "personified abstractions" is the designation for what correspond in poetry to "allegorical figures" in painting (9:72–73). But a personified abstraction is the projection of a strictly mental entity into an imagined physical world, and so in poetry forms a bridge between the narrated fiction and the mental realm in which the reader's actual experience takes place; the judicious use of allegory *intellectualizes* the fiction, which, as a result, is more easily merged with our supposedly actual experience of reading and thinking about the words. It follows now, incidentally, that when we speak of the inner experience of the reader, we must not exclude abstract thought; otherwise allegory would be excluded from poetry. Experience, in the sense that I claim summarizes Lessing's poetic reflection, is a single process in which conceptual thought and emotional response cannot be clearly differentiated. We have already remarked that the very form of Laokoon is calculated to suggest the idea of *critical* thought as an experience, not a detached cogitation.

We can go deeper into the poetics of experience by way of the distinction between natural signs and arbitrary signs, which is not prominent in the published "First Part" of Laokoon, but was meant to play a crucial rôle in the continuation. Natural signs, which are principally the signs of painting, are signs dictated (or "motivated") by the nature of the referent. The redness of an object must be represented by red pigment; the shape of an object that presents a circular aspect must be represented by a circle. No other color or form will do. Arbitrary signs, by contrast, are primarily words, and their

---

[16]This perception does not require access to Lessing's manuscripts. Herder, for example, makes it on the basis of the printed text alone (SW, 3:139).

correspondence to objects is dictated not by the nature of the object but by the conventions of the language to which they belong.

In *Laokoon*, however, it is clear from the notes that Lessing intended to *question* the distinction between natural and arbitrary signs; for we hear of situations in which painting may be said to employ arbitrary signs and poetry natural signs (L-M, 14:382–83, 427–35). The argument on painting is suggestive but undeveloped, not going much beyond the idea of the work's physical dimensions; but the argument on poetry is crucial. There are two main cases, says Lessing, in which the signs of poetry become "natural": when the sound of a word represents onomatopoetically a sound in reality, and when the sequence of words represents convincingly the sequence in which things or thoughts or feelings occur in our actual experience (14:428–29). The second possibility especially, which is touched on in the published book (9:110), leads us back to the center of Lessing's thought. For the sequence of words is the single textual feature that is most directly relatable to a property of the reader's supposed inner experience as he reads; the sequence in which the words are printed is presumably the exact sequence of our reading them. And the existence (if it could be shown) of natural or normal sequences in experience, to which a sequence of words might correspond as a "natural sign," would support Lessing's contention that in poetry the words as such disappear from the reader's consciousness, leaving our experience here and now, in reading, to merge with the experience represented.

But then Lessing suggests yet a third way in which poetry's signs tend toward the natural. In *metaphor*, he argues, though the signs do not actually become natural, still they achieve the "value" ("Werth") of natural signs:

> Da nehmlich die Kraft der natürlichen Zeichen in ihrer Aehnlichkeit mit den Dingen besteht, so führet sie [die Poesie] anstatt dieser Aehnlichkeit, welche sie nicht hat, eine andere Aehnlichkeit ein, welche das bezeichnete Ding mit einem andern hat, deßen Begriff leichter und lebhafter erneuert werden kann. [L-M, 14:429]

> [Since the power of natural signs resides in their similarity with things, poetry, instead of this similarity, introduces a different similarity, between the thing represented and another thing of which our conception can be more easily and vividly renewed.]

At first glance this appears merely a playing with words. The "similarity" between red and red or between a circle and a circle, after all, is quite different from the "similarity" between, say, Menelaus and a well-bearded lion (*Iliad*, 17.109). In fact, Lessing's remark makes sense only if we understand it as a *denial* of any fundamental difference between these two types of similarity, hence as the assertion that even our reading of a painting—and by extension, *even our "reading" of the direct sensory experience of real objects*—contains an inherent verbal metaphoricity. Precisely the arbitrariness of the verbal sign, in other words—which is reflected and dramatized in the arbitrariness of any comparison, like Menelaus and the lion, that we might call metaphor as distinct from metonymy—precisely this arbitrariness is the *natural* sign of an unappreciated arbitrariness inherent even in our supposedly immediate experience, even, for example, in the identification of the color red.[17]

The illusion of experience in reading poetry thus does not merely *approach* some unattainable actuality of experience itself, but rather *surpasses* actual experience, at least in the qualities of completeness and intensity. The supposed immediacy of "actual" experience is in truth constituted by a variable degree of blindness or delusion: by a *failure* to experience the arbitrary component of the process, which in poetry is represented by the arbitrariness of the verbal sign and of the practice of metaphor; by a *failure* to experience the subjective component of the process, which is represented in poetry by the recognition that "motion" has always already become an intentional or purposeful "action"; and by a *failure* to experience the abstract or intellectual component of the process, which can be represented in poetry by the figure of allegory.[18] There is thus an exact parallel be-

---

[17]Todorov recognizes that "as a constituent feature, resemblance is *not* the same in metaphor as in motivated signs (such as images or onomatopoeia); the two are equivalent only from a functional point of view." But he still insists that for Lessing, "metaphor is a motivated sign created by means of unmotivated signs" (p. 143). This is not the case. The crucial feature of metaphor is that it is *un*motivated, hence arbitrary, hence a natural sign of the arbitrary in experience. Wellbery reads Lessing here in essentially the same way as Todorov, but without seeing any difference from the thought of J.J. Breitinger and J.G. Sulzer (p. 195). The particular example that Wellbery chooses from Lessing, however, Homer's mist as a metaphor for becoming invisible, works against him. Is there really an "associative path of similarity" (p. 196) from the idea of mist to that of invisibility? Is it not true that metaphor operates precisely by our sense of *dissimilarity* between its terms? And is Homer's mist not thus a metaphor par excellence, insofar as invisibility cannot be "similar" to anything at all? Jacobs's discussion of the mist metaphor (pp. 503–8) is more to the point.

[18]The argument on natural and arbitrary signs explains Lessing's difficulty in developing his thought on allegory. The exclusion of allegory in painting is deduced from the inappropriateness of mixing arbitrary signs with the natural signs normal in that art form (L-M, 14:430), whereas the general argument on signs tends toward the conclusion that such mixing is not only permissible but necessary. Already in 1764, Lessing is groping for a way

tween Lessing's view of poetry and Goethe's of science, the view that what we take to be our actual and immediate contact with the world is in truth always already confused by an uncontrolled theorizing, that only by passing through the complications of an avowedly verbal and social process (poetry or science) do we ever arrive at anything approaching the direct experience of our own process of experiencing.

The Proto-Kantian Critique of Experience in Lessing's Poetics

I do not claim to have established as a certainty this reading of *Laokoon*. I claim only the following: first, that given the inherent limits of poetic theory, Lessing's failure to elaborate systematically the ideas I have presented is not an argument against the validity of these ideas as a description of his poetics; second, that my argument is supported by its resonances with similar arguments on Goethe and Hölderlin, not to mention resonances with Kant, resonances that suggest that the ideas in question did belong to the contemporary communicative force of Lessing's text; and third, that the presence of a number of sticky questions practically compels us to read Lessing with wide detours into the inexplicit—questions like: exactly what do people like Herder, Goethe, and Friedrich Schlegel see in *Laokoon*? why does Lessing manipulate the form of his critical work as if it were a narrative? how shall we deal with passages that appear to say nothing at all, such as the passage on metaphor?

The passages in the published text of *Laokoon* that I think support my argument most directly are those in which Lessing asserts that in reading poetry, we lose altogether our awareness of the verbal medium and respond directly to the fictional experience (L-M, 9:92, 101). The radicality of this formulation of the theory of romance reading, I contend, operates as a *provocation*, which lays bare for a moment the irony upon which the validity of any such theory depends. For if experience already exists, prior to our reading, and is merely expanded or developed in the reading process, then what Lessing says is nonsense; as Iser points out, a "division" in the reader must

out of this dilemma (14:383); and if it had been a crucial point, he probably could have managed. But in the published "First Part" he simply avoids the issue.

be posited, between a persistent actual self and a fictionally fluid self, and this division *is* an awareness of the verbal medium. But if, as I have suggested, Lessing's point is that experience in a strong sense *first arises* in reading, if reading is more fully experience (experience with less delusion) than experience itself and is thus *an enactment of the origin of personal or individual experience*, then verbal mediation—between the text and the preexisting subject, or between segments of the subject—is no longer a factor; the verbal medium *has* in effect vanished, if perhaps only by becoming all-encompassing.[19] It would in any case be difficult, without this distinction of a hidden level of meaning, to account for Lessing's historicizing or fictionalizing of the structure of his own expository text—despite the suggestions I have made above. But now a good account can be provided. Given the text's fictional structuring, it must be true that the idea of the supersedure of the verbal medium can be applied to *Laokoon* itself. And what can this idea possibly refer to, in the case of a nonfictional, nonnarrative text, if not to the supersedure of the argument's superficial meaning, hence to the operation of a radical *irony*?

What is now still puzzling about *Laokoon*, therefore, is not its deep quasi-narrative structure, but its superficial structure, especially the comparison of poetry and painting. If *Laokoon* is primarily a poetics, and especially if it is a poetics on the level of ironic subtlety I have argued for, doesn't the ostentatious symmetry (especially of chapter 16) merely confuse matters?

I contend that whatever Lessing's original design may have been, in the finished *Laokoon* the argument on poetry and painting operates to unveil dramatically a philosophical point that is crucial to the idea of poetry as an enactment of the origin of experience. For the symmetrical presentation in chapter 16, on analysis, *clashes* with the customary distinction (in its Lockean or its Wolffian form) between sense data themselves and the subject's response to such data. Whereas the natural signs of painting represent nothing but raw sense data, the signs of poetry represent inner events that are part of our *reaction* to sense experience; "bodies" are real objects, whereas

---

[19]The difference between my argument and Wellbery's development of the "advantages" of the verbal medium (pp. 134, 196, 213, passim) is contained almost entirely in this move—in the recognition of a verbal metaphoricity that belongs inherently even to our "immediate" experience—which I contend is *Lessing's* move. Once this step is taken, practically all of Wellbery's arguments in detail can be mobilized in support of its consequences.

an "action" always includes a subjective element, a judgment (that it is not merely "motion") on the part of the perceiver. Our mental process in observing a painting, therefore, moves as it were in the same direction as in our dealing with reality; first we receive raw sense impressions, then we contribute enough from our own subjectivity to infer the action that the artist has suggested "by implication." But in poetry this process is reversed; first we receive the pattern of our inner response, then we must infer *backwards* toward the raw sense impressions suggested. Does this not place poetry at one further remove from experience than painting?

The insistent symmetry of Lessing's argument thus requires us to *question* our basic psychological notions, especially the distinction between raw sense impressions and subjective responses. That Lessing himself has doubts about this distinction appears in the *Hamburgische Dramaturgie*, where we read of the incomprehensibly infinite variety of "nature" as such, which is perceivable only by an "infinite intellect"; "in order for finite intellects to participate in the enjoyment of this spectacle," the text continues, "they had to be endowed with the ability to set limits to nature which nature herself does not possess" (L-M, 10:82). Note the decisiveness of this formulation. In perceiving the world, we set limits *to nature*, not merely to our perceptions; as far as we are concerned, nature simply does not exist without the subjective structuring by which we make sense of it. This is close to a Kantian recognition that there is no way to distinguish *in* our experience between the effects of raw objective reality and the effects of rational structures that characterize our thinking.

(It is significant, incidentally, that Lessing's formulation of the problem of what happens when we *see a thing* [L-M, 9:101–2]—which he borrows from Mendelssohn [14:345]—is strikingly hermeneutic, suggesting an ineradicable residue of uncertainty in the determination of the object. "First," he says, "we observe its parts individually, then the relation of the parts, and finally the whole." That the hermeneutic circularity implied here—how can we perceive parts or their relations except by reference to the "whole"?—did not *escape* Lessing [or Mendelssohn] is clear from the haste with which both insist on the "astonishing speed" of our supposedly carrying out these separate operations in perception. But why raise the question in the first place, especially since the obviously ad hoc concept of "speed" ["Schnelligkeit"], which is needed to answer it, recalls uncomfortably the equally shaky idea of "swiftness" ["Geschwin-digkeit," L-M, 9:101] in our reading poetry? Why raise the question if not as a provocation, if not to reveal a level of radical *self*-question-ing in the text, if not to create an opening onto the argument's *irony*?)

The distinction between phenomena ("Erscheinungen") and sub-jective feelings ("Empfindungen"), which Lessing makes in the *Dra-maturgie*, is thus an empirically reasonable distinction, but not an empirically demonstrable or locatable one. From our feeling of being in contact with an outside world we deduce a separation between objective and subjective realms; but in practice we can never distin-guish any particular effect that belongs to one realm or the other. Otherwise we would have direct knowledge of the purely objective, which Lessing denies is possible. But if we did not still have a vague, yet undeniable sense of the differentness of subject and object, we would have no conception of personal being, hence no possibility of experience to begin with. Empirically, we seem to know *that* there is a difference between subjective and objective effects; but we cannot know exactly *where* this difference lies. Experience, in other words, involves *the positive awareness of a combination of separate objec-tive and subjective effects, along with the inability to separate the two in detail.*

Hence the importance of the structure of the argument in chapter 16. The image of symmetry suggests the idea of an *equivalence* be-tween poetic and pictorial representation, which suggests in turn that the poetic evocation of sense impressions ("bodies") by implica-tion from a given progression of motions and thoughts or feelings ("actions") reproduces experience no less exactly than does the pictor-ial evocation of feelings by implication from a given pattern of sense impressions. Again, it is impossible to say whether, or exactly where, in experience, direct perception precedes subjective composition or vice versa; therefore the artistic process in one direction is every bit as vivid a representation as that in the other. This is the point made by the rhetorical figure, the *metaphor*, of exact symmetry between poetry and painting. The reversible relation between poetry and painting signifies the reversibility of the relation between raw sense data and our subjective contribution to sense experience. Once the reversibility of the latter relation is understood, it follows that poetry produces not the same kind of illusion as painting, but no less a *degree* of illusion—as Lessing says in the definition of "poetic paint-ing" quoted earlier.

The rest of the systematic argument in chapter 16 now also falls into place. For in order to create the illusion of experience, art is under no obligation to arrange subjective and objective effects in any particular order; it need only create the sense of an inextricable intertwining of such effects. In painting, this end is accomplished by imposing on the spectator's consciousness from without (objectively) the images of bodies, but bodies caught in a "fruitful" position by which the spectator is induced to supply from imagination (subjectively) the actions necessary to complete a sense of actuality—necessary because "bodies exist not only in space but also in time," and in the pattern of cause and effect that makes an "action" (L-M, 9:95). And in poetry, correspondingly, the illusion is created by imposing on the reader's thoughts and feelings, as he or she reads, a pattern or progression arising from the poem's action, while leaving for imagination the impressions of the physical objects presupposed by that action. Thus both painting and poetry seek to produce in us the *combination* of objective and subjective effects that we recognize as experience.

The Structure of Originary Experience

Mendelssohn says that the state of being "aesthetically illuded" includes the recognition of illusoriness;[20] and for Lessing too, an essentially theoretical moment is embedded in the "swiftness" of artistic illusion. But more is at stake for Lessing than for Mendelssohn, and more than in the convention of romance reading. If Lessing were concerned with the manner in which poetry increases the *range* of our experience, he would have no trouble with terminology and no need of an ironic or esoteric level in his argument. Nor is Lessing concerned, like Iser, to offer the reader a kind of vacation from the strict separation of subject and object. For Lessing, rather, it is clear that a complex and potentially theorizable *critique* of the operation of subject and object—without any pretense of somehow suspending that operation—must be woven into the very fabric of the experience of reading, must thus be carried, so to speak, a step beyond system or theory. The parallel with Goethe's science is significant. The introduction into experience of an element of theoretical *mediation*

[20]See n. 12.

must be managed in a way that produces, paradoxically, an increased *imm*ediacy of experience, originary experience, experience as if new-born, bursting (literally bursting, not perfected or whole or in re-pose) with the critical knowledge of its own complexity.

And if this form of the argument seems fanciful, at least the fancy is Lessing's own, operative especially in the discussion of Greeks and Germans at the very beginning of *Laokoon*. It is true that Lessing lacks the terminology for even attempting a positive formulation of what Hellenic experience was in itself. But Greek literature, espe-cially Homer and tragedy, still serves him as a reference point by which to measure the *decay* of experience (its loss of immediacy) in modern European, particularly German culture—our hypostasizing of the "cogito," not merely in theory, but in a way that suffuses our very identity with the sense of a strictly integral subject, constituted by its incessant resistance to whatever threatens the subject/object separation. The passions of fear, pity, and grief are especially endan-gered for us; whatever happens to us in the real world, we barbarians insist, is merely objective and must not be permitted to touch the core of our own person. Experience is thus subject to thorough his-torical conditioning, at least to the extent of being able to decay; and experience, for us, therefore *needs* re-originating. The task of the artistic illusion of experience is not to imitate the constrained, in effect theorized, narrowness of our accustomed experience, but to give us practice in a more inclusive or complete experiencing—as tragedy gives us practice in pitying the truly pitiable, comedy in laughing at the truly laughable (L-M, 9:303). The similarity of this thinking to Schiller's on the function of artistic beauty is clear, as is the relation to Hölderlin's or Goethe's recognition of the need for a newly originated version of the social or conversational. As in Höl-derlin, the poem, for Lessing, must in a strong sense become life itself, or indeed *more* life than what nowadays passes for life "itself."

Therefore, to return to the practical side of Lessing's argument, the artistic illusion of experience requires at least (1) that both sub-jective and objective components be present in our relation to the work of art; (2) that the boundary between these components *not* be clearly locatable; and (3) that our failure to locate that boundary—the failure that stands, as a negative image, for our potentially theoretical critique of experience—be incorporated and profiled as a prominent and integral part of the process. These points enable us to under-stand why both painting and poetry must maintain a "comfortable relation" with their subject matter.[21] For in both cases, the boundary between objective and subjective coincides easily with the difference between "bodies" and "actions," which in turn defines a fundamental structural characteristic of each art form: the painting *is* a physical body; our reading of the poem *is* an action. In the abstract, therefore, the boundary between subjective and objective is clearly marked. But for the actual viewer or reader, if the work is properly conceived—even for the critical reader, provided he or she attends to *the work*—there is no experiential field within which to locate that boundary; no matter how closely we examine the work, we cannot find *in it* the categorical divide by which representation announces itself, since the work *is* of the same category as what it represents. If, however, the painter goes too far, and attempts to impose on us too specific an idea of action, or if the poet dwells on an object in too much detail, the situation is altered. Now we do discover *in* the work a sign of the difference between the subjective and objective components of our relation to it; the boundary now *appears* clearly located (which is what counts), and the illusion of experience is broken.

But the symmetry of the argument of chapter 16 is still really only a rhetorical figure, a metaphor for the reversibility of categories in experience. And the actual asymmetry or poetic bias of Lessing's thought on the illusion of experience becomes clear when we consider the third basic requirement for such illusion. In order to profile our significant failure to locate the boundary of subject and object, artistic illusion must include a move of self-reflection on our part; and in the case of painting, this move must conflict with the illusion by involving a pronounced temporal component, since reflection in effect *is* time. But in the case of poetry, first, the temporal effect of reflection coincides with and reinforces the temporal structure of the artistic object. Second, the *reversed* relation in poetry between supposedly raw sense impressions and subjective inferences (reversed with respect to the rigid idea of experience that precisely a modern subject brings to reading) engenders a form of post-Cartesian doubt in which the very possibility of a boundary between subject and object becomes questionable. And third, the reflection on subject and

[21]The standard interpretations of the concept of "comfortable relation" tend to insist upon Lessing's *separation* of an aesthetic from a nonaesthetic realm, which seems to me wrong-headed. See, for example, Karlheinz Stierle, "Das bequeme Verhältnis: Lessings *Laokoon* und die Entdeckung des ästhetischen Mediums," in *Das Laokoon-Projekt: Pläne einer semiotischen Ästhetik*, ed. Gunter Gebauer (Stuttgart, 1984), pp. 23–58, esp. pp. 39–40.

object activates the ontological problem implied by the very idea of "the work" or "the poem." For whereas a painting simply is a physical body, the poem—in order to *be* that "action" which (precisely in the illusion of experience) it is—must in its being straddle and obscure the relation between "itself" and our reading of it, which is again the relation between object and subject.

In the case of poetry, therefore, our failure to locate the boundary of subject and object can, in principle, thrust itself up prominently in the midst of the illusion of experience, which thus becomes originary experience in the sense of incorporating its own whole problematics *as* experience. Lessing's thought does not imply that this effect can be empirically demonstrated whenever a person reads a poem. The reader need not reflect on (or in) this problematics in the first place; and the reflection, even if it occurs, is capable of detaching itself systematically from the experience, as in the preceding paragraph. What we are talking about is a *structurally given possibility* in the art of poetry, of the same order as the structurally given possibility of the community as a reader in Goethe or Hölderlin. And it is the resonance among these ideas, not the question of their practical efficacy, that I claim supports my discussion of the poetics of the age in eighteenth-century Germany, the importance of enactment-of-origins and community-as-reader as interpretive categories.

In any event, we can now formulate one further answer to the question of why Lessing applies to this expository text, *Laokoon*, the compositional principles he derives from a discussion of narrative poetry. For if the crucial idea of reading as an illusion of experience is to have any actual validity, then we, as readers, must be able to think the whole of Lessing's thought *as* experience; we must be able to do exactly what the text of *Laokoon* does, unfold that thought for ourselves as a process in time without detaching ourselves from it by means of a systematic formulation. We cannot avoid systematizing; but we must find a way of restricting our system to the value of metaphor—or of theorizing with irony—in the manner of Lessing's symmetrical system of relations between painting and poetry.

Lessing and Hölderlin: The Poem as Process

There are, then, a number of deep resonances among the texts we have looked at. But do these resonances reflect the existence of a practical poetics, a method for producing and understanding works of literature? It is important that there also be relatively superficial parallels, that Goethe's novel, Hölderlin's poem, and Lessing's treatise arrive at the idea of enactment of origins by roughly the same route. For example, does Lessing's poetics directly support our interpretation of "An die Parzen"? The idea of the poem as a process figures here, the idea that the content of the poetic utterance actually changes from sentence to sentence, or from word to word, in response to its implications on several different levels of self-reflection. This idea is required for a perception of the poem's monodramatic and dialectical meditativeness in Hölderlin, which in turn makes possible a dramatic unveiling of the social dimension of language. And it is also required in Lessing's discussion of beauty and ugliness. Ugliness in poetry "so to speak ceases to be ugliness," because its constituent elements are disassembled and presented one after the other; but this disassembly could not have an effect on the general impression of ugliness if it were not true that each element somehow changes its nature when, in the forward-moving poetic process, it slips into the past. Or further, the denotative operation of *word order* in Hölderlin recalls the discussion of Homeric word order in *Laokoon* (L-M, 9:110). The relatively free syntax of Greek enables the order of a poem's words to observe a detailed correspondence with "the natural order of thought," the mental process, instant by instant, by which we normally shape our recognition of what the senses perceive. And although Hölderlin is not attempting to create a "poetic painting," still the retardation of the phrases "gesättiget," "dann mir sterbe," and "gelungen" in "An die Parzen" serves an exactly analogous purpose, the representation of successive instantaneous phases in a complex mental process.

The process-aspect of Lessing's poetics would be immediately recognizable as a theoretical equivalent to Hölderlin's practice if it were not for Lessing's concentration on narrative or "graphic" poetry, whose meaning is conveyed primarily by way of a well-developed fictional situation or action. In the case of graphic poetry, the reader's mental process, to which the poem's verbal process must correspond in detail, is the perception and recognition of events in a physical world. But it is still entirely a *mental* process; otherwise poetry could not reproduce it. If Lessing had expanded his discussion to include lyric poetry as the verbal representation of a process presumed to be under way in the speaker's mind, the application to Hölderlin would have been obvious.

Nor do we need to rely entirely on speculation to make this point. On one of the occasions where he does go beyond narrative poetry, Lessing says of Ewald von Kleist and his poem "Der Frühling":

> If he had lived longer, he would have given the poem an entirely different form. . . . He was pondering how he might control that great quantity of images—which gave the impression of being detached at random, now here and now there, from the infinite panorama of rejuvenated Creation—so that they would come into being and succeed one another, before his eyes, in a natural order. . . . Out of a string of images, only sparsely intermingled with feelings [Empfindungen], he would have made a succession of feelings only sparsely interwoven with images. [L-M, 9:106–7]

The "natural order" of images in Kleist's poem is not provided by the progress of a fictional action; but this does not trouble Lessing. He falls back without hesitation upon the idea of a natural order that originates in the "succession of feelings" experienced by the poetic speaker; the images will achieve poetic power by arising "before *his* eyes*," the speaker's (my translation is exact here), as elements of a developing process of consciousness which we perceive to be taking place inside him. The distance to Hölderlin's practice is no longer very great at all.

We can follow this parallel further, into the *problems* of the idea of poem as process. For in Lessing, as we have seen, our reflection upon the question of what the poem "is"—upon the manifest inadequacy of the statement that the poem "is" an action—feeds back, by way of a quasi-dramatic unlocating of the subject/object separation, into the illusion of experience, the enactment of originary experience, that the poem as action or process engenders. This feeding back of reflection into experience is itself in turn dramatized in the form of *Laokoon*, in the embedding of critical reflection in a text that acts as if it were poetry of experience—and, in fact, by not strictly "being" poetry of experience, enacts even the inevitable internal explodedness of an experience that contains its own radical critique. The situation in Hölderlin is no different. The effect of the poem as process—of such questions as *when* is the word "noch" spoken? *when* is the end of strophe 2 declarative?—is to make the situation of the individual reader into an insoluble problem, which enables us to recognize the unveiling of the social component of the language, whereupon the whole reflection feeds back into a situation in which the poem is process after all, but only in the form of an actual, uncontrollable ironic game in society.

The specific textual signs of this complexity are similar in Lessing and Hölderlin, especially the embedding of surprisingly simple formulations in problematizing contexts. When Lessing says that the reading of narrative poetry must sweep us along with it, that poetry must move forward with such "swiftness" that our responses never develop beyond the stage of pure feeling, we cannot take these assertions seriously. They conflict not only with common sense, and with Lessing's own insistence elsewhere on the reader's imaginative freedom, but with the very possibility of an adequate critical reading of poetic texts, which is what we and Lessing were supposed to be engaged in. And yet we cannot simply disregard what Lessing says. We must find a way to take him seriously after all—much as we must find a way to regard the aphorisms in the *Wanderjahre* as true—which means, as far as I can see, that we must develop the idea of an illusion of experience that is exploded *into* experience (as its origin, not a mere imitation) by incorporating our critical reflection upon it. The difference between experience as instant response (being swept along swiftly) and experience as critical reflection—or rather, the centering of our experience on the need for that difference—must be suspended. (To the extent that Wellbery's argument is valid, the suspension of the difference between painting and poetry that he speaks of [p. 198] operates as a *metaphor* for this larger metaesthetic suspension of difference in our experience.)

In Hölderlin, correspondingly, we must find a way to take seriously the surface meaning of statements of the type "Once I lived like the gods," which imply belief in the existence of pure feelings and in the irretrievable uniqueness of certain experiences. At least we must recognize that we are not in a position to claim we do *not* believe these things; for precisely the deeper level of "godlike" knowledge depends on our maintaining that pretense of belief— maintaining it to the extent that we can no longer legitimately call it a pretense. The meditative and communicative aspects of "An die Parzen," again, are strictly interdependent; if, in some real sense, we do not receive the poem *as* meditative language, then the ironic or communicative force of the utterance is lost.

The relation of Goethe's narratives to this argument, finally, emerges from the relation of the theory of romance reading to the idea of the poem as process. As in Lessing and Hölderlin, the literary

work (for Goethe here, the novel) *is* in the final analysis a process
that belongs to the large historical process of communal composition
(writing and reading) by which the scripture of a new religious age
comes into being. And as in Lessing and Hölderlin, it is our inevitable failure to circumvent the problems created by a narrower idea of
literature as process (romance reading) that compels the reassessment of our own reading by which we gain access to the historical
and social vision.

In sum, then, we are not merely talking about ideas that different
authors reach by different routes. We are talking about something
more like a method. We are talking about a poetics.

Experience, Society, and the Critique of Cartesian Individuality

Does this poetics make sense in intellectual history? Can we account for its arising precisely in the German eighteenth century? In
opening this question, I will speak of the Cartesian idea of the "individual," and avoid for the time being the notion of the "subject." The
immediate question is that of the relation in *priority* between the
individual and the social. Who is it, exactly, who reads, or writes? To
what extent is this question answered by Descartes's argument, in
part 5 of the *Discourse* or in the second *Meditation*, that "I" can have
no doubt concerning "my" existence? We will come to the question
of the "subject" in the next chapter.

In Hölderlin the critique of the Cartesian ego, although recognizably modern, still has a form characteristic of the late eighteenth century. Hölderlin's method is to set up an ironic situation in which the
empirical ego—the conception, developed by the individual from experience, of his or her own individuality—is *reconstituted* by the
very process of being called into question. At the end of "An die
Parzen," the reader is left in a dramatically augmented aloneness
with the written text. "Once"—despite the unspecifiability of
when—he or she had "lived like the gods," in the uncircumscribed
and uncentered state characterized by a meditative speaking voice
that (via lyric "identification") had overleaped individuality and expressed no particular "cogito." That the words "Once I lived like the
gods" are still in a sense spoken by that voice, which is both ours and
not ours, now only marks the disintegration of that happy state and

my imprisonment in a condition that is strictly mine. But this inescapable individuality is now also not merely a condition; it is a free act of renunciation carried out by a god, and enacted by us in the form of irony—precisely the ironic move that I project into the text, in order to read of it there—in every moment of a conscious and necessarily social existence. We still are particular individuals, and we know ourselves as such; but our social condition embodies the unformulable recognition that we are this and know this because we insist on it, not merely because that condition is fact.[22]

This manner of dealing with the Cartesian sense of the individual is typical of the pre-Romantic or pre-Kantian period. The Romantic period itself is generally characterized by a more direct approach, along two routes. The Romantic feeling for nature (already suggested in *Hyperion*) entails a collapse of the barrier of doubt that separates ego from object. The objective world is no longer the domain of doubt, as distinct from the proposition that I exist and the propositions that follow from it; but rather my own self-certainty is now achievable only in the form of universal certainty, in a sense of joyous unification with all things that are. And Romantic despair, the despair of the heirs of Werther, breaks down the barrier of doubt from the opposite direction. Now even the self, as well as the external world, is flooded with doubt. Werther does not yet actually doubt his own existence, although characters who do are not long in appearing, in Jean Paul for example. But he does find himself incapable of making the neat Cartesian distinction between the propositions "I am" and "I am not perfect." The first proposition, for Descartes, provides a solid ground from which the second can be viewed with relative equanimity and recognized as a proof of the existence of God.[23] For Werther, however, the knowledge of personal imperfection, that disunity of the self which originates precisely in our search for the self, poisons existence at its root; the knowledge that "I am" tantalizes me with the *possibility* of myself as a stable and unified object of contemplation but denies me the *actuality*, and suggests suicide as the only possible test of the matter.

[22]On the Trinitarian structure of this thought, including a parallel in Augustine, see my "Trinitarische Humanität: Dichtung und Geschichte bei Schiller," in *Friedrich Schiller: Kunst, Humanität und Politik in der späten Aufklärung*, ed. Wolfgang Wittkowski (Tübingen, 1982), pp. 164–77.
[23]René Descartes, *Discours de la méthode*, part 4, in his *Oeuvres et lettres*, ed. André Bridoux (Paris, 1953), pp. 147–50.

But Hölderlin's pre-Romantic reconstitution of individuality in irony reflects no less radical a dissatisfaction with the Cartesian idea, a dissatisfaction we will also trace in Klopstock and Herder, as well as in Rousseau's version of the social contract. Or we think of Goethe's conception of "daimon," which appears to set up the individual as a governing principle in its own existence, but actually, by being distinguished from "chance," "love," "necessity," and "hope," raises profound questions concerning what I mean, or can mean, when I say "I." The case that concerns us now, however, is Lessing, where a reflection of the general situation in intellectual history is combined directly with the poetics we have outlined.

Die Erziehung des Menschengeschlechts, on first glance—to take a text in which poetic theory does not appear to be a factor—strongly presupposes Cartesian individuality. The idea that God instructs the human race by a method analogous to our method of instructing our children suggests that we arrive at a notion of the perfect and undeniable being of God by direct extrapolation from our own equally undeniable but imperfect being as individuals. And the idea of education as measurable progress from each stage to the next, whether in the life of the pupil or in history, requires the existence of an ego sufficiently definable and unalterable to serve as a foundation for the structure of knowledge erected on it. The presuppositions of this text can thus be read out of Descartes practically verbatim.

But the logical effect of *Die Erziehung des Menschengeschlechts* is to disintegrate the Cartesian individual. If the goal of God's education, a morality of reason in which humans do the good for its own sake, is not accessible to reasonable minds in *every* historical age, if there is a basic imperfection in human nature, a barrier of doubt between our thinking as such and the moral application of its results, then it is not clear how God's purpose can ever be achieved at all. It follows, if Lessing's vision is to be rescued, that the time and culture into which I happen to be born make a substantial difference in what "I" am, a difference precisely in my ability to achieve my own proper destiny as a thinking being, which relativizes what is meant by "my" existence in the first place. When I say "I," it now appears that I am referring mainly to a set of historical conditions; my *cogito* has become a *cogitatur*. Thus the consequences of the argument conflict with its presuppositions, which is part of the problem Lessing claims to circumvent by introducing the idea of metempsychosis at the end. But whether this idea is a serious logical conclusion or a staged provocation, an ironic vehicle for thoughts (the argument itself suggests this) that ought not yet to be expounded in public, the result, as far as the idea of individuality is concerned, is the same. Either the Cartesian presuppositions are a concession to the reader's cultural limitedness, hence the sign of precisely a preter-Cartesian relativism; or else the propositions "cogito" and "sum" are torn asunder by an immense forgetting (§99, L-M, 13:435) and no longer have even the same grammatical subject.[24]

The result of the irony, in either case, is the same as in Hölderlin's poem, the retention of the Cartesian ego even in its disintegration, which is in turn a radical anatomy of irony as such. On the one hand, irony is not its own concept, not realizable, except in the domain of the social or intersubjective. Irony is a thinking that cannot be exchanged for the bankable currency of discourse because it does not *belong* to its thinker; it is a wedge driven between "cogito" and "sum." But on the other hand, irony also establishes and isolates the individual. Irony requires the intersubjective, but it *exists* only for the individual, as an individual experience, like the imperceptible pelagic swell that becomes a breaking wave only at the shore. Irony in fact is *the* experience of individuality, the happening in experience of the utter incommensurability of the self, the experience of a communication whose content is nothing but its own impossibility, the fusion of "cogito" and "sum" into a single needful defense against the else all-devouring sea of discourse.

This form of critique of Cartesian individuality is found throughout Lessing, not only in *Die Erziehung des Menschengeschlechts*. It is derivable from Lessing's theory of dramatic character and from his actual creation of characters.[25] It appears from time to time in extremely simple devices, such as the use of the word "I" in the essay "Pope ein Metaphysiker!" which was written in collaboration with Mendelssohn. That "I" is disintegrated by the actual plural authorship but still persists as a discursive necessity; and this paradox is

[24]For a detailed treatment of the logical difficulties in the *Erziehung*, see my "Reason, Error, and the Shape of History: Lessing's Nathan and Lessing's God," *LY* 9 (1977), 60–80.

[25]For a discussion of the semiotic construction of individual character in Lessing's idea of drama, see Stuart Barnett, "'Über die Grenzen': Semiotics and Subjectivity in Lessing's *Hamburgische Dramaturgie*," *GQ* 60 (1987), 407–19. For a discussion of the character Philotas and his construction in scenic space, see Peter J. Burgard, "Lessing's Tragic Topography: The Rejection of Society and its Spatial Metaphor in *Philotas*," *DVLG* 61 (1987), 441–56. For the relation between alienated individuality and theatrical posturing, see my "Generic Constant in Lessing's Development of a Comedy of Institutions and Alienation," *GQ* 56 (1983), 231–42.

kept open by the essay's explicit focus on the relation between system and statement. Especially important for our purposes, however, is the relation of this philosophical critique to the *Laokoon* poetics. For irony, as a radically individual experience that nevertheless fails to belong to the individual, ranges itself alongside the artistic illusion of experience as an enactment of the *origin* of individuality.

The social component of this thinking is still not worked out. Lessing does not take the leap into formulations like Hölderlin's "conversation" that we "are" or his "communal soul" or Herder's "soul of the race" (*SW*, 5:115). The bridge Lessing erects between the situation in intellectual history and his own poetic concerns is made almost entirely from the concept and problematics of experience, which tends to obscure his significance. For we are accustomed to looking at the eighteenth century, especially its critique of Cartesian thought, in the mirror of Kant; and Lessing's idea of experience implies a rejection at least of Kant's systematic method. Again, system operates as *metaphor* for Lessing, a metaphor that reveals not totality but uncertainty or rupture. The system of poetry and painting in *Laokoon* reveals an asystematic incompleteness, hence a constant need for re-origination, in our very sense of world; the systematic logic of the *Erziehung* exposes the incommensurability of its own presuppositions and conclusions. But Kantian systematics strives for transparency with respect to the qualities of totality and closure in our experience. From a perspective like Lessing's, the system of the *Critiques* merely reformulates the Cartesian propositions "I am" and "I doubt and am therefore not perfect," while reversing their order: I cannot know everything, but I can and do know the structure and limits of what I can and do know.

Lessing's poetics implies that Kantian systematics will be positively damaging, since the crucial task of poetry and philosophy is not to establish the results of Kant's argument as theorems but rather to uncover and profile, to activate and empower those results *in experience itself*, to reveal in experience a repeatedly originary, quasi-Hellenic condition in which no Kant will be needed. To the European barbarian, who spends half his life digging artificial gulfs between subject and object, and the other half speculating on how these gulfs are traversed by his perceptions and thinking, Kant's work comes as a revelation. But Lessing suggests—and to judge from the ancient use of the words πραγμα and χρημα, he may be right—that a Greek would have wondered why. The notion that phenomena are *not* conditioned radically by my manner of perceiving them, responds the Greek, is absurd; it would deny the fabric of explosive problems that reveals itself anew every morning when I open my eyes. The phenomenal world is where I live; all my experience is a collision with it and in it. When I succumb to it, and weep with sorrow or shriek in pain, what happens is not substantially different from when I assert myself as a thinker or builder or governor or fighter. What sort of language is it in the first place that can even imagine arguing about the "thing in itself," about things without the effects of my presence, without humanity, without language? I am present, I am human, I do speak.[26]

This hypothetical Hellenic response to the as yet unwritten *Critiques* is of course logically as well as historically impossible. But it makes the point that Lessing, who died in the year of publication of the first *Critique*, was a *contemporary* of Kant, that the difference between them with regard to areas of concern they shared can in fact be reduced largely to a difference between genres of writing—a crucial difference, it is true, but not the radical historical difference that Kant himself thought his work had created. And it is out of this contemporaneity, out of an intellectual situation characterized on a large scale by the complicated critique of Cartesian thought I have sketched, that Lessing's poetics arises.

The Defense of Poetics against Aesthetics

The main point of the preceding section remains valid even if not all the arguments are accepted in detail. The force of Cartesian individuality as an *issue* in Lessing's time, if it is admitted, is sufficient to provide a plausible intellectual background for the *Laokoon* poetics. But why a *poetics?* Kant, for example, does not feel called upon to develop his thought in this direction. To what specific issues in the area of poetics is Lessing's thought a response?

This question is answered by the conspicuous absence in *Laokoon* of the term "aesthetic." That Lessing was dissatisfied with the thought (and worried about the influence) of Alexander Gottlieb Baumgarten, to whom we are indebted for the term "aesthetics," is evident from a slighting aside at the very beginning of *Laokoon*. But the

---

[26]For essentially this response to Kant, see Herder's *Metakritik* (SW, 21:87–91).

matter goes deeper. Baumgarten's terminological innovation became generally accepted very quickly. When an author in the 1750s or 1760s, such as Lessing, fails to refer to the study of art as "aesthetics," it is not because he does not know the word—by then he has already heard it ad nauseam, even from friends like Mendelssohn—but because he deliberately avoids it.

The basic distinction implied by the term "aesthetic" is between two types of knowledge, the objects of which, in Greek, are νοητά and αἰσθητά, intelligibles and sensibles. This distinction between higher and lower mental faculties, between the rational and the sensitive, which had been more or less codified by Wolff, is applied by Baumgarten, who argues that the task of art, in particular of poetry, is to aim for a perfection of sensitive knowledge in the reader or hearer, which means not a mediation between sense perception and reason but rather a perfection of the sensitive in its own sphere. A number of good minds, including Herder, were impressed by this general approach because of its suggestiveness; the perfection of the sensitive in its own sphere might even be taken to imply the idea of an enactment of the origin of experience.[27] But most minds were attracted by Baumgarten's implied claim to have established rational principles for the judgment of artistic beauty in terms of its effect on a percipient individual. In order to understand art within its own realm, it is felt, rather than merely justify it extrinsically, we must first understand the distinguishable mental faculties that are directly called into play in the perception of a work. Just this claim, in the form in which Baumgarten suggests it, produces an obvious weakness in his argument; as Lessing observes, and as Kant later points out, Baumgarten attempts to systematize a priori in an area where judgment is necessarily empirical, where our experience needs to be refined and reinvestigated, not deductively ordered. Thinkers like Mendelssohn, therefore, while retaining the general "aesthetic" approach as well as the term, tend to relax the strict logical distinctions among types of mental activity and response.

But there is a more important difficulty in the very idea of "aesthetics," in that the field of study defined by this term does not con-

---

[27]On Herder's inclination to develop suggestions in Baumgarten's terminology, see Knodt, pp. 25–26. Compare also Herder's "sinnlich vollkommene Rede" (*SW*, 3:138; sensorially perfect discourse), with Baumgarten's "oratio sensitiva perfecta" (perfect sensory discourse). See Alexander Gottlieb Baumgarten, *Meditationes philosophicae de nonnullis ad poema pertinentibus*, ed. Heinz Paetzold (Hamburg, 1983), sections 7 and 9, p. 10.

tain a means of understanding the *construction* of a work of poetry. Eighteenth-century aestheticians have ideas on this subject—Baumgarten does—but their ideas are necessarily vague. If a poem has the requisite effect on its reader, we shall perhaps be interested in how it achieves its effect; but we arrive quickly at a level of technical detail where it can no longer be maintained that a differently constructed poem could not work just as well. The disciplines of aesthetics (how art affects us) and poetics (how poems are made) therefore tend to diverge. And in the eighteenth century, precisely this divergence makes aesthetics attractive, since it appears to liberate the study of poetry from that mechanical enumeration of rules into which poetics was commonly seen to have degenerated.

Actually, however, the divergence of poetics and aesthetics is a danger, for it entails a *separation* between the actual craft of the poet and the operation of poetry in society. If the minute details of the poet's craft are not an integral part of its social achievement, how will the craft develop, or even merely avoid deteriorating, especially since history is not usually careful about whom it appoints the arbiters of taste? It has always been a problem for European poets—we all have our Cani Grandi and are lucky if we have not worse—that the fine points of their craft are not generally appreciated; but the establishment of aesthetics as the governing study of poetry lends an intellectual or at least academic sanction to this state of affairs and makes it even more difficult than necessary for the poet to imagine any actual value in being a *miglior fabbro*.

Laokoon reflects an awareness of this danger and attempts to counteract it. All its major arguments have a direct bearing on questions of poetic technique: questions of word order, of the proper quantity and disposition of adjectives, of fictional events and their pacing, of conventionally disagreeable images, of the function and use of metaphor or allegory, and of the verbal positing of typical progressions in the dynamics of mental life. If we try to consider *Laokoon* as a work of aesthetics, any number of questions come to mind that should have been treated: the nature of beauty in a verbal work, the type of actual profit an individual may expect from reading poetry, and so on. The idea of an enactment of the origin of experience, for that matter, if worked out in sufficient terminological detail to give the (delusive) impression of being a *criterion* of literary quality, would tend to promote an aesthetic approach to literature—which implies yet another reason for Lessing's development of an ironic method.

Laokoon is a work of poetics, not aesthetics; but the contemporary receptive atmosphere in which it had to communicate its meaning was dominated by aesthetic preconceptions to the extent that any logically complete argument, any argument presenting itself as a finished object, would inevitably have been assimilated to the aesthetic habit of mind. An ironic or fictionalized text is the only possible response to this situation, a text that does not so much state its purpose as *signal* it—even in such apparently objective and neutral features as the disturbingly lengthy discussion of the question of priority between Vergil's Laocoon and the sculpture, which is ultimately a poetic question, the question of priority, in the structure of experience, between the verbal and the sensory, hence the question of the metaphysical leverage afforded the poet by his verbal medium. Lessing's book *is* "performance" (Jacobs) because its primary concern is performance—not reception, not response, not consumption, not aesthetics.

That Lessing takes up the cause of poetics against aesthetics, moreover, belongs to the critique of Cartesian individuality. The assumption that poetry requires, or admits, an aesthetic justification, presupposes the strict distinguishability of ego and object, as well as the locatability of their boundary, which is where poetry must impinge on its recipient. And it is only in a world of Cartesian individuals, the world, eminently, of division of labor, that the dangerous separation between poetics and aesthetics can occur. In such a world, the non-poet, the consumer of poetry, has no direct use for poetics, any more than a college professor or even a baker (though both are interested in bread) has use for the operator's manual to a combine-harvester. But if we can imagine a world in which poetry *lacks* an "aesthetic" component (as *Laokoon* lacks the word), a world in which our individuality is not the vessel but the *product* of what I have called "experience" (which idea cannot occupy a terminological slot in Lessing's scrupulously ironic discourse of "imitation"), if we can imagine a world, therefore, in which poetry, as an enactment of the origin, admits no passive perspective, and in which poetics is therefore in turn also activated into a kind of anthropology as "performance" (not the drowsy "anthropology" feared by Foucault but an anthropology whose object, at its touch, explodes into incommensurable individuals), then the latent social aspect of Lessing's thought appears after all. The poem, even as I read and understand it, is now an act in which I participate, yet strictly speaking neither *my* act nor (since passivity is excluded) someone else's. It is an act that has no Cartesian individual as its author and so becomes *in experience* a knowledge of the priority of the communal.

A word is required here about Schiller. For the effect of the "aesthetic state" he discusses is to create a bridge between the active and passive tendencies in our nature, which (despite the terminology) is not inconsistent with the results of Lessing's poetics. Schiller attempts to traverse the same ground Lessing had—to describe artistic creation and communication with a kind of activated anthropology (as "play")—but also apparently to carry out this task with Kantian exactness. And in view of what we have said about the rôle of irony (not exactness) in a project of this type, we might be tempted to dismiss Schiller's method as hopeless. I think this point is disputable. But for our larger purposes, it does not particularly matter whether or not Schiller develops his own version of Lessing's irony. Even if the aesthetic letters are an attempt to *remove* irony from poetic theory, still, precisely the existence of such an attempt testifies to the depth of establishment in the period, and the breadth of effectiveness, of the poetic views we have discussed in connection with Goethe, Hölderlin, and Lessing.

Lessing and the Theory of Poetic Genres

Before *Laokoon*, in the correspondence with Mendelssohn and Nicolai, and afterwards in the *Dramaturgie*, Lessing devotes a great deal of effort to the genre of drama; and in 1769 he asserts that the continuation of *Laokoon* will demonstrate the superiority of drama (letter to Nicolai, 26 May). In *Laokoon* itself, and in the extant notes for the work, there is no suggestion of any preference for drama and only the barest mention of distinctions that must be made among literary types in general. But it is during the *Laokoon* period that Lessing also writes and revises *Minna von Barnhelm*; and in 1769, after working long and hard on the *Dramaturgie*, he is struck by the idea of using his half-finished treatise on painting and poetry as the start for a theory of drama. How would this have worked?

In fact, the letter to Nicolai enables us to see how a complete *system* of genres could have been developed from the basic categories in *Laokoon*. Victor Anthony Rudowski points out correctly that the crucial passage is the assertion that "the highest genre of poetry

. . . is the dramatic; for here the words cease to be arbitrary signs and become the *natural* signs of arbitrary objects." He then goes on to refute the more or less standard idea of what this assertion means, the idea that Lessing is referring to the "gestures and expressions of the face" that one sees in the theater.[28] On the contrary, Lessing says that the *words* become natural signs in drama, and this means that the superiority of drama "must be attributed solely to qualities which are inherent in its written form" (Rudowski, p. 50). But Rudowski's own interpretation of the passage, his idea that words become natural signs by revealing "character in action" (p. 76), is unnecessarily complicated and does not clear up the matter.

Lessing's meaning is extremely simple. Red pigment is a natural sign because it represents the color red, the circle is natural by representing a circle, and words become natural signs *when they represent words*, namely in drama. (This also explains the idea of reference to "arbitrary objects," which words are in a manner in which nothing else is.) When Homer compares Menelaus to a lion, the word "lion" refers to a real thing in the world, and the sign is arbitrary; it happens that Homer uses the word λις (*Iliad* 17.109), but the word λέων, or even the English word "lion," would have had the same referent. However, when Shakespeare writes, "O, the blood more stirs / To rouse a lion than to start a hare!" (*Henry IV*, Part I, I.3.197–98), his word "lion" represents *the word* "lion" as used by the character Hotspur; the sign is natural, because if Shakespeare had used a different word, then the object signified, the word used by Hotspur, could not have remained the same—just as the painter cannot change a circle into a square without changing the shape of the object depicted.[29]

This is what Lessing means by claiming special status for the words in drama; this is all he *can* mean, given the definition of a natural sign, plus the restriction, which Rudowski does not account for, to

[28]René Wellek, *A History of Modern Criticism: 1750–1950*, 7 vols. (New Haven, 1955–), 1:165. Rudowski's argument is on pp. 34–50 (see n. 12) and deals not only with Wellek but also, for instance, with Elida Maria Szarota, *Lessings "Laokoon"* (Weimar, 1959). Wellek especially (1:163–65) makes Lessing's letter into a source of confusion. He even suggests an emendation: "der Ton der Worte . . ." for Lachmann and Muncker's "der Ton, die Worte, die Stellung der Worte, das Sylbenmaß, Figuren und Tropen, Gleichnisse u.s.w." This is wrong; "die Worte" means "the *choice* of words," and the list of poeticizing devices in language would hardly be complete without it.

[29]Todorov (p. 144) grasps this point but does not develop its significance. Knodt (pp. 116–17) goes further into the metaphysical ramifications of the idea of language's representation of itself.

"arbitrary objects." And this interpretation also implies a strict limit on the use of narration in drama, which is the crux of Rudowski's argument; for if a dramatic character narrates at length and if our attention is not held by his words as such, by the question of why he speaks exactly as he does, then our attention must be captured by *what* he narrates, whereupon the words, for us, become arbitrary signs.

More important, however, is how the letter on signs illuminates and completes the potential theory of literary genres in *Laokoon*. The idea of experience requires that the subject matter of poetry be some sort of action comparable to the action of speaking or reading, a temporally developed process constructed in a manner that encourages a judgment concerning its purpose. But in *Laokoon* and in the letter to Nicolai, Lessing distinguishes three *types* of poetic subject matter: (1) chains of events in the physical world, imagined as being perceived by the senses ("Handlungen"); (2) chains of events in the mind, imagined as a response to the world ("Empfindungen," as in what Kleist's "Der Frühling" would have become, according to Lessing); and (3) chains of words, speeches, dialogue. Obviously this threefold distinction corresponds to the distinction of epic, lyric, and dramatic genres. It also follows from the *Laokoon* poetics that drama may be regarded as the highest of the three types. For the *obvious* sense in which words are natural signs in drama betokens the profound sense in which poetry of every type, as the enactment of originary experience, reveals the quality of the natural sign in *all* words, reveals that precisely the arbitrariness of words is the natural sign for a metaphysical quality in objects that we merely conceal from ourselves in our supposed actual experience.

Lessing's thought in and around *Laokoon*, therefore, on being thought through, blossoms into a complete and detailed system of poetics; it manifests a systematic potential without which the term "poetics" would hardly be applicable. But as I suggested earlier, this system cannot be regarded, even after the fact, as the ground or germ of its thought. It is, rather, a kind of happy accident, the homecoming of a prodigal speculation to the actual conditions of literary history, a triumphant flourish by which the poetics of irony proclaims itself without defining or limiting itself. It is an "allegory" that turns out to be "anything but an unveiling of meaning" (Jacobs, p. 521). In fact, the allegorical relation of the system to its metaphysical referent is itself allegorized in the *Dramaturgie*, in which Lessing argues that the playwright must not make his plot depend on "the incomprehensible ways of providence" but should rather create his own "plan," his own systematic "whole" as a suggestive shadow or "silhouette of the whole created by the eternal Creator" (L-M, 10:120). For if we read this passage alongside the earlier passage about our inevitable setting of "limits to nature, which nature itself does not have" (10:82), it becomes clear that the allegorical "shadow" does not in any sense *reveal* the eternal "general plan" (10:120). Our allegorizing, rather, is precisely the condition of our existing in the presence of the still intractably incomprehensible.

And why, finally, does Lessing not himself *carry out* this system of poetic genres, this obvious capstone to the *Laokoon* poetics? The reason, it seems to me, is that the system, for all its allegorical quality, still embodies in its hierarchical structure a deactivated and falsifying relation to truth. For the establishment of drama as the "highest" genre, in which language imitates language, has the effect of reducing the *Laokoon* poetics to what it in a sense actually is, a poetics of language or discourse, a poetics that perfects itself by the simple expedient of reducing the whole world of things to nothing but the operation of that verbal metaphoricity which things after all *are*. The result, however, is then not a poetics at all, but a kind of scholastic theology of language, from which—despite Heidegger—there is no way back either to our experienced existence or to the construction and operation of actual poetic initiatives. Lessing's ironic "performance"—the arbitrary suppression of the system, the arbitrary deviation from final truth into a poetics of "experience"—is therefore required in order to grasp that universal metaphoricity *as* metaphoricity, as itself sufficiently arbitrary to ground precisely its function as a "natural" sign and make drama possible. It follows in fact that *experience itself*, every moment of individual existence, *is irony*, is a poetic deviation from the system of poetics, an act of renunciation (as in Goethe or Hölderlin) for the sake of the integrity of precisely the system, the poetics of language, that it denies.

CHAPTER FOUR

Ironic Conversation and the Communal Soul: Goethe on and in Language

Lessing's poetics is "complete" only in the sense that it engages the whole range of poetic literature. It is not a poetics *of* totality or closure. The illusion of experience—by incorporating a criticism that attacks any structure comparable to the subject/object distinction, any structure that might support a recognition of boundary or closure—is from the outset *not* complete and lacks all hope of completion. This idea of course resists its own terminology; the "incorporation" of criticism suggests that the result is a "corpus," which I claim it is not. And the reason for this difficulty is the separation of our theoretical perspective from Lessing's own resolute refusal to adopt a comprehensive theoretical point of view—his refusal, speaking historically, to make the Kantian move. Again, it is the mirror of Kant, and the appearance of inevitability in Kantian systematics, that confuses issues here. In eighteenth-century Germany, I contend, we have the concrete example of a complete and well-communicated poetic theory that *depends* (as in Lessing's treatment of drama) on avoiding the Kantian move. We now need to look more closely at how that poetics is communicated and how it is related to literary practice.

Irony and the Subversive

By suggesting, as I did earlier, that its irony makes Goethe's narrative "radically subversive," subversive with respect to any possible determination of its content, I do not mean to leap over actual historical conditions into a realm of harmless generality. The ironic poetics and ironic practice of eighteenth-century Germany, I contend, are effectively subversive even with respect to the bourgeois ideology that in time collected about such supposedly dominant ideas as "symbol" and "totality."[1] Only in the *Sturm und Drang*, or in certain Romantic texts, only in either the pre- or the post-"Classical," do we ordinarily speak of a subversive questioning of the developing bourgeois value-system. My contention is that this political map of the period needs to be redrawn. Even in Goethe, even in the "classical" Goethe—even, for example, in *Hermann und Dorothea*—there is a powerful subversive movement with respect to actual social and ideological conditions.[2]

Statements of this sort, however, are always made questionable by their unavoidable theoretical component, since theory by nature domesticates everything it touches. How shall we understand, or even merely identify, the subversive without subjecting it to an order in which it loses its quality *as* the subversive? For example, if the analogy I drew in Chapter 1 is correct, between the implied community of readers of Goethe's *Wanderjahre* and the community of modern literary studies, then it appears to follow that the operation of that text is now represented by an actual quasi-political establishment, which would contradict my argument on the text's radically subversive quality. That argument can still be rescued, since the idea of a "community" of literary studies does not actually *imply* an establishment. When we (in literary studies) call ourselves a "community" and

[1]Especially important in the development of recent historical preconceptions concerning late eighteenth-century Germany is the revaluing of the distinction between symbol and allegory, mainly in the wake of Walter Benjamin, *Ursprung des deutschen Trauerspiels*, ed. Rolf Tiedemann, 2d ed. (Frankfurt am Main, 1982; orig. 1928), esp. pp. 138–46. See also Paul de Man, "The Rhetoric of Temporality," in his *Blindness and Insight: Essays in the Rhetoric of Contemporary Criticism*, 2d ed. (Minneapolis, 1983), pp. 187–228, who treats "irony" as a more or less strictly nineteenth-century development. David Wellbery's insistence on the quasi-visual transparency of poetic language for Lessing belongs here as well (see his *Lessing's "Laocoon": Semiotics and Aesthetics in the Age of Reason* [Cambridge, 1984]). For a summary of Marxist views that as a rule affirm German Classicism as a pioneering of bourgeois ideology in its time, see Walter Hinderer, "Die regressive Universalideologie: Zum Klassikbild der marxistischen Literaturkritik von Franz Mehring bis zu den *Weimarer Beiträgen*," in *Die Klassik-Legende*, ed. Reinhold Grimm and Jost Hermand (Frankfurt am Main, 1971), pp. 141–75. On Brecht see, in the same collection, Walter H. Sokel, "Brechts marxistischer Weg zur Klassik," pp. 176–99.

[2]See Frank G. Ryder and Benjamin Bennett, "The Irony of Goethe's *Hermann und Dorothea*: Its Form and Function," *PMLA* 90 (1975), 433–46. My own view now is still more uncompromising.

refer to more than just the group that agrees on some particular issue, we are really only invoking the analogy with such entities as the
body of readers of the *Wanderjahre*, those Christian Europeans who
trace their literary descent to Hellenic antiquity yet now recognize
themselves as a community only in the cryptic mirror of the Jews.
But problems of this type do not go away for being answered in a
particular case.

Let us approach the matter via the relation between *irony* and the
subversive. We speak of irony, to begin with, when we recognize
that an utterance "appears" to mean M but "really" means X. Irony is
not the same thing as ambiguity, where the different possible meanings of the utterance have approximately equal value or plausibility.
An ironic vehicle is definitely *subordinated* to the meaning that it
"conceals," which produces problems of definition. For once we have
recognized the irony, once we see through the vehicle M, the utterance has in a strong sense ceased to be ironic and (for us) simply
"means" X. Of course X alone, stated directly, is not exactly the same
utterance. But the *subordination* of one possible meaning to another,
which for most practical purposes makes X equivalent to the original
utterance, is part of what we mean by irony in the first place. (It
should be noted that the statement of this problem can easily be
adjusted to refer to any type of linguistic "act" or "force," say, the
constative or the performative, the illocutionary or the perlocution-
ary.)

Therefore, if irony is more than just an occasional ornamental
flourish in the production and communication of meaning, we must
seek it in cases where the principal or concealed meaning can no
longer be clearly identified as X, associated with some alternative
non-ironic utterance. Meaning M is still subordinate, but we are no
longer in a position to say *what it is subordinate to*. In order to
recognize the utterance as ironic, we must in some sense "know"
what is concealed beneath its surface, but we now find that this
knowledge is excluded from the system of possible utterances implied by the historical situation of our language. We find that any
attempt to pin down this knowledge in a direct statement *necessarily*
misses the point. The use of statements or terms "under erasure,"
the attempt to say something without committing oneself to the saying of it, is a strategy for avoiding what would otherwise be irony in a
radical sense—and is thus itself, in turn, actually an ironic procedure, since what it performs superficially, *first* statement and *then*

erasure, conceals an operation that is strictly beyond the limits of what *can* be performed in writing.

Irony, then, is the point at which language somehow "means" beyond the range of its own possibilities; it is "a *language problem*, a struggle in language against the hypostatization of thought, against the impossibility of bringing together what language itself has already irrevocably separated."[3] Or in other words, irony is a *subversive* movement with respect to language considered as a self-limiting semiotic system. We need not concern ourselves now with the question of where this subversive movement originates, where the extralinguistic fulcrum is located by which it gains its leverage in linguistic meaning. The term "genius," in the eighteenth century, seems sometimes to refer to the possibility of irony; and the separation between "thought" and language in Hölderlin tends in that direction as well. But notions of this sort involve the concept of the subject or subjectivity; and the poetics of irony with which we are concerned calls into question, among other things, the priority of the subject with respect to language, thus also the possibility of a subjective anchoring of its irony. We will come later to the question of where irony is located. For the time being, it is sufficient to recognize that the existence of the ironic, if it can be shown, keeps open at least the possibility of the radically subversive.

Language Is Music

In Friedrich Nietzsche's *Birth of Tragedy*, the nouns most often modified by the adjectives "Apollonian" and "Dionysian," respectively, are "illusion" and "wisdom," which produces a strong asymmetry. For whereas "wisdom" refers to a condition of the subject— much more exclusively of the subject than, say, "knowledge"—"illusion" refers to a quality of objects, and in fact, in the context of Nietzsche's book, to a quality of objects *as such*. How must we complete the pattern? What form of the object is associated with the Dionysian "drive," what subjective condition or process with the Apollonian?

If we attend to Nietzsche's insistence on strict symmetry and reciprocity between the drives, and if we recognize that the drives do

---

[3]Eva Knodt, *"Negative Philosophie" und dialogische Kritik: Zur Struktur poetischer Theorie bei Lessing und Herder* (Tübingen, 1988), p. 85.

not originate in preexisting individuals but generate human individuality by their own prior operation, then I think it becomes clear that
the concepts we need are "creation" and "truth." The Apollonian implies not merely our subjection to illusion but our active insistence
on such subjection, our desire to continue dreaming; and at its point
of highest intensity, among the Greeks, when confronted with the
correspondingly culminating Dionysian in tragedy, it arrives at the
realization of existence as an act of original quasi-artistic *creation* relative to the world as a whole, including our own suffering individuality. The only possible frame (or non-frame) for this originary creative act, however—and the final object, in turn, of Dionysian
cognition—is truth in the sense of absolute nothingness, the *truth* of
the utter void of nonentity yawning behind all phenomena.[4]

Nietzsche does use the terms "creation" and "truth" in this text—
and in contexts that strongly suggest their definitive force. But he
does *not* use them to define the "drives." And this avoidance of direct statement seems to me a uniquely clear instance of radical irony.
For although a statement can be made that characterizes the Apollonian in terms of originary world-creation—or, to push the paradox to
its limit, *repeatedly* originary creation[5]—still the statement in this
form also necessarily misses its own point, fails to say what it means,
since the very concept "world" is an act of submission on the
speaker's part to an organization of things that is not his or her own
creation. What we have here is not merely a logical contradiction but
a speech act that cannot possibly accomplish what it "means," since it
already makes nonsense of itself *as an act*. The statement that "truth"
is the Dionysian object violates the minimal integrity of language acts
in exactly the same way. For truth in the sense of ultimate nothingness cannot be "known" or "perceived" or "encountered" or "dealt
with," cannot be any sort of object, except by being *negated* or *denied*, since the happening of any object refutes nothingness. And
such negation would violate the positive linguistic act that is embod-
ied in the concept "truth." With regard to the eighteenth century,
this case is especially interesting, because a similar radical irony is
suggested by Lessing's parable of the right and left hands of God in
Eine Duplik.

    [4]For a detailed argument on these points, see my "Nietzsche's Idea of Myth: The Birth
of Tragedy from the Spirit of Eighteenth-Century Aesthetics," *PMLA* 94 (1979), 420–33.
    [5]Deadly negativity is overcome "fortwährend von Neuem" in the artistic creation of the
Olympians; the vision of tragedy occurs in repeated "discharges." See *NW*, pp. 32, 58.

The ironic move by which certain logically necessary statements are erased—*actually* erased, simply not there—in the text operates to produce a special historical integrity in the act represented by *The Birth of Tragedy*. The philosophical "battles" of the age, Nietzsche says, are not such that we can be merely spectators to them (*NW*, p. 98); and his book, accordingly, pulls itself together as a historical act, resists the temptation to embark on a Hegelian adventure in upward-spiraling formulations that claim eventually to *say* everything. But it does not follow that the inherent problems of irony are left out of account.

How does radical irony "mean" in the first place? Given two ironic utterances, we cannot say specifically how they *differ* in meaning without specifying in some degree the meaning of each, hence denying their irony, the exclusion of their concealed content from the realm of language acts. Does this imply that all radical irony means the same thing, or that it means nothing at all? Either conclusion would be absurd, since irony is by definition a vehicle of meaning, and meaning *is* difference. Nietzsche recognizes, however, that a way to confront this impasse, if not to escape it, is offered by the idea of *music*, where the problem of meaning is almost exactly parallel. For music, as a sign system and a social proceeding, evidently both signifies and communicates; and musical forms or pieces evidently differ in meaning. But the specificity of musical meaning, or indeed the specificity or identity of the musical signifier, nonetheless remains an entirely intractable problem, no matter where one positions oneself on the scale from, say, record-liner rhetoric to Schopenhauer's idea of an "immediate representation of will" (*NW*, p. 100). Music does not solve the problem of meaning in irony. But Nietzsche's emphasis on music is itself an ironic reference to the radical irony in his discussion of what he sees as the ironic form of tragedy, a form that can never in any sense say what it means (pp. 60–67, 105–6). From the point of view of radical irony, Nietzsche suggests, and with regard to the question of meaning, language itself is music and nothing but.

Nietzsche thus also serves as an example for the manner in which radical irony is dialectically and historically self-replicating. Irony breeds irony, since any adequate critical or interpretive discussion of a radically ironic text—such as Nietzsche's interpretation of Greek tragedy—must itself be radically ironic. And thence arises in turn the possibility, indeed the inevitability, of *ironic conversation*.

Why, for example, in *Ursprung des deutschen Trauerspiels*, does
Walter Benjamin attack Nietzsche as vehemently as he does, in the
very process of recognizing that the idea of tragic "Schweigen" (silence), which he borrows from Franz Rosenzweig, is central to both
his and Nietzsche's conceptions of "Tragödie" (Benjamin, pp. 88–89)?
It seems to me that this attack is itself evidence that the element of
agon, which Benjamin claims Nietzsche is blind to, is already inevitably present in radical irony *as a practice*. For the shaping of a
radically ironic statement or position, the basic process of articulation, can never be disinterestedly transparent with respect to an im-
personal or ahistorical meaning. Such a statement or position cannot
happen in the first place, cannot distinguish itself as itself, except as
a form of response or dialogue or polemic. We find ourselves operating in a distinctly Bloomian universe. The point Benjamin misses—
and he must miss (or erase) *some* point in order to articulate his
position—is that his own conception of an inevitable, historically
conditioned conflict in tragedy is breathed forth by the very structure of Nietzsche's discourse.

The particular instance of ironic conversation that will occupy us
most is the *Laokoon* debate, especially between Lessing and Herder.
But first we must have a firm grasp of the idea of a silence, a tragic
"Schweigen," *in* discourse, a deaf-mute spot in language, so to speak,
which is still sufficiently substantial to serve as a basis for the communicative and the radically subversive. Such silence is not literal
silence, which is simply not there, but a silence like the silence before "An die Parzen," which does not appear except by *re*appearing
in the poem's speaking, or like Kierkegaard's silence, in the very
midst of speech, the silence that Nietzsche recognizes in the most
talkative of all tragic figures, Hamlet (*NW*, p. 106), a silence for
whose manifestation, as Rosenzweig points out, the apparent competition of semiotic systems in drama is especially well suited.[6] And this
point brings us again to the German eighteenth century. For both
Benjamin and Nietzsche, in the specific historical organizations they
propose, and in their focus on a relatively narrow philosophical notion of the tragic, blind themselves to (or erase) the coincidence of
ironic silence and dramatic form in the works of—at least—Lenz,
Lessing, Goethe, Schiller, and Kleist. Even in extremely verbose

[6]For Kierkegaard's "silence concealed in a most striking talent for conversation," see
Søren Kierkegaard's Journals and Papers, ed. Howard V. Hong and Edna H. Hong, 7
vols. (Bloomington, Ind., 1967–78), 6:522.

plays like *Nathan der Weise* and *Torquato Tasso* and *Die natürliche Tochter*, the volume of talking in the end only shows forth the gulf of silence that it proves insufficient to fill, a silence which, by existing *in* language, inevitably infects the whole, marks its origin and bounds, and gives language as such the character of articulated speechlessness, which is to say, music.[7]

Is Language Meant to Mean?

Benjamin suggests, as a specification of the content of tragic silence, the idea of *a knowledge that we are better, or more, than our own gods* (Benjamin, p. 90). This knowledge is quintessentially silent—silent even if we shout it at the top of our lungs—for it combines an acknowledgment of unconditional subordination (contained in the very concept of a god) with an assertion at least of defiance, if not of dominion. We think of Goethe's "Prometheus," or of Blake: "All deities reside in the human breast." The ironic utterance (*M*) shows a similar structure; it carries out an act of subordination relative to a meaning (*X*) that persists in the universe of discourse only by virtue of that act (*M*) considered as *power* (the power to express *X*, which would otherwise be absolutely silent, or nonexistent). The gods live on our sacrifices, suggests Goethe.

But the idea of deities or divinity is not necessary here. Ironic silence obtains when the act of utterance would (or does) at once both acknowledge and violate the historical conditions of its own meaningfulness. (A violation of the strictly logical conditions of mean-

[7]There is room for some misunderstanding here, given the ideas in Rousseau's *Essai sur l'origine des langues* and Paul de Man's commentary in "The Rhetoric of Blindness," in his *Blindness and Insight*, pp. 102–41. De Man is correct in asserting that "the avowed thesis of the *Essai* equates music with language and makes it clear that, throughout the text, Rousseau never ceased to speak about the nature of language" (p. 131). The trouble is that he takes Rousseau's equation of music and language as evidence of a somehow *valid* (non-logocentric) view of the latter: "The sign is devoid of substance, not because it has to be a transparent indicator that should not mask a plenitude of meaning, but because the meaning itself is empty; the sign should not offer its own sensory richness as a substitute for the void that it signifies. Contrary to Derrida's assertion, Rousseau's theory of representation is not directed toward meaning as presence and plenitude but toward meaning as void. . . . Music becomes a mere structure because it is hollow at the core, because it 'means' the negation of all presence" (pp. 127–28). My point about Nietzsche is that the image of music, among other things, signals precisely the *impossibility* of a directedness "toward meaning as void," or of "the negation of presence." And I am not sure that this point would not yield a better argument on Rousseau. In this general connection, I will draw a parallel between Nietzsche and Herder.

ing, with no sense of the utterance's historical subordination, its involvement in a historically developed semiotic fabric, produces only the relatively trivial phenomenon of paradox.) And it follows that on a very high level of generality, we may say that radical irony arises from the silent knowledge that we are in some sense better than, or more than, *our language*. It is this knowledge, I think, that flashed into Herder's mind when he saw the prize-essay topic proposed by the Berlin Academy.

Herder himself, in his letter to Hamann of 1 August 1772, speaks of the "mask," the cloak of concealment, the "Leibniz-Aesthetische Hülle," he had employed in his *Abhandlung* on the origin of language. But this letter asserts at most that the prize essay is characterized by what we might call trivial irony. My contention is that in its outline and in its detailed execution, the essay is radically ironic. Herder's main thesis is that the single "positive" force that makes up human nature receives its direct and inevitable and *complete* manifestation in language, that there is no such thing as humanity without language or prior to language, that language therefore *constitutes our world*, our "Kreis," our circle or horizon, the whole of existence as we experience it. Without language, our existence—if one could call it that—would be nothing but helpless exposure to a perfectly chaotic "ocean of feelings" (SW, 5:34), which is a state we cannot even imagine, since imagination would already articulate it linguistically. This thesis excludes the possibility of our having been "given" language by God, since the human creature to whom language is supposedly given cannot exist, cannot be in a position to receive the gift, without already possessing language. Therefore, if we agree that language has an "origin" in the first place, it follows that humankind must somehow have *invented* language—in the words of the Academy. And this conclusion is a form of the silent knowledge that engenders irony. For it is based on an act of strict historical subordination—our existence is conditioned in its entirety by language, which must therefore be prior to us—but then unmasks that act as an act of power, control, generation.

One of Herder's main targets in the *Abhandlung* is Johann Peter Süßmilch's "Attempt to demonstrate that the earliest language took its origin not from men, but from the Creator alone."[8] But Herder does not reject Süßmilch's thought *in toto*. He accepts the argument

[8]*Versuch eines Beweises, daß die erste Sprache ihren Ursprung nicht von Menschen, sondern allein vom Schöpfer erhalten habe* (1766), presented to the Berlin Academy in 1756.

that he calls an "ewiger Kreisel," an eternally spinning top—the argument that the invention of language presupposes the prior existence of reason in linguistic form—and even develops it by pointing out that the reception of "divine instruction" would also presuppose language (SW, 5:38–42). What he quarrels with is Süßmilch's conclusion from this argument, which merely avoids the complexity of the problem by unloading it onto God (2:68, 5:144–45). Herder suggests, in other words, that the structure of even Süßmilch's treatise could conceivably be regarded as ironic, that its conclusion merely *masks* the insoluble problematics, the silent knowledge, that it purports to resolve. (Exactly this strategy, the ironic attribution of irony to one's opponent, is used more explicitly by Goethe against Kant.)[9]

This type of problematics, I contend, is what above all concerns Herder. For what is the advantage of the thesis that human beings "invent" language? Süßmilch's "Kreisel," which refutes the idea of invention in any *strict* sense, remains in force. Herder himself concedes that although "Besinnung" or "Besonnenheit" or "Reflexion" is strictly coincident with language, still this moment of reflection must have been *preceded* by a moment of "self(?)-collection," a moment of "Sammlung" into humanity that was under God's control alone (SW, 5:95). And what prevents this "Sammlung" from being regarded as a kind of divine instruction? Is it that God gives us only the *capacity*, the "Fähigkeit" for language? Herder himself earlier ridicules this concept as a mere terminological phantom, a "Gespenst von Worte" (SW, 5:42). The idea of invention solves nothing. What it does—and this makes all the difference for Herder—is *keep the problem open*; it comes closer to realizing and manifesting the potential for radical irony that is already there even in the structure of Süßmilch's thought.

Moreover, what does it mean that we are *able* to theorize about the origin of language? The "Kreis" of any animal, its sphere of perception and operation, in effect its world, is determined mainly by its senses. But the enormously larger "Kreis" of human experience is conditioned mainly by language, which Herder therefore calls "dieser neue, selbstgemachte Sinn des Geistes" (SW, 5:47; this new, self-made sense of the intellect). The difference here, which underlies the paradoxical formulation, is that the physical senses, which are given directly by God to the animals, can never become objects of their own operation. Neither we nor any other animal can see our

---

[9]See "Anschauende Urtheilskraft," in WA, pt. 2, 11:54–55.

sight or hear our hearing in the way we *can* talk about our language, in the way we in fact already are doing so in Herder's treatise.[10] And although Herder clearly knows what the "Kreisel" implies—that it is impossible, on objective grounds, to decide between divine influence (instruction or infusion) and human invention as hypotheses concerning the origin of language—still, it now also becomes clear that objective grounds are not needed, because we have *already made* a decision in the process of raising the question. Our theorizing about language, as an operation of language upon itself, is an *enactment* of the human invention of language—which necessarily means the making of language *by* language ("selbstgemacht" being nicely ambiguous)—impossible as it may be to imagine that event as having happened, originally, at some point in the past. This enactment, moreover, is a *historical* act. It cannot be retracted; the parallel between language and the merely God-given physical senses would always be rebroken precisely by the attempt (in language) to restore it. To insist on the divine origin of language is wrong not in the sense of being inaccurate but in the sense of being a hypocritical retreat from one's own theorizing considered as an irrevocable act.

Herder is thus a radical ironist in almost exactly the sense Nietzsche is, motivated by a concern for the historical integrity of his own text considered as an act. This view can be supported not only from his linguistic theorizing but from his historical theorizing as well, where the relativistic component, which implies subordination to our historical condition, combines with the act of intellectual control, the systematic description of history, to produce the silent knowledge I have spoken of.

But let us return to the *Abhandlung*. Herder discusses language as power, as the structure of experience, and as history in great detail. But especially part 2—like Lessing's *Erziehung des Menschengeschlechts*, which it resembles in outline—says a great deal with what it does *not* say. For Herder gives practically no account of linguistic *meaning*. He does assert, earlier on, that a "Merkwort," a marking or mnemonic or designating word, is also necessarily a communicating

[10]Compare Jacques Derrida on "s'entendre parler," in *Of Grammatology*, trans. Gayatri Chakravorty Spivak (Baltimore, 1976), pp. 7–8, and in *Speech and Phenomena: And Other Essays on Husserl's Theory of Signs*, trans. David B. Allison (Evanston, Ill., 1973), pp. 16, 76–80. Derrida's argument is prefigured in the submerged operation of Herder's. The structure of presence ("s'entendre parler") already includes its *rupture* and the decision in favor of a ruptured discourse, based on the idea of "invention," which all Herder's historical speculation cannot (and does not really want to) put together again.

word, a "Mitteilungswort" (SW, 5:47); and he does privilege verbs historically (5:51–52), verbs being that type of word in which the transition between what the word does and what it signifies is most direct. But Süßmilch's "Kreisel," in a developed form, still prevents the derivation of definite communicable meaning from these ideas, since a signified or a referent must already *have been* coded semiotically before it can ever operate as the object of a "Merkwort." That this difficulty apparently does not disturb Herder suggests that the communication of definite meaning, in his view, is not an important function of language to begin with. The business of language is to generate the identity and experience of the individual, the cohesion and endurance of the community, the history of the species, *not* to convey meaning from one self-present mind to another.

And yet, language must operate *as if* it communicated meaning, must have definite meaning (so to speak) on its surface; its individual and social and historical functions all depend on this pretense, which is to say that language, as such, is radically ironic. Herder actually goes into the question of language as meaning only in his discussion of animal language, where he compares the nervous system to a musical string that vibrates sympathetically with the emotional cause of the cry it hears (SW, 5:6–17). The only kind of thing we can say about meaning in language, that is, turns out to be the kind of thing we say habitually about meaning in music; with regard to the question of meaning, language for Herder, as for Nietzsche, is music and nothing but. It means, but only in the problematic sense of radical irony.[11]

Lessing Plus Herder Equals Nietzsche

We are still left with the question of the *status* of our own observations on irony. The discussion of irony in this or that particular text, provided we are speaking of irony in the radical sense, necessarily involves statements that have a peculiar provisional quality, since their operation as statements is called into question by their inter-

[11]If meaning or communication is regarded as the *telos* of language, then the development of ironic discourse can be understood as part of a widespread suspicion of teleology—in Herder's *Gott* (SW, 16:492–93), in Goethe's science, along with such followers as Georg Büchner in the "Schädelnerven" essay, in Kant's *Kritik der Urtheilskraft*, and so on.

pretive content (concerning the limits of what language *can* do, in the mirror of the text under consideration) and vice versa. And this provisional quality leaves plenty of room for alternative interpretations of the same material, interpretations that have an enormous advantage over the idea of irony, since the introduction into the discussion of any *authority* whatever—especially the supposed authority of the author's hypostatized mind or intention—is an anti-ironic move that decides the issue before it is even debated.

It is still possible, however, to get at the phenomenon of radical irony by way of its *symptoms*. We have seen that the necessary generation of irony in the perception of irony must produce, in the history of discourse, relatively well defined ironic conversations; and we have looked at an instance of such conversation in Benjamin's response to Nietzsche's theory of tragedy. Benjamin introduces the idea of tragic "silence" as a citation, but not a citation from Nietzsche, even though he does quote some of the passages in *The Birth of Tragedy* that suggest the idea. He thus announces a kind of agreement or consonance with Nietzsche but without locating (without, as it were, triangulating) that metaphysical *point* of agreement (the knowledge that we are better, or more, than our gods) which is characterized precisely by an abyssal silence that must prevent its location. And in denying Nietzsche's perception of the agonistic in tragedy, Benjamin sets up an agonistic relation *with* Nietzsche that reveals the inevitability of agon in the discourse as Nietzsche had initiated it, thus significantly undermining the operation of his own (Benjamin's) concept of agon as an objective or essentialist characterization of tragedy.

But let us return to the eighteenth century, and the *Laokoon* debate, especially the exchange between Lessing and Herder's *Erstes Wäldchen*. The ironic quality of this exchange has been treated in great detail by Eva Knodt in her *"Negative Philosophie" und dialogische Kritik*. Knodt simply takes seriously, and follows in their implications, both Herder's insistence on his basic solidarity with Lessing, despite his objections to the working of Lessing's argument, and Lessing's affirmative response to Herder's criticism. Or rather, she takes these assertions humorously, with a sense for the complicated game to which they belong. After all, if the *whole* ground of Lessing's argument is faulty, as Herder insists, what difference does it make *who* "builds on" that ground? (*SW*, 3:144). "Only he," only Lessing, could build what is built in *Laokoon*, says Herder, which in this context logically requires that the word "Lessing" refer not to a particular person or subject or type of subjectivity but to a modification of the very idea of critical argument (see Knodt, pp. 54–55). And Lessing then returns the compliment when he plays games with the question of who wrote the *Erstes Wäldchen* (L-M, 17:287). "One asks oneself: on what level is communication happening here?" (Knodt, p. 49).

It is especially important that Herder does not fail to appreciate the fictional manipulation of form in *Laokoon*, but compares Lessing's own procedure to Lessing's idea of Homer's (*SW*, 3:12). For in Chapter 3, I proposed at least seven different answers to the question of why Lessing reproduces narrative or poetic structure in his critical work: to suggest the idea of critical reflection as a type of experience; to maintain a poetic bias by avoiding development toward a system of all the arts; to preserve, in the texts and examples under discussion, that quality of resistance to criticism which criticism itself requires in order to generate meaning; to signal the operation of irony via the implied reflexive operation of the idea of the vanishing verbal medium; to demonstrate the problematics of reading poetry, the inescapable arbitrariness of the reader's asystematic approach; to dramatize the feedback of subject/object reflection (via the question of what the poem "is") *into* the illusion of experience; and to avoid establishing the idea of quasi-originary experience as a *criterion* for poetic quality, which would shift the discourse from poetics into aesthetics. The trouble with these answers is that there are too many of them. Formulations such as "Criticism . . . is a theorizing that *reflects on itself in the act of its own presentation*" (Knodt, p. 61) summarize the situation only by disarticulating it. There is *no* reason for Lessing's procedure, because "reason" gets lost among the mirrors by which it constitutes itself. And when Herder then adds more mirrors, by not only recognizing but also both imitating and parodying Lessing's procedure, he thus justifies (and also undermines) his deep critical disagreement with Lessing, by agreeing on the absence of a target for agreement. Irony now does all the talking, and theory has become "speechless" (pp. 63–65).

But "even if, in fact, the actual communicative process in this controversy unfolds *behind* the text, on a non-discursive level of suggestive allusions and ironic gestures, still the existence of a discursive line of argument *in* the text cannot be denied" (Knodt, p. 64). And Knodt, in following this line of argument, shows that it turns out to be a *single* line running through both texts. "Herder reads *Laokoon* as a work that includes, so to speak, its own self-criticism, in the ironic discrepancy between systematic content and fragmentary form. . . . Behind the break between presuppositions and consequences [in Lessing] Herder uncovers a conceptual vacuum that requires the transition to a theory of poetic imagination as linguistic creativity [in our terminology: enactment of origins]. . . . Lessing's project reaches a limit where it logically presupposes the existence of a linguistically articulated world, which Herder argues has to be thought of as the product of poetic imaginative 'force'" (p. 7). But it does not follow that Herder's thought thus simply corrects and completes and supersedes Lessing's. On the contrary, Herder's notion of "force" ("Kraft") *requires* its adversarial relation to Lessing in order to receive contour as a concept, to become anything other than an empty word. "It gains concreteness *only* in its dialogical relation to that terminological vacuum that Lessing makes visible at the basis of the aesthetics of the time" (Knodt, p. 119).

In terms we have used above, Lessing produces, at least *in potentia*, a complete poetics, which Herder, *by* completing in a particular way, shows to be based on a radical impossibility of completeness that now undermines his own argument (and also verifies that argument by avoiding the illusion of completeness, the quality of "work"). This is what I mean by ironic conversation, the indices of which are much more unambiguous in their intertextual unfolding than the indices of irony in a single text.

Especially interesting, however, is that the single large argument that emerges from the relation between Herder and Lessing almost exactly parallels the ironic argument of *The Birth of Tragedy*. (See the diagrams in Knodt, pp. 100, 104.) Lessing supplies, so to speak, the Apollonian component, the understanding of existence by way of an insistent (if easily undermined) visual metaphor (see Knodt, pp. 92–95), the neat separation of space from time that enables an individuality to *be* even while it is changing. And Herder, who factors into the discussion, among other things, the idea of music (*SW*, 3:133–38), supplies the Dionysian component, which explodes the visual metaphor (the postulate of imitation, the comparison of images) while at the same time rescuing it by giving it a new sense (poetry's operation as a *force* producing objects in space [3:137–38]). This process is comparable to tragedy's explosion and reinstitution of visible myth for Nietzsche—and to the disintegration of the Cartesian individual as fact, that it might be revived as act, in Goethe and Hölderlin and perhaps in Schiller's "aesthetic state."

The parallel with Nietzsche can be followed to considerable depth. The concealment of the concept of originary illusion (of the "esoteric subtext" in which sign and referent are identical [Knodt, pp. 110–11]) behind a relatively trivial concept of aesthetic illusion, in *Laokoon*, is more than just parallel to the concealment of "creation" behind "illusion" in Nietzsche's terminology for the Apollonian. And the esoteric aspect of the Dionysian in Nietzsche, the idea of truth as a nothingness so perfect that it can be thought only by being denied, is detectable at a number of points behind the rational and sensible façade of the *Erstes Wäldchen*, behind its calm reconciliation of Lessing and Winckelmann, its ostensibly regretful unfolding of Lessing's inconsistencies.

Chapter 9 is especially significant. Having pointed out that nothing in nature ever holds still, that space is not even hypothetically detachable from time, Herder says, "Metaphysically, therefore—"and then interrupts himself (*SW*, 3:75). He had apparently been about to continue, "there are no objects in nature; nature is pure energy" (Knodt, p. 103), which means, nature *is* not anything at all, has no contour, no articulation. But in a Nietzschean move that denies the void, he actually continues, "But let us not talk metaphysically; let us talk from the point of view of the senses. And in the range of our vision, are there not enough constant, enduring objects for art [here, especially painting] to imitate? Of course there are." These objects, however, are usually "dead"; and the transitoriness of whatever vital quality art infuses them with must inevitably conflict with the painting's permanence as a "work" (*SW*, 3:78–79). Therefore the objects must possess, above all, the quality of "beauty" (3:79–81), which turns out, however, to depend on a compromise between "dead inactivity and exaggerated effectiveness" (3:80) that leaves *our* imagination as much play as possible—so that it is always really only *we* who are at fault, our "human weakness, the flabbiness of our senses, the unpleasantness of a long effort of attention" (3:78–79), when art's "ewiger Anblick" (3:81; eternal gaze), fails of its realization. Through all the rifts and fissures in this argument, in the language considered as either vehicle or performance, seeps Dionysian truth, the utter devouring void against which humanity as the poetic imagination desperately enacts its ever uncompleted origin and repeatedly constitutes itself by the images it brings forth.

"Language is music." This statement, by which we have referred
to the ultimate semiotic unaccountability of language in Herder and
Nietzsche, can be applied more broadly, if we agree with Knodt
about language's having no natural referent—in Lessing's theory of
poetry—except itself (Knodt, pp. 116–17). And this language-music,
in Lessing and Herder, like music itself in Nietzsche's theory of tragedy, operates in such proximity to the absolute universal identity of
nothingness that it can exist only by bringing forth repeatedly its
exact opposite, images, visions, contours, stories, the articulation of
space and time, frames of reference, individuals. "Metaphysically,
therefore—" says this music, and then always suddenly changes the
subject. But especially in Herder's Dionysian thinking, the metaphysical is never very deeply submerged. The arts, for Herder, operate not *in* space and time but rather "by means of" or "by way of"
("durch") space and time, which thus become not their precondition
so much as their instrument or medium, indeed almost part of their
created content (*SW*, 3:136; cf. Knodt, pp. 106–7). Or we recall the
notion of "negative philosophy" in the *Fragmente* (*SW*, 2:17), a philosophy that manages actually to encounter nothingness, while also
suggesting, interestingly, the figure of Socrates. And Knodt points
out that the critique of individuality in Herder arrives at a reestablishment of the subject in a form that calls to mind both Dionysian
community and Goethe's community as reader (Knodt, pp. 29–30):
"We believe ourselves alone, but never are; we are not even alone
with ourselves" (*SW*, 16:37).

But what is the significance of the equation: Lessing plus Herder
equals Nietzsche? In the first place, it gives contour and concreteness to the effacement, by irony, of the distinction between text
(Nietzsche) and intertext (the Lessing-Herder dialogue)—or by analogy, between subject (reader) and intersubject (community as
reader). Strictly speaking, the very concept of intertext effaces that
distinction; if the idea of the intertextual means anything at all, then
it must mean a quality of every actual and possible text, by which the
text (in being made, ultimately, of nothing but quotation) calls its
own isolable identity into question. My point, however, is that in
eighteenth-century Germany this otherwise harmless theoretical ver-
ity is made to operate as part of a subversive poetic program. The
quality of nonclosure in texts, which is crucial in any argument on
irony, is impossible to demonstrate by interpretation, since inter-

pretation *effects* closure.[12] But in the case of eighteenth-century Germany, we can achieve at least an increase in cogency by speaking of a poetics that is articulated *in* one text only by that text's nonclosure with respect to *another* text.

In the second place, the relation with Nietzsche supports our interpretation of the Lessing-Herder dialogue by suggesting a further intertextual operation, the possibility of regarding Nietzsche's theory of culture and tragedy as the articulation of a pattern of thought in German intellectual *tradition* since the eighteenth century. Nietzsche himself is more clearly aware of Schiller as a predecessor than of Lessing or Herder, or for that matter Goethe. But Schiller—in his position as something like a conversational intermediary between Goethe and Hölderlin, or in the relation to Lessing that we discussed in the previous chapter, or especially in regard to the theory of drama—is quite sufficient as a link between Nietzsche and the ironic poetics of the eighteenth century.[13]

And in the third place, Nietzsche helps us deal with the Kant problem, the problem of the systematic articulation of the content of ironic communicative strategies. Does Kantian systematics successfully establish a stable and transparent metadiscourse by which the ironic complexity of (what German intellectuals are fond of calling) the "pre-critical" eighteenth century is rendered unnecessary, obsolete, in effect merely opaque? That the Lessing-Herder dialogue, with all its ironic depth, reemerges in Nietzsche—and then also finds its way into new intertexts, Nietzsche-Benjamin, Nietzsche-Artaud, Nietzsche-Derrida—at least casts doubt on the idea of system as the final resting place of theory. Nietzsche, moreover, not only postdates Kant but also *ironizes* the systematic Kantian method (which he calls by the oxymoron *"Dionysian wisdom* in conceptual form" [*NW*, p. 124]); he drags Kant into the ironic operation of his own discourse, and mounts him as it were, invisibly but inevitably, behind Schopenhauer on the horse in Dürer's engraving

[12]On nonclosure in *Faust*, see my *Goethe's Theory of Poetry: "Faust" and the Regeneration of Language* (Ithaca, 1986), pp. 310–29. For an extensive and probing discussion of the general problem, see Alice A. Kuzniar, *Delayed Endings: Nonclosure in Novalis and Hölderlin* (Athens, Ga., 1987).

[13]For material with which to fill out this picture of tradition, see Knodt's final chapter (on the *Hamburgische Dramaturgie*), my "Nietzsche's Idea of Myth," and my *Modern Drama and German Classicism: Renaissance from Lessing to Brecht* (Ithaca, 1979), esp. chap. 7 on Schiller.

(p. 127). The relation between system and irony, the systematization of irony and the ironizing of system, thus itself becomes yet another form of ironic intertextual operation.

Scraps of Conversation, Discourse Boundaries, the Discursive Unconscious

The *Laokoon* discussion does not end with Lessing and Herder. Goethe's contribution, especially in the essay "Über Laokoon," attempts, like Herder's, to develop the intertextual situation by reevaluating and reenergizing the dialogic relation with Winckelmann. And like Herder, Goethe employs Lessing's text as a kind of foothold, to gain leverage against both the very idea of system and the inevitable exposure of his own writing to an interpretation in the form of systematic closure.[14] Herder, meanwhile, who had popped the cork on Lessing's poetics and opened it to its own native atmosphere of ironic conversation, has a similar service done for him in Hamann's critiques of the *Abhandlung über den Ursprung der Sprache*. Once we understand Herder's relation to Lessing, it is obvious that we can analyze Hamann's relation to Herder in the same way, except that the huge open text or intertext that emerges, in this case, is caught up later not in *The Birth of Tragedy* but rather, perhaps, in Kierkegaard's *Either/Or*. Hamann may even have intended his criticism of Herder as a parody of Herder's criticism of Lessing.

Or let us consider the general idea of "poetic painting." There is much talk in eighteenth-century Germany, in Bodmer and Breitinger, in Klopstock, in *Sturm und Drang* authors, about the sensual or evocative "power" ("Macht") of certain words and combinations of words, the ability of language to create vivid imaginary sense experiences for a reader. What is meant most often is the power of metaphor considered as a sign of affect or passion (*EG*, 276–313). But Breitinger, in a passage quoted (disapprovingly) by Lessing (L-M, 9:103), insists that a long passage in Albrecht von Haller's *Alpen* is superior, in its effectiveness as a description of its object, to any actual painting. And this challenge to Dubos's by then standard view of the greater "power" ("pouvoir") of painting's natural signs is repeated not only in Lessing's exposure of the arbitrary in painting

---

[14]See Peter J. Burgard, "The Serious Game: Essaying Goethe's Essays" (Ph.D. diss., University of Virginia, 1988), pp. 238–62.

but also, in an entirely different register, by Johann Caspar Lavater: "The *poet* is a *painter* and a *musician* at the same time, and more than both together. . . . Who is the *poet?* . . . A spirit who feels he can create and does create—and whose creation not only pleases and enraptures him *inwardly*, as *his* work, but also, as Creation, is proclaimed by *all tongues*: 'Truth! Truth! Nature! Nature! we see what we never saw and hear what we never heard—and still, what we see and hear is flesh of our own flesh, bone of our bone.'"[15] Poetry, it seems, enables us actually to *see*, in a manner that mere painting cannot duplicate.

But no one claims that language actually *transmits* an experience that the reader had not previously been capable of imagining; no one claims that the arbitrary signs of language can *determine* a visual experience to the same extent that what we see is determined when we observe a painting. The poetic "power" of language is the power to awaken our own imagining, to assemble in our mind an experience of which we had already possessed all the constituent elements. We think here of ironic Socrates, the intellectual "midwife" who always only reminds his collocutors of what they already know—and of the eighteenth-century German fascination with Socrates, in Mendelssohn, in Hamann and Herder, in Wieland's dialogues and Lessing's, in Goethe's and Hölderlin's plans for dramas.[16]

The discussion of poetic painting thus suggests a *structure* similar to the structure of ironic discourse. The principal meaning of the utterance, the image we "see" as if it were painted, develops on a plane that is distinguished categorically from the plane on which the utterance unfolds as discourse. The utterance is in a strong sense *preceded* by the communicative act that it supposedly carries out; if we do not already know the meaning, if we have not already done the seeing we are meant to do, then the actual utterance does not mean, for us, what it means. (Lessing, we recall, says that metaphor "renews" an image.) Moreover, if we assume that this structure in poetic language reflects the operation of radical irony, then it follows that the critical discussion of poetic painting is characterized by a similar irony. In order to make an argument on irony in the critical discussion—hence on the pervasive, not merely sporadic, quality of

[15]Johann Caspar Lavater, *Physiognomische Fragmente, zur Beförderung der Menschenkenntniß und Menschenliebe*, 4 vols. (Zurich, 1968–69; facs. of 1775–78), 3:205.
[16]See Goethe's letter to Herder of January 1772 and Hölderlin's to Neuffer of 10 October 1794.

ironic conversation in eighteenth-century Germany—it is therefore necessary only to show that graphic poetic language is *regarded* as ironic.

The trouble is that an entirely different manner of accounting for the structure of both poetic painting and its critical discussion is available, an account in which the notion of irony does not figure. In Wolffian epistemology, objects of sense perception are represented in the mind by preverbal intuitions that function more or less as the objects' natural signs, to which the arbitrary signs of language then refer. And especially in Baumgarten, it appears that the relation of sign to referent is corrigible and perfectible at both the intuitive and the verbal stages of the process, since the referent, at both stages, is fully determined in itself and strictly prior to the sign. All that is needed, therefore, in order to produce a complete theory of "poetic painting" is the possibility of interaction between the stages, the possibility that a well-chosen combination of verbal signs (a metaphor, say, or a new or revived compound) might produce a relation among intuitions by which the intuitions themselves are perfected. The question of what is or is not (or is *and* is not) beyond the limits of language, the question of irony, does not then arise; the limits of language are simply given, if perhaps only as asymptotes.

This strictly "semiotic" account—if the argument of this and the last chapter holds—does not work for the idea of poetic painting in Lessing or Herder. Here we require a "hermeneutic" account, in which the historical conditions of understanding come under scrutiny, and in which the unavoidable concept of pre-understanding threatens an infinite regress that opens at least the type of space in which irony operates.[17] But how shall we locate exactly the *boundary* between an older discourse, limited by the idea of semiosis as imitation, resemblance, substitution, and a newer, potentially ironic discourse, in which the rôle of the extralinguistic has become a problem? How shall we locate the point where one and the same idea, "poetic painting," stops meaning what Wellbery finds in it (the ambition to reachieve in linguistic signs the picture's transparency to intuition) and begins meaning what I have suggested (an intimation of

---

[17]This use of the terms "semiotic" and "hermeneutic" is found in Wellbery, p. 2, passim, and also, for instance, in Robert S. Leventhal, "Semiotic Interpretation and Rhetoric in the German Enlightenment 1740–1760," *DVLG* 60 (1986), 223–48. Wellbery locates the boundary between discourses at the difference between Lessing (semiotic) and Herder (hermeneutic). Leventhal discusses semiotic culture in greater depth, but does not attempt to place Lessing.

hermeneutic complexity and radical irony)? Wellbery finds "astonish-ing" the "close proximity" between Breitinger's poetic thought and Lessing's (p. 203) but then explains it by arguing that both men in-habit the same basic discourse, that Lessing merely develops it fur-ther toward "the theory of aesthetic representation as a global and intuitive representation" (p. 208), toward the idea of a *"totalizing re-gard within the present instant"* (p. 213). If we recognize the opera-tion of radical irony in Lessing, however, and assume that Breitinger still works in the shadow of Wolffian thought, then our sense of prox-imity between them becomes a problem. Where is the boundary, the mutation in discourse?

What do we make of Klopstock, for instance, when, in talking about newly coined poetic words and their relation to their context, he says, "Especially in this case the reader constantly makes a com-parison, a very quick but still exact comparison, between the thought and the word. He feels what we have wanted to say, what we have said, and what we have not said" (*AW*, p. 1021). In the essay "Von der Sprache der Poesie," this remark could probably be dismissed as reflecting an imitative view, if it were not for the idea of "what we have *not* said." What difference is made, in a Wolffian conception of graphic language, by intuitions from sense experience that are *not* called into play? Must we not think here in terms of an ironic com-munication between author and reader concerning the *strategy* of utterance—a strategy of inclusion *and* exclusion (what we do not say), which articulates the historical process of inclusion and exclu-sion by which the language as a whole constitutes itself, the structure of blind spots by which it sees?

In the "physiognomic fragment" quoted above, Lavater has un-questionably left imitative aesthetics behind. Language, he insists, can be reduced—by eliminating that artificial "tone and manner" which sometimes infects even Homer—to the point where it be-comes practically identical with a newborn nature that we *see*, in a seeing that operates not by the comparison of intuitions to things, but by sympathetic inspiration, which opens the way to an intermin-able hermeneutic reflection. And Johann Heinrich Merck—who also contends, in "Über den Mangel des Epischen Geistes in unserm lie-ben Vaterland,"[18] that language can achieve graphic transparency by eliminating the artificial—appears to be operating on the other side

---

[18]Johann Heinrich Merck, *Werke*, ed. Arthur Henkel (Frankfurt am Main, 1968), pp. 385-91.

of the division between discourses. What makes natural speech so
vivid, he says, is "das Umständliche," the circumstantial, the slow
pace and loving attention to detail by which both the common people's narration and Homer's narration are characterized. If we but
talk long enough, if we but keep working verbally on the object or
event to be imitated, eventually the object will be fully there for our
hearers. But then, as his final flourish, Merck praises the "little
events," narrated in great detail, that are woven into the texture of
Tristram Shandy! The criteria are still the same, but an area of puz-
zlement, if not contradiction, is opened between the examples, since
the main point about Homer and the common people is that neither
the personal nor the verbal "medium" intrudes. And when it is then
conceded that "the practically real, living people" in Sterne—Trim
and widow Wadman are mentioned—are *known* by us to be "creatures of the author's brain," when the distinction between fantasy
and reality is thus clouded, we become still less certain about the
historical gulf that seems to separate this discourse from Lavater's.

Exactly where is the boundary between discourses? This question
is bedeviled by the inevitable failure of discourse and terminology to
keep step with one another. Indeed, the emergence of a transparent
terminology is a reliable sign that the discourse to which it is transparent has already been superseded. This consideration illuminates
not only the irony of *Laokoon*, but also the more compact complexity
of Hamann's *Sokratische Denkwürdigkeiten*: "The relationship and
agreement of concepts in a demonstration are no different from what
the interaction and symmetry of values and sounds are in a musical
composition, or that of lines and colors in painting. The philosopher
is as much subject to the law of imitation as the poet" (MiN, 2:74).
The terminology of imitation here develops the idea that philosophical proof never proves anything not already "believed" (2:73), which
contradicts the Wolffian idea of "symbolic" knowledge, hence also
the structural consonance of mind and world on which exactly the
rhetoric of imitation is founded. And this contradiction in a sense
substantiates Hamann's initial anti-Cartesian proposition: "Our own
being and the existence of all things outside us must be believed and
can be decided upon in no other way" (2:73), in which the concealed
implication of a *self*-grounding "belief"—how can "we" believe, before even our existence is assured?—is the symptom of a new discourse in the very bosom of the old.

There is no way to locate the discourse boundary we are interested in. The relation of Herder to Baumgarten, for example (poetry as "sensorially perfect discourse" or "perfect sensory discourse"), only confuses the question of the historical distance between them, and perhaps, on Herder's part, is *meant* to confuse this question.[19] Irony in general does not respect boundaries or limits or historical separations. Once we admit the operation of radical irony in text *A*, then any relation whatever with text *B* (including even disagreement, opposition, ridicule) implies that radical irony cannot be excluded as an interpretive possibility in *B*. We have observed this dynamics in the relation of Herder not only to Baumgarten, but also to Süßmilch, and in that of Goethe to Kant[20]—not to mention the relatively unambiguous instances of ironic conversation discussed above.

It does not follow, however, that irony is therefore not a well-formed concept, that it cannot be talked about. There is no localizing irony in particular texts; but there is, in the history of discourse, a definite *resistance* to radical irony, by which the latter can be located as a phenomenon. Discourse in history (including especially the discourse *of* history) attempts constantly to articulate and periodize itself, to establish large boundary structures that imply eventually the boundedness or closure or "meaning" of particular texts. And this historical mechanics—which is embraced by hermeneutic theory as the very matrix of meaning—seems both a natural and a necessary component of our intellectual existence, until, from the perspective of irony, we ask what it is opposed to, what it excludes, what it *resists*. The parallel with the rôle of the ego in psychoanalysis is interesting, with that apparently natural and necessary component of our personal existence which becomes a puzzle only from the perspective of the unconscious, whence it is resolved into "instincts" that appear principally as "resistances" to analysis.[21] For the time being, in fact, it may be useful to think of radical irony as a kind of *discursive unconscious*.

In any case, from the point of view of our own historical and interpretive concerns, this state of affairs is definitely double-edged. The ironic conversations of eighteenth-century poetics, by opening their discourse unreservedly with respect to the future as well as the past, authorize us to conduct the discussion without needing to make a

---

[19] See Chap. 3, n. 27.
[20] See "Anschauende Urtheilskraft," in WA, pt. 2, 11:54–55.
[21] See *The Standard Edition of the Complete Psychological Works of Sigmund Freud*, ed. James Strachey, 24 vols. (London, 1966–74), 16:350, 19:17.

relativist leap into conventions we admit from the outset are alien. But at the same time, insofar as our participation in those conversations turns out to be *constitutive*—if not of their bare existence, then at least of their limits and consequences and depth of local penetration in particular texts—we are threatened by the possibility of a history that we cannot talk about without its talking back, without its avoiding and countering our formulations by talking about *us*. Lacan says of the unconscious "that its status of being, which is so elusive, so unsubstantial, is given to [it] by the procedure of its discoverer."[22] Is the "status" of irony not given to it by its critical discussion in exactly the same way? And in fact, given the "fragility" of such status "on the ontic plane," how different is the assertion of this parallel from the assertion of an identity?

Why the Eighteenth Century?

Where, then, is the value of discovering in the eighteenth century a poetics that grows up around the operation of radical irony? If irony, for all we know, is constituted by our discussion of it, then such a poetics could be found anywhere in history. This problem, however, is not wholly created by the concept of irony; it arises in any discussion of the poetics of an "age." For every poetics either makes or implies a claim to be *universally* applicable—even at the cost of excluding from the realm of poetry whole past ages or cultures. And if the critical discussion of a given poetics does not to some degree accept this claim, then it has not penetrated the target system of thought to the level at which the latter *is* a poetics to begin with. A poetics (unlike, say, a philosophy or a political theory) does not attract our attention *as* a poetics except to the extent that we recognize in it a successful or fruitful poetics.

Hence the question, why the eighteenth century, especially in Germany? There are three main factors that justify our looking for a poetics of irony and enactment-of-origins in this particular age. First, it is not only argued in this book, but also generally acknowledged, that the eighteenth century is characterized by at least two widely disparate discourses, whose meeting or conflict is a major crisis of

[22]Jacques Lacan, *The Four Fundamental Concepts of Psycho-Analysis*, trans. Alan Sheridan (New York, 1981), p. 33.

Cartesian thought. "Classical" and "Romantic" are the terms used most often to describe this opposition; "semiotic" and "hermeneutic" occur, as do "pre-" and "post-critical," with reference to Kant's *Critiques*; "aesthetic" and "ironic" would perhaps fit my argument best. Foucault argues for the reduction of this conflict to a more or less orderly shift of *epistemes*. But in German literary history, even the standard terminology insists on the *problem* of the boundary. For between the two terms that unambiguously describe the major discourses, "Enlightenment" and "Romanticism," are inserted two further concepts, "Sturm und Drang" and "Classicism," which tend to associate themselves with the major discourses in reverse chronological order.

The second factor that shifts that problematic boundary to increase the territory of the ironic at the expense of the aesthetic is the prevalence in the eighteenth century of reflection on language as such—as opposed to reflection on the rôle of language in some larger system. In the aesthetic or Wolffian model of poetic thought, language is not a problem. The arbitrariness of the linguistic sign gives rise to certain specific problems in both philosophy and aesthetics; but language itself cannot yet become the kind of governing problem that it is for Condillac, Rousseau, Maupertuis, Süßmilch, Herder, Hamann, or Goethe. This factor also draws our attention especially to Germany. For in Germany, where the literary language in the eighteenth century is in the process of a highly self-conscious "emergence"—as the title of Eric Blackall's classic study on the subject has it—the urgent and profound reflection on language is by no means confined to linguistic treatises. Especially thinkers on poetics are as a rule clearly aware that their task is to *decide the fate* of their language and literature. Hence, in Hamann and Herder for example, the direct connection between the question of the origin of language and specific questions of style in the present, questions which they not only discuss but also dramatize in the style of their discussion. There is nothing abstract about the question of the origin of language in Germany, for the Germans themselves are experiencing an analogous process of linguistic origination and growth. Even where the connection between poetics and the question of the origin of language is not as direct as in Hamann and Herder, the reflection on language is in general far too active and radical to support the idea that poetic thought, except in certain pockets of resistance, is actually contained within aesthetic-Wolffian categories.

The third factor, finally, that I think tends to validate the present endeavor, is the opening of French Enlightenment thought in theoretical debate of the last couple of decades, especially Derrida's ambivalent inhabiting of Rousseau in *Of Grammatology*. Derrida gives us what we might call an ironic Rousseau—it being understood that irony by no means implies the absence of "blind spots"[23]—a Rousseau whose utterances, in various discursive genres, repeatedly penetrate the territory of what language in the end cannot get away with (i.e., the achievement of presence, the effacement of the trace) yet never take the step of ensconcing themselves systematically in that territory, but are always expelled and drawn back to it by yet another route, in a process that lays bare precisely the impossibility of their desire, a process that thus doubles paradoxically and in a sense validates Derrida's own constant precarious return to "a certain exteriority in relation to the totality of the age of logocentrism . . . a knowledge that is not a knowledge at all" (Derrida, pp. 161, 164). I do not mean simply to take Derrida's word for Rousseau and then draw firm conclusions about Germany. Our project, again, is to sketch a poetics of the age, which means, in practical terms, to show the relative plausibility of particular interpretive approaches to a group of texts. We are talking, in other words, relativities, not facts or certainties, a web of relativities in which, for example, Nietzsche evidently participates, and from which the recent discussion of the French eighteenth century cannot be excluded.

The Subject and the Social

The groundwork, then, or as much in the way of groundwork as can be expected, is there. And in order to understand how Goethe's work figures in the eighteenth-century discourse we are describing, we must refine our concepts, especially with regard to the entity we have called, after Hölderlin, "the communal soul," but which also appears in Klopstock as "the soul of language" (AW, p. 979), and in Herder as the supposed communal author of folk-poetry or as "the soul of the race" in the *Abhandlung* (SW, 5:115). In particular, we must distinguish the "communal" from the "social." The latter refers

[23]Derrida, *Of Grammatology*, p. 163. De Man objects in "The Rhetoric of Blindness."

to the community considered as a *plurality* in which we participate, whereas by the "communal" (especially in its quality of "soul") we now restrict ourselves to meaning the essentially *singular*, if extra-individual, entity that must be posited as knowing extralinguistically the knowledge behind irony. The communal is that ideal subject whose experience is the perfect origin of experience; it is the "god in us," the true agent of the act of renunciation that is manifest in the poem as writing.

The trouble with this idea of the communal is that as soon as we recognize its necessity—in our consideration, for example, of poetic irony—we are tempted to identify it with a particular structure of subjectivity. Schiller's "aesthetic state" risks becoming such a conceptual shortcut, as does the supposed reader of romance reading. In a consistent development of the thought of eighteenth-century German poetics, however, the correlative of the subject, to which the subject is related as signified to signifier, is not the communal but the *social*.[24] Poetry is an act of renunciation (for the communal) only by way of its being "a game in society" for the subject. And if reading the *Wanderjahre* is religious in the sense of being an affair of the communal, then this is so not by way of our solitary reading, but by way of our reading in the presence of (over the shoulders of, in conversation or debate with) other readers. This "by way of" is still a problem; the correlation of the subject and the social always includes a gesture toward the communal as its presumed ground. But the concepts must be kept separate.

[24]There is room for confusion here, since semiotic terminology is also used in connection with the idea of the subject by Lacan and his followers. The signified, when Lacan distinguishes it from the signifier, ordinarily means something more substantial, more an object of reference, less fully included in language, than the signifier. (See, for example, Jacques Lacan, "The agency of the letter in the unconscious or reason since Freud," in his *Ecrits: A Selection*, trans. Alan Sheridan [New York, 1977], pp. 146–78, or "A Jakobson" and "L'amour et le signifiant," in *Le Séminaire de Jacques Lacan: Livre XX: Encore* [Paris, 1975], pp. 19–27, 39–48.) I use the terms, by contrast, in their strictly semiotic sense, the sense suggested by Saussure's famous image of the two sides of a sheet of paper. That the subject is a signified says nothing whatever about its existence or substantiality or ontological status, but addresses only its relation to the signifier, hence the manner in which it is *accessible* to us. My point is that when we speak of the subject, we are really only describing structures that have become manifest to us in the domain of the social or conversational signifier. (In other words, I propose a discourse *different* from "le discours analytique" in which the subject is "le départ" [Lacan, "L'amour et le signifiant," p. 48].) There are theoretical complications here that I will leave to one side for the time being, especially C. S. Peirce's recognition of the need for *three* components in the signifying relation. I account for these complications in Chapter 6, in the discussion of the semiotic value of the ego and the communal.

Let us return to Hölderlin's "Friedensfeier" for a charting of this
state of affairs.

> Viel hat von Morgen an,
> Seit ein Gespräch wir sind und hören voneinander,
> Erfahren der Mensch; bald sind wir aber Gesang.

[Much, from morning onward—since we are (or have been) a conversation and hear of each other—has man learned or experienced; soon
however we are (or will be) song.]

The pronoun "wir" (we), despite its grammatical number, clearly operates here as a *singular*, as can be seen by transposing the statement into the third person. To say "people, in the plural, are constituted as a group by their conversation" is to state the obvious. What
Hölderlin suggests is "the existence of an individual person [signified
paradoxically by "wir"] is somehow grounded in conversation, in a
conversation in which the individual is heard *of*, not in the type of
direct contact with others that would constitute being *heard*." The
word "wir," in other words, *names the subject* (is a kind of quasi-"I")
and succeeds in naming the subject precisely because (as a plural) it
avoids naming the subject. For the subject as such is unnameable.
What is named as the subject from the point of view of the subject
(grammatical first person)—and every utterance is made from the
point of view of *some* subject—is never actually the subject but always (by being the object of naming) at most the *ego*, in a sense not
widely at variance with the Freudian.

The word "wir" therefore names the subject by naming the manifest signifier—the social, the element of "conversation"—that signifies the subject. (Hence, as in "An die Parzen," the importance of the
written medium, which makes the poem itself into an instance
of "conversation," language originating in a subject who is heard *of*,
not heard.) But it turns out now that the relation of signifier and
signified opens the possibility of *learning* ("Viel hat . . . Erfahren der
Mensch"); for this signifying relation is also an incurable wound
(since the subject cannot be named directly), a gap, a defect, which
is precipitated as the experience of *time*, an experience that is defec-
tive and self-wounding exactly to the extent that it is self-reflexively
cumulative, that the "now" is enabled to know itself as different from
its past or its future. And since the only *object* available to our learning in time is the originary act of signification that makes it possible,

it follows that our learning is always a learning *of the communal*, of the primordial ground of identity (which does not need to "exist" in order to be learned) upon which the signification of the subject by the social arises. The communal—which Hölderlin names "song," the resolution of the plural conversational sign into a single voice that signifies its own unified, no longer alienated voicing—is thus the impending future state inherent in the very structure of temporal experience.[25]

And yet, even assuming that this reading of Hölderlin's text is to the point, what does it mean that the subject and the social are related thus? The suggestion of an answer to this question is contained in the philosophical theory of "the Other" or "others"—in Jean-Paul Sartre, for example, where the discussion starts out from the experience of shame: "Thus the Other has not only revealed to me what I was; he has established me in a new type of being which can support new qualifications. . . . [S]hame is shame *of oneself before the Other.* But at the same time I need the Other in order to realize fully all the structures of my being. The For-itself refers to the For-others."[26] Sartre's entire "Being-for-Others," considered as a play on the structure of person, number, and case in the personal pronouns, might reasonably be regarded as a map of the subject.

But "others," in their mute Sartrean "looking," are not yet the social, not yet a "conversation." And the missing linguistic element in an argument of the general shape that Sartre proposes is supplied by the discussions of *irony* I have suggested in earlier chapters. One cannot be ironic in solitude, because one's meaning cannot be hidden from oneself in exactly the manner in which ironic meaning is hidden. And yet, even though the ironic therefore presupposes the element of the social, irony does not actually *happen* except as an experience of the isolated individual subject, indeed as *the* experience (of not being fully present in conversation) by which the subject experiences its individual isolation. If it were possible to restrict ourselves to the social interplay of utterances and their interpretation by various individuals, without going into the subjective experience of

---

[25]Hölderlin's "von Morgen an" suggests the idea of *awakening*, hence an interesting parallel in Lacan, *Four Concepts*, pp. 56–60, on "the phenomenon, distance, the gap itself that constitutes awakening" (p. 57), and on "the other reality hidden behind the lack of that which takes the place of representation," the Freudian "*Trieb*" (in our terms: the communal) which "we may have to consider . . . as being only *Trieb* to come" (p. 60).

[26]Jean-Paul Sartre, *Being and Nothingness: An Essay on Phenomenological Ontology*, trans. Hazel E. Barnes (New York, 1956), p. 222.

interpretation, our discussion would not be able to differentiate between irony and *misunderstanding*. *That* there is irony (and not merely misunderstanding) is therefore grounded in the experience of the individual subject; but irony can become *what* it is only in society. Which is to say that society and the subject are related, by irony, as signifier (the pointer, the identifier of "what") and signified (the pointed-at, which has no separable qualities of its own, but only adds the "that which" to the act of pointing).

It is true that in this chapter, we have worked with a different account of irony, in terms of the intrusion of the extralinguistic into language, the historical limits of what a speech act *can* do. And this account does not have room for the idea of a subject constituted anywhere except in language itself, which seems to imply that the whatness of irony can be situated in the subject after all, or even that that whatness, as the operation of the extralinguistic, *is* the subject. If "we" means the subject, and if "we" *are* "a conversation," then the conditions of conversation, including irony, cannot be excluded from the subject. But this account is really only the adoption of a different point of view. The crucial consequence, that one cannot be ironic with oneself, or ironic in solitude, still holds, except that now this proposition follows from the quality of irony as the destruction of the whole illusion of solitude, as the subject's elusive but undeniable access to the linguistically impossible, to the one thing that it can never say about itself (or, in a Cartesian sense, even think about itself), except perhaps in the disguise of a "we": namely, that it is constituted nowhere except in language considered as conversation. The argument has simply been turned around; it no longer arrives at the idea of the subject as signified, with respect to the social, but it begins there.

Or let us return to the indistinguishability of irony and misunderstanding on the level of the social or conversational sign. If we begin by agreeing that conversation is founded upon misunderstanding, that the dynamics of conversation is the dynamics of misunderstanding, that the gesture of conversation toward the goal of an understood and verified understanding—like the gesture of science toward a perfect and perfectly adequate theory—is a gesture toward its own death: then it follows that misunderstanding participates centrally in the signifying relation of the social to the subject. In particular, misunderstanding signifies irony, signifies what it can be distinguished from only in the operation of that larger signifying relation. In fact, insofar as the larger relation (social to subject) is presupposed in the signifying of irony by misunderstanding, it can be said that the latter signification (provided it can be summarized and identified as a sign) *signifies* the former.

Nor is this argument merely abstract. For there exists in the domain of the literary a specific device by which the plane of conversation-as-sign is isolated from all subjectivity, from all possibility of a categorical distinction between misunderstanding and irony that would prevent the one from signifying the other. That device is the dramatic stage. In narrative, it is impossible to say anything at all about a character, in either the third or the first person, without opening the character's subjective dimension. But in the theater, when the performance begins, all narrative is ritually excluded, even the essentially narrative text that is being performed, and we are confronted (even in soliloquies) with nothing but conversation. Or at least this statement is true in *semiotic* terms. In "reality," one can argue, a narrative text still operates for the theater audience; the audience do inevitably make inferences about characters' subjectivity. But the sharp distinction, however questionable, between what a narrative text is (a window into subjectivity) and what a theatrical performance is (ritual imposture, people saying things not dictated by their actual subjectivity) still serves to *profile* for us the whole of conversation-as-sign, to make it available to us *as a sign*.

And this point suggests a special significance for the pervasive misunderstanding in eighteenth-century German drama. The interplay of verbal misunderstandings, which is already extremely complex in Lessing—and never fully resolved at the play's end[27]—engenders what might be called an idiom of misunderstanding in Lenz, and reaches in Goethe a pitch at which it becomes possible to read *Torquato Tasso* or *Die natürliche Tochter* on the assumption that no character ever understands anything at all of what the others say. This convention in dramatic language is the high wire on which Heinrich von Kleist then balances; and by the time we reach Georg Büchner's *Woyzeck*, the characters no longer even try to understand one another.

It is in drama, however, as in no other form, that the signifying

[27]See my "Reason, Error, and the Shape of History: Lessing's Nathan and Lessing's God," *LY* 9 (1977), 60–80; "The Idea of the Audience in Lessing's Inexplicit Tragic Dramaturgy," *LY* 11 (1979), 59–68; and "The Generic Constant in Lessing's Development of a Comedy of Institutions and Alienation," *GQ* 56 (1983), 231–42.

tendency of misunderstanding, in the direction of irony, is most clearly marked. For misunderstanding among dramatic characters is available as a perception to the spectator in a theater only to the extent that he or she *understands* the ground of that misunderstanding, and understands it *directly* (from the conversation in which it occurs), not by way of such intermediate terms as the understanding of a narrator's or character's understanding. But the directness of this relation—especially in Lessing, Lenz, and Goethe, where no satisfactory summary of the characters' "real" relations is articulated for us on the stage—entails the recognition that the basis of our spectatorial understanding, the complex of pre-understood factors (prejudice, convention, evidence, etc.) that produces it, is *structurally indistinguishable* from the basis of the misunderstanding that it supposedly understands. Thus our confidence in the validity of our own understanding is undermined, but only by way of precisely the continuing assumption that our understanding is valid—which is not a logical contradiction, but rather an irony, a gap in the fabric of discourse, an interpretive language act whose very impossibility, its subjection to no order, to no rule for development or modification, makes it irrevocable.

And yet, it is not only in the dramatic genres that misunderstanding as such operates as a signifier. Goethe's Werther, in his first letter, derives comfort from the recognition that misunderstanding is a greater source of confusion in the world than malice. But malice is at least a force that can be struggled against, whereas misunderstanding, as a condition even of innocence, points the way toward an ironically complicated subjectivity for which there is no cure—if a cure is what we wish—except suicide.

The Golden Touch

Werther's adventure in subjectivity must not be taken as a metaphor for that text's operation in its discursive and cultural environment. In general, even though the actual operative poetics of eighteenth-century Germany represents a definite abandonment of what is normally meant by "Enlightenment" discourse, still that poetics is also not yet "Romantic," not yet focused on hermeneutic complexities and the problem of subjectivity. It is a poetics, ultimately, of the "communal soul," which is present to it mainly by way of irony, or by way of the subject considered not as a primary entity (however problematic), but as the signified of the social.

What must this poetics give rise to, how shall it be manifest, in poetic *practice*? Herder and Lessing, in their ironic debate, outdo one another in setting what appear to be impossible conditions for poetry. And Hamann does not help matters when he says, in the *Aesthetica in nuce*: "Speak, that I might see Thee!—This wish was fulfilled by Creation, which is an address to the creature by way of the creature" (MiN, 2:198). All nature, in other words, is a single verbal act in which we participate by being as well as by speaking. And if we have managed to garble the original poetry of that act (into "Turbatverse und disiecti membra poetae") by taking too seriously the process of individuation in which it involves us, then our task now is to rediscover and reconstitute it—evidently in our own poetry. But in what *kind* of poetry?

We have looked at Goethe's narratives, which do require the community as a reader and do more or less satisfy the demands of a poetics of the enactment of origins—but only speculatively, only on condition that their idea of the general history of narrative prove adequate. And we have looked at a poem of Hölderlin's in detail, a poem that proves useful as a kind of summary of the poetics of the social sign. In Hölderlin, however, even in "An die Parzen," the language tends to have more the quality of an individual achievement than that of a common idiom. And in later Hölderlin this quality is increasingly marked, the quality of interpretation or summary (or perhaps epitaph) with respect to an inferred basic idiom in which the text now participates not naturally so much as hieratically. But where is the basic poetic idiom *itself*?

When Blackall speaks of "the golden touch," he means Goethe, in the sense that Goethe manages to pull together what exists elsewhere, in his time, in the form of linguistic and poetic theory, into a poetic practice that is so thoroughly integrated with itself that it gives the impression of a natural phenomenon *prior* to the theoretical discourse surrounding it. There are limits to this view. It is true that a number of major figures in the period, including Lavater, Herder, Lenz, and Schiller, who were in direct personal contact with Goethe, tend on occasion to regard him more as a phenomenon than as a person. And it is true that Goethe's poetry is the principal standard by which we recognize a certain poetic idiom in the period. But is this idiom *the* idiom implied by the poetic theory of, say, Lessing and Herder?

To look at Goethe's early poetry in light of this question would require another whole book. But there are a couple of later poems in which the basic Goethean idiom is combined with questions of language and poetics in an interesting way. As a kind of envoi to a collection of occasional poems, the "Inschriften, Denk- und Sendeblätter," the following little poem is added:

> Worte sind der Seele Bild—
> Nicht ein Bild! sie sind ein Schatten!
> Sagen herbe, deuten mild
> Was wir haben, was wir hatten.—
> Was wir hatten wo ist's hin?
> Und was ist's denn was wir haben?
> Nun, wir sprechen! Rasch im Fliehn
> Haschen wir des Lebens Gaben.
>   [WA, 4:71]

[Words are an image of the soul—not an image! they are a shadow! They say harshly, interpret mildly, what we have, what we had.— What we had, where is it gone? And what we have, what is it? Well, we speak anyway! Quickly, in escaping, we snatch life's gifts.]

The sense of the poem as a self-conscious process is so obvious here as almost to be comic. The word "image" is no sooner spoken than it is criticized and retracted; the idea that replaces it, "shadow," is developed by the ideas of "what we have" and "what we had," whereupon these ideas are in turn also questioned; and finally the whole process of questioning is questioned, for we will speak anyway, no matter how questionable our speaking is. Thus, to stretch a point, there is a relation here to the dialectical structure of Hölderlin's "An die Parzen." Or is this really stretching a point?

The first two lines of the poem illustrate their own content. Words are intended, when we speak them, as an image of our soul, of what we wish to express; but by uttering the words and contemplating its own reflection in them, the soul develops beyond its initial state, so that the words are no longer a true image. They have become a "shadow," a shade, a ghost of something that is now dead, or a shadow in the sense of a reproduction (like a profile in silhouette) that lacks one dimension of its original, as words lack the dimension of development by which the soul escapes them, or a shadow in the sense of something that follows along behind. "What we have," in the very process of speaking, is superseded, becomes "what we had"; and this idea is then developed as a psychological perception in lines 3–4—provided we may associate the first verb in line 3 with the first object-clause in line 4, and the second verb with the second object. "Harshly" and "mildly" express, first of all, a distinction in types of judgment; we judge harshly of what we possess, whereas we place a mild interpretation on what we have lost. Of "what we had" the poet asks nostalgically, "where is it gone?" but of "what we have" he asks, "what is it?" with the suggestion of, "what use is it?"

This perception, however, does not exhaust the self-mirroring complexity of the opening lines; nor does the distinction between attitudes of judgment exhaust the suggestions of the adverbs "herbe" and "mild." "Herb," in normal usage, refers primarily to a harsh or acid sensation of taste; and although German "mild," as a sense adjective, is usually tactile, referring especially to air temperature, still, when directly contrasted with "herb" (which is never tactile), it can also suggest a pleasurable taste in the mouth. Moreover, "herb" is often used figuratively in connection with the idea of disappointment. Thus the poem suggests that when we "say" directly ("sagen") what we now possess, the words, in our mouth as we speak them, have the sharp taste of disappointment—for by speaking them we supersede or lose what they refer to—whereas the words by which we "interpret" ("deuten") what is irretrievably past have a pleasing taste, for such interpreting is a repossession of something that, in its new intellectualized form, cannot be lost again. We think of the *Faust* "Zueignung": "Was ich besitze seh' ich wie im Weiten, / Und was verschwand wird mir zu Wirklichkeiten" (What I possess I see as if in the distance, and things that have vanished become realities for me).

But there is yet a third suggestion in the opposition between "herbe" and "mild." "Herbe Worte" are harsh words and "milde Worte" are mild or conciliatory words, from the point of view of the person addressed. Harsh words tend to separate individuals; mild words tend to join or reconcile them. The words that "say" what we now possess are thus harsh in the sense that they set us off from others, define and defend our private domain as individuals, whereas words that "interpret" what we have lost are conciliatory, for by appealing to a community between speaker and hearer in the experience of transitoriness, they bring us together (since interpretation generalizes) as sharers in loss. Thus the distinction between "herbe" and "mild" has meaning in each of the three relations that make up the act of speech: the relation to the speaker (taste in the mouth), to the object spoken of (type of judgment), and to the person addressed (defensive or conciliatory).

But this point leaves us with a set of paradoxes. With relation to the speaker and the object, the "harsh" aspect of language suggests disintegration of the self—our self-lacerating scorn of "what we have"—whereas with relation to the person addressed, it asserts and defends the self. And the "mild" aspect of language, which, with relation to speaker and object, reintegrates or stabilizes the self, also aims beyond the self, at conciliation, with relation to the person addressed. It appears that the defense of the self is a process of self-loss, whereas a willingness to relax the self's limits enables us to reintegrate the self.

> Man knows himself only to the extent that he knows the world, which he perceives only in himself, and in which he must perceive himself. Every new object, well examined, unlocks a new organ in ourselves.
>
> Most profitable to us, however, are our fellow humans, who have the advantage of comparing us with the world from their point of view and thereby achieving a more exact knowledge of us than we are capable of.
>
> Therefore, in my mature years, I have paid great attention to the matter of how well others might know me, in order that in them and by them, as by means of mirrors, I might achieve greater clarity concerning myself and my inward being. [WA, pt. 2, 11:59–60]

Only by relinquishing its exclusive claim to self-possession and self-knowledge can the self ever actually achieve possession or knowledge of itself.

This paradox helps explain, in the poem, the word "wir" (we). If communication is as difficult as it appears, if the soul's transmitted image in words is falsified by the very act of speaking, if "what we have" is either lost before we can lay hold of it verbally or else becomes a wedge between self-protecting individuals, then how can the community of experience implied by the word "we" be assumed? In order to say "we," we must be at once both separated (plural) and together (a unit); in order to justify the poetically universal "we" of this poem, which subsumes an introspective "I" on the part of each reader (thus meaning the subject, as in Hölderlin), our separateness must somehow be an integral part of our togetherness, and vice versa. And a fulfillment of these conditions is adumbrated in the idea that the self achieves true integration only by seeking beyond its own limits.

In itself, however, this idea is only speculative. If, in our "mature years," we adopt the attitude that Goethe prides himself on in the passage quoted, then presumably the "we" of the poem will make perfect sense to us. And the prose passage, taken by itself, makes it appear that the adoption of such an attitude is entirely natural. But the dialectical development of the poem suggests exactly the opposite, that the achievement of a stable point of view from which to utter the word "we" is not only difficult but impossible. From the outset, the speaker attempts to establish contact with us, in words as an image of the soul. But in making this attempt, he sees he is wrong. Words are not transmitters of a content provided by the soul; they have a taste of their own, harsh or mild, that is produced by the Protean changeableness of the soul that says them. At least the general shape of our experience, however, the different taste of words in our mouth as time passes, ought to be something we have in common and can communicate about; hence the appeal to the reader, the first "we," in line 4. But in order for us to communicate on this basis, the shape of our experience, the difference between "what we have" and "what we had," must be relatively constant; and the next two lines recognize that this is not the case. What we had is simply not there ("where is it gone?"), except insofar as in some sense we still have it; and if what we have is in the process of passing, then "what is it?" how can it be differentiated from "what we had"? We are reminded of Werther: "Can you say, *That is*, when everything passes?" Or of Faust: "Und was du nie verlierst das mußt du stets beweinen" (And what you never lose you must mourn constantly). What we have, in our very having of it, has become what we had; what we had, to the extent that we know of it at all, is something we have. The interchangeability of the concepts is reflected in the chiasm of their appearance in lines 4–6. The temporal structure by which the "we," in communicating it, must validate itself, is thus itself subject to a kind of dialectical time that has always already disintegrated it. Trying to communicate is like trying to throw a ball of water (cf. "Lied und Gebilde," in WA, 6:22).

Thus the poem faces us with an insoluble problem, a problem of linguistic limits, of irony, like the problem of the necessary but impossible expression of human godlikeness in Hölderlin. The pattern of paradoxes makes clear what is required of us in order to justify our "we," whereas the dialectical structure makes clear that we cannot satisfy these requirements by way of our sense of our own being. And yet, it is evident that the problem *has* a solution, for "we are speaking anyway"; even as readers we are engaged in a process of verbal communication that is somehow not nonsense. The only way to resolve this contradiction is to turn the problem inside out. The subject must be recognized as nothing but the signified of the social. The process of speaking must be the prior reality (simply, "Nun, wir sprechen!"), whereas the separated "souls" that speak, and their togetherness in the speakable experience of time, the poles of the paradox that creates the word "we," are in truth only secondary phenomena by which language (conversation, considered as a sign) realizes itself. The "we" is not derivable from our sense of individual being; in truth it is our sense of individual being that is derived, by way of the "we," from the prior reality of our speaking. (In a precise statement of this idea, the concepts of "priority" and "truth" would have to be relativized semiotically. For all we know, the subject might have substantial existence. But our *access* to it depends on the sign-system of language and the signifying force of the social, the word "we."[28])

In any case, "life's gifts"—now we understand why Goethe places this poem at the end of a collection of occasional verse—are *occasions for speaking*, which means, as far as "we" are concerned, either individually or collectively, occasions for renewing our relation to existence. "Quickly, in escaping," we snatch these occasions; and it is

---

[28]The problems of terminology become unnecessarily burdensome here if we insist on complete precision. Therefore, I will not attempt to eliminate all slippage or contamination between the ideas of essential priority (the distinction between a prior and a derived or secondary "reality") and semiotic priority, which is the priority of signifier to signified. (Signification, where the signified is secondary in the sense of being *accessible* only by way of the signifier, must not be confused with *reference*, where the referent is prior and the sign added to represent it.) In fact, the contamination of terminologies makes an important point here. The idea of the subject as the signified of the social includes the idea that what we take to be the structure of reality is actually a semiotic structure—or at the very least *becomes* such to the extent that our thinking relation to it entangles itself inevitably in the question of modes of accessibility. But this proposition (that real structure is "really" semiotic structure), no matter how we state it, always in a sense contradicts itself by becoming a proposition *about reality*—which we can reduce to a semiotic proposition only on the basis of yet another proposition about reality. The terminological blurring of boundaries can be thought of as a constant acknowledgment of this difficulty.

never entirely clear in life, as it is not clear in Goethe's syntax, whether it is the occasion that tends to escape us (while we, like Werther, confuse ourselves with the idea of elemental subjectivity) or whether it is we who, by speaking, supersede and so escape the occasion. But in the midst of this unmitigated flux, the first three syllables of the poem remain valid: "Worte sind," words *are*.

Thus it is possible to interpret this little poem in terms of a theory of social language similar to the one implied in Hölderlin's "An die Parzen." And this interpretation is supported strongly by the idea of language set forth in Goethe's scientific works. The important difference from Hölderlin, again, is that in "Worte sind . . ." we have the sense of an established and at least potentially shared poetic *idiom*, an idiom that reflects and realizes the poetics of such thinkers as Lessing and Herder. The idea of the social as a sign for the subject is not infused with the power of incantation, as in "Friedensfeier," but arises with deceptive ease as the simple psychological consequence of colloquial speaking in a language that at least presents itself as the kind of language practically anyone might use.

Poetic and Scientific Language: We and Objects

In Chapter 1, we had occasion to discuss Goethe's view of science and the social. Let us reopen that discussion and look at the texts in more detail. In the foreword to *Zur Farbenlehre* we read of

> the extremely curious requirement . . . that we should present experiences without any theoretical connection, and leave it to the reader or pupil to form for himself, in his own way, some conviction. For the mere glimpsing of a thing cannot profit us. Every viewing leads to an observing, every observing to a contemplating, every contemplating becomes an associating, and thus one can say that we already find ourselves theorizing with every attentive glance into the world. To intend and accomplish this theorizing, however, with awareness, with self-knowledge, with freedom, and, to use a daring expression, with irony: such agility is needed if the abstraction we fear is to be rendered harmless, and if the inductive results we hope for are to be endowed with true vitality and usefulness. [WA, pt. 2, 1:xii]

If it were not for the word "irony," we could interpret this passage to mean that the scientist, by being aware of the influence of theory on our perception of facts, must remain in control of theory, always in a position to reassess its appropriateness, never an unwitting slave. But the idea of irony has a necessary *social* dimension. What Goethe is concerned with here—as is clear from the rest of the foreword as well, as soon as we think of it in these terms—is not merely how we should talk about natural phenomena, but how we should talk *to each other* about natural phenomena.

The word "irony" presupposes a social situation. And if we are talking about a language that is focused on its *content*, like scientific language, then the social situation in question must be characterized by the assumption that the content of our utterance is already known to our hearers. (Thus scientific language becomes *imitative*, a kind of painting, in more or less the sense in which Hamann suggests that philosophical language is imitative.) The scientist's task is not to *transmit* an accurate idea of phenomena, but rather to foster by irony a conversational (if need be, polemical) state of affairs in which our common pre-knowing is brought to the fore. We think of the poet's closing words to his companion in "Metamorphose der Thiere":

> Freue dich, höchstes Geschöpf der Natur, du fühlest dich fähig
> Ihr den höchsten Gedanken, zu dem sie schaffend sich aufschwang,
> Nachzudenken. Hier stehe nun still und wende die Blicke
> Rückwärts, prüfe, vergleiche, und nimm vom Munde der Muse,
> Daß du schauest, nicht schwärmst, die liebliche, volle Gewißheit.
>   [WA, 3:91]
> [Rejoice, highest creature of nature; you feel yourself able to rethink
> the highest thought she achieved in creating. Stand quietly here and
> turn your eyes back, experiment, compare, and receive from the lips
> of the Muse—that you are seeing, not dreaming—the delight of full
> certainty.]

The scientist does not teach us what we see or how to see, but reminds us *that* we can see, with a seeing whose validity is guaranteed by our *belonging* to nature, which is the object seen. The method of science is ironic; it speaks as if describing and explaining, whereas in reality its aim is achieved somehow in spite of this theoretical discourse. The speaking of science is always two speakings at once, the second of which, in "Metamorphose der Thiere," is ascribed to "the Muse." Can we associate this second, concealed speaking with the speaking of a "we," in the sense of the poem "Worte sind . . .," rather than the speaking of an "I"?

Or to begin with another question: how can we be convinced that we see truly, if, as Goethe insists, a theoretical element intervenes between ourselves and phenomena every time we open our eyes? The "Schlußbetrachtung über Sprache und Terminologie," in the *Farbenlehre*, opens: "We cannot remind ourselves too often that a language is actually only symbolic, only figurative, and never expresses objects immediately, but only as reflections" (WA, pt. 2, 1:302). We then hear of various types of verbal or quasi-verbal "formulae" that science uses, and of their faults, whereupon Goethe continues: "It would be most desirable, however, if the language by which we designate details in a general area were taken from that area itself, if the simplest phenomenon were treated as a basic formula, and the more complex phenomena were derived and developed from it" (1:304–5). This seems a contradiction. Language can never "express objects immediately," and yet science ought to aim for a verbal formula that not only expresses but *is* "the simplest phenomenon."

The conflict here is resolvable by the distinction between objects ("Gegenstände") and phenomena ("Erscheinungen"). Goethe suggests that we must incorporate into our language an experience of the world *as phenomena* (as a process of appearing), not as objects, which is in keeping with what he describes as his concrete or natural way of understanding Kantian philosophy (WA, pt. 2, 11:47–53). We live in a world of phenomena that are inevitably codetermined by our manner of perceiving them; the attempt to pass beyond phenomena, to the strict object or thing-in-itself, leads to mere confusion, to an infinite chain of theories criticizing theories, to the building, as it were, of a fortress so complicated that it is uninhabitable (1:xiii–xiv). What Goethe has against Newton's theory of light is mainly that it pretends to be more than imitative with respect to our perception of light and darkness as phenomena.

But phenomena, by the very nature of the process of appearing, appear to us *in the form* of objects, *as if* they were objects—"Gegenstände," taking a stand somehow over against "us"—which objectification is intensified in a discourse of image ("Bild") that cannot even maintain neatly the division between "what we have" and "what we had" (what is or is not actually in the process of appearing). Therefore, in order to imitate *phenomena*—or in order to *be* "the simplest phenomenon"—scientific discourse must include in the very process of imitation a radical critique of its own imitativeness.

(We are reminded of Lessing and the illusion of experience, or of Hamann's pushing the idea of imitation in discourse beyond the possibility of a simple binary relation.) A critical theory of theorizing, for example a Kantian theory, can do no more than persuade us that the theoretical shape of our discourse is logically inevitable. What we require is a discourse that actually rejoins the phenomenal by dismantling its own unavoidable pretense to be more than the phenomenon.

It is important therefore that at the end of the last passage quoted, Goethe is leading up to the idea of "polarity" (WA, pt. 2, 1:305–6)— his own candidate for "simplest phenomenon" and "basic formula"— and that (in a manuscript note) the first two examples of polarity that occur to him are "We and objects, light and darkness" (11:164). Neither in the note nor in the *Farbenlehre* is there any attempt to establish a logical connection between these two polarities. But the suggestion is clear nonetheless, and exposes what we may call Goethe's scientific credo: that the true shape of experience—"we and objects," as the dialectical or interactive polarity that can be regarded as *producing* phenomena—is revealed to us by analogy *in the shape of phenomena themselves* (e.g., "light and darkness"), provided we take a simple enough view of it. This belief, that the shape of phenomena reveals allegorically (not "symbolically," in Goethe's usage) the shape of the process of their emergence, implies the possibility of scientific irony, of communication concerning the non-difference in kind between even the "highest thoughts" of nature and our own thoughts. By embarking on an explanation of phenomena (thus *setting into operation* the polarity "we and objects"—"we" as the element of discourse, "objects" as what phenomena inevitably become in the imitative operation of discourse), and by theorizing on the simplest available phenomena (which reveal in themselves an *analogous* polarity), the author holds up a mirror to our (author's and reader's) actual relation with nature, that relation which is the happening of the phenomenal.

"We and objects" is the basic polarity, not "I and objects" as for Fichte. It is *we* who discover that we and nature "think" in the same way; if *I* discover this, there is no way for me to distinguish my discovery from mere fantasy. It is crucial to the operation of scientific discourse that we enter that discourse as a dialogic collective, not as separate individuals. And curiously enough, it is precisely the apparent *disadvantage* of our discourse—that its theorizing presents phenomena as if they were objects—that serves us well here. For whereas the pure phenomenon is correlated only to the individual subject (which is its point of emergence), objects are by definition there in the same way for any and all subjects, subjects in the plural. It does not matter whether we are *actually* in any sort of contact with *actual* objects. What matters is that the theorizing presentation of phenomena as objects *presents us to ourselves* as a "we," which opens the polarity of we-and-objects that we then see represented allegorically in the shape of even the objectified phenomenon, whereupon this resonance or simultaneity of our seeing and our being now in turn *symbolizes* (as it were, "from the lips of the Muse") our true and valid seeing, the seeing that is constituted by our belonging to what is seen. Thus we arive at the pure phenomenon after all—or rather, we discover it (with its locus, the subject) *in* our discourse, as a symbol—but only by way of the signifying function of the "we." Again, we have access to the subject only as the signified of the social.[29]

But not all scientific discourse operates in this manner. The discourse of the Newtonians, for example, denies its imitativeness with respect to phenomena, thus denies itself access to its own inevitable theoretical distortion of phenomena, and so blocks its own symbolic path back to the true phenomenon, to nature. And as part of the same (in Goethe's view) anti-scientific move, the Newtonians' insistence on exclusive validity for their theory cuts off the process of conversation or debate, the unresolved competition of theories, by which the crucial "we" is maintained in discourse. The Newtonians fail to observe the categorical imperative of science, "Geselle dich zur kleinsten Schar" (Join yourself to the smallest company), which prevents discourse from lurching into the *merely* theoretical and so preserves precisely its theoretical depth, a depth that is similar to the depth revealed in an aesthetic discourse of imitation when it is impregnated with the poetics of enactment of origins.

The Goethean Scheme

Terminology is unavoidably a problem in the treatment of a positively anti-systematic poetics, a poetics beyond theory, like that of the German eighteenth century. In the present chapter, we have

[29]Germs of this thought can already be found in the relatively early essay, "Der Versuch als Vermittler von Object und Subject," especially in Goethe's emphasis there upon science as a community endeavor, upon the importance of "das Interesse mehrerer auf Einen Punct gerichtet" and of "Mittheilung, Beihülfe, Erinnerung und Widerspruch" (WA, pt. 2, 11:25–26).

had to replace the vague idea of the individual with the idea of the subject as signified of the social, which idea is meant to embrace all subjective effects (conscious or not) in experience considered as the relation of subject and object. This all-inclusive subject is the subject of irony, within which meanings can be operative yet perfectly concealed, in a manner analogous to the manner in which concealed meaning operates in conversation. There is no contradiction here with the argument on the impossibility of irony in solitude. For it is understood, in the proto-Kantian critique of experience, that the entirety of subjective effects *cannot be isolated*, that the subject of irony therefore cannot accommodate the attribute of solitude, cannot be "with itself" in the first place. The subject in this sense is not manifest in experience, and is not known *except* as the signified of the social. If we attribute existence to it, then we do so only as a logical consequence of the experience of radical irony. This is a paradox, but not a contradiction. Precisely our experience of alienation in the element of the social permits the attribution of existence to a subject for which such an experience is unthinkable.

(It is important, incidentally, that its nonsupport of the attribute of solitude or isolation—hence of definition—also implies that the subject of irony may not be regarded as the *locus* of irony, as that incursion of the extralinguistic into language from which irony receives its leverage in meaning. The question of the locus of irony remains to be dealt with.)

It will help if we now understand the *ego* as that component or aspect or function of the subject, that subjective region, where the possibility of solitude *arises*—which accords well enough with the Freudian ego's resistance to analysis.[30] We might then use the corresponding Latin pronoun "nos" to refer to what has been called above "the 'we,'" the element of the social or of conversation. For the nos, in this sense, is related to the communal—as the component or aspect or function or region where the possibility of conversation and especially misunderstanding arises—in a manner approximately parallel to the relation of the ego to the subject of irony. In fact, it is not clear that the concept of the communal soul and that of the subject of irony can be distinguished from one another except by way of the images of the nos and the ego.

[30]See Freud, 16:350, 19:17. And consider the curious passage, in *The Ego and the Id*, on the id's ability to be "inherited," by contrast with the personal singularity (potential solitude) of the ego (Freud, 19:38).

The nos and the ego, however, pose a problem in priority. For the nos, in which misunderstanding must be possible, *presupposes* the ego as the possibility of isolation, separation from others. But if the ego is thus prior to the nos, then it appears that the nos must have come into being *through* verbal communication among egos. And although it may be true that the scientific content of language is known to every individual before speaking, still irony, the scientific way of talking about this shared knowledge, cannot arise until it is known *that* our knowledge is shared. (The argument of the preceding section does not work without this assumption.) The nos, therefore, if it were an accumulation of egos, would require at some point a verbal communication *without* irony, which means either a direct self-expression of the ego or a complete verbal grasp of unchanging "objects," both of which possibilities Goethe denies. "By words we express fully neither objects nor ourselves" (WA, pt. 2, 11:167), he says under the heading of "Symbolik." It follows that the nos is in some sense prior to the ego, not derived from it by multiplication.

The notion of "Steigerung" (intensification, or heightening) is Goethe's way around conceptual difficulties of this sort. Further on in the note on "Symbolik," we read: "By way of language there is born as it were a new world, which consists of necessary and accidental components." It emerges in the sequel that by "necessary" and "accidental" Goethe means here something close to "natural" and "arbitrary," as these terms are applied to the signs of language; types of money are used as a metaphor, ranging from gold (the sign of value that possesses value, thus participates, as a natural sign, in the qualities of the referent) to paper money (as an arbitrary sign of value). There is not a great deal to go on in this manuscript note; but if we take into account the first sentence, that words express "neither objects nor ourselves," then it is clear that the "new world" of language lies *between* objects and the nos and combines elements of both— natural signs being referable to objects, arbitrary signs to the nos. That is, the world of language *is* the world of phenomena, of interactivity between arbitrary human thought and the strict object. Indeed, without this identification it is hard to see how it can occur to Goethe to speak of taking the "simplest phenomenon" *as* a "basic formula," or how language could hope to keep alive the knowledge that we see truly. We recall the thrill of approval Goethe felt (WA, pt. 2, 11:58) when his intellectual procedure was characterized by J. C. A. Heinroth, in 1822, as "gegenständliches Denken" (object-bound thinking, or thinking in objects), a thinking of which the medium, language, dissociates itself minimally from the material. In any case, it is *the natural identity of words and phenomena* (as two guises of the interaction between mind and objects) that is obscured by theory but still, in its persistence as the content of irony, makes science possible.

The question of priority between language and its users or content, then, is in a sense answered. If language is the same as the phenomenal world, it clearly cannot be derived from either the nos or objects, for its existence would then presuppose our *direct* knowledge of objects as an original impetus. The nos and objects, rather, must be regarded as the two sides of the necessary *polarity* by which language "enters into appearance" (WA, pt. 2, 11:166); and the ego then arises from (or within) the nos by "Steigerung." The relation of these ideas to Goethe's thought in general can perhaps be made clear by a diagram.

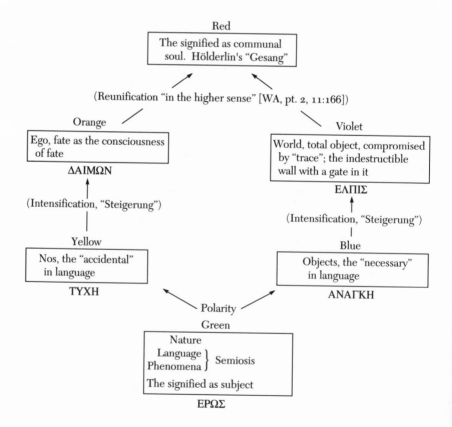

This diagram, which I call "the Goethean scheme," in a sense tends to stabilize Goethe's thought, but only by bringing to light its persistent instabilities and problems. The basic polarity, first of all, is *itself* both "necessary" (required by the very idea of phenomenon or signification) and "accidental" (as a deviation, a *clinamen*, with respect to its own primordial wholeness). That is, the fundamental polarity, "we and objects," of which phenomena such as "light and darkness" are an allegory, cannot be considered an absolute origin, but is itself always the allegory of an analogous prior polarity (of the necessary and the accidental). And correspondingly, although the diagram suggests relations of essential or ontological priority, this suggestion is thwarted by the semiotic component of the thought, the recognition that the apparent ontological origin, considered as the subject of irony, is accessible *only* as the signified of the nos. As long as we consider this signification from without, as a kind of reference, the signified retains its priority over the signifier, and the signifying force of the nos is regarded as our access to the primordial. But then, at the level of the supposedly primordial, we encounter not a transcendental signified, but rather—as the content of radical irony—precisely semiosis, the polarity-in-identity of signifier and signified (language and phenomena). Thus we may not regard the signification of the nos as a kind of reference after all, for we are trapped *within* the semiotic process, where priority (however tenuous) belongs to the signifier. Whereupon the whole idea of the primordial disintegrates.

I have developed this structure, moreover, by adding to it the Greek stanza-headings of the poem "Urworte. Orphisch," which represent the general shape of conscious experience for the individual, moving counterclockwise from "Ego." Thus matters are complicated further. For the shape of experience, unfolding from the experience of immutable self or "daimon," is an intimation of the shape of existence as a whole, unfolding from a polarity (self and world) grounded in the subject of irony. But precisely to the extent that this intimation is valid—as represented by the fitting of the poem into the scheme—the shape of experience and the shape of existence *fail* to coincide, either in point of origin or in the structure of their unfolding. This inherent confusedness in the ego's recognition of itself as origin—which can become irony in speaking, or the empirical self as *imitatio Christi* in Hölderlin—is also played with in Goethe's "Xenien," 371–84 (WA, 5/1:259–61).

Nor is it eccentric on my part to associate "daimon" with "ego" (rather than "subject"). The "demonic" in Goethe is not a mysterious natural or metaphysical force separate from the sphere of consciousness but rather is regulated, if not constituted, by conscious ego-structures.[31] And the association of Eros with the ground of polarity, or with nature or the phenomenal world, is easy enough via Aristophanes' idea of love, in the *Symposium*, as an undoing of polarities, or via the cosmogonic Eros in Hesiod, Parmenides, and Empedocles, all of whom show something of Orphic belief, or via Goethe's own utterances: "Nature's crown is love. Only through love does one come close to her" (WA, pt. 2, 11:8). And if there is some question about quoting a text like "Urworte. Orphisch" in a context that attributes significance to such "accidents" of language as the fact that "moi" and "toi" are similar whereas "ich" and "du" are not (11:169), then perhaps it is worth noting that the German word "Dämon," if we unpack the "e" in the umlaut, is an anagram of "Monade." And is it an accident, or what kind of "accident" is it, that the Roman transliteration of the fifth stanza-heading in the poem, ELPIS, is an anagram of the German word "Spiel"?[32]

Goethe and the Temple of Poetry

We have looked at the poem beginning "Words are"; let us now look at the poem beginning, "Poems are."

[31]See the argument in my *Modern Drama and German Classicism*, pp. 127–34, which distinguishes between "daimon" and "the demonic," the latter being a conscious self-multiplication of the former. But can "daimon" happen *without* that multiplication? What is the rest of the "Urworte" poem otherwise?

[32]I have made the diagram, but I do not claim to understand it fully. It appears, for example, that the ego (in its derived and emphatic singularity) signifies the communal in much the same way that the nos (being plural) signifies the subject. And the ego is coordinated dialectically (by polarity) to the total object (singular) in a manner parallel to the relation of the nos and objects (plural)—since the object is never totalized, never "world," from the point of view of the nos, but is always reconstituted in conversation. In any case, "the indestructible wall with a gate in it" (the intractable, totalized object and the trace of its differential genesis) is the actual image used in the fifth stanza of "Urworte." On the whole idea of thinking in diagrams, and on the importance of this idea *in* linguistic thought of especially the German eighteenth century—which I take as support for my procedure—see Ulrich Gaier, *Herders Sprachphilosophie und Erkenntniskritik* (Stuttgart-Bad Cannstatt, 1988), pp. 57–61, 157–65, and passim, on "Hieroglyphe" and "Schöpfungshieroglyphe." Gaier's thought supplements my argument on Goethe and ties it back more firmly to the discussion of Herder. Gaier himself, in fact, expands his thought to include Goethe in a talk "Dialektik der Vorstellungsarten als Prinzip in Goethes 'Faust,'" given at the conference *Interpreting Goethe's "Faust" Today*, University of California, Santa Barbara, August 1992. The "dialectic of representational modes" spoken of by Gaier is composed not of quasi-historical relations so much as of hieroglyphic or diagrammatic relations.

Gedichte sind gemahlte Fensterscheiben!
Sieht man vom Markt in die Kirche hinein
Da ist alles dunkel und düster;
Und so sieht's auch der Herr Philister:
Der mag denn wohl verdrießlich sein
Und lebenslang verdrießlich bleiben.

Kommt aber nur einmal herein!
Begrüßt die heilige Capelle;
Da ist's auf einmal farbig helle,
Geschicht' und Zierrath glänzt in Schnelle,
Bedeutend wirkt ein edler Schein;
Dieß wird euch Kindern Gottes taugen,
Erbaut euch und ergetzt die Augen!

[WA, 3:171]

[Poems are stained-glass windows. If you look into the church from the market, everything is dark and gloomy there; and thus the Philistine sees it. He may as well be bad tempered and remain bad tempered his whole life. But you, enter it now! Greet the sacred chapel; suddenly all is colorful and bright, story and ornament gleam immediately, a noble glow (or illusion) has the effect of significance. This will have value for you children of God, edify yourselves and delight your eyes!]

The image of the market and the verb "taugen" (be of use, be worth something) suggest, as a focus, the question of the *value* or *use* of poetry.

The meaning of the poem's main metaphor is obvious. If we inquire about poetry from an external perspective, if we expect from the poet an attempt to convince us objectively of the value of the endeavor, we will be disappointed. From such a perspective, poetry has no value; its value becomes apparent only from inside the sacred chapel, to those who already believe in it. The idea of children of God ("Gottes Kinder" in Luther's Bible, as in the poem) is a reference to Paul: "For ye are all the children of God by faith in Christ Jesus. For as many of you as have been baptized into Christ have put on Christ. There is neither Jew nor Greek, there is neither bond nor free, there is neither male nor female: for ye are all one in Christ Jesus" (Gal. 3:26–28). Only through something analogous to an unconditional Pauline faith, only through a direct relation of the soul to its divine source, not by any sort of persuasion, can the value of poetry be grasped. Paul's words themselves, transplanted by the allusion into the context of our argument, manage to suggest the concepts of nos and communal soul, as well as an understanding of the subject-ego relation as *imitatio Christi*. But these ideas are kept beneath the surface in the poem.

For the poem is addressed to believers, believers who may have strayed but still at least profess belief, not heathens, not utter Philistines. The poem opens with a metaphor in the form of unqualified predication: poems *are* stained-glass windows. The Philistine might be persuaded that in some respects poems are *like* stained-glass windows; but this poem is not aimed at persuading Philistines. No attempt is made to show a connection between the instructive and decorative aspects of poetry, between "story" and "ornament," or to meet the obvious Philistine objection that giving the impression ("wirken") of significance is not the same as actually having significance. The poem sets out as if to present a unified intimation of what poetry is; but it ends merely by opening, and leaving open, all the difficult questions.

Like Hölderlin's "An die Parzen," however, Goethe's poem makes its own failure significant, its failure to overcome the need for that *anticipatory* understanding of itself which the image of stained-glass windows locates in the nos, not the ego, in our sharing with others an objectively available point of view (an actual place, inside the chapel). And if we agree that the difference of nos and ego operates here, then our reading of Goethe's science becomes applicable, especially the idea that the shape and nature of our existence, as a process, are known to us allegorically in the shape of phenomena, that language, the means by which we come to grips with the phenomenal world, is in origin identical with that world. In our verbal dealing with "superficial situations or relationships," the content of an utterance is apparently transmitted from ego to ego; but poems, especially the poem we are considering, are constructed to show that we must already possess the content of the utterance, its "spirit" (Rom. 8:14–16), in order to receive it, indeed that *all* language, insofar as it touches "deeper relations" or "the inner relations of nature," is "poetic" in this sense (WA, pt. 2, 11:167). We still talk from ego to ego, but with an irony by which the very idea of the ego is transcended; "well, we speak anyway!" but only by knowing that our speaking never says or does what it pretends to.

Thus the content of the poem "Gedichte sind . . ." may be said to arise from its lack of content. In telling us what "poems are," the speaker does not go beyond what a "Philistine" could (if disapprovingly) agree with. He offers no defense against the Philistine's objection that poetry's decorativeness is useless, its significance mere illusion. But precisely this lack—considered as an act of restraint, a poetic "veiling" of truth, which the truth itself requires (WA, 1:7)—is what enables the poem to operate as a poem, by leaving its content to be "supplied" in reading, thus compelling us (as nos) to treat its language as the articulation of a knowledge we already possess. By failing to give an adequate account of itself as poetry, Goethe's poem becomes poetry; by lacking the content we seek in it, it receives its content via the process of reading, its content being not *what* we supply when we read, but rather *our ability and inclination*, as such, to supply a meaning, hence our understanding of the existence of shared knowledge that precedes any particular utterance, our participation in the nos.

Once we have arrived at this stage in our understanding, however—and *only* by understanding the poem in this way—we discover that it has a content after all. Like all poems, it is in reality nothing but "decoration," unsupported by any useful statement. But if we accept it anyway, and accept its pretense of significance, then precisely this acceptance *gives* it significance, by involving our acknowledgment of a truth about language by which we are "edified." Thus the disconnection between the decorative and the edifying disappears. The source of our edification may even reasonably be spoken of as a "story" or "history" ("Geschichte"); for the truth we acknowledge has a strong genetic or developmental component, the idea that language is not a tool of the ego but rather its matrix, a prior world in which the ego first originates. The truth is that "story" of which the first sentence gives Faust so much trouble: "In the beginning was the word." Again, the Philistine in the marketplace and the believer in the chapel both see the same thing, the light of day, except that the believer has positioned himself so as to see it through an artistic filter. But it is this positioning alone by which the believer, while still using language as money, like the Philistine, makes of it a money that means not only its face value, but also the symbolic processes through which it receives its value (WA, pt. 2, 11:167–68).

Let us go further into the relation of the poem to the *Farbenlehre*, where we read: "Colors are doings of the light, doings and sufferings.

In this sense we can expect them to reveal something about light. Colors and light stand in a very exact relation to each other, but we must think of them both as belonging to nature as a whole: for it is nature as a whole that tends to reveal itself through them, in a particular way, to the sense of the eye. . . . Color is nature, or natural laws as a totality, with respect to the sense of the eye" (WA, pt. 2, 1:ix–x, xxxii). Color is therefore to the eye what language is to the understanding: it *is* the phenomenal world. Like color, language is ordinarily thought of as only one component of our surroundings. But if we pay attention to language, to what it contains *as* language (rather than to the apparent content of utterances, their face value), we discover that, like color, it *is* nature (as semiosis).

Still, how shall we bring it about that language makes this revelation? In real life, language is never detached from particular utterances, any more than color is ever detached from the physiological or physical or chemical process by which it becomes manifest. And theory, the detaching of the general from the particular, is even more misleading in the case of language, since it proceeds, by way of the theorizing ego, directly away from the original phenomenality of language. What is required is what Goethe calls "higher empeiria" (WA, pt. 2, 11:221), or "experience of a *higher type*" (11:33), experiences that we achieve by setting up series of related experimental situations, from which the sought-for empirical principles gradually emerge of their own accord.

In the *Farbenlehre* no special experimental use is suggested for stained-glass windows. But Goethe does make the point a number of times that colors are more colorful, more expressive of their "nature," more fully themselves, when they are seen in a strong light passing through them from behind (e.g., WA, pt. 2, 1:232–33), which is how the colors in stained glass are seen. And this idea, that it is color *as color* that fills our perception in the "sacred chapel," not color merely as the attribute of objects, is also suggested by what must otherwise appear a rather awkward line in the poem: "Geschicht' und Zierrath glänzt in Schnelle." If the words "in Schnelle" mean "all at once" or "suddenly," then they are redundant, because of the "auf einmal" in the preceding line. But if we consider the intense colorfulness of color in stained glass, the "in Schnelle" makes sense. The figures in the windows represent a "story"; the task of the colors is to manifest the story visually. But a story takes time to comprehend, whereas the specially intense colors of stained glass against sunlight take effect instantly, "in Schnelle"; the colors as colors thus overpower their own historical content in the contest for our attention. We have contrived for ourselves a situation in which, by the *contrast* (the semiotic difference) between color itself and what it is the color of, we approach the experience of color in its identity with nature—which is concealed in the marketplace. It is possible that "Zierrath" (ornament) is here a pun on Greek κόσμος (ornament, or *world*).

This experience, taken literally, is not a valid scientific experiment; but it does explain the metaphorical sense in which "poems are stained-glass windows." A poem is an utterance whose meaning (in the sense of "story," or allegorical meaning) is overpowered by the symbolic quality of language as language. We have discussed various ways in which this is accomplished in both Hölderlin and Goethe. The narrative meaning of the utterance is hedged about with ambiguity and metaphorical suggestiveness in such a way that its very existence becomes questionable and language appears a "game"; the utterance maneuvers us into an ironic position with respect to it (inside the "chapel"), from which the question of what it *is* radiates through the question of what it *says*. Poems are experimental verbal situations contrived, we might say, to make language as intensely "languageful" as possible. In our reading of poems we develop, with respect to language, a "higher empeiria" by which the whole semiotic order of nature—including, indispensably, our own rôle as perceivers—becomes available to us.

Two concluding remarks are necessary. First, this reading of "Gedichte sind . . ." makes clear that the relation between symbol and allegory, for Goethe, is not simply one of preference for the former, but a *dialectical* relation, a relation of interdependence. Without our immediate (or anticipatory) apprehension of the language as language, on the level of symbol, what the poem says, its allegorical content, is not understandable. But precisely the allegorical gesture toward a content, and the failure of that gesture, are what profile the symbolic for our apprehension to begin with.[33] And second, the use of the idea of color suggests the metaphor of static visual arts, which reminds us that the discourse here does not yet pretend Roman-

[33]On symbol and allegory, see my *Goethe's Theory of Poetry*, pp. 61–82, 153–58, in which I argue that in *Faust* the allegorical function *as such* has symbolic value, and where the present argument—that the symbolic, as revelation, is itself an allegory of the inherently temporal unfolding of nature as semiosis—is suggested, but not yet carried out.

tically to be revelatory in a literal sense, to be saturated with the symbolic—the poem is easily late enough (1827) to operate with these categories—but rather is still basically an imitative discourse content to compare itself (if in irony) with painting. It is thus still the common poetic *idiom* of the eighteenth century.

CHAPTER FIVE

Instability and Irony:
The Real Eighteenth Century

Our argument so far is framed between discussions of Goethe, and provokes the question: are we talking about the eighteenth century or about a "Goethean scheme" for the eighteenth century? As I have suggested, I do not think these alternatives exclude each other. But the present chapter will spread the focus, allowing other important players in the game to appear more or less independently.

Family Resemblances and Hidden Strains

One can imagine an argument with nearly the same content as that of the preceding chapters, but operating in an entirely different manner. We might, for example, have begun with Wittgensteinian "family resemblances" among main figures. Goethe and Lessing have in common a theoretical interest in the ideas of irony and the esoteric; Goethe and Herder an interest in the genesis and "natural history" of language. Goethe and Hölderlin are humane christologists; both want to understand the apparent "actuality" of experience as an act of divine self-sacrifice, an *imitatio Christi*. Lessing and Herder, in their turn, are inveterate polemicists, and prepared to defend on conceptual grounds the idea of intellectual life implied by this attitude. Lessing and Hölderlin have in common an idea of syntactic or dialectical time. And Herder and Hölderlin share a penchant for intellectual mythology, the construction of sweeping historical narratives that are self-validating and self-undermining at once, in that the conditions of the story's telling are themselves a chapter in it.

Schiller could then have been added to the pattern, along with such figures as Lenz, Hamann, and Lavater. And from the *types* of resemblance that make up the pattern, we might have put together a reasonable inductive argument for the operation of radical irony as a primary communicative mode in the period. But the argument in this form would have obscured its own problems by trivializing the idea of irony, taking irony as a historically locatable phenomenon. It is true that historical analyses are always in principle subject to hermeneutic criticism, which must be kept within bounds lest it confuse the focus of the original analysis. But the idea of irony—by insisting on the *operation* in texts of a meaning that it also insists is not *present* in those texts—has already initiated a radical hermeneutic self-reflection (on its own operation with its texts) that cannot be aborted without robbing the original idea of its very substance.

Instances of ironic conversation are the best actual evidence we have looked at, especially the extended two-way conversations between Lessing and Herder and between Herder and Hamann. Interesting points could also be made about the relation between Goethe and Schiller—which is an education in irony for the latter—not to mention the very curious relation between Goethe and Eckermann.[1] And if we admit the possibility of one-way ironic conversations, the idea that a text can draw an earlier text into ironic conversation without any direct engagement between the two authors (as Benjamin does Nietzsche, or Nietzsche Kant), then the eighteenth-century German instances multiply: Lessing/Ewald von Kleist, Lessing/Winckelmann, Goethe/Winckelmann, Goethe/Lessing, Goethe/Kant, Herder/Baumgarten, Herder/Süßmilch, even (for all its bitterness) Herder/Kant, have been suggested above.

But the discussion of these "conversations" always requires speculation about the thought-processes of at least one extratextual *subject*. For as I have pointed out, if subjectivity were entirely bracketed, if we could talk about the intertextual with no tinge whatever of the subjective, it would become impossible to distinguish irony from misunderstanding.

<hr/>

[1]See my "Trinitarische Humanität: Dichtung und Geschichte bei Schiller," in *Friedrich Schiller: Kunst, Humanität und Politik in der späten Aufklärung,* ed. Wolfgang Wittkowski (Tübingen, 1982), pp. 164–77. On Goethe and Eckermann, see Avital Ronell, *Dictations: On Haunted Writing* (Bloomington, Ind., 1986).

And in fact, whatever the situation with irony, misunderstanding *is* demonstrably an important phenomenon in the period we are looking at. Especially Herder had a talent for reading his own intellectual affinities so as to make personal estrangements of them—with Hamann, Goethe, Schiller, Kant.[2] The thought of Spinoza, in the various misunderstandings to which it was itself subjected, became an occasion for confusion, misalliance, needless division, and failed communication involving, among others, Jacobi, Lessing, Mendelssohn, Goethe, Herder, Kant, Fichte, Schelling, and the memory of Leibniz. Figures such as Hölderlin and Heinrich von Kleist, despite what seems to us the obvious historical place of their writing, were never recognized by the potentates in Weimar and Jena, who themselves, in turn, practiced a surreptitious subversiveness that positively courted misunderstanding by its difference from the outright subversiveness of the *Sturm und Drang*, a difference that wears thin in Schiller's last plays and in works such as *Die natürliche Tochter*. The focus on misunderstanding in drama, it appears, was an image of actual intellectual life at the time.

Nor is it difficult to see why the second half of the eighteenth century, particularly in Germany, should be characterized by a special complexity of misunderstanding. The presence of a deep historical discourse boundary—of which writers at the time were by no means unaware—plus the tendency of that boundary to obscure its own exact location, had as a consequence that texts found themselves side by side in the same terminological environment with no basis for confidence that they were speaking the same language. And the situation is complicated further, I will argue, by a collision between abstract *types* of discourse. Can the idea of ironic communication, a communication effective enough to be regarded as grounding a cohesive poetics, still be rescued here?

Discourse Types and Their Confusion: Spinoza and Kant

By *anchored* discourse I mean a discourse that employs primarily its relation to its object or referent in order to stabilize itself as a me-

[2]On Herder and Schiller, where it is perhaps not obvious that there ever was a real affinity, see the notes and commentary in Schiller, *On the Aesthetic Education of Man*, trans. Elizabeth M. Wilkinson and L. A. Willoughby (Oxford, 1967).

dium of communication. By *collected* discourse I mean a discourse that seeks stability mainly in its relation to itself, in that this relation forms a structure. (The criterion here is not self-reflexivity. Anchored discourse can reflect profoundly on its relation to its anchoring; collected discourse can *be* stable in its structure without reflecting on its stability.) I do not offer this distinction as a general theory of discourse. It is an ad hoc distinction that becomes interesting in the case we are discussing.

In most science and scholarship, anchored and collected discourse are closely intertwined without producing any marked instability. In natural science, the collectedness of the discourse and its anchoring in experimental results must be coordinated. The discourse of literary criticism and theory is collected in that it belongs integrally to its own object, literature, but anchored in that it posits a canon of "primary" texts as referent. Legal discourse requires social reality as a referent, but refers to it only in a theoretically tailored form. Even mathematics, which appears the prime example of a strictly collected discourse, reveals its anchoring in response to the question of why particular forms of collectedness arise at particular times. Are the achievements in foundations of mathematics in the last century or so not a *representation* of the problematics of Romantic subjectivity? Whence else the popularity of *Gödel, Escher, Bach?*

But the ideas of anchored and collected become useful in discussing the debate between Spinozists and Kantians in the eighteenth century. For the discourse of both Spinoza and Kant claims to be strictly *anchored*; each writer maintains that the details of his exposition are ultimately accidental in relation to the truth that governs them, that other forms of expression might possibly contain that truth more completely and lucidly.[3] And yet, as soon as we adopt any critical distance at all, it becomes clear that especially the *Ethics* of Spinoza and Kant's *Critique of Pure Reason* are examples of *collected* discourse, in which the effect of anchoring (the *effect*, as distinct from any supposed actual referentiality) is reduced to a minimum. Both texts begin in an accepted philosophical terminology, but then attempt to pull their ladders up behind them by developing a log-

---

[3]See Spinoza's reply to Burgh in Epistle 76, "ego non presumo, me optimam invenisse Philosophiam, sed veram me intelligere scio," and the section on method and truth in the *Tractatus de intellectus emendatione*, in Spinoza, *Opera*, 4 vols. (Heidelberg, 1925), 4:320, 2:17. And see Kant's foreword to the second edition of the *Kritik der reinen Vernunft*, in *KW*, 3:23.

ically closed system from terminological refinements that themselves in turn belong to the system as definitions.

And why then, in the late eighteenth century, did the century-old text of Spinoza and the brand-new text of Kant arouse so much interest and controversy? Why these systematic texts, this eminently collected discourse? The controversy between Spinozists and Kantians was focused primarily not on the cohesion of the systems, but on the manner in which the discourses are supposedly anchored; most of the participants in the controversy did not in fact trouble to master either of the two systems, *as* systems, in detail. (Goethe, who attempts to give both philosophers their due, is candid on this point.)[4] The question of Spinoza's idea of God is debated mainly with reference to specific passages, indeed often with reference to Spinoza's life; and the details of Kant's method are usually not indispensable in the discussion of nondogmatic rational support for morality and religion.

But this does not mean that the collectedness of Spinoza's and Kant's discourse did not play a part in the controversy. On the contrary, the quality of each text as system is frequently used *against* either Spinoza or Kant by advocates of the other. Herder, in his conversations on God, systematically de-systematizes Spinoza by analyzing his thought into a pattern of direct natural perceptions and intuitions, by stressing the relation of his thought to his life and to the lives of the fictional discussants, and by introducing parallels from poetic literature. And Kant's thought, in the process, is reduced to the status of mere unanchored speculation, *mere* system, an abstract web of "human knowledge without and before all experience . . . sensuous perceptions without and before all sensation of an object, ordered according to implanted forms of thought which no one had implanted . . . symbolical words without ideas and without objects," a web of criticism that "has no more basis than if I wanted to hear colors, taste light and see noise."[5]

Friedrich Heinrich Jacobi, however, two years earlier, had attacked Spinoza on almost exactly the same grounds. "Every course of

---

[4]On Spinoza, see Goethe's letter to Jacobi, 9 June 1785. On Kant, see the series of sketches in *Zur Morphologie* (WA, pt. 2, 11:45–57). Also see Goethe's letters to Reichardt, 25 October 1790, to the Herders, 7 June 1793, to Schiller, 5 June 1799, all of which show the concern to establish a *position* on Kant.

[5]SW, 16:513–14, 521. In the case of this work, I use Frederick H. Burkhardt's translation in Herder, *God, Some Conversations* (Indianapolis, 1940).

demonstration ends up in fatalism" (*HS*, p. 178); and since Spinoza's discourse (according to Jacobi) is not anchored, but depends for its supposed validity on its collectedness alone, on its quality as "demonstration," it follows that Spinozism is merely "atheism" (p. 173). Never mind that in *On the Improvement of the Understanding*, Spinoza defends himself against such attacks with a notion of the *intuition* of truth that is very like the idea Jacobi himself later quotes approvingly from Pascal (p. 185) in a passage whose denial of "a priori knowledge" reads very much like a Herderian attack on Kant. Like Herder, Jacobi here twists both Kant and Spinoza out of shape. And when Kant himself, whom Jacobi had apparently expected to support him,[6] enters the fray—in his essay on "orienting oneself" in thought (an idea Herder mocks in the *Metakritik* [*SW*, 21:32])—he does in a sense agree with Jacobi, by opposing to Spinoza's mathematical pretensions (his collectedness) a notion of "rational faith" that he presents as the true result of "healthy reason" (*KW*, 7:143, 133); but he quotes this last idea from Jacobi's opponent Mendelssohn (thus trumping one Jew, Spinoza, with another?), and manages to blame Mendelssohn and Jacobi *together* for imputing Spinozism to his own *Kritik der reinen Vernunft*.

The situation is thus confused, to say the least. But its very confusion suggests a diagnosis. Precisely the relation between anchored and collected discourse tends to become a *problem* in the vicinity of the historical discourse boundary we have spoken of. "Hermeneutic" discourse includes (or leans toward, or shudders away from) the recognition that discourse can never really be anchored, since its meaning is never really prior to it, but in effect (not in actuality, which we cannot know) arises only in being interpreted. Therefore the works of Spinoza and of Kant must become attractive *in their collectedness*, since collection is now the only possible route to discursive stability. But the anchoring of discourse, which in Enlightenment ("semiotic") writing cooperates with collectedness, cannot simply be given up; for at least our whole practical sense of the meaning of discourse depends on it. And especially the appearance of competing philosophical systems makes clear our *need* for an anchor as the criterion by which to choose between them—whereupon exactly the collectedness of Spinoza and Kant, which had at first attracted attention, is rejected as *mere* collectedness, and anchor after anchor is manufactured for whichever system one favors.

[6]See Jacobi's letter to Hamann of 24 March 1786, and Hamann's answer of 9 April.

This particular controversy cannot last forever. Thomas McFarland lays out clearly the process by which, over time, the search for anchoring formulations resolves itself into the choice between two basic philosophical attitudes—the "I am" and "it is" of Coleridge—whereupon this choice itself operates as a kind of anchor (defining the subject matter of the discourse), and things quiet down.[7] But the problem itself remains: an anchor for discourse is both indispensable and absent; strict discursive collectedness is therefore both needful and pointless. And hermeneutic theory, accordingly, continues to act as if discourse could in a sense be anchored precisely by its lack of an anchor, while systematic philosophy (especially in Hegel) develops its collectedness toward a hoped-for completion that will become substantial enough (as absolute spirit) to anchor retroactively its own discursive genesis.

For our purposes, however, it is crucial that the emergence of anchoring and collection as a problem not only explains the welter of misunderstanding that in the late eighteenth century might easily be mistaken for irony, but also opens, in the midst of those misunderstandings, precisely the space or matrix of irony. For it is obvious that the only conceivable *solution* to that problem would be a discourse that manages somehow to be *neither anchored nor collected*, a radically unstable, ironic discourse—although the problem does not immediately imply how such a discourse could exist and communicate.

Discourse Types and Instability: Rousseau

We have already looked at some examples of discourse that is neither anchored nor collected. Lessing's *Laokoon*, for instance, begins by presenting itself as strictly uncollected, a series of simple responses to its author's reading. Then, in chapter 16, it pretends to discover an underlying collectedness in itself and pulls itself together into structure, but into a markedly *faulty* structure (especially in the definition of "actions") that opens onto a problematics of subject and object, which, in turn, undermines the ostensible anchoring of the discourse in its reference to the artistic imitation of the real—an anchoring that Jacobs shows had already been rendered suspect by

---

[7]Thomas McFarland, *Coleridge and the Pantheist Tradition* (Oxford, 1969), chap. 2, "The Spinozistic Crescendo," esp. pp. 53–57, 61 (on Coleridge), 67 (on Schelling), 71 (on Fichte), passim.

Lessing's pose of trying not to wander from his path and by the tendency of his examples and concepts always to say a bit more than he (in interrupting himself) says about them.[8]

And Herder's response to *Laokoon* then prevents our mistaking Lessing's procedure for an instance of the normal *interaction* of anchoring and collectedness in scientific discourse. For Herder, by never actually agreeing with any of the statements he quotes from *Laokoon*, denies that text's anchoring, while at the same time he approves of what is "built" on its unsound foundation, and so implies that the text has stability only as structure, only in its collectedness. The structure he means to affirm, however, is not logical but (in precisely Lessing's sense) *poetic* structure, the manner in which we "see" the text's "becoming," its coming into being, as an action. And from the point of view of the discourse considered strictly as text, this collectedness turns out, after all, to be a kind of *anchor* in the immediate experience of the author, but an anchor that provides no stability, since the experience in question is nothing but the process of producing exactly this text. The discourse is *collected* only if we regard discourse as communicative activity (not just text), whereupon that collectedness takes the form of an extreme self-reflexivity (discourse on its own genesis as discourse) that is also inherently unstable, both in its temporality (as Lessing's own argument suggests) and in the inevitable self-conscious confusion of subject and object (as reflected in Lessing's overstepping of his own distinction between poetic writing and "prose"). Moreover, the availability of these two disjoint points of view, discourse as text and as activity, suggests an innate instability in discourse as such. And Herder's own discourse, in raising these possibilities, cannot itself escape infection.

Discourse, in any case, cannot simply *lack* either anchoring or collectedness (let alone both) unless it is mere gibberish. The instability of ironic discourse, rather, requires that anchoring and collectedness be made to *interfere* with themselves and each other. Nietzsche's *Birth of Tragedy* is a clear instance. Its discourse is anchored ultimately in two statements—concerning the Dionysian truth of the void and the Apollonian activity of world-creation—that cannot be made, or even known, without disrupting the collectedness of the discourse by introducing a type of language act that the discourse itself (which names itself "aesthetic science") excludes; and con-

[8]Carol Jacobs, "The Critical Performance of Lessing's *Laokoon*," *MLN* 102 (1987), 483–521.

versely, the exclusion of those language acts in the text as it stands not only robs the discourse of its anchor, but also creates a gap in its collection at the implied but unanswered questions of Dionysian object and Apollonian activity.

Or to stay within the eighteenth century, let us consider Rousseau. I have already suggested that Derrida, in managing at once both to dismiss and to inhabit Rousseau, in effect offers us an ironic Rousseau. And I think it can be argued that Paul de Man, precisely in disagreeing with Derrida, yet again lays bare the irony in Rousseau's writing. De Man claims to have "tried to show . . . that Rousseau's use of a traditional vocabulary is exactly similar, in its strategy and its implications, to the use Derrida consciously makes of the traditional vocabulary of Western philosophy. What happens in Rousseau is exactly what happens in Derrida: a vocabulary of substance and presence is no longer used declaratively but rhetorically, for the very reasons that are being (metaphorically) stated. Rousseau's text has no blind spots: it accounts at all moments for its own rhetorical mode."[9] This passage appears to say what I said earlier about Lessing's use of the traditional aesthetic vocabulary of imitation, except that I should probably have opposed "ironically" to "declaratively." And my argument also stressed, in Lessing, the development of a theory of poetic writing that "accounts for" the structure of the expository text in which it is developed.

But I did not claim that this "accounting for" its rhetorical mode removes all "blind spots" in Lessing. On the contrary, the resonance in *Laokoon* between the shape of the text itself and its theory of poetry is a *problem*, and is part of the reason that that text *is* blind (however clear-sighted its author) until responses like Goethe's and Friedrich Schlegel's, and especially Herder's, plunge it into a dialogic or intertextual element that is the light it requires to see by. Even if we admit a reduced and tightened version of de Man's argument (which I do), I do not think Rousseau's texts actually find the intertextual element in which their blindness might be washed from them—except belatedly, in certain German readers like Goethe and Hölderlin, in Derrida, in de Man himself.

But in order to argue that the structure of irony, as it were the desire of irony, is actually present in Rousseau, that the lamp is there waiting to be lit, we must argue *against* de Man even while admit-

[9]Paul de Man, "The Rhetoric of Blindness: Jacques Derrida's Reading of Rousseau," in his *Blindness and Insight: Essays in the Rhetoric of Contemporary Criticism*, 2d ed. (Minneapolis, 1983), pp. 138–39.

ting his basic perceptions. For de Man's vision of a perfected Rousseau—as well as his assertion that "the myth of the priority of oral
language over written language has always already been demystified
by literature" (p. 138)—involves a resolute confusion of the ideas of
signification and reference.

> We are entitled to generalize . . . by giving Rousseau exemplary value
> and calling "literary," in the full sense of the term, any text that im-
> plicitly or explicitly signifies its own rhetorical mode and prefigures its
> own misunderstanding as the correlative of its rhetorical nature; that
> is, of its "rhetoricity." It can do so by declarative statement or by
> poetic inference. "To account for" or "to signify," in the sentence
> above, does not designate a subjective process: it follows from the
> rhetorical nature of literary language that the cognitive function re-
> sides in the language and not in the subject. The question as to
> whether the author himself is or is not blinded is to some extent irrel-
> evant; it can only be asked heuristically, as a means to accede to the
> true question: whether his language is or is not blind to its own state-
> ment. [Pp. 136–37]

This passage says "signify," and it wants very much to *mean* "signify"
(not "refer"). Hence the insistence that the blindness of the language,
not that of the "subject," is at issue: it is the language that signifies,
the user of the language who refers.

But for all his implied protestations to the contrary, de Man is
actually talking about *reference.* Otherwise he could not talk about
the things "his" (Rousseau's) language does that presumably not all
other language does—certainly not the language of "Lukács,
Blanchot, Poulet, or the American New Critics" (p. 102). One could
conceivably say that language as such, in the form of literature, reveals itself as signifying its own rhetorical mode. Or as Knodt puts it:
in Lessing's view, poetry imitates language.[10] This is perhaps an aspect of what de Man has in mind. But from the point of view of an
individual text, that text's "rhetorical mode" is coded as a sign only in
some metasystem, not in the system with which the text actually
operates, and *cannot become a textual signified.* In any case, de Man
himself insists on the primacy in Rousseau of an "allegorical mode"
(p. 135), a "rhetoric of temporality," in which the founding semiotic
move must after all be *referential,* conceding priority in time to its

[10]Eva Knodt, *"Negative Philosophie" und dialogische Kritik: Zur Struktur poetischer
Theorie bei Lessing und Herder* (Tübingen, 1988), p. 117.

object.[11] (The question of whether the object, the text's "rhetorical mode," is *actually* prior to its being "accounted for," does not arise. The "allegorical" rhetoric must *treat* it as prior, which makes the process reference, not signification.)

And yet, how can a text possibly refer to "its own" rhetorical mode? A text can refer to *a* rhetorical mode (any such mode); but the only conceivable guarantee (beyond interpretive opinion) that that mode is "its" mode would have to reside in its *signifying* that mode, constituting the object of its own reference, after all. Reference thus presupposes signification here; but signification is impossible. Or more precisely, signification presupposes reference, the identification of the object (the text's "own" rhetorical mode) in order that it be available for coding in the first place. Nor, in this case, can we imagine signification and reference happening simultaneously—in a kind of symbolically revelatory, quasi-visible burst—without throwing away everything de Man says about the allegorical and the temporal. Therefore *neither* signification *nor* reference can happen, since each gets in the way of the other. This dilemma is a form of the *Laokoon* problem as well.

But if we shift the terminology a bit by recognizing that reference is the relation between a discourse and its anchor and that signification is the relation that makes up its collectedness; and if we agree with de Man that "Rousseau's famous statement 'Commençons donc par écarter tous les faits . . .' cannot be taken too radically" (p. 132); and if we agree, therefore, that no anchor or principle of collection is possible for Rousseau's discourse *except* its own rhetorical mode: then it follows that that discourse (at least in the *Essai* and the second *Discours*) is *neither anchored nor collected*, in a sense that opens the space of irony. De Man sees very clearly the outline of what he is talking about. But he identifies it as a solution, a cure for blindness, whereas it is in truth only the beginning of the problem, of a typical eighteenth-century ironic groping into the intertextual.

Discourse Instability as a German Phenomenon

No one, I think, not even a modern Kantian, can fail to be entertained by Klopstock's attack on Kant in his "Grammatical Dialogues":

[11]In a footnote, de Man here refers to his own essay "The Rhetoric of Temporality," in his *Blindness and Insight*, pp. 187–228.

"If one gives the words 'understanding,' 'reason,' and 'judgment' widely differing meanings, and if one does so without taking account of the existing subtle distinctions among them, then one has made of those words mere mumblings, or words that cannot mean what they ought to mean. Why can't the meanings that are foisted on those words simply be designated One, Two, Three, or *A*, *B*, *C*, so that the hearer, when the words recur, is not constantly reminded of the violence that has been done them?"[12] Indeed, a Kantian will be the more easily amused for having recognized that Klopstock has no idea of what Kant is getting at. But this fact, had it been pointed out to him, would not have troubled Klopstock. The idea that before judging a book, we must read it through to the end and understand it on its own terms, would have appeared at least questionable to him. On the contrary, an author is obliged, first of all, to speak in *our* terms, which means not that he must lower himself to the level of the vulgar mass, but simply that he must act as a responsible citizen of that "Republic of Learning" about which Klopstock wrote a witty, ironic treatise, which was greatly admired, for example, by Goethe (letter to Schönborn, 10 June 1774).

In this treatise, moreover, Klopstock distinguishes carefully between "inventing" and "discovering" ("Erfinden" and "Entdecken"), and speaks of "*The Guild of Philosophers* or investigators of first causes and of the whole extent of morals. They are inventors when they *demonstrate* new propositions or propositions that had already been considered probable" (*AW*, p. 882). Philosophy, that is, is the *invention* of well-shaped verbal processes (demonstrations) by which our existence is clarified for us; and from this point of view, Kant's claim to have *discovered* a system of thought that remains valid despite any faults in its verbal presentation must be rejected. For Klopstock there is no universally valid system of philosophical thought capable of being discovered and transmitted. The anchoring of discourse, rather, is always conditioned by qualities of the *natural language* in which discourse is conducted, by customs and common knowledge as represented in the operation of an accepted vocabulary. Philosophical invention merely brings that common knowledge to the fore, and if possible develops it, by playing the accepted language game with special skill.

In Klopstock's view, therefore, discourse is *anchored* in the *col-*

---

[12]*Klopstocks sämmtliche Werke*, 10 vols. (Leipzig, 1854–55), 9:310–11.

lectedness of a particular natural language, in that language as a game, as an evolved semiotic structure that operates independently of any supposed referential validity. And as long as discourse and language can be clearly distinguished—discourse being artifice, a more or less consciously constructed communicative technique subject to ideological criticism, unlike language, which operates as a natural communicative environment, traceable to no form of origin—this view is not problematic. But if the boundary between discourse and language becomes uncertain, then a collision between anchoring and collection, as in Rousseau, cannot be avoided, and the space of irony is opened. My contention is that the situation of the German language in the eighteenth century produces, in the culture as a whole, a blurring of that boundary between discourse and language.

In arguing this point, I will quote mainly from Eric A. Blackall's *The Emergence of German as a Literary Language.* (This procedure is suggested by the same considerations as the analytic procedure of Chapter 2. I mean to show that my argument is separated by no great conceptual distance from a historical view, Blackall's, with which I assume the reader is relatively comfortable.) When Klopstock reads Kant, we have seen, he does not attempt to master the substance of the argument; his attention is captured by the mechanism of expression and formulation, by the dangerous relation between discourse and its language. And one accomplishment of Blackall's work is that it shows not only how widespread and deep-seated this attitude was in eighteenth-century Germany but also the factors that favor specifically the development of ironic discourse. The points in Blackall of greatest interest to us are the seminal position of philosophical language in the eighteenth-century development of German as a whole, especially by way of Leibniz, Christian Thomasius, and Christian Wolff; the abiding significance of J.C. Gottsched's contribution to modern German, both despite and because of the opposition his ideas aroused; and the characterization of the anti-Gottsched front as a "revival of metaphor."

Both Leibniz and Thomasius are ambivalent toward German as a medium of philosophical discourse (*EG*, p. 14); but both still advocate philosophical German in order to counter what they perceive as the "scholasticistic" quality, the obscurity of technical philosophy, in other languages, especially Latin (pp. 8–9, 21). They envisage in philosophy a true popularization, an opening up to every intelligent person of the mysteries now guarded by a clique of initiates. Leibniz mentions "popularity" as a desideratum in philosophical language; and Thomasius goes so far as to say that philosophy as such is "easy" when not obscured by terminology (pp. 9, 20). What is aimed at, therefore, is not merely a philosophical language that will be lexically and grammatically German, but a philosophical idiom that will be integrated with normal and natural German *usage* (*EG* on "claritas," pp. 8–9).

But in the domain of usage, as both Leibniz and Thomasius are aware, every language has its own peculiar character, so that philosophy in German will bear a different stamp from philosophy in French or Latin. And the usefulness of this new philosophical stamp will be to provide a better *anchoring* of philosophical discourse, although neither Leibniz nor Thomasius yet envisages an anchoring of the discourse in the collectedness of the language. What both men have in mind is an anchoring of philosophical discourse, so to speak, not *in* the language but *through* the language, in a form of reality that is made accessible precisely by the relatively *un*collected state of the German language of the time, its anchoring in a reality that is positively obscured by the over-collectedness (divorced from living referentiality) of philosophical Latin (*EG*, pp. 19–24). Leibniz in fact specifically attaches value to German's propensity for naming only *realia* (p. 9).

Exactly to what extent German of the early eighteenth century *was* a fragmented or uncollected language is not as important as the fact that it was *regarded* as being so. For philosophical discourse, especially in an age when philosophy is strongly influenced by mathematics, needs a fairly strong collectedness in its medium. And if that collectedness is assumed not to be already present, then it must be supplied by philosophy itself, which means that the natural language as a whole—since its collectedness (supplied by philosophy) is now recognizable as artifice—*itself takes on* (or is felt to take on) *the character of discourse*. Which means, in turn, that the dangerous idea of a discourse anchored in its own collectedness, a discourse in which anchoring and collection therefore tend to interfere with one another, a discourse that opens the space of irony, is ready to emerge. In Germany, where it appears necessary to *create* the natural language as a philosophical medium, the strict difference between language and discourse ceases to operate, and the same problem that we encounter in Rousseau's texts takes shape on a national scale.

Wolff becomes important here. It is no accident that both Kant and Hegel pay tribute to him as a pioneer of logical thought in German, thought freed from the supposed vagueness of the language as used by nonphilosophers (*EG*, pp. 26, 46–47). In his reform of German philosophical terminology, Wolff does his best to retain contemporary usage, but only up to the point where it begins to conflict with his own mathematical idea of what constitutes a definition; and once he has defined a term, he prides himself on never using it in any but the strict sense (pp. 37–38). That is, his activity balances between the repair or revival of a natural language (the German idiom he regarded as particularly "suitable" for the sciences [p. 38]) and the creation of a technical discourse, thus obscuring the distinction between these categories. In a revealing comparison of passages, Blackall shows that the "German" of Wolff's philosophical treatises was not the language he actually used in social intercourse, or even in personal meditation (pp. 40–41). Wolff's philosophical idiom is at once *both* a "natural" German, in its attentiveness to usage and its elimination of unnecessary foreign borrowings, *and* an obviously contrived and self-contriving discourse. Nor is this combination of characteristics at all improbable in this period, which strives, as Wellbery puts it, toward "a perfect philosophical language," a systematics that would be *more* natural than natural languages, in that "it would coincide with reason itself."[13]

In Leibniz and Thomasius, then, we begin to sense the idea of anchoring discourse in language, and in Wolff the boundary between language and discourse begins to blur. These two tendencies, it is true, do not yet seem to meet in the combination that favors ironic discourse; but two factors operate to bring them closer together. First, the blurring of the boundary with language in precisely that philosophical discourse which in the course of the century, down to Kant's *Der Streit der Facultäten*, increasingly assumes the dignity of a *master* discourse in whose collectedness all other scientific discourses are anchored—to the extent, especially, that their referential relation to real objects is called ever more into question. And second, the peculiar situation of the German language, which is regarded *both* as eminently "natural"—less corrupted than others by cultural contrivance, therefore useful for anchoring discourse—*and* as a deliberate cultural product (in respect to consistency, expressiveness, precision), hence itself still *in need* of anchoring.

These factors bring us to Gottsched, who was basically in sympa-

---

[13]David E. Wellbery, *Lessing's "Laocoon": Semiotics and Aesthetics in the Age of Reason* (Cambridge, 1984), p. 35.

thy with Leibniz and Thomasius in that he also wished to allow the German language to find its own shape and level by usage. But unlike those two philosophers, Gottsched undertook the practical task of unifying German grammar; and as Blackall points out, he inevitably assumed the rôle not only of preserver but of "legislator for the language of the whole nation" (*EG*, p. 115). There was no way of deciding objectively among various dialect usages. At some point arbitrary decisions had to be made—decisions that, by being arbitrary, and known to be arbitrary, infected the quality of language with that of discourse—and Gottsched, because of the basic soundness and wide acceptance of his grammatical opinions, was in a position to make them. Moreover, his avowed debt to Wolff (pp. 47–48)—plus the perception of that debt among his literary opponents, who recognize that the *Critische Dichtkunst* of 1730 lacks all sense for "poetry [as] anything more than conveying thought" (p. 231)—associates the language as a whole with the idea of a philosophical master discourse.

In fact, opposition and debate *favor* the tendencies already present in Gottsched's writing. It is true, for example, that "*Aufklärung* Germany . . . owed far more to French theories and discussions of style than has been recognized by German scholars" (*EG*, p. 170). But it is also true that any debate concerning the conflicting claims of, say, dignity and clarity, in France, was a debate about how the language should be used, whereas in Germany, because of the (actual or perceived) state of linguistic development, it became a debate not about how to *use* a language, but about how to *have* one, how to have a coherent and above all *natural* communicative medium of the sort that in France or England (it was supposed) served precisely to anchor such debate. The hopeless circularity of a discourse anchored in nothing but itself now evidently arises as a threat, all the more for thinkers whose opposition to Gottsched included the idea that even the naturalness of an established natural language is not necessarily permanent but can be corrupted (as supposedly in France) by the very culture it anchors.

In any case, the actual opposition to Gottsched, in Breitinger's *Critische Dichtkunst*, for example, takes the form of a "defense of metaphorical diction"; and the value of metaphor in turn is that it "gives a new face to things that are well known" (*EG*, p. 287). This "new face," however, is new *to us* only because our culture has obscured its primitive or aboriginal quality. Hamann merely radicalizes widespread contemporary thought when he says: "Senses and passions speak and understand nothing but images. Images make up the whole treasury of human knowledge and happiness" (MiN, 2:197). And access via language to this primitive level of experience, Bodmer suggests in his treatise on "poetic paintings," is provided by metaphors or figures of speech in general, which are defined as "symptoms or accesses of feelings, as these burst forth in speech and reveal their nature, quality, energy, and degree. They are settled forms in which feelings appear according to type" (EG, p. 294, my translation). That the operation of figurative language in this sense is *referential*, moreover, emerges from Breitinger's remarks about synonyms, which form an interesting contrast with Herder (pp. 282–84, 456). Metaphors may therefore be regarded as *anchoring*, in a minutely differentiated structure of direct emotional experience, the discourse or language that they apparently only embellish.

What happens, however, if the use of figurative language in poetry must be explicitly advocated as part of a *program* of language reform, such as Bodmer and Breitinger's? The basis of that very program is the idea that in the ordinary course of events, the anchoring effect of metaphors in poetic discourse is achieved by way of the operation of the same metaphors as a natural anchoring of *the language* in experience. But if those metaphors—or the requisite degree and prominence of metaphoricity—only find their way *into* the language by way of their deliberate creation in poetic discourse, the result is an attempt to anchor language as a whole in the collectedness of a particular discourse, which puts a great deal more strain on both ideas (anchoring and collection) than does, for instance, the reverse process as suggested by Klopstock.

Again, therefore, the anchoring and the collection of discourse threaten to interfere with one another profoundly, in a manner that is especially well marked in Germany. And in this general situation, it is hard to see how thoroughly ironic forms of discourse, radically unstable, incomplete, dialogic discourses, discourses neither anchored nor collected from the point of view of the individual text, could *fail* to arise.

Kant's Difficult Position

When I speak of Kant's "difficult position," I refer both to difficulties he *causes* and to difficulties he *faces*. We have already said something about the former. The systematic move in philosophy, the move that (although not unprecedented) is epitomized for the nineteenth and twentieth centuries by the *Critiques*, is a summarizing and totalizing move that suggests seductively convenient articulations in intellectual history, articulations that tend to obscure, especially, the eighteenth-century poetics we are concerned with. And it is also primarily the mirror of Kant that inclines us to read the rhetoric of totality and unity and the organic, in German Classicism, not as a functioning and relativizable rhetoric, but as an exact summary of the spirit in which it is written. Even the concept of irony is infected. Since we assume with some justification that Friedrich Schlegel's theory of "Ironie" has to do with Kantian systematics by way of Fichte, we are encouraged to think of irony itself as a totalizing move, a controlling move, rather than a subversive move.

These difficulties repeat difficulties that Kant caused in his own time. First, the *Critiques* are hard books to attack. Their sheer size and intricacy provide every point with multiple lines of defense; everything is hedged and qualified so as to give under pressure without breaking. (Klopstock complains of this in his extended "Grammatische Gespräche" [*Werke*, 9:308].) Second, if the task in hand is a defense of the practice of irony against the Kantian practice of system, how shall one approach this task without *explaining* one's irony and thus violating it? Third, the abstract structure of Kant's thought is uncomfortably similar to exactly that structure of thought for the sake of which Kant must be attacked. In both Herderian irony and Kantian systematics, the principal question is what kinds of statement *can* be made? In Herder: How—without perpetrating impossible language acts that can produce nothing but misunderstanding—shall one account for the tendency of discourse, when it reflects upon itself (as it must), to arrive at formulations that violate the historical conditions of its own effectiveness? And in Kant: How—without adopting an untenable dogmatic position—shall one account for the tendency of reason's inexorable critical reflection upon itself to arrive at the choice between dogmatism and an empty skepticism that would violate the historical conditions of its own effectiveness? Fourth, the Kantian idea of *freedom*, and its location in the autonomous individual subject, appears to offer a simple ground or fulcrum for irony, thus preempting the delicate reflection upon irony that reduces the subject to the status of the signified of the social and opens ideas like "the community as a reader" as ways of accounting for ironic communication. How shall a stable and cohesive anti-Kantian position be articulated under these circumstances?

Klopstock, we have seen, attacks Kant on the grounds that Kantian discourse violates the natural character of the language in which it operates. And he sends a copy of his dialogue to Herder, who develops its ideas in the *Metakritik* and *Kalligone*, especially in the latter, where we read:

> The language of men contains their *forms of thought*; we think, especially on an abstract level, only in and with language. If your ideas, as you say, are such as to require special new schemata, then leave our language alone and invent special symbols; do your schematizing in Tibetan. The spirit of all cultivated European peoples has *one* philosophical idiom; from Plato and Aristotle it continues to Locke and Leibniz, to Condillac and Lessing. A gobbledygook that associates foggy new concepts with words that are otherwise universally understandable is and remains gobbledygook. [*SW*, 22:7]

Leibniz had already been quoted on the subject of "gobbledygook" ("Rothwelsch") in the *Metakritik* (*SW*, 21:319).

But there are still problems here. Even assuming that Klopstock and Herder are both attacking Kant's failure to anchor his discourse in natural language, it is not clear whether natural language itself is to be regarded primarily as anchored (in the referential, representational, "semiotic" view) or collected (as a system of communicative conventions, in the "hermeneutic" view). Still less is it clear whether Kant's apparent anchoring of his discourse in its own collectedness is rejected simply as unnatural, or as obscuring—by appearing to solve it—the *problem* that opens the space of ironic discourse. And especially in Herder, it is no longer even clear that natural language is the issue. The idea of natural language does provide leverage for attacking Kant, which Herder had employed in the *Metakritik* by quoting Leibniz on the subject of philosophy in German (*SW* 21:70–72). But can we speak of a "discourse" in the first place, if we insist too strongly on its being anchored in a particular natural language? How can we recognize philosophical discourse to begin with, if it is not translinguistic, the "*one* philosophical idiom" Herder speaks of? And once we admit this point, we are dangerously close to the idea of a self-anchoring philosophical master discourse—which, again, masquerades seductively as the foundation of a free subjectivity, as an extralinguistic ground for something like irony.

I will take up later Herder's entirely radical manner of dealing with the problem of the relation of languages and discourses. But there is more to say about the complexity of contemporary reactions to Kant, which is a measure of the difficulty he caused. I have mentioned Goethe's little piece "Anschauende Urtheilskraft," which opens by suggesting that Kant was being "mischievously ironic" in setting strict limits to human understanding (WA, pt. 2, 11:54). Goethe is not concerned here with interpretive accuracy; he is attempting to develop Kantian *language*, in this case an actual quotation (*KW*, 5:407–8), toward the idea "that by contemplation of a ceaselessly creating nature, we have made ourselves worthy of intellectual participation in her productions" (WA, pt. 2, 11:55), which is the idea of a language capable of refining itself toward reestablished unity with the phenomenal world. That this entirely un-Kantian idea is what Goethe has in mind is clear from the sketch that immediately follows in the serial *Zur Morphologie*, "Bedenken und Ergebung," where we read that the separation between what we see and what we think or say must be healed, or at least soothed, by poetry (11:57).

Here, as in yet a third *Morphologie* essay, "Einwirkung der neuern Philosophie," Goethe appears to defy Herder's arguments directly by emphasizing the acceptability of a Kantian use of *language*: "And so I accustomed myself gradually to a language [that of Schiller and the Kantians] that had been entirely alien to me, and in which I could orient myself all the more easily for being enabled, by the higher idea of art and science that it favored, to regard myself as nobler and richer" (WA, pt. 2, 11:53). But Goethe's ways of *developing* Kantian thought, he admits, are regarded by Kantians as peculiar, if not exactly wrong (11:51–52); and the difference between Goethe and Herder is thus not as deep as it might seem. Herder's position is that of philology, the love of language and the need to protect it against the supposed non-language of Kant, whereas Goethe's may be described as "logurgy," the conviction that language must always be developed, never protected. For Goethe, when people (even Kantians) speak to each other, they simply cannot, by definition, be using non-language; our task is therefore not to reject their terminology, any more than the serious botanist can reject an existing flower, but to develop it (perhaps by "peculiar" Goethean paraphrases) toward what I have called the languageful language of poetry. And languageful language is the goal of Herderian philology as well. The trouble with Herder—Goethe mentions him in the essay quoted above (11:49)—is that he is apparently not ironic enough, that he becomes illiberal, that he allows Kant to put him off balance.

Even in Schiller there is an undercurrent of doubt about Kant. I refer for brevity to an argument made in my *Modern Drama and German Classicism*: Schiller's Kantian thought of the philosophical and aesthetic essays of the 1790s has consequences for poetry, especially the technical theory of tragedy, that he himself finds unacceptable, although he retains the basic outlook of those essays on matters of character and action. The result in the late plays, from *Wallenstein* on, is a procedure that has the structure of Goethean logurgic irony. In order to approach those plays, we must carry out at least a rudimentary Kantian analysis of limits and types of mental activity; but then our participation in the theatrical proceeding is made continuous with a participatory relation to the natural as such, which bursts the Kantian scheme. The Fichtean criticism of the thing-in-itself, as sketched in *Über die ästhetische Erziehung des Menschen*, perhaps plays a rôle here. But precisely this work moves more in Goethe's orbit, and even in Herder's.[14]

For all this confusion in the reaction to Kant, however, there is also a considerable unanimity of *resistance* to him, even among his apparent allies, such as Jacobi. And this resistance, in turn, feeds the confusion in its own bosom by providing Kant's thought with an ever more undeniable *historical* existence, which is especially tenacious when the resistance is based precisely on the idea of the historically given (e.g., the character of natural languages) as opposed to the rationally given. There is no antidote to Kant once history has him in its blood. Fichte, Hegel, and Schelling, although they all disagree with Kant, and despite Schelling's interest in nature, myth, and poetry, are all still Kantians in the definition that would be applied by Herder; and of the German Romantics it might be said that they developed irony into a system in its own right, and so did not maintain a Herderian metacritical position. Perhaps, within a decade or so on either side of 1800, the only effective protest against Kantianism, if one had not the public position and personal composure of a Goethe, is represented by Heinrich von Kleist's suicide, or by the attempted suicide mentioned in Klopstock's letter to C.M. Wieland of 7 August 1797.

But neither does the opposition to Kant, the need for a move beyond system or beyond theory, disappear from the historical scene in the long run. Schopenhauer to an extent de-terminologizes the sys-

[14]See nn. 1 and 2, and my *Modern Drama and German Classicism*, pp. 175–228.

tem; Kierkegaard and Nietzsche testify by implication that Herderian irony was at least as prophetic as it was futile. And if the resistance to Kant was thus a Thermopylae of the intellect, the true Leonidas is probably not Herder but Herder's mentor, the German incarnation of William Blake, Johann Georg Hamann. The very idea of a "Meta-kritik," centering on the relation between Kantian "purism" and language, comes to Herder from Hamann. And even if Herder's influence on German thought is not really reducible to the spreading of a Hamannian "epidemic,"[15] it is still true that Hamann's direct influence surfaces later at some very significant points in intellectual history, in Kierkegaard almost as strongly as in Goethe, to an extent in Nietzsche, in Benedetto Croce, and in a revealing essay by Hegel. For Hegel's inadvertently megalomaniac remark that Hamann had failed "to take the same trouble God had taken," by not unfolding his thought into a Hegelian "system," is a defense against the recognition, forced upon him by Hamann, of a need unfilled by his own systematic undertaking.[16]

There are also misunderstandings between Hamann and Herder, which, though they predate the *Critiques*, still have to do with a conception of language that belongs to the anti-Kantian resistance and so form part of the confusion in that resistance. Hamann, after his initial negative reaction to Herder's *Abhandlung*, soon accepts the substance of Herder's thought after all; and Herder, after reading *Des Ritters von Rosencreuz letzte Willensmeynung*, in which the idea of language as originally identical with the whole phenomenal world is suggested strongly (MiN, 3:32), feels that a basis for communication has been reestablished (letter to Nicolai, 2 July 1772). On 1 August 1772 he writes to Hamann, explaining that the "Leibnizian-aesthetic cloak" of the *Abhandlung* had been merely a necessary "mask"; and Hamann, in the *Philologische Einfälle und Zweifel*, responds with an outpouring of ironic praise—but in its very irony, genuine praise—for Herder's irony (MiN, 3:41, 51–53). He still subjects the *Abhandlung* to a vigorous *reductio ad absurdum*—does Herder not see man's lack of instincts as itself a natural instinct to invent language?—but in such a way as to place it, by implication, alongside his own absurd attack on the absurdities of the age. If this is the form taken by reconciliation or agreement in the anti-Kantian

---

[15]Josef Nadler, "Hamann, Kant, Goethe" (orig. 1931), in *Johann Georg Hamann*, ed. Rainer Wild, Wege der Forschung 511 (Darmstadt, 1978), p. 213.

[16]Georg Wilhelm Friedrich Hegel, "Ueber: 'Hamanns Schriften,'" in his *Sämtliche Werke*, ed. Hermann Glockner, 26 vols. (Stuttgart, 1927–40), 20:252–53.

camp, this bouncing of minds against one another "like billiard balls" (as Goethe says of Jacobi to Eckermann, 11 April 1827), then surely we have no right to expect a coherent doctrinal alternative to Kant, and no right to use the absence of such an alternative as an excuse for underestimating the strength and depth of the resistance.

Two points are crucial. First, we are talking not about a *reaction* to Kant—which would leave unchallenged the idea of the *Critiques* as marking a primary epistemic divide in history—but about the *resistance* to Kant that arises in a preexisting eighteenth-century culture of irony. And second, this resistance does not collapse in the face of Kant's success. It persists throughout the nineteenth and into the twentieth century in the form of a resistance to system, a subversive appetite for irony, the need for a communicative move beyond theory. If our project were to write a history of this resistance, the next chapter—dealing, at least, with Kierkegaard, Nietzsche, Derrida—would probably be titled "Hegel's Difficult Position." For Hegel's thought, like Kant's, resonates uncomfortably *in structure* with the ironic questioning of its own systematic pretensions. But our concern, for now, is to anchor this subversive tradition in the eighteenth century. And one witness still waiting to be called is Kant himself.

Kant and the Conflict of the Ironies

We have not yet said much about difficulty in the sense that Kant *encountered* it; and we have not yet gone very far into the political aspect of eighteenth-century irony, into how to distinguish between its potentially subversive quality and its potentially disinterested or secretly conservative quality. Both of these matters are illuminated by Kant's little stitched-together book, *Der Streit der Facultäten*, which contrives to be at once both arrogant and obsequious in its placing of the intellect in political life. Is its obsequiousness a mere pose, a mere yielding to necessity? The first two sections, after all, had been denied publication for years by direct government censorship; and Kant prefaces the book with a copy of the letter of 1794, from Friedrich Wilhelm II of Prussia, forbidding him to publish on the philosophy of religion (*KW*, 7:6–7). But Kant himself, in letters, positively boasts of his scrupulousness in obeying the law (see, for example, *KW*, 7:339); and I am not sure that actual censorship was not secretly of value to him in his work—as an opportunity to obey the law at some personal cost, as a kind of negative anchor (a testimony of referentiality) for a discourse that would otherwise be anchored only in its own collectedness.

The arrogance of Kant's position appears in his dismissal of the faculties of theology, law, and medicine as mere guardians of written canons. "All three upper faculties base their doctrines (which are entrusted to them by the government) upon *written documents*; this is as it must be in the situation of a populace placed under the guidance of learning, since without these documents there would be no unvarying norm, available to everyone, for the people to follow" (*KW*, 7:22). But the question of the *validity* of religious or legal or even medical doctrines—and what other interesting questions are there?—is the province of the "lower" or philosophical faculty.

> The philosophical faculty can therefore lay claim to all doctrines, in order to subject them to the test of truth. It cannot be placed under a governmental interdict, save when the government acts against its own real and essential purpose. And the objections and doubts brought forward publicly by the philosophical faculty must be tolerated by the upper faculties, a necessity they will certainly find bothersome, since without such critics they would be able to enjoy undisturbed their property (however defined and proclaimed) and in fact govern it despotically. [7:28]

Censorship, to be sure, has its place, but not the censorship of professors.

> Only the practitioners of those upper faculties (e.g., clergy, officials in the legal system, physicians) can be prohibited from publicly contradicting the doctrines entrusted to them by the government. . . . These officials, e.g., preachers and lawyers, if they felt the urge to direct at the populace their objections and doubts concerning spiritual or secular law, would be inciting the people against the government. But the faculties only direct these doubts at one another, as scholars; and the populace, for practical purposes, take no notice, even when these matters come to their attention, since subtle reasoning is not their business, and they feel constrained therefore to accept what is proclaimed by the appointed officials of the government. [7:28–29]

This passage sketches a complete, if hardly realistic vision of the orderly operation of society from the point of view of scholarly learning. But its real theme is the philosophical master discourse, and especially the protection of that discourse from censorship. Censorship of the philosophers, in their critical debate with their colleagues, not only works against the government's own best interests but is also not worth the effort, since no one listens to the philosophers anyway.

The master discourse (we are told) is thus at once both too powerful and too insignificant to be censored. Armed with an unconquerable truth, by which it is entitled to act as an uncompromising arbiter in its own "lawful" disputes (*KW*, 7:33), the master discourse must still beg its local government for permission to be heard in public. And as I have said, I think this paradoxical situation serves a secret expressive purpose for Kant; the arrogance and the obsequiousness it favors add up to Kant's own version of precisely the *subversive irony* of his opponents, an ostentatiously harmless discourse that in the very act of knuckling under to the state's power, actually invalidates and undermines that power. This irony comes close to the surface in the second part of the *Streit*, where we read that the supposedly dangerous philosophical "enlighteners" are not really dangerous at all, since "their voice is directed not *familiarly* at the populace (who take little or no notice of them anyway, or of their writings) but rather *respectfully* at the state, which latter is thus implored to take to heart the people's lawful needs. And this cannot happen by any means other than that of publicity, if a whole people is to put forward its complaints" (7:89). And a few pages later, Kant insists that the progress of humanity can only be effected "*from the top down*" (7:92), by a state or government whose wisdom he basely flatters by comparing it to the wisdom of "Providence" (7:93).

The trouble with these genuflections to the state is that they immediately follow a discussion of the French Revolution as a *philosophical* phenomenon (*KW*, 7:85–87), which is to say (although Kant avoids saying it), an instance of the people's listening to philosophers after all, an instance of moral and ideal and philosophical reform *from the bottom up*. Kant's submissive entreaties to the state thus take on the quality of a warning, indeed a veiled threat, which is very nearly articulated as such in the words:

> For such a phenomenon in human history [the French Revolution] *can never again be forgotten*, since it has uncovered in human nature an aptitude and a power for betterment, of a sort that no politician could ever have inferred from the earlier course of events, and which only nature and freedom, united according to inner principles of justice in the human race, were in a position [by way of philosophers?] to

prophesy—although, in the realm of temporal actuality, they could promise it only in an undetermined form, as a result of historical accidents. [7:88]

Kant himself is speaking prophetically here—a prophetic or "soothsaying history" (7:84) being, after all, his stated main concern in the second part of the book. But he prophesies with irony, and concludes his book with a discussion of the supposed conflict between the faculties of philosophy and medicine, a discussion which is *really* harmless, not much more than Kant's meditations on his own habits and infirmities.

Moreover, if Kant is really aiming at a subversive irony, then the actual censorship of his work has played into his hand, by showing the state's awareness of the power of philosophical writing. It seems to me, however, that what we have here is still not radical irony in the sense of the arguments in earlier chapters, but rather a discursive procedure that at best flirts with radical irony. By a lucky accident, which Kant takes advantage of in his preface, this particular text manages to be both censored and uncensored. But its irony is exhausted in this paradox, in the paradox of a threat to the state that the state itself validates unwittingly. It is not an irony built into the discourse itself, not an irony of the sort that still eludes de Man in that second *Discourse* of Rousseau which, de Man says, insists on its own misunderstanding.

It is, especially, not an irony that generates ironic conversation; and Kant himself appears to concede that it is not really subversive when he compares the upper faculties to the government party (of the right) and the philosophers to the opposition (on the left) in "the parliament of learning" (*KW*, 7:35). The subversiveness of the *Streit* does not infect its own discourse, but stops at a point where it can still (at least in imagination) be *institutionalized*—which means: not subversive at all. It is a *dream* of subversiveness, and as such a significant dream, Kant's dream of membership in the party opposed to his own systematic (therefore inherently institutional and conservative) initiatives in discourse. It is the founding instance of nineteenth-century regret for a lost ironic communicativeness.

Censorship and the Institution of Meaning

If a sign is needed to distinguish between the dream of subversive irony and subversive irony itself, then Kant's own procedure suggests one; for subversive irony, in the sense I mean, tends neither to submit to censorship, nor even to resist it, but to *advocate* it. We think of *Wilhelm Meisters Wanderjahre* and the excluded Jews who are *us*. Or we recall that in the *Social Contract* of Rousseau, not only the next-to-last chapter, "On the Censorship," but also the last, on civil religion, recognizes a rôle for the state in the shaping of citizens' opinions and beliefs.

In the chapter on censorship, Rousseau insists that the office of the censor may not in any way decide or determine public opinion, but merely declare it (JJR, 3:458). That this text is not to be taken strictly at its word, however, becomes clear at the end of the chapter, in the story of the Lacedaemonians and "certain drunkards from Samos" (3:459). In the edition of 1782, for the benefit of readers who do not know Plutarch, there is an author's footnote admitting that the island in question was not really Samos, but another island whose naming the "délicatesse" of the French language prevents (3:1497). The mere possibility of a vulgar pun on the name "Chio" (English "Chios") and the word "chiottes" (shit-house), thus censors out the name—and precisely in doing so, *suggests* the pun!—whereupon the footnote itself becomes a criticism of public taste (hence an act of censorship) directed against the fastidiousness of the French language. Not only the efficacy of censorship, therefore, but its very possibility, is called into question. *Which* act, the act against the pun or the act against the customs of the language, rightly declares public opinion?

In view of these complications, one might ask why Rousseau raises the question of censorship to begin with. Or why, in the following chapter, he opens the even bigger can of worms marked "civil religion," which requires, in order to be dealt with honestly, the actual formulation of religious principles conducive to good citizenship and the empowering of the state to *enforce belief* in those principles—at least negatively, by banishing all those who do not believe (JJR, 3:468). It is true that by assigning this power only to "the sovereign," Rousseau avoids the difficult question of which particular *agency* of the state will enforce belief. But the question does not go away, especially in the immediate context, where it is clear that Rousseau is talking about a Christian Europe composed of existing states, not about conditions at a state's founding. The concluding generalizations about the toleration only of tolerant religions (3:468–69) are thus merely a distraction from the implied advocacy of an extremely difficult and all too easily perverted form of censorship.

Why, then, does Rousseau go out of his way to advocate censorship? Why not, for example, admit the possibility of tolerating even intolerant religions, as long as religious pluralism is maintained? On what grounds is it asserted, to begin with, that "sentimens de sociabilité" (JJR, 3:468) must take the form of religious belief? Or is this assertion an instance of ironically self-compromising Genevan self-censorship, a recollection that under Calvin the citizens of Geneva, *as* citizens, were in fact compelled to make a prescribed profession of faith—and in terms considerably different from those proposed by Rousseau? Was Calvin, or his church, markedly tolerant? Where is the line between logic and tautology in the statement that intolerant religious dogma is "*good* [my emphasis] only under a theocratic government" (3:469)? We recall the footnote to the chapter "The Legislator," in which Rousseau, in insisting on a distinction between the author of the *Institutes* and the recodifier of Geneva's laws, opens precisely the question of how deep that distinction goes (3:382).

Exactly how the elements of meaning and irony are distributed here need not concern us. It is enough to recognize that against the background of tangled implications in these final chapters of the *Social Contract*, the advocacy of censorship (hence the denial of strict freedom of speech or conviction) emerges as a highly problematic yet still apparently unavoidable social or communal act. And it seems to me that the reason for this position, or this act, is stated in the opening words of the chapter on censorship: "In the same way that the declaration of the general will is made by the law, so the declaration of public judgment is made by censorship" (JJR, 3:458). What is important here is the *analogy* between censorship and lawgiving, since it is only by way of this analogy, only by way of censorship as an *enactment* of lawgiving on a reduced scale, that the origin of law in an act of collective will can become *an object of knowledge*. For when it is regarded objectively, rather than in process as analogical or metaphorical reenactment, the law cannot but appear to the individual in the form of mere constraint.

If we agree that there is no prior sanction in "natural" law for the social contract, or for the laws that are erected upon it, then it follows that precisely where government is at its best, where the state is "ruled by laws" (JJR, 3:379–80), the law will appear as an overpowering, quasi-primordial *fact*, not as an action by those who are ruled. Indeed, even at their inception, the laws must appear in the form of divine edicts transmitted by an inspired "legislator" (3:380–84). For if

I go but a short step too far in *thinking of* the law as my act or my will, the inevitable result will be confusion and the loss of precisely my freedom—even though, in truth, the law *is* my own act. "When the view contrary to mine wins [in a legislative vote], this proves nothing but that I had been mistaken in my assessment of the general will. If my own particular view had won, I would have done something other than what I had really willed, in which case I would not have been free" (3:441).

The law in truth *is* my own free and ultimately arbitrary (unsanctioned) act; but I cannot *think of it* in this way without contradicting its efficacy as an act. The situation is thus typical of situations that engender the silent knowledge of irony. I cannot know the law as an act except in the process of acting it out, reenacting it on a small scale, which is the rôle of censorship, the significantly arbitrary (not strictly legal) enforcement of public judgment or belief. In exactly the same way—we argued earlier—the question of the origin of language does not open itself to anything like knowledge, except insofar as we recognize, in our very reflection upon it, an enactment or model of the invention of language.

Or in terms closer to discourse theory, the social contract itself, if entirely without prior sanction, would have the character of an *institution of meaning*, the absolute inauguration of a potentially universal meaningfulness or communicativeness in discourse. The absence of a prior sanction, in a matter as decisive as the social contract, implies the absence of even the possibility of such a sanction, the absence of any "natural" fabric of meanings in which even the question of a sanction could arise. Knowledge of the social contract, therefore—however hypothetical that knowledge ("Let us begin by putting aside all the facts" [JJR, 3:132])—implies the knowledge that meaning *is* an institution, an arbitrary human act, not a natural property of our existence. And this knowledge, in turn, is another instance of the silent knowledge of irony, since any adequate articulation of it would place the absolute origin of meaning in a prior context of meanings. Meaning itself, for a discourse incorporating this knowledge, can therefore provide neither an anchor nor a principle of collection, and the discourse is perforce radically unstable.

Censorship, however—or even the mere advocacy of censorship—is capable, to an extent, of mastering this difficult knowledge by enactment, since censorship is an arbitrary restriction of meaning, thus as it were a reinstitution of meaning, within an *existing* discourse.

The analogical structure is perhaps not as perspicuous as in the case of censorship and law; and I will argue later that the enactment of the institution of meaning, and of the social contract, is perfected only in the novel as a genre. But at least the negative form of the equation adds up; we cannot grasp the institution of meaning *except* by way of a scaled-down enactment such as censorship. Kant, we have seen, accurately perceives a connection between censorship and irony, which he tries to exploit in *Der Streit der Facultäten* by setting up censorship as the paradoxical object of both acceptance and resistance. But discourse, for Kant, is still not unstable enough to *desire* censorship. It is not yet a discourse plagued by the institution of meaning, but still a discourse that can afford (as it were in spite of itself, like a socialist millionaire) to desire *freedom*, a discourse still anchored (now, as it were, in spite of itself) in the chimera of a pure reason that *guarantees* meaning.

Let us conclude by returning for a moment to Lessing's *Laokoon*, where the place of Kant's paradox, acceptance and resistance, is occupied by the paradox of a desire for censorship that puts its own object out of reach. Carol Jacobs's observations are again useful, especially her development of Lessing's argument on the disgusting. The text of *Laokoon*, in this view, attempts to stabilize itself, to set limits to itself and its object ("poetry"), by a "ventriloquistic" act of self-censorship (censorship as if from without). But the text's exclusively self-referred dynamics—its lack of an anchor, which makes censorship necessary in the first place—entails that even the category excluded by censorship, the "disgusting," exists as an excludable category only by making sense in terms of the imitation of experience (a process in which, we recall, "experience" is as much a product as a given), the imitation of an experience that Lessing then brilliantly identifies as "hunger." The result of this development of the concept of imitation, however, is a self-compounding "disruption in the logic of representation" that now disqualifies that concept even as a principle of textual collection, so that the act of censorship in the end articulates only the radical instability that had made it desirable.[17]

Or more specifically: In chapter 2 of *Laokoon*, Lessing affirms the acts of governmental censorship by which, in antiquity, certain states excluded all imitation that was not "beautiful" (L-M, 9:12–14). Then, however, he dismisses his remarks as a mere digression: "But I am

---

[17]Jacobs, p. 501. The terminology here is mine, the argument hers. See Jacobs, pp. 495–501.

straying from my path. I only wanted to establish that for the ancients beauty was the highest law of the pictorial arts" (9:14). In fact Lessing *has* stepped out of bounds here, for the juxtaposition of the concepts of law and beauty, plus the absence of a positive definition of beauty in his own argument, suggests the possibility that "beauty" is, after all, *nothing but* a variable legal concept, the result of an arbitrary act of exclusionary censorship. "Only what is beautiful is permitted" is uncomfortably close to "Only what is permitted is beautiful."

But then Lessing gets back onto his path, so that by chapter 9 we read: "If one wishes to compare the poet and the painter in particular cases, one must consider above all whether the two have possessed complete freedom, whether, without any external compulsion [i.e., censorship], they were able to work toward the highest effect of their art" (L-M, 9:65). And the contradiction that arises here—with the idea, from chapter 2, that pictorial art and its "highest law" of beauty *are* subject to censorship—would perhaps not even be noticeable, if Lessing, by referring from footnote to footnote on the subject of the Furies (9:67–68, 14–16), did not himself insist on calling it to our attention. The idea of censorship thus produces a real problem in his argument, which he apparently seeks to reduce by attenuating the idea of the artist's necessary "freedom." It is enough, he now says, if the marks of religious censorship are not "too noticeable," if the beautiful at least "can seem" to overpower the merely meaningful (9:67). But the trouble with this attenuation is that it makes necessary *a second level of censorship* before we can arrive at a judgment of "free" artistic beauty; now the strictly objective "antiquarian" can be overruled by the "connoisseur," who makes that judgment on attenuated, qualified, therefore ultimately arbitrary grounds (9:67). Freedom itself thus in a sense becomes the result of *two* moves of censorship; and at this level of complication the parallel with Rousseau becomes clear, in the operation of a discourse that must advocate censorship in the very process of admitting its loss of control over the manner of its being censored.

Herder and the Use of Censorship

We have already said a certain amount about the *Abhandlung über den Ursprung der Sprache*, which is one of Herder's most successful texts, in which the relation of the concept of "invention" to what the text actually does, its linguistic reflection upon language, produces an exceptionally clear and simple ironic structure. But this structure depends on the recognition that the concept of invention is a response to *censorship*, or arbitrary predetermination of meaning, in the form of the question posed by the Berlin Academy: "En supposant les hommes abandonnés à leurs facultés naturelles, sont-ils en état d'inventer le langage? et par quels moyens parviendront-ils d'eux mêmes à cette invention?" (Are humans, left to their own natural faculties, capable of inventing language? and by what means shall they arrive of themselves at that invention?) Why is Herder so enthusiastic about this supposedly "excellent, large, and truly philosophical question" (letter to Hartknoch, April 1769), this question which, he later complains to Hamann, forces him to adopt an uncomfortable "Leibnizian-aesthetic" pose?

Herder stresses, as the center of his argument in the *Abhandlung*, the idea of the strict unity of all mental faculties in any given organism. Every "soul," whether animal or human, is characterized by a single "positive force" (SW, 5:28, 30)—the terminology is clearly Leibnizian—to which justice is never fully done by an analysis into components. "That we have classified certain mental operations in certain broad categories, for example wit, perspicacity, imaginativeness, reason, does not mean that a single action of the intellect is ever possible in which wit or reason is acting alone . . . but in every case it is the whole undivided soul that is acting" (5:30). In particular, reason is never absent from human thought or action. "If man existed for but one instant without reason, then I cannot see how he could ever in his life think with reason, without altering his whole soul and the whole economy of nature" (5:30). And the name given by Herder to the one central "force" in the human soul, of which "sensualness, instinct, imagination, and reason" are but aspects or manifestations, is "Besonnenheit," which means roughly the process of "taking thought" or the state of having taken thought.

This basic act of reflection, by which we enable ourselves to exist, happens "when, in the whole hovering dream of images that sweep past his senses, man can collect himself in one instant of waking, when he can remain voluntarily with *one* image, observe it clearly and calmly, and separate from it the features that distinguish it as this object and no other" (SW, 5:35). This idea is related to the Leibnizian distinction between perception and apperception (see SW, 5:35, with a footnote referring to Sulzer). Perception, in a human

world not preformed by instinct, cannot happen without apperception, the reflective act by which, in effect, the perceptible object is
made to present itself to us. And this is the point at which Herder
cries "Eureka!" For the unity of the soul implies that the act of apperception, by which an ordered phenomenal world is born, is *already* in essence language. "This *first distinguishing feature in our
taking thought was a word of the soul! With this word human language is invented!*" (5:35). Otherwise it would be necessary to postulate a *second* mental faculty, separate from original reflection, that
could devise and arbitrarily apply verbal signs to the raw appercep-
tions reflection had produced. This is the basic logical structure of
Herder's argument: unity of the soul implies that reflection and language and existence in a phenomenal world are in truth merely different ways of regarding one single operation of "force."

The idea of "invention" appears to have no place in this structure.
Herder stresses that language simply *is* human nature, and at one
point even says: "Language thus becomes a natural organ of the understanding, *a sense of the human soul*, in the same way that the
power of sight constructed an eye for that sensitive soul of the ancients, or in the same way that instinct constructs a cell for the bee"
(*SW*, 5:47). How can a strictly natural process (like the bee's cell-
building) include a move of conscious "invention"? In fact the analogy, understanding is to language as sight is to the eye, is obviously
inexact; for the relation between sight and its external organ is that
between the mental and the physical, whereas language (Herder is
emphatic on this point) is fully in existence even where it is not
physically manifest. The one element in the genesis and operation of
language that has a necessary physical existence is humanity itself,
and does this not imply that humanity is the organ of language? If
humanity simply does not exist without language, if language is humanity's "*defining characteristic from without, as reason is from
within*" (5:47), does it not make sense to argue that nature, in order
to become a phenomenal world (not merely a machine of instinctive
reactions), requires language and therefore produces humanity as the
vessel of language? An argument in this direction is suggested
strongly by the four "natural laws" at the end of the *Abhandlung*,
which seek to explain the whole of human existence in history as the
result of nature's interest in the genesis and development of language.

Language, then, in a sense produces humanity, or nature produces humanity through language. But the Academy had made it clear that they wanted to hear how humanity "invents" language, and Herder obliges by constructing his argument on two entirely separate levels. He borrows from Mendelssohn's critique of Rousseau the image of the bleating sheep (MM, 2:106), and argues that humans first hit upon the idea of using spoken words when it first occurred to them to take natural sounds as the distinguishing features of objects, and then to imitate those sounds (SW, 5:35–37). By comparison with the deep logical argument on a single natural human "force," this hypothesis is distressingly naïve. How is the bleat distinguished as *one* sound, separate from the rest of the noisy world? At what stage does the idea of the sheep's *producing* the bleat enter? And the direction in which Herder then continues, toward another question dealt with by Mendelssohn, the question of how language can name objects that are perceived by senses other than hearing, appears in the end simply to leave the sheep behind.

"What are all our senses if not types of image-formation that belong to *one* positive force of the soul? We distinguish them from each other, but we do so only by means of the senses; we distinguish types of image-formation by types of image-formation. With much effort we learn to separate them in using them—but at a certain depth they still all operate together" (SW, 5:62). This radical synesthesia, if it were too intensely manifest in our actual experience, would produce a kind of insanity (5:61); but it remains true nonetheless that there is never a human experience in which any particular sense, for instance hearing, does not participate. The superficial level of argument, signaled by the concept of "invention," again obtrudes for a moment in the statement: "Since man receives the language of instructive nature only through hearing and otherwise cannot invent language, it follows that hearing in a certain way has become the mean among his senses, the true door to the soul and the bond of relation among the other senses" (5:64). But when Herder then goes on to develop the special characteristics of the sense of hearing—its range, clarity, vital intensity, progressiveness, expressive urgency, and developmental fruitfulness (5:64–68)—his argument is clearly a demonstration that the very existence of the human senses (hence of a phenomenal world) *already presupposes* their languageful organization with respect to the sense of hearing. Superficially it is argued that our recognition of the articulative usefulness of the sheep's bleat, and of similar phenomena, leads to the development of the special rôle of hearing. But on the deeper level it is argued that the special relation of the human senses to hearing is equivalent to the existence of an articulable phenomenal world and belongs to human nature before ever a bleat is heard.

The trouble with this separation between levels of argument is that, taken by itself, it is *too logical a structure*. Herder's deep argument, that the whole phenomenal world is conditioned by our situation in it as "the *speaking animal*" (SW, 5:47), has no relation to our actual experience. When I look out my window, I see trees and clouds, not words; I hear a dog barking, not a subject verbing. It may be true, theoretically, that language gives us our world; but it is still *a world* that language gives us, and precisely our nature as verbal creatures thus requires of us that we take it as a world, not theorize our way out of it. Excessive theorizing (or in Goethe's terms, failure to theorize with irony) is what Herder holds against Leibniz when he rejects the idea of "egoistic monads" (5:5) or of the "dreaming monad that *could think entirely without words*" (5:100), that is, the individual who attempts to think beyond the limits of the world of experience in which his words inevitably place him. This means, however, that the deep theoretical argument *implies logically* the superficial argument, the idea of a world that is simply there as experience, in which an "invention" of language can be imagined. And this logical implication, in turn, *absorbs* the superficial argument into the deep argument, so that the crucial tension between them, which produces irony, diminishes in the very process of our understanding it, and eventually disappears altogether.

Or at least this conclusion would follow, and collapse the text's irony, if the idea of invention *were* strictly a logical consequence of the deep argument, if it were not—*in fact*—imposed on the text from without by an act of censorship. What we have, in the two levels of argument, is not a dialogue between Herder and the Berlin Academy, but an arbitrary exercise of power; the Academy puts a word into Herder's mouth that he has no choice but to use. That he in the end uses it to his own advantage, as it were ventriloquistically, is irrelevant. The issue is one of fact. Even the *logical* reason for the superficial argument on "invention," after all, is precisely a need to account for our experience of the world as fact, not as a product of the operation of language; and that the existence of that argument, in turn, can itself be accounted for on the level of fact, preserves its categorical difference from the theoretical argument that otherwise threatens to absorb it. Or in the terminology we used earlier: the fact of censorship is a kind of anchor for the text, but an anchor that interferes with the achievement of theoretical collection, just as the still undeniable move of the deep argument to absorb the superficial argument interferes in turn with that anchoring. The result is an instance, if a precarious or temporary one, of radical instability in discourse.

Herder's Difficult Position: The Uses of Contradiction

We must recall that Kant's exploitation of the real censorship of his works is not the sign by which we distinguished his procedure from that of radical irony. What makes the difference in Herder is an implied *advocacy* of censorship, the absorption of the act of censorship into the basic logical structure of the discourse. For Herder, however, as for Kant, the act of censorship must still be extra-linguistically real. Our argument on ironic discourse in Rousseau, or in Lessing, was differently focused; but in neither case did we attempt to show a *self-contained* ironic discourse—which would be an absurdity anyway. Could the irony of the *Social Contract* operate without our knowledge (from the title page, if need be) of Rousseau's Genevan citizenship? Could Lessing's irony operate without the large act of censorship represented by the terminology of artistic imitation, or without the dialogic relation to Herder's response?

And yet, Herder's procedure is different from that of a Rousseau, a Lessing, or a Goethe; it is more desperate and episodic, less amenable to analysis in terms of the development of discursive strategies in the course of a work, or from work to work. For all their insistence on various forms of the idea of "Humanität," Herder's writings never resolve themselves (or avoid resolving themselves) into a career, into a shape consistent with the idea of setting and carrying out some definable historical task. They remain a *collection* of writings, which engage their various historical situations in different ways and are characterized above all, in structure and in detail, by the figure of *contradiction.*

Contradiction, as a figure with positive value, not merely the sign that a given line of thought must be rejected or abandoned, is well established in Western thought and literature. Does Nietzsche contradict himself? Then the reader must understand that there are criticisms and reinterpretations of intellectual tradition that cannot be *stated* without submitting to misinterpretation by precisely the tradition they criticize, and so can only be *enacted* in the form of contradiction. For our purposes, however, it will be useful to look at a kind of locus classicus in Montaigne: "Tant y a que je me contredits bien à l'adventure, mais la vérité, comme disoit Demades, je ne la contredy point" (MdM, p. 782; It may well be that I contradict myself from time to time, but the truth—as Demades said—I do not contradict).

The immediate context of this statement seems to justify our reading it to mean simply: I (Montaigne) always say exactly what I think in any given situation; if my statements conflict, it is because the conditions under which they were made (including, for all I know, my very character) differ from case to case. But this reading accords only uncomfortably with the form of the written and printed book as we have it before us. For writing, in general, is the vehicle not of *thoughts* (arising, we suppose, spontaneously in given situations) so much as of *second thoughts*, thoughts belonging to a broader perspective in which both we and the eventual reader survey our thinking. The statement we are looking at is itself an obvious instance of such second thought. This difficulty, moreover, which can be circumvented in theory, is forced upon us in the particular case when we explore the context in detail. For Demades, in the passage from Plutarch's *Life of Demosthenes* to which Montaigne alludes, claims not "truth" as the reason for his self-contradictions, but rather "the public good," the πόλις (Plutarch, 851f).

Demades' self-contradictions, that is, if we take him at his word, are *not* spontaneous; they are calculated political decisions. And passages elsewhere in Montaigne (also suggestive of Plutarch) imply specifically that contradiction in the service of *truth* may be a quasi-political operation, a strategy to ensure that truth have its proper effect in the world (e.g., MdM, p. 1055). But why suggest this idea, in the passage we began with, by *mis*quoting Plutarch, and in fact misquoting the words of an individual whom Plutarch himself is evidently accusing of mere sophistry, mere political opportunism? Is this procedure (this violation, in a sense, precisely of truth) not the sign of an inescapable difficulty in its own content, is it not an intertextual enactment of the impossibility of ever distinguishing clearly between strategy and capitulation? "Even truth does not have the privilege of being used at any time and in any way," says Montaigne;

for "the use of truth, noble as it may be, has its proper domains (*circonscriptions*) and limits" (p. 1055). But once we have put this recognition into practice by tailoring or trimming the truth to suit particular conditions: by what standard (a standard that must be somehow beyond truth) do we decide where we must stop in order to avoid *sacrificing* truth to those conditions?

And how shall we judge the truth or falsehood, now, of Montaigne's own assertion that he never contradicts truth? For this assertion can claim to be true only by running the palpable risk of becoming false—indeed, in a sense, only by actually being false. Demades, Montaigne indicates obliquely, shows us that the idea of the compatibility of contradiction with public good (let alone truth) is *inherently* liable to be used as a mere excuse for unworthy actions—which contradicts the idea of a strategy in the service of truth. And yet this form of falsehood is derived from precisely that helpless exposure of statements to circumstances which *validates* the original assertion. Or yet further: The form of the printed book gives the lie to Montaigne's pose of spontaneity, shows it to be merely a form of calculation. But the complex allusion to Plutarch implies that we can never calculate far enough, that the line between strategy and capitulation can never be drawn clearly, hence that our calculation is always infected with arbitrariness and so becomes a kind of spontaneity after all. Montaigne's statement on contradiction thus itself produces a multiple infinite regress of contradictions—which implies (by structural resonance) the operation of some form of truth. But exactly where?

Any number of passages in Herder could be subjected to a similar analysis. Let us consider just one, which we have already looked at, and which also involves the move of quotation. In the story of the bleating sheep in the *Abhandlung* (*SW*, 5:35–37), which refers to an example from Mendelssohn's argument against Rousseau, does the intervention of several *texts* between Herder's present writing and its supposedly concrete originary object (the encounter of human with sheep) not signal the recognition that *in* the story, the event narrated could not really happen without the intervention of some form of text, some preexisting language, between human perception and the actual animal? And is this structure not replicated in the intervention of the *Abhandlung* itself—as a text, as belonging to a culture of language in which meaning is in principle reducible to quotation—between itself and its object, between itself and any possible conception of a condition external to language in which language might have originated? Precisely this fabric of contradiction, however, this operation of our talking, as talking, against its own ostensible object—so that the very word "contradiction" contradicts itself by becoming a pleonasm, a tautology—precisely this *mise en abîme* also *demonstrates* Herder's point (thus contradicting itself yet again) that the invention of language is the invention of the whole scope of our existence, leaving us no external territory from which to survey it. And at the same time, these contradictions also *establish* an external perspective on language—as the site of precisely the idea that the nature of language makes such a perspective impossible—and so make possible the whole paradoxical idea of an "invention" of language, which is where the chain of contradictions had started.

Plenty of passages like this can be found. But I am more interested now in the pattern of contradictions that characterizes Herder's work on a larger scale, contradictions that have to do mainly with the idea of a systematic or disciplinary *closure* of discourse. Various compromise answers have been suggested to the question of whether Herder's view of history is strictly relativistic or systematically explanatory and normative. My contention is that it is both, and that the contradiction between these views is what matters. Or we might consider the *formally* systematic quality of Herder's writing, which is suppressed in such texts as the *Fragmente*, the *Kritische Wälder*, the "Torso" for Abbt, but then surfaces in the prize essays, including the essay on the origin of language, where it is dictated in each case by the occasion. And although the content of the prize essays always contrives to resist the form in which they are organized, systematic articulation nonetheless characterizes, thenceforward, practically all of Herder's work. This tendency culminates in the *Ideen*, where, despite the plural title, the content borders on becoming identical with the text's systematic architecture, and on thus producing a vision of human history that is unified in a reductive, dogmatically European Enlightenment sense. It is true that in the fifteenth book, which closes part 3, Herder insists that "the purpose of human existence is fulfilled" in every human individual (*SW*, 14:247). But how can any actual particular individual *interpret*, in this manner, the enormous, teleologically focused system of "ideas" in which his or her individuality is here subsumed?

What we have in this view of the *Ideen*, it seems to me, is not a difficulty or paradox, but the sheer impassable gulf of contradiction, a gulf that is insisted upon by the *categorical* separation between the articulative modes of its opposed elements, between statement (each individual is the purpose of human existence) and structure (supraindividual progress, God in history [*SW*, 14:207]). This use of structure to produce contradiction is developed yet further in Herder's writings against Kant. It is true that in the preface to *Kalligone* we read of "oppositions," between the *Metakritik* and Kant's *Kritik*, that do *not* form a "system"; "for the aim of the *Metakritik* was to liberate the reader from [Kant's] categorical despotism, not to bend the reader under a new terminological yoke" (*SW*, 22:7). But precisely the type of "word yoke" suggested by the idea of the "categorical" is in fact then employed by Herder in the *Metakritik*, in his imitation of Kant's category-tables, an imitation that actually surpasses the original in systematic perfection, in that the scheme of fourfold divisions is replicated exactly from level to level—or at least more exactly than in Kant.

Herder can insist all he likes on the difference between his own "schematics" and Kant's; he can scorn Kant's categories as mere tea leaves for fortune-telling (*SW*, 21:124), while proclaiming his own categories as "an *act* of the *understanding* itself" in language (*SW*, 21:112), indeed as an "actus purus" (*SW*, 21:126). The *structural resonance* between his own schemes and those he repeatedly reproduces from the *Kritik der reinen Vernunft* is still too strong. And the categorical difference between an act and a text is too great—between something that is what it is (namely, an act) only to the extent that I experience it as the direct expression of my own subjectivity, here and now, and something (the text, especially a text with diagrams) that possesses inescapably the quality of a visible object impinging on my awareness from without. Herder himself says, referring to the young reader of Kant: "As long as the author's obscure or concealed *schematism* does not contradict ours, we go along with him; only when the two come into conflict do we ask, 'How could the author say that?' We model ourselves upon him, we follow his manner of using words, and many a disciple or advocate has never asked that cardinal's question, [or 'cardinal question'] 'dove ha pigliato?'" (*SW*, 21:122).[18] Surely the reader of *this* book (the *Metakritik*) is not

---

[18]The quotation "dove ha pigliato?" (where did he [or you] get it?) is to an extent explained in *SW*, 1:265, as a question addressed to Ariosto by "the cardinal d'Este," which would have to be Ippolito d'Este. But I do not know the source of the story; and as far as I can tell, neither does any editor of Herder.

meant to suppress the question "Where did he get it?" or the inevitable tension and disagreement (the contradiction between act and text, hearing and seeing, temporal and spatial) that that question must produce. Especially *this* book—which begins by pointing out that a book that calls itself a "critique" itself insists on being read "critically" in its turn (*SW*, 21:17–18)—especially this *Metakritik* therefore demands a reading of exactly the same sort that it carries out upon Kant.

I am not suggesting that Herder does not "mean" what he says in the *Metakritik* and *Kalligone*. Obviously he does mean seriously the set of basic ideas and assertions that we recognize from his other works: the idea that the human soul is unified not as substance but as force ("Kraft"); the idea that thought is coextensive with language; the idea that philosophy errs when it does not treat "Humanität" as a unit notion. My point, rather, is that on the level of *structure*, these books are calculated to engender a situation of *radical contradiction*—contradiction not merely in the sense of a proposition and its negative, but in the sense of a text that requires, in order to be understood, not reading but dismantling, a text that literally "speaks against" every possible reader—even the reader who believes what it says—a text that attacks Kant not by pushing him off the cliff of his errors, but by embracing him and jumping off *with* him. In this sense, in the sense of being "against" the reader, the *Metakritik* and *Kalligone* to an extent take on the character of "action" after all.

Beyond Theory: Herder's Leap into the Body

The use of "contradiction" as an interpretive category is limited by the definiteness of negation it implies, which keeps it from being operative *in* the textual system where it occurs. (We recall the problem in the idea that Rousseau's texts "account for" their rhetoricity.) Contradiction—unlike paradox or tension or difference—needs a strict metasystem for its definition; and the interpretive relevance of such a metasystem is never decidable. The best we can do is ask: Does it *make sense* that Herder should be interested in the production of radical contradiction?

The diagrams below attempt to summarize what seems to me a crucial aspect of Herder's early thought, especially in the *Fragmente*. The first diagram illustrates the basic grid of languages and what I

will call "disciplines"—Herder most often uses the word "Wissenschaften." The meaning of this grid is suggested in passages like
the following: "The matter I am writing about: that language is [1.]
the tool of the disciplines, [2.] their content, and [3.] in a sense the
pattern to which they are cut, is so immense, even for the purpose of
merely sketching points of view, that in all I have said, I seem not
yet to have said anything of what I wanted to say" (SW, 2:20). Language, which means here every particular natural language, is (1) the
tool of the disciplines, insofar as each discipline uses different languages, and by using a language also changes it, adds to what that
language is capable of expressing; and (3) the form to which the discipline is cut, insofar as the language *affects* every discipline that
"dwells in it" (SW, 2:20), so that the discipline is never entirely the
same in two different languages. The idea (2) of language as the content of the disciplines mediates between these opposites by suggesting that in the process of representing its presumably real objects in
discourse (thus compromising their reality and receiving precisely
discourse as a "content"), a discipline also inevitably becomes subject
to the particular cultural conditions of its discourse (i.e., the natural
language it is using).

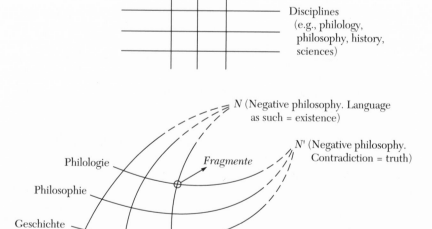

N.B. Point $N = N'$. Herder's objection to Kant's *Critiques*: Kant claims to have reached N'
without contradiction.

But what is so daunting, so "immense," about these ideas? In the first place, they contain a contradiction. The first grid above makes sense only if each discipline and each language is a stable unit, having the same value at each node (like an abscissa or an ordinate), which is precisely what the meaning of the grid denies. Hence Herder's "allegory" of the land surveyor who is dizzied by the problem of dividing language into fields (SW, 2:14). But in the second place, this contradiction, this vertigo, is an inescapable condition of any approach to truth on the highest level, to the truth that our being is indistinguishable from our being-human, and that our being-human, in turn, our "Humanität," our existence, experience, and history, is exactly coextensive with the invention, operation, and development of language. That this truth must be available to us, moreover, that we must have access to it, is *part* of our humanity, since otherwise language would be merely an enveloping "Kreis" to our existence, not qualitatively different from the enveloping element constituted for an animal by the range of its instincts.

Our access to truth, however, depends first on the existence of a *plurality* of natural languages (SW, 5:129–34, 141–42), without which we should have no perspective upon the co-determination of language and thought, upon the manner in which language is thought's form as well as its tool. And this perspective, in turn, the object-status of one language with respect to another, would be useless without the existence of intellectual disciplines, in the sense of translinguistic, object-oriented discourses that attempt to organize our existence systematically. For it is only against what ought in principle to be the strict uniformity of the discipline from language to language (guaranteed by the unity of its object), that the actual differences between languages can be measured. Furthermore, in order to operate as a gauge of the shaping of thought by language, each intellectual discipline must be radically developable, capable of critical distance with respect to itself, or differentness *from* itself, which is made possible exclusively by the discipline's differentness from language to language. (We think of Herder's repeated return to Leibniz's ideas about how the discipline of philosophy will benefit from the German language.) And the differentness of a particular language from discipline to discipline, in turn, is a token of *the language's* developability, of its dynamic character, its quality as an intimation of the identity of our existence with language as such.

The grid of languages and disciplines is thus the necessary mechanics, however contradictory, of our relation to truth. But the idea that languages and disciplines must be radically developable suggests a second diagram, which turns out to be a geometrical impossibility, since the two hypothetical, never actually attainable points, N and N', are *the same point*. The hierarchical arrangement of languages and disciplines implied by this diagram, incidentally, in which German and philology are closest to the goal, must be understood not as absolute, but as Herder's assessment of historical conditions in his own time.

And yet, what *is* Herder's situation in his time? where is his work situated in the grid? The *Fragmente* take as their point of departure the junction of philology and German, but only as their point of departure. For Herder's intellectual ambition directs him to a site *beyond* the grid, from which to view it as a whole. This ambition is in fact already asserted in the *Fragmente*, if cryptically, in the vision of "the true sage of language" who will unlock an ultimate "semiotics" (*SW*, 2:13), the "philologist of the nation" who would combine philosophy, history, and philology, and would explore the secrets of all foreign tongues while still somehow remaining "a true idiot," a man of *his* people (2:13–14). But especially we think of the "negative philosopher," who would operate at the very limit of human knowledge, and although perhaps unable to *see* into the "free air" beyond such knowledge (beyond the grid), would still as it were stretch forth his hand and proclaim: "Here is emptiness, here is Nothing!" (2:17).

This is Herder's ambition—to stretch forth his hand into the void—and it is the reason he cannot be content to operate *within* any intellectual discipline, even one of his own invention. The object of his thought is always the grid *as a whole*, in all its dizzying paradoxical complexity, whence it follows that the presence of radical contradiction in his work does make sense. Not that he seeks contradiction as a goal. But the nature of his endeavor entails that every particular inquiry be prosecuted at least to the point where it arrives at contradiction, since any systematically closed (i.e., putatively noncontradictory) discussion of an aspect of human existence or experience, or any discussion that even admits the possibility of systematic closure, belongs by definition *within* a "Wissenschaft," an intellectual discipline, either actual or conceivable.

It is still absolutely necessary—for the sake of our access to anything approaching precisely that complete view of the human condition which Herder desires—that the intellectual disciplines exist, that they be practiced and developed with as much rigorous consistency as possible. Herder's thought does not claim to be more *general* than normal scientific or scholarly thought; it does not claim either to rectify or to render obsolete the existing practice of any intellectual discipline. (In Herder's view, Kant is the one who makes this type of untenable claim.) But Herder's own work nevertheless traces a path that locates itself, by contradiction, outside all disciplinary boundaries, a path as it were perpendicular to the intersecting developments of language and discourse. And to be "outside" is the only general claim that it makes or implies, to stand as a token or witness of the mere *existence* of such an "outside," the existence (not the attainment) of point *N-N'*, which is equivalent to the existence of truth, of ultimate purpose, in our intellectual activity.

Herder's work, in other words, is not general at all, but eminently particular. He presents, in the final analysis, nothing but *himself*, as "a true idiot," an ἰδιώτης, which means not only a relatively independent proprietor within the community but also a lay person, the practitioner of no organized profession. He presents himself as precisely that individual of the *Ideen*, in whom the whole of humanity is fulfilled, and who, for this purpose, must be precisely *a* particular individual, "ein wahrer Idiot," not *the* general form of the individual. His use of contradiction thus in the end brings us back to the passage from Montaigne with which we began, which is also where Montaigne insists that his work presents nothing but himself ("Mes-huy c'est fait"), nothing but "Michel de Montaigne," and where he says, "If the world complains that I talk too much about myself, I in turn complain that the world does not even *think* about *itself*" (MdM, pp. 782–83). Herder's work, similarly, is not an attempt to "form humanity," not an attempt to describe or organize the world, but rather a gesture, a token, a witness, a perpendicularity, an idiotic martyrdom (in the etymological sense of these words), at which the world of disciplines and languages and apparent progress, the developing grid of developments, is meant for a moment to pause and take thought of *itself*.

What name shall we give to the version of "himself" that Herder (or Montaigne) thus injects into the scheme of languages and discourses? What we mean is obviously not the "ego," which is the self *in the form of discourse*, or presented as an object or meaning or content of discourse. But it is also not the "subject" that witnesses and suffers here; for the subject, as we have used this term, cannot be "Herder's" to begin with, but exists only as the signified of the social, or by extension, the signified of irony in discourse. The only concept, as far as I can see, that means "himself" (of Herder or Montaigne) in a manner sufficiently particular and sufficiently nondiscursive, is the concept of the *body*. It is his body that Herder repeatedly reinhabits in his writings and forces between the stones of language and discourse in the huge mill of truth. It is his very body upon which the authentic interpretation of his writings is written. This phenomenon, this writing upon the body, is not exclusively Herderian in the age of radical discursive instability with which we are occupied; but it tends elsewhere to appear in the compressed form of crisis. In Herder, by contrast—who thus repeats the rôle of Montaigne in an earlier age—the body is compelled to *survive* and become legible, under conditions that otherwise produce the madness of a Lenz or a Hölderlin, the suicide of a Kleist.

Klopstock as a Witness

Let us conclude by taking the testimony of one further witness to the ironic communicativeness of the age we are examining in Germany, a witness who is the more effective for being unexpected. In Herder and Lessing, as in Hamann and in some works of Goethe, we are struck by a cabalistic quality in the writing; not only *is* there more than meets the eye in the *Abhandlung* and the *Ideen*, in *Laokoon*, and especially in *Die Erziehung des Menschengeschlechts*, but specific devices draw our attention to what is hidden. This quality is entirely absent in Klopstock's prose, which requires an extremely attentive reader to penetrate its apparent straightforwardness, a reader like Lessing. In discussing the essay "Von der Nachahmung des griechischen Silbenmaßes im Deutschen," which was printed in 1755 as a preface to the second volume of *Der Messias*, Lessing says:

> One sees that not everything has yet been said; but what has been said is excellent. The reader, however, must himself have pondered ancient metrical forms if he wishes to understand all the subtle remarks that Herr Klopstock appears merely to toss off in passing, rather than present by design. This is what happens when a *genius* is full of his subject matter and knows its deepest secrets; when he has to talk about it, he will seldom know where to begin; and when he does begin, he will presuppose so much that the common readers will con-

sider him obscure, while readers of a somewhat better sort will criticize him for superficiality. . . . I am uncommonly pleased with the prose of our poet; and this treatise in particular is a model of how to write about grammatical trifles without pedantry. [L-M, 8:44–45]

The last remark makes it clear that Lessing distinguishes *three* classes of reader, not two. The common reader finds Klopstock's elliptical arguments obscure, because explicit demonstration is missing. The reader "of a somewhat better sort" recognizes the possible presence of sound argument behind what Klopstock says, and assumes that the argument itself, fully developed, would increase the accuracy and validity of the statement, which, as it stands, is still superficial. The third type of reader, however, who is Lessing himself, understands that precisely the elliptical character of the presentation reflects knowledge, a knowledge too ironically self-referential to offer any adequate starting point for systematic discussion.

Precisely what knowledge is concealed in Klopstock's prose? Let us look at one long passage from the essay Lessing admires:

The thoughts in a poem are separate; and the euphony is separate. The two have no relation to each other except that our soul is entertained by aural sensations at the same time that it is occupied with the poet's thought. If the harmony of the verse pleases the ear in this way, then we shall have achieved a great deal, but not quite everything that we could have achieved. There is a certain type of euphony beyond this, which is connected with thoughts and helps express them. But nothing is harder to describe exactly than this highest refinement of harmony. Grammarians have called it "vivid expression," and tend to discover it in Vergil and Homer only where it is exaggerated, thus stripped of its proper beauty, the principal element of which is its subtlety; or there are other passages where the poets never dreamt that scholiasts would come along and credit them with a beauty of this type. Different degrees of slowness or swiftness, something of soft or violent passions, a few subtle indications of what principally deserves to be called action in a poem: these things, by vivid expression, can be imitated distantly. When the poet does this, he employs (or rather he depends on the fortunate cooperation of) some of his most delicate elaborative devices, which are correspondingly likely to miscarry as soon as he applies them too purposefully, or as soon as his imagination too eagerly expands the limited range of these subordinate touches, thus abandoning the harmony of a poem in favor of music. I will admit that there are cases where vivid expression must say emphatically what it wants to say. But as a general rule, vivid expression, in this sense, should be approached rather than achieved. [*AW*, pp. 1042–43]

It is easy to see how this passage might be considered obscure, for the main concept in it, "vivid expression" ("lebendiger Ausdruck"), is neither defined nor illustrated by examples. This poetic device, we are told, involves a "connection" between sound and sense in language. It perhaps includes onomatopoeia, but must include other devices as well, for Klopstock would evidently consider most instances of onomatopoeia excessively "purposeful." And yet, on the other hand, to the extent that we do more or less understand what "vivid expression" is—a subtle combination of pace and rhythm, along with the quality of specific sounds, harsh or smooth, flowing or abrupt, as these correspond to qualities of thought—Klopstock's treatment appears superficial, since general practical rules are asserted with no justification.

There is, however, a coherent chain of reasoning here, which has to do with the idea of music. The emotional expressiveness of music is a commonplace; and for Klopstock, who regards "the depiction of passion" as a main task of poetry (*AW*, p. 1021), the quality of emotion brings poetry and music into a potentially dangerous proximity. For in truth the two arts are not only different, but belong to different classes of intellectual activity, music to *beaux-arts* ("schöne Künste"), poetry to *belles-lettres* ("schöne Wissenschaften"), both these terms being understood in their eighteenth-century meanings.[19] If the sound of poetry makes too strenuous an attempt to express the whole sense, then poetry is in danger of losing its character as poetry; the language of the poem risks ceasing to function as language, with an ethical or moral dimension that is its normal advantage over the nonverbal arts (see *AW*, pp. 986–90). The special character of language is that it speaks *directly* to the heart, not by way of the senses (p. 985); if the meaning of a poem becomes too entirely audible, this advantage disappears.

But then why does Klopstock permit "vivid expression" to begin with, even in a controlled form? Why not prohibit it altogether? Let us look at the ode "Die Sprache," which is much later than the essay but develops the same basic thought (*AW*, pp. 131–32). The poet

---

[19]See "Von dem Range der schönen Künste und der schönen Wissenschaften," in *AW*, pp. 981–91.

here warns against "separating" language from its favorite "play-mates," who are identified as "euphony and meter":

> Harmonie zu sondern, die so einstimmet,
>   Meidet, wer weiß, welcher Zweck sie verband:
>   Die Trennungen zwingen zu viel
>   Des Gedachten zu verstummen.

[The sundering of a harmony that so fits together will be avoided by anyone who knows the purpose for which it was created: such separations compel too much thought to be silent.]

If language, "the twin of thought," is separated from the seemingly nonessential devices by which it is made into poetry, then it appears that somehow a large portion even of its "thought" will be stifled. And the importance of poetically regulated language has to do with the idea of *audible speech*. Two strophes earlier, the poet addresses a hypothetical "inventor," the first person who had understood language deeply enough to conceive of it as a system recorded by signs:

> Doch, Erfinder, täusche dich nicht! Für dich nur
>   Ist es gedacht, was zum Laute nicht wird,
>   Für dich nur; wie tief auch, wie hell,
>   Wie begeisternd du es dachtest.

[But inventor, do not deceive yourself! For you only is thought what does not become a sound, for you alone, no matter how deeply or clearly or enthusiastically you thought it.]

The written word is a kind of magic by which the otherwise transitory sounds of language are made permanent ("durch Zeichen . . . hinzuzaubern den Hall"); but if the written word, in its turn, is not actualized as a sound, then the thought contained in it has not yet really become community property. Hence the indispensability of poetic regulation, which, even in written language, calls our attention to the sound of the words, thus "awakening" the sound, and the thought, for us.

The idea of "thought" in this context, however, does not refer to material supposedly transmitted by language from one individual mind to another. The image of the inventor is first introduced in the sentence: "Dem Erfinder, welcher durch dich [i.e., language] des Hörers / Seele bewegt, tat die Schöpfung sich auf!" (To that inventor who by language moved the soul of his hearer, all Creation opened into bloom!). The invention of communicative speech, in other words, is a revelation more for the *speaker* than for the hearer—this clearly reminds us of Herder—and the "thought" that is lost when poetry fails to preserve the sounding quality of language, consequently, is a portion of the speaker's (or the writer's) *own* thought, not material lost in transmission. Creation is revealed to us not by language as a vehicle from which we receive transmitted knowledge, but in the process of our *using* language; there is an essential difference between our thought as such, "for us alone," and our thought as we send it forth in soundable language, a difference from *our* point of view. By developing our thought as actual or potential sound, we advance actively into the world and bind ourselves to it ("das Wort . . . heiliges Band / Des Sterblichen"—note the singular), whereupon the world is first truly thrown open to us. And it follows that the heightening of thought in which we receive this revelation, the heightening of thought which differentiates communicative speech from silent or bookish meditation, is thought that *belongs to language itself*, not to the thinking individual. As in Herder and Goethe, with respect to our percipient and active situation in a phenomenal world, language is prior to individuality; it is language that employs the speaking individual for its realization, not the individual who employs language in order to transmit his or her fancies.

Now the ideas in the long prose passage we started with fall into place. The sound of language, merely by being sound, becomes the bearer of thought, not in the sense of formulable propositions, but in the sense of a basic area of interaction between what Goethe calls "us and objects." And a principal function of poetry is to keep this thought alive (as in Goethe, to remind us *that* we see the world) by preserving and elaborating language in the form of auricular enjoyment. Therefore "vivid expression," in Klopstock's sense, is useful; for the connection between sound and meaning in detail—when the sound helps express a particular degree of swiftness or passion, or a particular type of "action" (elsewhere defined as "the application of will power toward the attainment of an end" [AW, p. 1033])—increases our receptivity to the relation between sound and thought in general. By understanding particular cases of "vivid expression" we carry out a mental exercise toward comprehending the great general meaning of poetry as such, the self-revelation of all nature to humankind as the user of language, our poetically mediated rediscovery of our own native world.

But on the other hand, if the poet goes only a short step too far in "vivid expression," the effect will be to interfere with the function of poetry; sound will now give the impression of *transmitting* what the poet has in mind. Therefore Klopstock stresses that "vivid expression," strictly speaking, should not be *employed* by the poet, but should occur only as a happy coincidence on which the poet can subtly capitalize. When the sound of the language generates meaning, in other words, it must always remain clear to the reader or hearer that this meaning, and this expressive ability, *belong to the language as such*, not to the mind or talent of a particular individual. The poet must avoid usurping the position of language itself as the poem's ultimate speaker, for poetry is always a revelation not of one individual's thought or feeling, but of the whole world that language calls into being when it is truly language.

There is no need to dwell on the consequences of this thought; we have already done so in connection with both Goethe and Herder. What is interesting here is the faith Klopstock apparently has in the reader's grasp of the thought necessary to make sense of his argument. In both Lessing and Herder there is a much more complex and strenuous irony, a greater expressive urgency. In Goethe, alongside the familiar cultivated insouciance, or indeed as an integral part of it, there is a certain resignation to the possibility that what he is saying will never be understood in its entirety. In Hölderlin, whose formative years come a good deal later, this melancholy approaches desperation and produces not only several incomprehensibly complicated attempts at self-explanation in essay form, but also the incomprehensibly simple poetry of statement that we have sampled in "Friedensfeier."

In Klopstock, however, all of this is absent. His prose is ironic in the sense that its logical cohesion depends on a deliberately submerged level of argument. But there is no cleverness or virtuosity in his irony; he simply says what can be said, given the limits on direct formulation entailed by a complex ironic view of language, and says it as clearly as possible, leaving the rest to be supplied by the reader. This attitude is important because it implies Klopstock's opinion that the submerged knowledge in his prose was relatively *common* knowledge in his time. At the cost of some effort and complication, in developing the ideas of anchored and collected discourse, we arrived at a similar conclusion above: that an ironic poetics of the age was practically inevitable in late eighteenth-century Germany, a poetics lying beneath the surface of the various particular doctrines and practical principles espoused by major figures; and that not only the resistance to Kantian terminology among older writers but also the systematic hypertrophy of the ironic in the post-Kantian poetics of Romanticism are natural reactions indicating the depth at which that ironic poetics had established itself. But in Klopstock's calm certainty that his deep theory would be understood, we find a more direct witness in support of this argument.

The unstrained quality of Klopstock's thought, combined with his innovations in poetic form, earned him an almost unclouded reputation among the best contemporary minds. Not only Bodmer and Breitinger, the poets of the "Göttinger Hain," Wieland, Lessing, but also Hamann, Herder, and Goethe, despite occasional disagreements, evince a remarkably deep and constant respect for Klopstock; even Schiller is wary of committing *lèse majesté*, though it is evident in *Über naive und sentimentalische Dichtung* that he has little taste for *Der Messias*; and Hölderlin, in whom the influence is especially obvious, speaks unaffectedly of "father Klopstock." For his contemporaries as well as for us, Klopstock is a witness and, as it were, a star by which to navigate on the sea of ironies and misunderstandings, an unfailing reassurance that the new poetics, however difficult to explain or agree upon in detail, was a well-rooted and fruitful communal presence. Herder, the tormented body of the age, whose talent for contradiction included a talent for alienating the friends he needed most, left behind at his death no fewer than sixty-six handwritten copies (most copied by himself) of odes by Klopstock; and I do not think it is unlikely that Klopstock's death in 1803 (followed by Wilhelm Heinse's later the same year) contributed to the sense of perfect abandonment that sealed Hölderlin, once and for all, in his mental tomb.

CHAPTER SIX

The Genres of Mind and Contract:
The Theater, the Novel, and the Jews

If the argument of the preceding chapter is diffuse, it is so with good reason. Its conclusion is not one that can be established by a direct and continuous interpretive process; it can be made plausible only by being shown to exhibit explanatory power in relation to different phenomena viewed from different perspectives—the more different, the better. One key question, however, emerges repeatedly. Where exactly does the thinking of radical irony happen, if the idea of a thinking individual is too specific and if the idea of a thinking community, of "the community as a reader," is not specific enough?

Theater of the Mind

Marian Hobson, in her article "Du Theatrum Mundi au Theatrum Mentis," starts from Derrida's perceptions about the Cartesian "cogito" and argues that "theater," as a metaphor, always signifies a "clôture" or "totalisation" of our actions, perceptions, experience, a totalizing that in turn presupposes a consciousness able to encompass the total object, a spectator, who in the case of the world theater is the infinite spectator or God.[1] In the course of the seventeenth and eighteenth centuries, however, the divine spectator is supplanted by a human spectator; the theater of the world becomes a theater of the

[1] Marian Hobson, "Du Theatrum Mundi au Theatrum Mentis," *Revue des Sciences Humaines*, n.s., no. 167 (1977), 379–94.

mind, in which the individual is situated vis-à-vis the totality of his or her own experience. This development seems to me a direct consequence of the metaphor itself, whose very existence implies an identification of the human mind that conceives it with the divine mind it postulates; the metaphor, as a verbal act, is a totalizing act of perception on *our* part, and the psychologizing of its content is practically inevitable. Exactly this process in the natural life of the metaphor is reflected, in eighteenth-century Germany, in the idea that the *actual* theater affords its spectator a measure of identification with the divine mind; both Herder, in his "Shakespear" essay, and Lessing, in the *Hamburgische Dramaturgie*, arrive at this idea by way of the notion of world-closure.[2]

At certain historical junctures, as in the speculations of Herder and Lessing, our idea of the actual theater is not merely nourished by reflections of (and on) the evolving metaphor of the theater but constituted by such reflections. When I say "our idea of the actual theater," moreover, I mean simply "the actual theater"; for in the case of the theater, the distinction between the thing itself and our "idea" of it collapses incessantly. Housed as it may be for centuries in the same stone edifice, loaded down as it may be with the physicality of actors, properties, and stage machinery, trivialized as it may be by the majority of its visitors, for whom it operates as either an appetizer or an aid to digestion, enmeshed as it may be in the reassuringly sluggish institutional organization of this or that society—the theater, the actual theater, is itself still in truth never anything but a tissue of metaphor. For the theater, in all its materiality, *is* not what it is except in the act of becoming repeatedly something *other* than "the theater," something never fully determined by any conceivable general definition of "the theater." It is a kind of Platonic Receptacle (*Timaeus* 52d). Metaphor is not only enacted in it, but is its very substance, which is why the conventional metaphorical associations in which "the theater" participates, with the dreaming mind and with the world, are so remarkably ambiguous with regard to the direction of the tenor-vehicle relation—is the theater like the world? or the world like a theater?—by contrast with the conventional metaphorical associations of such concepts as "rose," "heart," "machine," "book."

---

[2]See Herder on Shakespeare's handling of his characters as God handles mortals (SW, 5:219–20, 222, 223, 227), and especially on Shakespeare's placing us in a position to observe from the divine perspective (SW, 5:221). In Lessing's *Hamburgische Dramaturgie*, see no. 79, the argument on how the design of the "mortal creator" (the dramatist) should imitate, in completeness or closure, the design of the "eternal creator" (L-M, 10:120).

In fact, I think it can be argued that in European tradition, the theater, by being at once both entirely a real material object and entirely a metaphor, is the unique location in the community at which the idea of *the metaphoricity of the real* is adequately expressed or understood or known. This idea is inevitably misunderstood in the arena of abstract philosophical discussion, for it requires that we distinguish radically between its two elements in order to understand precisely their identity. The uniqueness of the theater, however, its special cultural function, is that its quality as an institution and the quality of the rituals performed in it combine to circumvent this philosophical difficulty, to make the truth, by enacting it, not only ideally but also actually true.

These are large assertions, and by being made in the name of "our" idea of the theater they open themselves to the charge of dogmatism. Why not let the theater be either a simple given, an object or class of objects about which people can have whatever ideas they please, or else perhaps a family of ideas that bear various significant relations to one another but form no enduring structure? My position is that the "theatrical" itself, in the sense of a striving for totality or closure, has the effect of *resisting* any such dismissive pluralism; that the actual dramatic theater is always an instrument of intellectual focus, never merely the expression of some supposed unphilosophical vitality; that the theater, even in the decay of its focus upon "world," develops not toward the innocent plurality of mere objects but toward that problematic nonlocality, vis-à-vis the object as such, which is opened by the "cogito" and its critique. The theater, we have seen, is *where* the social signifies the subject. Among people who work in the theater and people who write for it, many insist on a strict disjunction between the chill of intellect (where, supposedly, any "idea" of the theater must dwell) and the warmth of real life (as artistic exuberance or social concern). But the theater itself, in which centuries of complex philosophical metaphor are repeatedly clothed with living flesh, in which actual solid things become semiotically translucent and put on their very solidity as a mask, the theater itself always at least calls that disjunction into question.

Any number of historical instances suggest themselves. Frances A. Yates, in *Theatre of the World* and other works, shows the existence in the Renaissance of a fundamental interaction between the theater as an institution and the philosophical metaphor of the theater. In the nineteenth century the dramatic theater pollinates itself by way of Schopenhauer, Hegel, and Nietzsche; it lives and sustains itself, *as* theater, in the form of a latent metaphor in philosophical tradition.[3] And now I will argue that the idea of a "theater of the mind," of the theater as a model or projection of the problematic interior life of a human individual, was not only present in eighteenth-century Germany, but in fact had the status of an axiom, an idea so evident that it required practically no systematic formulation and is visible to us now only (or mainly) in the artistic practice built on it.

That the idea is present is clear enough. I have mentioned Herder and Lessing, the idea of the theater as the site of our self-conscious participation in a divine mentality, hence as a revelation of the divine aspect of our own mentality. The case of J. M. R. Lenz is interesting, especially the relation between his own plays and his "Anmerkungen übers Theater." The "Anmerkungen" do not actually say anything *about* plays like *Der Hofmeister* and *Die Soldaten*, but rather the plays are the same type of text as the theoretical remarks, in effect an extension of the theory's own problematic unfolding, so that the distinction between drama and reflection upon drama tends to dissolve.[4] And in Goethe we recall his remark about theatrical tragedy and its "inward directed" hero, his vision of a literally self-reflecting theater in "Über Wahrheit und Wahrscheinlichkeit der Kunstwerke," and the constant intertwined playing with both theatricality and interiority in *Faust*.[5] But again, my point is not merely that the idea of a theater of the mind is important in eighteenth-century German dramatic thought. My point is that it is an axiom, brought along by theatrical tradition as a whole. What we observe is not merely the "German" imposition of introspectiveness upon an otherwise unphilosophical institution. The theater has a fundamental introspectiveness of its own and never moves, never lives, except in intimate contact with its own brooding image.

The Plot of *Stella*

The plot of Goethe's early play *Stella* is improbable to a degree that cannot but be meant to attract our attention. Many years before the

---

[3]See my *Modern Drama and German Classicism: Renaissance from Lessing to Brecht* (Ithaca, 1979), chap. 8.

[4]Regina Marz, "J. M. R. Lenz, 'Der Hofmeister': Ein Drama im Zusammenhang mit der zeitgenössischen theoretischen Diskussion" (unpublished), makes this point.

[5]See WA, 41/2:221, 47:257–66, and my *Goethe's Theory of Poetry: "Faust" and the Regeneration of Language* (Ithaca, 1986), esp. chap. 8.

play's action, Fernando had married Cezilie, stayed with her long enough to father a child, then abandoned her to search for his lost freedom. But instead of freedom he had found another, younger woman, Stella, then "no older than sixteen" (WA, 11:134), whom he had enticed away from her parents in order, under the pretense of being married, to set up housekeeping with her at an aristocratic residence near the town where the play is set. After about five years and the death of their infant child, however, he had become restless again. True to form, he had abandoned Stella and, after a futile attempt to locate Cezilie, gone off adventuring. Cezilie, meanwhile, having fallen (naturally enough) upon hard times, is forced to seek employment for her and Fernando's daughter Luzie; and in spite of the geographical distance that must be involved, she *just happens* to have found a position for Luzie in Stella's service, without of course knowing anything about Stella and Fernando. And on the very day that she and Luzie arrive at Stella's town, Fernando *just happens* to arrive as well, having decided to return to Stella. In the case of a farce we would perhaps be willing to accept these coincidences. But in a sentimental "Schauspiel für Liebende"?

The plot not only is absurdly improbable in itself but also draws our attention to other incongruities in the work. First, and most important, why do the two women love Fernando as they do? Where is that inner amplitude, the "große Seele" (WA, 11:145) Stella claims to perceive in him, or the "Geist" (11:130) recalled admiringly by Cezilie? When he first appears, he delivers a passionate self-searching monologue on his need for Stella (11:137–38). But only a few moments later he begins flirting with Luzie, who he does not yet know is his daughter, but who he does know plans to become a servant in *his* household—obviously a dangerous position for a girl of Luzie's age. And if this is not enough to convince us that Fernando is an individual with no firmness of character—except perhaps in his taste for female teenagers—then surely his conversation with his old servant, now Stella's estate manager (11:160–62), tips the balance. Stella and Cezilie are both powerful characters, Cezilie in her self-sacrificing practicality, Stella in her utterly committed love and kindness; but the man they have both fallen in love with does nothing but vacillate between a compulsive gnawing at his uncomfortable self-knowledge and various attempts to escape from it. When Stella calls him playfully a "Bösewicht" (11:157) she is flattering him; in reality he has not even the substance of a decent scoundrel.

Fernando, in other words, is close to being a strict nonentity, an empty space in the middle of the play's action; and the two women's love for him is therefore perhaps understandable after all. The object of their love is not really Fernando, but rather something they project imaginatively into the empty space he constitutes, into a space that receives such projections all the better for being empty of any character of its own—like Plato's Receptacle, which is here imagined as masculine, not feminine. This process of projection is represented graphically in the last scene, in which Cezilie engineers a solution to the play's problems by telling the story of the Graf von Gleichen with his two wives, a story that fits the present situation well enough *except* with regard to the character of the man, the noble crusader who is everything Fernando is not. And in the final tableau it is obviously the two women who have found each other, whose natures truly complement each other; Fernando, in the middle, is merely the vehicle of *their* union. He is the *stage*, the empty space, on which Stella and Cezilie act out their love; he is a self-reflexive allegory of the theater, a Platonic *chora* that is never itself except by being other than itself.

In any case, the quality of *allegory* is brought to the fore by the otherwise farcical coincidences on which the plot is built. The fiction does not imitate some possible reality about which we are then meant to think, but rather its structure means nothing if it does not represent directly, or allegorically, a structure of concepts. And the content of the allegory is clear. The play enacts *the operation of self-consciousness*. Fernando represents the focus of self-consciousness, the never-quite-entity that we refer to when we say "I," the object that can never become entirely an object because its nature vacillates constantly, refusing to be located at a distance from the perceiving subject, the object whose only enduring quality is that of an empty space into which images are projected incessantly and always instantly falsified. And the structure of the play represents the structure of self-consciousness, constantly poised and torn, like Fernando, between the experience of implacable reality, contingency, and obligation (Cezilie) and the experience of the ideal, of freedom, immortality, and quasi-divinity (Stella).

Among the documents in which Goethe develops this idea of self-consciousness, the most interesting for our purposes, because it also focuses on the genre of drama, is the little speech "Zum Shakespeares Tag," which contains the assertion that Shakespeare's plays all revolve about "den geheimen Punckt, |:den noch kein Philosoph gesehen und bestimmt hat:| in dem das Eigenthümliche unsres Ich's, die prätendirte Freyheit unsres Willens, mit dem nothwendigen Gang des Ganzen zusammenstösst" (WA, 37:133; the secret point— which no philosopher has yet seen or determined—where the uniqueness of our ego, the pretended freedom of our will, collides with the necessary operation of the whole). Obviously this "point" is not located anywhere in reality, as the point, say, at which an individual's intention is thwarted by circumstances; for then there would be nothing "secret" or philosophically indeterminable about it. It is, rather, a point in the soul, in our mental economy, at which the two absolutely irreconcilable aspects of self-consciousness manage for a moment to coexist and so to constitute a total or quasi-divine self-consciousness. Fernando's wanderings and confusions represent the characteristic oscillation of the mind between a belief in our absolute freedom and an acknowledgment of the helplessness of our actual finite condition. And the climax of the play, the sharing of Fernando by his two women, represents that miraculous "point" or moment in the soul where the totality of our nature, at once both perfectly free and strictly limited, is present to us in the form of experience, that "secret" moment which *cannot* happen, since its two aspects exclude each other both logically and naturally, yet also somehow *must* happen, since without it there would be no such thing as self-consciousness to begin with, no center for self-consciousness to take shape about, no ego, no "I! Who am all to myself and know everything only through myself!" (37:129). I do not mean that this moment occurs in *Fernando's* experience, that Fernando is thus a character worthy of Shakespeare. Far from it. My point is that the fiction *as a whole* represents allegorically the inward process by which the eternally originary "point" of human totality (which is also, eternally, a "collision" and a disruption of totality) is eternally reachieved in human experience. The stage *as a whole* has become a model of the interior of a human being.

Theater as a Working Model of Consciousness

But then why does *Stella* not look more like an allegory, the way scenes in *Faust* do? Why are normal mimetic conventions generally observed in action and dialogue? Why the form of drama in the first place? And why is the work called "Ein Schauspiel für Liebende"? How is this psychological-philosophical allegory directed at lovers?

The question of drama and theater offers a starting point. The interest of the eighteenth century in the form of "drame" or "Schauspiel," as opposed to the tired conventions of tragedy and comedy, has to do with the idea that in the theater the isolation of the individual is overcome by a surge of sympathy or "Mitleid," which is established first between the spectator and the fictional character, but thence implies and so in a sense creates a true if temporary community among the spectators.[6] What Goethe does in the allegory of *Stella* is simply unfold before the audience the only possible ground or scene of their sympathetic community. A sympathy based on the supposed sharing of some particular feeling is out of the question, for the quality of feeling depends precisely on its inarticulable *privacy*; the process of recognizing in someone else the same feeling as one's own is structurally indistinguishable from the process of conscious reflection, which—in Werther, for example—destroys the feeling *as* feeling. But the "secret point" of fully developed, self-conscious humanity is more than just a feeling and provides a better focus for human sympathy. My heart is mine alone, says Werther (WA, 19: 111); but the "secret point," although still profoundly *my* experience, also belongs to nature at large, indeed *is* the universal experience of human nature.

(The situation is not quite as simple as this statement of it. The "secret point" locates not only a completion, but also a collision or rupture in our humanity; and the community or sympathy associated with a focus upon that point is therefore never achieved, but always still in the making. This qualification, however, does not invalidate the concept of community in this context, or of sympathy, since neither concept can be imagined as having a pure or fully achieved manifestation anyway. Community and sympathy exist *only* by being still in the making, with respect to the stubborn individuality that provides their indispensable vehicle, the individuality that would simply be superseded by their perfection. Again, the idea of sympathy as

[6]On the ins and outs of "Mitleid," see Hans-Jürgen Schings, *Der mitleidigste Mensch ist der beste Mensch: Poetik des Mitleids von Lessing bis Büchner* (Munich, 1980). Also see my *Modern Drama and German Classicism*, chaps. 2, 4, and 5; and my "Idea of the Audience in Lessing's Inexplicit Tragic Dramaturgy," *LY* 11 (1979), 59–68.

the sharing of a particular feeling fails by presupposing the disintegration of precisely that feeling's needful individual vessel.)

This consideration enables us to understand the designation "Schauspiel für Liebende." *Stella* is a Platonic lesson for lovers; it teaches that the true object of our love is not a particular individual or anything that can belong to an individual but rather the vision of our own fulfilled humanity, which we perceive *by way* of the beloved individual—by projection *onto* that individual, if need be. Exactly this lesson is later articulated by Leonore Sanvitale in *Tasso*—in a situation similar to the one in *Stella*—when she says to the Prinzessin: "We seem to love the man, and actually only love—with him—the highest thing that we are capable of loving" (ll. 215–17; WA, 10:113). The "Mit ihm" (with him) is of course questionable. In the case of Fernando, it is clear that the beloved does not join the lovers (Cezilie and Stella) in experiencing the "secret point" but simply becomes transparent, a nonentity, in relation to that focus. And in *Tasso* the problem is the opposite: Tasso refuses to become transparent, insists on his own difficult personal qualities in a manner that makes nonsense of the Platonic pretensions of both Leonores. In any case, we recall that the composition of *Stella* belongs to the time of Lili Schönemann, whose actual personal qualities Goethe found it difficult to imagine as the object of his feeling, and about whom he says only half jocularly, "If you don't know her, thank God for it" (WA, 2:87).

Still, why the *combination* of allegorical and sentimental-mimetic conventions in *Stella*, which both obscures the allegory and overstrains the fiction? It seems to me that the effect of this combination is to suggest a reflection upon reality itself *considered as convention.* "Individuum est ineffabile."[7] But at the top end of our individuality, so to speak, at the fullest development of our self-consciousness, the miraculous "secret point" occurs, where we are set free from ourselves and joined in sympathetic contact with all humankind. And correspondingly, at the bottom end of individuality, at the minimum of self-conscious complication, occurs *reality*, the implacable external order that contains and limits us and therefore *also* operates ultimately as a communicative convention, a vehicle of contact with

---

[7]See Goethe's letter to Lavater of September 1780. Also see Wilhelm Dilthey, *Gesammelte Werke*, 19 vols., 6th ed. (Stuttgart and Göttingen, 1966–82), 1:29.

others, a sharing now not of freedom but of bondage. Again we think of *Tasso*:

> Die Menschen kennen sich einander nicht;
> Nur die Galeerensklaven kennen sich,
> Die eng an Eine Bank geschmiedet keuchen.
>   [Ll. 3338–40; WA, 10:240]

[People do not know each other; only galley-slaves know each other, who suffer, tight chained, on *one* bench.]

The combination of allegorical and mimetic conventions is thus yet another version of the connection (or collision) of freedom and limitation, another intimation of the "secret point" about which the whole structure revolves.

The play's focus upon this *coincidentia oppositorum* is relentless. In the final tableau considered allegorically, Cezilie represents limitation, Stella freedom; but in the same tableau considered mimetically, Fernando's position between the two women is clearly a form of entrapment, whereas the idea of bigamy, the flouting of law and social convention, suggests an instance of utterly free human self-determination. Freedom is to limitation as Stella is to Cezilie, as bigamous freedom is to entrapment between two women, as allegory is to mimesis. And the next term in this series is represented by the theater itself, considered either as a physically determined reality somehow suffused with metaphor, or as a metaphor somehow loaded down with immediate reality. We can arrange these relations in a diagram:

	Freedom	secret point of collision	Limitation
1.	Stella		Cezilie
2.	Fernando the adventurer		Fernando the husband
3.	final tableau as bigamy		final tableau as entrapment
4.	allegory		mimesis
5.	metaphoricity of theater		materiality of theater
6.	"Stella" in theater as mind		"Stella" in mind as theater

The last item suggests both an answer to the question of why the whole play is called after Stella, even though she apparently represents only one side of its central tension, and an incorporation into the play's structure of the *reversible* metaphorical relation between mind and theater. In the theater considered as mind, Stella represents the aspect of freedom. But the mind considered as theater is a *process of representing*, which represents, and so compromises, even its freedom; freedom is now "prätendirte Freyheit," "arbitrium liberum praetentum," freedom literally "held out" where it can be seen, hence transformed into a distant object of striving, a "star" ("stella"), in relation to which the quality of our condition as *limitation* is brought to the fore.

In any case, the diagram shows the *dynamic* quality of the play's structure. The whole relation between Fernando as adventurer and as husband (level 2) belongs to the realm of mimesis (level 4), whereas the relation between the two possible views of the final tableau (level 3) belongs to the realm of allegory; the whole relation between allegory and mimesis, in turn, belongs to the metaphorical quality of the theater (level 5), even though, paradoxically, the relation between the metaphorical and the material can also be considered part of the play's allegory; and Stella, who is one of the colliding aspects on level 1, is the theme of the whole collision on level 6. The "secret point" is not simply locatable in a symbolic topography, but *happens*, incessantly and self-replicatingly, throughout the play's unfolding. In this sense, the theater attempts actually to *be* the mind; it is not a picture but a working model.

Die Räuber and the Moral Subject

Schiller's *Räuber* is theater of the mind in a manner sufficiently different from that of *Stella* to compel our attentiveness to the quality as such. Exactly what does Karl Moor mean when he says at the climax of the play's early version, "daß *zwei Menschen wie ich den ganzen Bau der sittlichen Welt zugrund richten würden*"? (SA, 3:155). Why should *two* Karl Moors (but not one) imply the collapse of the structure of the moral world? If the moral world survives one Karl Moor today—as it apparently does at the end of the play—why should it not survive another Karl Moor tomorrow, or even two at the same time?

In order to understand what those words actually say, we must apply the notions of subject and object in the relatively strict philosophical sense they receive in Schiller's own "Philosophische Briefe," especially the very early "Theosophie des Julius." Young Julius has learned from his friend and mentor Raphael that there can be no valid objective basis for either religious belief or moral conviction, that the guarantee in such matters must be provided by reason alone, which he understands as the mind's operation on itself, our experience of self as subject. The only source of morality is the moral or self-determining subject; and Julius accordingly, in his "Theosophie," attempts to constitute morality on strictly subjective grounds, as a theory of love. Love, he argues, always profits the subject by appropriating and incorporating the beloved object; and since it would be irrational for the subject not to desire this development of itself, it follows that the subject is practically compelled to love as much as possible, hence to develop a natural morality.

These ideas were meant to be criticized thoroughly in the "Philosophische Briefe" as a whole. But the work was never finished, perhaps in part because the criticism of Julius's system is already carried out in *Die Räuber*. Karl Moor also attempts an entirely subjective constitution of morality, though not based on love. As long as he is merely a rebel, as long as his actions are primarily a negative response to objective moral corruption—even if this response involves a condemnation of the human race as a whole and the killing of uninvolved bystanders—he has put himself in the wrong, but he is not yet a danger to morality *as such*. For it is necessarily true, and to an extent therefore tolerable, that the objective or public aspect of morality (e.g., Karl Moor's own criminal acts) tends to become corrupt. But when Karl Moor swears his solemn oath to the robbers in Act 3, he goes a step too far. He now pretends to derive a *new* fabric of binding moral obligation from his subjective knowledge of the inadequacy of existing objective morality; he is no longer an *out*law, but attempts to assert his moral subjectivity as the center and origin of a *new* law.

Like Julius, he insists that the subject, in the logic of its internal operation, can give itself its own law. It is not difficult to imagine that Julius, if reality thwarted his universal love as it apparently thwarts Karl Moor's filial love, might also become a robber captain. And how could reality fail to thwart Julius? It is the very character of the object-world to oppose the absolute claims of the subject. This is what Karl Moor has learned when he says, "Oh what a fool I was to imagine I could beautify the world by terror and support the laws by lawlessness" (SA, 3:155). It remains true that the moral subject is the source of all morality, that written or objectively proclaimed laws are by nature corruptible and therefore morally empty. But the subject becomes a *moral* subject precisely by *restraining* itself vis-à-vis objective morality, by *renouncing* its apparent right to assert absolute values in reality. When the subject insists on self-expansion or self-assertion—even in the apparently innocent sense worked out by Julius—it ceases altogether to be a moral subject, since it now advances into reality as if it were one object among others, therefore comparable to objects and justifiable by the type of quasi-legal sophistry upon which Franz Moor, for example, erects *his* perverse moral theories.

(The terminology is different, but the thought here is not inconsistent with the idea of the subject as the signified of the social, which arises in the logical unfolding of the concept of irony. For the semiotic argument also excludes the subject from any particular situation *within* society, where it might take advantage of the inherently irrefutable superiority of subjective sincerity over actual social corruption. The thought of *Die Räuber* differs only by starting out from the idea of the subject as an inference from personal experience. Do I simply make the seductive but sophistical leap that endows my inferred subject with objective existence, or is my experience still sufficiently informed and restrained by its quality *as* inference, as semiosis, to permit the development of a moral subject?)

Hence the statement of Karl Moor with which we began. The "structure of the moral world" is sustained by the fact that in my experience *only one subject exists at a time*, namely my own subject. Other people, from my point of view, are objects, whatever moral obligation I may have to approach as closely as possible, by sympathy or "pitié" or "Mitleid," an experience or sharing of their subjectivity. And this uniqueness of the subject (the existence of only one subject at a time) is the whole source of that tension between subject and object which requires the basic moral act of self-restraint. If two distinct subjects could be experienced together *as* subjects, then the subject, with its uncompromising moral claims, would simply be a part of reality or the object-world, comparable with other objects;

the tension between subject and object would then disappear, the subject would have no reason not to assert itself in the objective arena, law would therefore become mere feeling, and the moral world would collapse. Of course a plurality of moral subjects can and does exist, in the sense that every individual can become such a subject. But *in experience*, in "my" experience, the subject is a strictly unique event, a singularity, an undeniable but also unlocatable "secret point"; and by having no spatial or temporal coordinates whatever, that point evinces a radical opposition to objectivity as such, an opposition that expresses its freedom, but also enforces the imperative of self-restraint (or self-determination) on which the "moral world" is built. The mere possibility of a plurality of moral subjects ("zwei Menschen wie ich," in the radical sense of "ich"), which would imply a location for the subject, a base from which to operate in objective reality, thus brings with it the destruction of that "moral world," and Karl Moor's statement acknowledges this.[8]

What is interesting for our purposes, however, is that at the point where Karl Moor actually commits his perversity, his objectification of the potentially moral subject, by swearing his oath to the robbers, *the stage changes in character*. The plot, as in *Stella*, now becomes unacceptably improbable. We are asked to believe that Amalia can have a long sentimental conversation with Karl Moor, in part *about* Karl Moor, without recognizing him. Can two years' separation and a suntan make that much difference? And then the robbers *just happen* to camp near a ruined castle where father Moor *just happens* to be imprisoned, a circumstance that is revealed by Hermann's *just happening* to arrive now with food for the old man. Again, as in *Stella*, mimesis is left behind, and the stage represents nothing but the operation of Karl Moor's subjectivity, his self-consciousness. The first thing that happens after he utters his oath is the arrival of Kosinsky, his exact mirror image, a self-reflecting allegory of his self-reflection, even down to the detail of having a beloved named Amalia. His project, the direct relegislation of reality by the moral subject, is thus refuted in the very instant of its inception. The stage at that point simply ceases to represent reality, and is engulfed by an allegory of the subject. Reality escapes. The moral subject and the

---

[8]Kant, in the *Kritik der reinen Vernunft*, also insists on the strict singularity of the subject (*KW*, 3:267), and on the consequent falsity of attributing substance to the ego.

object-world in which morality must be executed cannot exist together on the same plane, or, metaphorically, on the same stage.

Theater of the Mind as an Axiom

The theater-of-the-mind allegory in the second half of *Die Räuber* is
developed in considerable detail. The meetings with his beloved and
his father, in which Karl Moor conceals his identity but is then eventually recognized, represent the truth that an acceptance of the past,
of limits imposed by the temporal object-world (Karl Moor's established identity), is even subjectively necessary, that the idea of the
subject as its own creator and legislator is an absurdity that precisely
the subject cannot sustain. And on the allegorical stage Karl Moor
and Franz Moor, who never appear together, become essentially the
same person—as is also suggested in the dialogue between Karl and
his father (SA, 3:146). Karl's character is an unmasking of the self-
hating moral will behind Franz's desperate attempts to dispense with
morality altogether; Franz's evil is in turn an unmasking of the perversity of the self-asserting moral subject that Karl pretends to be.
And Franz and Karl together thus illustrate the argument with which
we began, as an allegory of the moral subject's futile attempt to develop itself as a self-locating plurality in the real world.

More interesting for our purposes, however, is the quality of *theatrical* self-reflection in the structure of *Die Räuber*. For the shift
from a mimetic to an allegorical convention in Act 3 not only reflects
Karl Moor's absurd commitment to the project of a subjective relegislation of reality, but also reveals the inherent moral character
and questionableness of the theater as an institution. Precisely in its
mimetic quality, in its pretending for a while to be reality, the theater also evidently attempts a kind of relegislation of the object-world.
In going to the theater, therefore, we come dangerously close to
involving ourselves in the same moral absurdity as Karl Moor. The
parallel here, provided we recognize it, is uncomfortably exact. Just
as the cohesion and spirit of the robber band represent an apparent
objective manifestation of Karl Moor's subjective moral will, therefore a delusive promise concerning the achievability of his relegisla-
tive project, so also the apparently unified, "sympathetic" attentiveness of the theater audience, as a group, offers itself as an objective

anchor for the subjective relegislation of the real carried out imaginatively by the individual spectator in his or her reception of the work.

The moral danger for the theater audience, however, is tempered by the theater's structural *self-reflexivity*, by the movement of self-reflection, relative to the question of the relegislation of the real, that is manifest in the shift of convention in Act 3. We are invited to participate not only in the theater's materiality, in its closeness to the real, but also in its metaphoricity, in its quality as a reflection *upon* reality, an uncommitted game. This is the idea Schiller gropes toward in his meditations on the theater as a "moral institution." The danger of becoming a Karl Moor, the need to relegislate reality, is always present; for the moral subject *is* in truth the origin of all morality. But the theater offers us an opportunity to relieve this need in the domain of play or metaphor—in the shadow, ultimately, of the truth of the metaphoricity of the real—without suffering the moral consequences. The inherent thought of *Die Räuber* on the moral function of art thus already goes beyond the "Schaubühne" essay in the direction of the idea of aesthetic education.

And yet, the operation of metaphoricity here is proper not to art in general, but only to the theater. The abrupt change of idiom in Act 3, from the mimetic to the allegorical, reflects back at us *our* actual situation in the theater. (We think of Goethe's "Über Wahrheit und Wahrscheinlichkeit der Kunstwerke.") It accuses us, so to speak, of participating in a ritual subjective relegislation of the real, insofar as we normally expect from drama, and in fact eventually receive in this play, a morally satisfying closure of the plot, a closure of the sort that precisely the moral subject must renounce in reality. But the metaphoricity of this accusation, its availability to us as an object of play, does not arise except, paradoxically, by way of the *materiality* of the theater. Only the physical distance between us and the stage keeps the allegory of mind in Act 3 from being simply a move of self-consciousness on our part, a move in exactly that process, on our part, that threatens constantly to objectify the subject and demolish the moral world. The supposed mental or conscious distance between reader and text, by contrast, would not be sufficient; for "distance" of this type simply *belongs* to self-consciousness, and is in fact exactly the illusory instrument by which the subject is pried free and presented to consciousness as an object. The same communally available materiality that, by way of our sense of the audience as a "sympathetic" group, opens the seductive possibility of subjective legislation, thus also resists that seduction. As in Goethe, the theater's materiality is *part* of its allegorical structure.

But are we, after all, really talking about *the theater* here, in either Schiller's case or Goethe's? In the first place, both *Stella* and *Die Räuber* were later revised by their authors—*Die Räuber* in fairly short order—to eliminate some of the textual features I have focused on. And in the second place, neither of the plays appears to have been conceived with the idea of theatrical realization in mind. Goethe circulates *Stella* in manuscript for his friends to read; and in both versions of the "Vorrede" to *Die Räuber*, Schiller claims to have superseded actual performance in his use of the "dramatic method." I think, however, that if my main point is understood correctly, these considerations tend to support it, not defeat it.

I mean to argue not that the metaphor of theater as mind was part of accepted theatrical convention in Goethe's and Schiller's time, but rather that the *idea* of the theater, as Goethe and Schiller both received it from tradition at a relatively early age (before they had begun to operate as professionals of the theater), includes the conception of a theater of the mind on something close to an axiomatic level. An argument of the type here advanced, if applied to works like *Iphigenie* or *Egmont*, or *Wallenstein* or *Maria Stuart*,[9] would be indistinguishable from an argument to the effect that Goethe and Schiller had imposed certain philosophical concerns on the existing institution of the theater. But if even *Stella* and *Die Räuber* possess a definite *practical* theatricality (whether or not their authors would have called it that) requiring the presence of an actual community in a real, material theater, and a theatricality, also, that turns upon the metaphorical relation of theater and mind; and if the source of this theatricality is precisely *not* yet a professional familiarity with contemporary theatrical exigencies, then, I contend, we are talking about an axiomatic element in the very idea of a possible theater as Goethe and Schiller received it. The revisions of the two plays, undertaken by their authors as a result of discussions with other people, perhaps suggest that the theatricality of *Stella* and *Die Räuber*, in the sense of the interpretations above, was not communicable (or not

[9]See my *Modern Drama and German Classicism* on these plays.

recognized as communicable) in actual theaters of the time. But this concession does not affect my point about the inherent theatrical quality of the original conception in each case.

Adam and Eve and Heinrich von Kleist

My concern is not the operation of actual eighteenth-century theaters, but the place of the idea of the theater in the expressive economy organized by late eighteenth-century poetic ironists, especially in Germany. And Heinrich von Kleist pushes this "invisible theater," this "theater that has yet to arrive,"[10] to a kind of limit. Let us look at *Der zerbrochene Krug*.

Since the content of the fiction is a legal proceeding, it seems to me that the audience at this play is encouraged to look at the fiction legalistically, to weigh evidence and ascertain facts. And when we ask, accordingly, what had actually happened between Adam and Eve on the night preceding, we must conclude that Eve's description of the event is evasive. She manages to suggest that she had allowed Adam into her bedroom only in order that he might write out the document she requires for Ruprecht (HvK, 1:243). But Frau Brigitte has testified that she had heard Eve and someone else (who we know had been Adam) arguing violently in the garden. "Pfui, shame on you, you're despicable" (1:233), Eve had said to him there. In other words, Adam had made his improper demands known *before* managing to get into Eve's bedroom, which means in turn that she had taken him there with every intention of paying his price for the false medical exemption. Indeed, it is not out of the question that she *still* intends to go to bed with him. At least she does not take the opportunity to accuse him of sexual extortion before the court inspector Walter. And we know that Kleist was fascinated by the scene between Isabella and Claudio in *Measure for Measure*, where the question between saving a life and losing a maidenhead is not unambiguously resolved.

At least one crucial fact in the plot—that Eve had intended to go to bed with Adam, which is crucial because it threatens both the marriage with Ruprecht and Frau Marthe's need to believe in her daughter's innocence—is therefore *never spoken of* by any character,

[10]These are Goethe's characterizations of Kleist's implied theater, in letters to Adam Müller, 28 August 1807, and to Kleist himself, 1 February 1808.

except cryptically by Eve herself when she tells Ruprecht that he ought to have believed in her even if he had seen her, through the keyhole, drinking together with Lebrecht the shoemaker (HvK, 1:216–17). This speech is full of duplicity. Eve admonishes Ruprecht: "You should have thought: Eve is good; everything will be resolved so as to preserve her good name, if not in life [where perhaps her virtue might be justifiably sacrificed?], then in the beyond, in the new day when we are resurrected." If Eve herself had really been willing to sacrifice "this life" (letting Ruprecht take his risks) in favor of the next, she would never have allowed Adam into her bedroom. She is playing a very complicated game here, and Ruprecht is perhaps in the long run not nearly so safe from the horns as he imagines when the play closes.

As I say, Eve's earlier willingness to share her bed with Adam is a *fact* in the plot, and a fact that is known to several of the characters, certainly to Eve herself and to Adam, probably also to the perceptive Licht, as well as to Walter, who is himself skilled at manicuring facts in language. "Upon my honor, that's a good foot," says Walter, with a nice ambiguity, when Adam shows him his club foot (HvK, 1:239). But no one ever *says* anything about the facts of Eve's behavior. And is a fact still a fact if it is entirely suppressed, if it is utterly denied any confirmation in language? This question leads to the central philosophical issue of the play.

Within the fiction, the facts concerning Eve are suppressed mainly for the sake of order, completeness, "clôture." Eve and Ruprecht will marry; Adam's resignation from office will be arranged as gracefully as possible; busy functionaries like Licht and Walter will be able to get on with their work. And *our* reason, in the theater, for participating in this suppression of fact, is essentially the same: closure, or at least the preservation of the illusion of closure, the completion of the comic structure, despite the reminder about unfinished business at the curtain. The suppression of particular facts in the plot thus stands for a suppression of the factual that we carry out *whenever* we go to the theater, the temporary suppression, for example, of the non-identity of actor and character. Once we have come this far, moreover, once we have understood the parallel between our present mental activity as an audience and a mental act carried out by several individuals within the play's fictional "reality," we cannot escape the suggestion that *reality itself*, outside the theater, is ordered, made compact and intelligible, hence in the end constituted, by the action

of our perceiving and understanding and (above all) editing or cen-
soring it. It follows, therefore, that what we suppress, in the theater
or in real life, is not merely a fact, but the *truth* concerning the
mental constitution of reality; for if this truth could ever be acknowledged publicly *as* the truth—not merely as theory—the result would
be the collapse of reality into an insane chaos of subjective fantasms.
(We think of Schiller, and of the needful self-restraint of the moral
subject.) Not only in the theater, but also in the world, the truth is
known by everyone—perhaps even by the Ruprechts among us—
and is suppressed for the sake of that "closure" which is the world's
very existence. The whole world is in essence a theater of the mind.

This brings us back to Eve, whose psychological situation now becomes a symbol of the human situation in general. She is playing a
complicated game, living in a secret labyrinth of thoughts, desires,
fears, memories, a labyrinth which, were she to display it, would
explode the order of her existence. (Lessing's Emilia Galotti, in a
tragic version of practically the same plot, does open the labyrinth
for a moment before she dies.) But we too, all of us, live in just such
a labyrinth by virtue of our self-suppressing self-consciousness; and
the theater of *Der zerbrochene Krug*, like the theater of *Stella* or *Die
Räuber*, is an allegorical diagram of our condition in this sense. The
artistic structure and mimetic cohesion of the work, its closure, as
such, represents that repeated suppression of the truth, on our part,
which is outwardly manifest as reality. But precisely this self-reflection of consciousness as a suppression of truth is by implication also a
representation *of* the truth, or of consciousness as a knowledge of
truth. Our recognition that the play's closure is contingent on a suppression of fact, in which we are implicated, also produces, for us,
the condition of nonclosure.

There are points in the play where the allegory comes almost to
the surface. Given what we know about Eve's behavior the night
before, it follows that Ruprecht, in breaking down the door, *had
prevented the sexual union of Adam and Eve*; that is, he had symbolically destroyed the humanly ordered world—and in the process had
broken the jug that represents human history—by preventing its *origin*. It is therefore up to us—in that we suppress that fact and so
refrain symbolically from breaking down the door, in that we accede
to the illusory conventions of the theater, as well as to the illusory
conventions by which reality is accepted as reality—it is up to us
now to reconstitute that human world, to make possible its origin,

thus in a sense to enact that origin, in the self-censoring mechanism of self-consciousness. Of course in the very process of thus leaving the door intact, we also inescapably do break it down yet again, do penetrate it, by knowing what it conceals, so that the operation of self-conscious self-restraint becomes necessary all over again. The human world, that is, must originate anew in every instant of self-conscious existence; the union of Adam and Eve is always both consummated and frustrated; the vessel of human history, like the jug in the play, is always both broken and whole, broken in its wholeness (since our experience of its wholeness, our knowledge of truth, is what breaks it), whole in its brokenness (since our acceptance of a finite, fragmented reality, our suppression of truth, is what realizes its whole order).

The Theater as Thinker

The allegorical relation between stage-space and the interior space of the mind in *Der zerbrochene Krug* is not as direct or perspicuous as in *Stella* or *Die Räuber*. It is necessary to grasp the work's philosophical purport, the idea of reality itself as a type of artistic closure enforced by our cooperation in suppressing the truth, before we can understand the manner in which the theater has become a structural equivalent of the thinking mind. The whole idea that the mind is like a theater—rather than like, say, a mirror or a window—the idea that reality is not merely given to the mind, but must first be staged (shaped, arranged, edited, censored) in order to become what it is for us, is derived from the idealistic speculation on the questionability of fact that is suggested by the fictional action and dialogue.

Without that speculation, it cannot occur to us to ask the question by which we recognize not only that the mind is like a theater, but that the theater is also like the mind. How, namely, can we *know* (or think we know) about the quality of reality as an artistic closure achieved only in our perception and verbal mastery of it? Since reality, in our experience, is always still there for us, it follows that that speculative truth, which threatens to produce nonclosure and a disruption of reality (just as a full revelation of fact would disrupt the comic closure of the play), is always *already* suppressed in our thinking. And where, then, is our present thinking *of* that truth located? This difficulty is not insurmountable in theory. It is met, for in-

stance, by the idea of the subject as a strict singularity, located nowhere at all in the object world, hence unaffected by any particular
conflicts between thought and experience. But theoretical resolu-
tions of this sort are specifically excluded in *Der zerbrochene Krug*,
in which our thinking of the truth is represented (via a process of
allegorical inference) by our knowledge of a *fact*. The subject, so to
speak, is not excused from the room—any more than Adam is, for all
his espousal of a theory of diabolical intervention—but must face up
to the paradox of its carrying out a speculation that implies its inability to carry out precisely that speculation.

We are thus compelled to recognize that the very idea of a strictly
singular subject, the whole experience of an individual mind, is nothing but yet another form of arbitrary artistic closure, another suppression of truth. We cannot have any conception whatever of how
the mind is constituted, except insofar as the theater in which we are
sitting, in all its materiality and communality, *is itself such a conception*: this theater, in which the perfect speculativeness of the truth
collides directly with the inevitable materiality of our thinking it, in a
collision from which the individual "mind" merely imagines itself ex-
empt; this theater, in which bright images unfold before an audience
space that represents subjective singularity by having no location in
the fictional coordinate system of the stage; this theater, which thus
imitates the experience of an individual mind closely enough to constitute a criticism of the whole idea of such a mind, a recognition that
our supposedly singular inner self-presence is in truth occupied by a
prior collectivity (which can be understood, for instance, as history),
by a huge silent audience for which the individual subject, our very
self, like the "character" on the stage, is nothing but a conventional
or contractual act of artistic closure, a semiotic signified; this theater
which, in its material intractability, is sufficiently unlike a "conception," sufficiently alien to what we imagine as our "thinking," to *be*
precisely our conception of the inconceivable; this theater, in sum,
which *is* the mind, by being our enactment of a thought that cannot
be adequately thought except in such enacting.[11]

---

[11]Compare Antonin Artaud, "La Mise en scène et la métaphysique," in his *Oeuvres
complètes*, 7 vols. (Paris, 1956–69), 4:45: "Je dis que la scène est un lieu physique et
concret qui demande qu'on le remplisse, et qu'on lui fasse parler son langage concret . . .
et que ce langage physique et concret . . . n'est vraiment théâtral que dans la mesure où
les pensées qu'il exprime échappent au langage articulé." Note that the argument on the
theater's imitating the experience of an individual mind becomes more obvious if one

The mind, then, is like a theater, and the theater is like the mind. But in the case of *Der zerbrochene Krug*, this metaphorical relation is mediated by a complex philosophical argument. And if we were only considering Kleist, we might therefore be inclined to speak of an idiosyncratic interpretation of the theater on the part of an individual who is known, anyway, for taking philosophical issues more deeply to heart than was good for him. The clear parallels with Goethe and Schiller, however, and especially with early works of these authors, suggest a different picture. Is it Kleist who thinks about the theater, or is it rather the theater that thinks, so to speak, *in* Kleist? This formulation requires only one refolding of the meaning of *Der zerbrochene Krug* back onto itself. German idealistic philosophy—already in Kant and Fichte, but then especially as it is later developed into the domains of history and language, and into semiotic and deconstructive idioms—always includes at least an implied criticism of the idea of the autonomous thinking subject. And if we take this criticism seriously, as seriously as Kleist did, then I think we will be less inclined to dismiss out of hand the idea of the theater, in both its immediacy and its history, as not merely a repository of thought but *an actual thinking organ*. The common insistence that it is philosophical "thought" which first somehow exists, and then is expressed or manifested in such ancillary mechanisms as the theater, is the insistence upon an analogue to exactly that autonomous thinking subject which, supposedly, is being subjected to a radical critique.

Where is thinking located? Where, in truth, is that "secret point" which, in practice, we find it impossible not to equate with our own personal self? This is the question that gives meaning to the idea of the inherent and pervasive metaphoricity of the theater. If we look back at our discussion of Goethe and Schiller, we find that the idea of the self-conscious or moral subject actually has only a heuristic function. All Goethe ever directly says about his "secret point," and all that can be directly inferred from the structure of *Stella*, is that that

---

imagines a dark auditorium (hence inward, subjective, anonymous) and a brightly lit stage. The practice of theater lighting was not uniform in eighteenth-century Europe, but it becomes clear in the writings of such authors as Leone di Simo, Angelo Ingegneri, and Nicola Sabbattini that the contrast between stage and auditorium lighting, including the use of footlights, was well established as a possibility by the middle of the seventeenth century, especially in court theaters. See also Hobson, pp. 386–89, on the camera obscura—which has a direct bearing on the discussion of Lenz later in this chapter—and her commentary on David Hume's use of the theater metaphor for perception, pp. 389–94.

unlocatable point is still somehow located, after all, *in the theater*—
in Shakespeare's, or, in a different manner, in Goethe's own. And in
Die Räuber, the idea of the moral subject as a strict singularity, located nowhere at all, is in the final analysis not the play's *meaning*,
but merely one of a number of available philosophical positions, and
a position that is called into question by the recognition that we, in
the theater, for all our philosophical perspective, are still at least
toying with the project, like Karl Moor's, of relegislating the real.
The moral subject is neither a given nor a conclusion, but a *problem*,
an exercise in thinking, and an exercise of which it obviously makes
less sense to say that it is carried out *by* that questionable subject,
than to say that it is located, that it happens, *as* thinking, in the
theater.

Where is thinking located? At least over the past two centuries, "I"
find myself willing to entertain the suggestion that "my" thinking is
located not (or not only) in "me" but in the order of objects that are
apparently only presented to my perception, or in the fusion of the
real and the fictional that makes up history, or in operations of language that incessantly undermine my own supposed operating with
language, or in the force of metaphysical suppositions that I find I
have bought into in the very act of criticizing them. The idea of *the
theater* as a location of thinking, however—by which I mean not
merely a place where thinking is done, but an entity, an organ, that
is more properly the subject-agent of "our" thinking than we ourselves are—is more concrete and specific, and (in its material arti-
ficiality) less easily infected with such debilitating concepts as "nature" or "divinity," than those other possibilities. The theater
therefore puts our philosophical seriousness to the test. Do we mean
what we say, or does our manner of prosecuting the critique of the
autonomous thinking subject not rather itself evince an irresponsible
acceptance of precisely that illusion, an irresponsibility that appears
especially in our restricting the discussion to a level sufficiently speculative and nonmaterial to be imagined as leaving our actual experience untouched? The theater, in this sense, poses for us a philosophical challenge, not only in the particular version of it that we happen
to have tickets for, but also in its whole historical existence.

Where is thinking located? My point is not so much that the theater, considered as theater of the mind, answers this question, as that
it keeps the question open. And keeping the question open, in this
case, is sufficient. For the question, in itself, is an outlandish one;

our thinking about it, "our" thinking, is constantly delegitimized by its own content. It is therefore perhaps the theater itself that thinks: this formulation, which is more outlandish still, is not at all senseless in the context of a discussion of the theater of the mind. It admits no demonstration; but it also, I think, requires none. What it requires is getting used to; and it *always* requires getting used to, even for its most committed student or practitioner. For it is an outlandish idea, as outlandish as that fusion of strict metaphoricity and strict materiality to which it refers. Or perhaps not even quite so outlandish after all. Natural evolution, we are fond of saying, assumes a new form in the era of rational humankind, whose history is marked by the repeated deliberate creation of *new* organs of locomotion, self-protection, perception, food-procurement, and so on. And in the age of the computer, we are told, even new organs of thinking become available, perhaps even organs of "intelligence." My point is that that special intellectual organ, which can think more and better than the individual natural brain, is perhaps not one of the newest human contrivances, but one of the oldest.

Beyond Theory: Lenz on and in Drama

The arguments on Goethe, Schiller, and Kleist, which anchor the idea of theater as thinker in the eighteenth century, are supported by the argument on Lessing in Chapter 3. For the imitation of language by language, which favors drama in Lessing's poetics, the word as a natural sign *in* its arbitrariness, enacts the truth of a verbally conditioned nature, which in turn is a version of the idea of the metaphoricity of the real. And Lessing's dramatic practice provides yet further support.[12] But considering the importance of the idea of the theater as a thinking organ in its relation to the question of where the thinking of irony is located, it is worth the effort to look at yet one more eighteenth-century figure, J. M. R. Lenz.

The simple questions about Lenz tend to be the difficult ones. Why, if he is as much an admirer of Goethe's *Götz* as he says, doesn't he write plays that resemble *Götz* more? Why, if he recognizes the fault of the Aristotelizing French manner in its focus on mere action, not on the active individual, does he himself write

[12]See my *Modern Drama and German Classicism*, chap. 3, "*Nathan der Weise*: Breakthrough in Practice."

mainly "comedies," in which "the personages are there for the sake of the actions" (*LW*, 2:669–70)? Or if the burden of his work is mainly social criticism, why are two of his major plays, *Der Hofmeister* and *Die Soldaten*, at least ostensibly focused on limited social malfunctions that might better be dealt with in essay form? And why, in turn, does *Der neue Menoza*, his other major comedy, *not* fit the same critical mold?

There is a deceptively easy way to answer these questions, using the concept of "handeln" (acting) in Lenz's essays. In the essay on *Götz*, Lenz points out that human life, objectively considered, is nothing but the operation of a small machine within the larger machine of the "world" (*LW*, 2:637), and that this unsatisfactory sense of our existence (as "merely a postponed death" [2:638]) is counteracted in us only by our own "active force," a power in us of which we learn "that it does not rest, or stop working, moving, raging, until it has gained us a space of freedom, room to act, good God, room to act, even if it were a chaos that You had created, desolate and empty, but at least freedom would dwell there and we could brood over it, imitating You, until something came forth—ecstasy! ecstasy! a godlike feeling!" Chaos itself, utter disorder, is preferable to any systematic knowledge of the world, however perfect or beautiful, if such knowledge impedes our free activity.

And Lenz then implies, after proposing the question of artistic "effect" (*LW*, 2:639), that *Götz von Berlichingen* is one of the few plays that can awaken "the Promethean spark" in us, the spark that inspires "convictions, deeds, and *actions*." But he does not assert that *Götz* will normally have this effect *upon spectators*. The point of the essay, in fact, is that we must first *learn how* to judge Goethe's play before its potential effect can be realized; and the method of learning suggested is not that we read or attend a performance but (we think of Brecht and his "Lehrstücke") that we ourselves *enact* the play, that we put on a performance. This move is logically unavoidable. For the notion of action in the radical sense in which Lenz means it cannot be grasped except *in acting*. The passive situation of the spectator or reader necessarily undermines this notion by attempting to pin it down objectively in a framework of conceptual relations and concrete examples, in a theory that merely reproduces and asserts the "machine" of the world, which in turn is precisely what action, in its preference for chaos, is unalterably opposed to.

Götz, in Lenz's view, is a work of genius, written in defiance of the

Enlightenment's insistence on a systematic view of world as "machine." But genius alone is not enough. It is not enough that works like *Götz* be written and performed; they must also be prepared for. *A new kind of audience* must arise—hence the enthusiastic, hortatory tone of Lenz's essays—a group of spectators and readers who will no longer be merely receptive, but will respond to a work such as *Götz* in the radically active spirit of the genius that created it. And it is clear from *Pandämonium Germanicum* that Lenz regards this preparation of the way for genius as his own special task. Klopstock, Herder, and Lessing, in that text, say of Lenz: "Good young fellow. If his achievement is small, at least his vision is great," to which Goethe responds, "I will do the achieving" (*LW*, 1:270).

But how is this task to be carried out? By expository essays, like the essay on *Götz* and the earlier *Anmerkungen übers Theater*, plus perhaps such pieces as "Über die Natur unseres Geistes," which also unfolds the difficult notion of "handeln"? The trouble is that the essay—even in the colloquial and idiosyncratically fragmented form of Lenz's *Anmerkungen*—is a *theoretical* genre, which requires of its reader not action but receptivity, which operates by creating relations among concepts that must come together in some form of "machine" if the work is to have meaning. Chaos, or the disruption of those machine-like movements of thought which seem to correspond to an actual world-machine, is beyond the range of the essay as a form. Precisely our understanding of Lenz's essays, the moment in which it becomes clear to us (say) that free activity is the whole key to our being human, is also the moment in which the equations of our conceptual self-understanding are solved, and so present us with a rigid structure of truth that impedes, precisely, our free or arbitrary activity.

It is tempting, therefore, to shift the burden onto Lenz's dramatic writing. If the form of the essay cannot open chaos for its reader, perhaps the form of drama can for its spectator. The meaning of a play does not depend on its having a conceptual structure we can associate with truth or understanding. Even the structuring force of the *authorial voice*—except in what Lenz regards as the perverted French convention (*LW*, 2:661–63)—is absent in drama. We are confronted instead with a multiplicity of voices—of personal attitudes, thoughts, actions—that need not combine to form an interpretable machine any more than real people do in real life. Indeed, drama can be realistic—that is, merely mimetic, governed by no clear concep-

tual structure—without even having an assumable level of *fact*. At
least this type of instability seems to be part of Lenz's aim in *Der
Hofmeister*, in which the chronology of the fiction casts doubt on
Läuffer's responsibility for Gustchen's child, and in *Der neue Menoza*, where the crucial question of who is whose brother or sister is
adjudicated by nothing but the repeated passionate outbursts of the
nurse Babet, who is an interested party.

And if we consider in addition Lenz's own view on the difference
between reading and theatrical realization—that the reader, "in the
midst of his clearest seeing" (*LW*, 2:657), is always distracted by irrelevant thoughts, whereas the direct sensory communication of performance *enforces* "seeing" in the spectator—then it seems to follow
that Lenz's plays attempt merely to confuse their audience, to impose the experience of radical disorder, hence the possibility of "acting," hence the ability to appreciate plays like *Götz*, on the theater-
goers of his time. *Götz* itself, for all its genius, is too well focused (on
precisely the idea of "freedom") for its own good; an audience of
enlightened eighteenth-century spectators must inevitably interpret
that focus as a conceptual order, as that type of "machine" by which
precisely the idea of freedom is rendered meaningless. ("Wehe der
Nachkommenschaft, die dich verkennt.") Such an audience must first
be trained in a theater like Lenz's to open itself to the possibility of
disorder. In this respect, Lenz's plays even include a kind of fail-safe
mechanism. The worst thing that can happen to a playwright, says
Lenz, is to be "performed and gotten wrong" (*LW*, 2:657). But in the
case of plays aimed at the experience of disorder, a mistaken performance can only *increase* the desired effect.

Drama and the Sensory Surplus

According to this line of reasoning, Lenz produces something like
negative drama, in a sense comparable to Herder's idea of "negative
philosophy," a drama that deconceptualizes and corporealizes the
foundations of its own form, and so is in a position to take up the
work of dramatic theory at the point where theory as such collides
with an untheorizably radical idea of action. But this answer to the
questions about Lenz we began with is deceptive. In itself, it is not
an answer at all. If disorder is required, in a sense radical enough (as
"chaos") to match the radicality of Lenz's idea of action, then the

mere accumulation of disparate personal points of view and the mere clouding of fictional facts is not sufficient. Nothing prevents even these features of a play from being accounted for in a cohesive interpretation. And if disorder is the aim, how can the use of plot structure be justified, a structure that must be internally consistent—as also in Kleist—if the questioning of its factual basis is to be perceived?

I still think the reasoning I have sketched is substantially correct, that Lenz's plays are meant to prepare the way for a drama of genius. But the argument requires a better foundation, which can be developed from another section of the *Anmerkungen übers Theater*. There are, says Lenz, two sources of poetry: the Aristotelian drive to imitate (*LW*, 2:645–46) and another source that has to do with the tendency of our reason to create a conceptual model of as much as possible (ultimately the whole) of our existence.

> We all try to reduce our complicated conceptions to simple ones, and why? Because our understanding can then comprehend them more quickly, and more of them at once. [*LW*, 2:647]

But this drive to reduce the world to a simple conceptual model is pointless in itself, for

> We would be inconsolable if in the process of conceptual reduction we were to lose the direct awareness, the immediacy of the original perceptions and cognitions. And the constant striving to unpack all our simplified conceptions and to peruse their elements, to make them vivid and immediate, I consider the second source of poetry.

Conceptual knowledge is pointless unless we constantly reconnect it with its basis in immediate experience. Or in general psychological terms:

> The Creator has hung a lead weight onto our soul, which, like a clock pendulum, by its downward force, keeps the soul in constant movement. This weight is, I hope, a device of the Creator for holding on to all our knowledge until it has become intuitive or vivid.

And the name of this lead weight of the soul?

The senses, yes the senses. Of course there are individual differences in the grinding of the lenses and in the size of the projection screen— but for all that, if the *camera obscura* has rents in it . . .

We will return to the image of the camera obscura in a moment.

For the sake of brevity, let me now attempt a summary interpretation of these passages, rather than follow all the detours of Lenz's actual method. First, the thinking here is based on drama's being the single literary type in which verbal communication is directly combined with sensory communication. In all other literary types, the sensory aspect is supplied by the reader's and/or author's *imagination*. ("The dramatic poet does not need to engage our senses with wit and trickery; that is done for him by the set designer" [*LW*, 2:658].) Second, the verbal aspect of literature normally operates to *semioticize* the sensory or imaginative aspect, to infuse it with a conceptual or visionary order (a kind of "machine") that we receive as the work's meaning. Third, only in drama can there be a *surplus* of sensory experience, beyond the order of meaning, since the imagined sensory experience, in other literary types, arises only in response to verbal stimuli, and is therefore always *already* semioticized. And this surplus of the sensory in drama, this unsemioticized, unordered "lead weight," is the only possible site for a literary experience of disorder, hence for the experience of the possibility of action.

Now the shape of at least two of Lenz's major plays becomes explicable. A play must *have* meaning; meaning cannot simply be eliminated, since interpretation will supply it anyway. But if the play is constructed so that its meaning is reducible to an extremely simple or narrow idea, then the sensory surplus of drama (beyond that narrowness) becomes more obvious, more an object of the spectator's awareness. Hence, in *Der Hofmeister*, the reducibility of meaning to the advocacy of universal public education; hence, in *Die Soldaten*, the idea that the institutionalized availability of sex for soldiers would prevent the play's problems. This is not to say that the meaning of either play is really reducible to the proposal of a simple social reform. The apparent reduction of meaning, the *gesture* of reduction, is sufficient to force upon the audience's awareness that sensory surplus which, in the theater, *is always there anyway*. An Enlightenment audience, by definition, will normally find a way to convince itself that everything in its theatrical experience has been integrated into the machine-like order of meaning. The task of Lenz's preparatory or theoretical theater is to interfere with this process, to allow the sensory surplus in experience to reassert its real existence.

Its real existence: not only in the theater but also in our daily mental life. The theater, in this sense, is a model of the mind. An enlightened age is an age in which the individual mind is trained to do everything it can to deny or eliminate the chaotic sensory surplus in experience. It punches holes in its camera obscura to admit as many crossing beams of light as possible, in the hope of having its sensory experience at last fully illuminated, fully integrated into the machine of rational philosophy—with the result, even if the philosophical goal is not achieved, that the senses are deprived of their proper function, their pinhole focus upon what is simply and intractably there, their operation (to change metaphors) as the lead weight that constantly unwinds our tight conceptual mastery of experience. And Lenz, by way of the theatrical model, attempts to restore the camera obscura to its original healthy condition, hence to restore the possibility of action in an age where the individual's highest hope is otherwise merely to find his or her place in the given universal scheme. The other arguments I have suggested, the other advantages of the theater over the essay, remain valid within limits; but they become cogent only in relation to the idea of a sensory surplus in the theater.

And what of *Der neue Menoza*? Does it fit the pattern? We do not need to look much beyond the play's title. Is there a need, indeed is there room, for a "new" Menoza? Lenz's direct reference to a tradition that includes not only Pontoppidan's novel, but also Montesquieu's *Lettres persanes*, Delisle's *Arlequin sauvage*, and even Voltaire's *L'Ingénu*, reminds us that the supposed radical criticism of European civilization from an imagined external perspective is itself a cliché *of* that civilization, embodying the claim of reason to be able to complete itself in a valid self-reflection. Thus the presumed meaning of Lenz's play, its commentary on enlightened Europe, is reduced even further than in the other comedies, to practically nothing. Indeed, the very possibility of a useful critical meaning in drama is called into question, since the civilization under scrutiny is shown to have a co-optive appetite large enough to engulf any critical perspective whatever. (Are Prinz Tandi's ideas any more effective, as criticism, than Beza's or Zierau's?) But Lenz's aim is not cultural criticism. It is the rescue of the sensory surplus in experience by means of the theater used as a model of the mind.

The parallel, therefore, between Lenz's project of sensory restoration and Goethe's science is clear. In both cases, the interposition between ourselves and the world of an artificial device—for Lenz the theater, for Goethe the procedure of experimenting and theorizing "with irony," which requires a social situation—serves paradoxically to restore our *immediate* relation to what Goethe calls "the true," to what is simply there. For Lenz, moreover, as for Goethe, that interposed device is indispensable. The individual mind—no matter whether it is historically conditioned in this respect—cannot carry out a de-conceptualizing or de-theorizing move; its very existence is constituted by moves in the opposite direction. It is the theater, again, the theater in its materiality, that must think our way back to the senses for us. For the theater is a *better* mind, a mind that is characterized, like ours, by the drive for conceptual or semiotic order, but in its quality as both strictly literary and strictly *material*, is unable to delude itself about the divide between that order and an irreducible chaotic surplus of experience.

And if this version of the idea of the theater as a thinking organ appears primitive alongside the structural subtlety of plays by Goethe, Schiller, and Kleist, we must not forget that a primitive theater, a device for training audiences, is exactly what Lenz wants. Moreover, the very possibility of a primitive or undeveloped form of the idea supports my contention that what we are talking about is not the startling philosophical reinterpretation of dramatic form by a secret society of geniuses, but something more like a latent axiom of the theater, which, if it fails to appear axiomatic to us, thus testifies again to *our* resolute forgetfulness of the eighteenth century.

Materiality, Irony, and Community

If there are grounds for arguing that in a significant segment of eighteenth-century literature, the theater assumes the function of a primary organ of thought, then the problem of the locus or fulcrum of radical irony, the question of how the knowledge behind radical irony can be known in the first place, appears to be answered. I say "answered," not "solved" or "put to rest." For from the point of view of my own inescapable experience of myself as an individual thinking subject—however illusory I "know" that experience to be—the problem is as intractable as ever. But now the realm of material reality—which is categorically different from the realm of subjective experience, where the problem merely festers—at least contains an "answer," a response that at least exists and has points of contact with the problem, even if the same categorical difference prevents any final judgment about its adequacy as a response. I suggest, then, that the theater is the locus of irony, the organ that can think the whole knowledge of radical irony. Again, the *materiality* of this organ is crucial, in the same way that it is crucial for Herder—in response to his own radical understanding of the problem of languages and discourses—to extend his actual hand into the void, to effect a revelatory rupture in discourse by using the equivalent of his own material body as a wedge.

But to what extent *is* this theater material or materialized, the theater of young Goethe and Schiller, and then of Kleist, which Goethe later calls "invisible," the theater at least of Lessing and of Lenz as well? Its materiality—which, for us, is only an interpretive inference—is probably sufficient to mark it as *an* answer to the problem of irony. But the question of how good an answer raises the question of what grounds we have for speaking of "materiality" here—as if materiality could be measured by a nonmaterial or conceptual test. Historical grounds, tracing the exact provenance of the axiomatic quality in eighteenth-century Germany of the idea of a literally thinking theater, would perhaps satisfy us, but would require another whole book for detailed treatment.

The other possible way of grounding conceptually the idea of a material theater involves the notion of community. The theater's material presence must be vouched for by its unrestricted communal availability; the "aesthetic" factor, the individual's subjective response, although unquestionably involved in the theater's operation, must be shown to be of no consequence in its *constitution*. But we have seen that the field in which the concepts of individual and community declare themselves in the historical period that interests us is composed mainly of genres other than drama. The relation between meditative and social language in poetry is important, as is, especially, the theory of the novel and of its history suggested in *Wilhelm Meisters Wanderjahre*.

Therefore I want to return now to the question of the novel, and to the question of how, and how solidly, the notion of community is grounded in the operation of the genre. Is the community of the novel's readers—or the community *as* a reader—really anything more than an idea, a fancy, that can be imagined as arising in the course of an individual reader's "aesthetic" response? The discussion of drama is not outside the range of this question. To the extent that the idea of community has substance in the literary domain, it supports the idea of the theater's materiality, and of its creating an ironic leverage in literature. But our concern now is the novel, and in particular, the question of its general textual *type*.

Rousseau's Political Texts as a Theory of the Novel

Paul de Man says, in *Allegories of Reading*, "The conceptual language of the social contract resembles the subtle interplay between figural and referential discourse in a novel. . . . *The Social Contract* is [Rousseau's] best novel."[13] This statement is subject to the same type of criticism as de Man's insistence, in "The Rhetoric of Blindness," that Rousseau's texts "account for" their own rhetoricity. But like that other statement, it also contains an important perception. Rousseau's political writings, especially the *Discourse on Inequality* and the *Social Contract*, can be read as implying a *theory* of the novel. Reading them in this way in fact relieves some of their logical difficulties.

The difficulties I mean begin in the preface to the *Discourse* with the question: "*What experiments would be necessary in order to arrive at a knowledge of natural humanity, and by what means could these experiments be carried out in the bosom of society?*"[14] "The greatest Philosophers," Rousseau continues, "will not be too good to direct these experiments, nor the most powerful rulers too good to carry them out" (JJR, 3:124). But the speculative knowledge those philosophers would need in order to "direct" their social experiments, which could not yet be the knowledge to be gained *from* the experiments, would perforce be a speculation on the best ways of "removing," *in* society, the "difficulties that conceal from us the real foundations of human society," hence the best ways of revealing our "natural right," which must by implication turn out to be ways of *improving* society. And precisely this speculation, if it goes but a short step further and formulates "rules," to which it "gives the name of natural law . . . with no other proof than the good we think would

---

[13]Paul de Man, *Allegories of Reading* (New Haven, 1979), p. 159.
[14]JJR, 3:123–24. That "expériences" mean "experiments" here, and not something closer to "experiences" or "inferences from experience," is clear from the sequel.

follow from their universal practice" (3:125), is then categorically rejected.

This difficulty disappears, however, if the gap between speculation and experiment is eliminated, which is the result if we take the idea of "experiments" figuratively, to refer to fictional narratives (quasi-novels) that by their plausibility, or lack thereof, test the cogency and consequences of the speculations on which they are based. The creation of this sort of narrative is the task Rousseau actually sets himself in the *Discourse*, in which he insists on the "hypothetical" quality (JJR, 3:133) of his account of human prehistory, yet still recognizes the obligation of "Philosophy" to supply such an account (3:162–63). The fictionality of his narrative becomes clearest in the account of the origin of language (3:145–51), which succeeds mainly in opening, in the form of unanswerable questions, a gulf between the states of nature and civilization that can be traversed neither by narration nor by speculation alone, but only by a form in which each relativizes the other to produce, as in Herder, a discourse of *enactment*.

The task of philosophical discourse, then, is not to describe or regulate humanity, but in a sense to *create* it, to *make* human beings as characters are made in a novel. And it follows from the "perfectibility" of human being (JJR, 3:142, 162)—from the mutability of our very nature (3:123, 191–94), which for Rousseau is a logical consequence of the existence of inequality—that discourse in this sense is by no means necessarily excluded from the domain of actual political cause and effect. But the *Discourse on Inequality* does not itself pretend to be the kind of novel-as-experiment it envisages. It is still primarily the theory of such a novel. Its insistence upon the state of nature, despite the gulf that separates us from that state historically and still lacks filling in, is as it were an anatomy lesson for novelists. Like the painter, the novelist must know how to draw the naked body (humans in the state of nature) in order to make his costumed figures plausible, their actions convincing and effective.

I do not mean that a theory of the novel is actually aimed at in Rousseau's political texts. My suggestion, like de Man's, is that *our* idea of the novel, when held alongside those texts, endows them with a special intelligibility—whether or not it can be traced to an "intention."

Especially the *Social Contract* shows a new side of itself when read in this way. For the ideas of social pact and general will require the possibility of a strict distinction between "contentious or debatable affairs," involving the relation to the public of "individuals with particular interests" (JJR, 3:373–74), and questions of law (in Rousseau's carefully restricted sense [3:378–80]) where the authority of the general will can be invoked. But cases that blur this distinction inevitably arise—Rousseau suggests this in his chapter "Suffrage" (3:440–41)—and by what authority will they be assigned to one or the other category? In the reading of nonreferential texts such as novels, however, an exactly parallel distinction is maintained with no effort or controversy: between debatable questions, which include all questions of "meaning," no matter how simple, and what we might call the "law" of the text, our prior agreement (even if only with ourselves, in solitude) to read exactly this text, without even imagining the possibility of changing it to suit our taste or advantage. The possibility of an "institution" in which "each individual submits necessarily to the conditions he imposes on others" (3:374) is highly questionable in the political realm. But in the case of fictional literature, whose meaning is to no degree decided by comparison with facts, just such an institution (our agreement on what text we are talking about) is the unquestioned ground of even the deepest-cutting debates.

Or we think of the figure of the "legislator," who is the weakest link in Rousseau's myth of the origin of the state, in part because he has to fill the largest logical gap, the requirement "that the effect become the cause, that the social spirit, which must be the work of institutions, preside at their very institution, that people, in advance of the laws, be already what they must become by way of the laws" (JJR, 3:383). Transposed into a theory of the *author* of the novel— whose business it is to set up the particular fictional "institutions" that for the time being materialize our subscription to the general contract of reading, who thus "persuades without convincing" (3:383)—the precarious idea of the legislator becomes hardly even disputable, and in fact evinces not only the author's necessary doubling (as discussed, for instance, by Kristeva) into subject of enunciation and subject of utterance but also the exteriorized and ambivalent condition of that doubling which characterizes fictional literature.[15] Precisely as subject of utterance, or signified, the lawgiving deity is

[15]Julia Kristeva, "Word, Dialogue and Novel" (orig. 1966), translated in her *Desire in Language: A Semiotic Approach to Literature and Art*, ed. Leon S. Roudiez (New York, 1980), pp. 74–76.

employed by the legislator as a sign signifying an inherently fugitive subject of enunciation.

And Kristeva's development of Bakhtin's novel-theory also includes a parallel to the cessation of all governmental jurisdiction in Rousseau's Assembly of the People (JJR, 3:427–28), an idea whose practical difficulties Rousseau sees clearly, and whose theoretical difficulties are unfolded especially by Derrida.[16] For it is just such an authoritative supersedure of authority that Kristeva names "*transgression giving itself a law*" (p. 71) in describing the specificity of the dialogic that informs the carnivalesque or polyphonic novel.

The Communal and the Ego

I am trying to prepare for the proposition that the novel shows a tendency, based in the eighteenth century, to *enact* the same thought that Rousseau, on whatever level of irony, attempts to capture systematically in his political writing. Crucial to this argument will be the concept of the ego, by which I mean, as before, the individual in its intersection with discourse, or in the form of discourse, as grammatical subject and object in a narrative that is its "fate." In its distinction from the subject as signified of the social, namely, (1) only the ego can possess "rights" or "powers," which presuppose discourse, (2) only the ego, as we have seen, can be solitary, hence in a position to "enter" the social pact, and (3) only the ego is meant as "the reader" in the convention of romance reading, and undergoes "division" (Iser) only *within* the discursive realm, as grammatical subject *and* object, or as signifier *and* signified in the textual situation (Kristeva's A_1 and A_2, p. 74).

Rousseau's insistence on the "social pact," on the contract that has no content whatever (no specific laws or requirements or prior sanction) except its quality as pact, as signifying the corporate unity of its subscribers, creates difficulties with respect to (1) and (2). For the pact in this sense, as we noted in connection with the idea of censorship, must be the *foundation* of that discourse in which the ego first becomes a bearer of the "rights" or "powers" it had supposedly surrendered in contracting (JJR, 3:360–61). In the *Discourse*, Rousseau attacks Samuel Pufendorf for asserting the individual's "natural" right

[16]Jacques Derrida, *Of Grammatology*, trans. Gayatri Chakravorty Spivak (Baltimore, 1976), pp. 295–302.

to keep what belongs to him, "but without explaining what is meant by 'belong'" (3:132). Surely the concept of "belonging" is applicable to "rights" and "powers" as well, at least applicable enough to justify the same attack *against* the Rousseau of the *Social Contract*.

The *Social Contract* can be defended against this attack only by the consideration that the validity of its argument does not depend on the objective historical existence of the pact it describes. (The pact, even if it did happen, would still not belong to "history," but would be prior to the very possibility of history.) What Rousseau actually argues, especially in the first five chapters, is that the experience and concept of the ego—which is presupposed by all questions of right or power, of liberty or submission or slavery—makes the idea of human community, hence of the state, incomprehensible *except* insofar as it is traced to an aboriginal contract. (The argument is not "qu'il y'a eu . . ." but "qu'il faut toujours remonter à une première convention" [JJR, 3:359].) Given our inescapable experience of the ego, in other words, we cannot honestly or logically *think* of our community except as the result of such a contract, whatever the (inherently inaccessible) facts of the case may be. Or in a terminology we used earlier: The ego, in the experiential and discursive situation to which we are irrevocably committed, unambiguously *signifies* the social contract. (To say that the ego "implies" the social contract would overstrain the concept of "ego," endow it with too objective and closed an identity. The identity of the ego is *only* that of a sign, that of the signified, for example, of the word "I.")

But the unity that results immediately from the social contract is not what we called "the social" in Chapter 4; it cannot yet be a plurality held together by "conversation," since the discursive environment in which conversation can take place has not yet developed. It is, rather, what we have called "the communal," human belonging-together not as a plurality unfolded in conversation, but as an utterly originary singularity, as a *"moi,"* a "public person" (JJR, 3:361), a huge individual human being, as Hölderlin's "Gesang," not "Gespräch." Thus our argument in a sense comes full circle. Just as the subject is the signified of the social, and is accessible to us only by way of this signifying, so also, and with the same limitation on accessibility, *the communal is the signified of the ego.*

The ego and the social, in this pattern, are the discourse-bound forms of human individuality and human plurality respectively. The subject and the communal are those forms of individuality and plu-

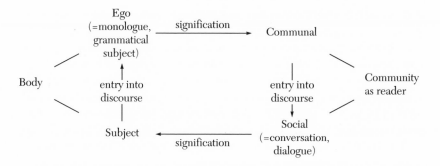

rality which, given the unavoidable insistence of discourse on its referential component, are posited as exterior or prior to discourse. (This positing, however, is strictly abstract. The subject and the communal only actually happen, for us, as semiotic signifieds.) I have included in my diagram the "body," in the sense of the discussion of Herder, which is no longer subject but not yet ego, and is *in* discourse, but only as a radically disruptive factor. And I have placed at a corresponding point in the diagram the concept of "community as reader," which is treated in the discussion of the novel that follows.

It is clear that the novel plays a crucial part in this structure of concepts. Just as drama is the literary genre in which the social is purged maximally of the "subjective" element that gets mixed up with it in our actual social life, and so emerges with maximal clarity as the signifier precisely of the subject, so also the novel, correspondingly—by means of the convention of solitary romance reading—frees the ego maximally from its interpersonal determinations, for the sake not of its indulgence as ego, but of its signifying power relative to the communal. Or at least this argument—which is also supported by the arguments in Chapter 1 on the presence of community in novelistic discourse *despite* the convention of romance reading—becomes possible if the parallels I have suggested between Rousseau's systematics and the novel as enactment can be sustained.

Contract and Constitution in the Novel

As before, we will restrict our focus to Goethe's *Wilhelm Meisters Wanderjahre*, considered as a theoretical and practical summary of the eighteenth-century ironic novel. A broad discussion of novels by various authors would perhaps in some respects be preferable, but, in the context and scope of the present project, is neither necessary nor possible. The structure of critical concepts with which we are operating has been anchored historically in several different ways. The business of the argument now is to show how that structure requires the novel, in exactly Goethe's sense, for its completion, and how it implies a useful critical approach to those eighteenth-century novels that the *Wanderjahre* claims to represent.

The question of the ego and the novel brings us back to the question of romance reading and to the problem of the work's *existence* as an aesthetic or intentional object in the age of autonomous art. In the so-called pre-autonomous age, the existence of the work of art is established by the web of doctrinal, liturgical, political, mythical, or generic relations that contains it; its intentionality is anchored from the start as a *function* in the communal order. In the age of autonomous art, by contrast, of art that insists on making its own laws not only from genre to genre, but (especially in the novel) from work to work, the only possible guarantee of the work's existence is the individual recipient's immediate experience of it, our seeing or hearing or reading it.

Thus the "aesthetic" view of art arises, which we have discussed in connection with Lessing, a view that depends on the idea of the recipient's *radical solitude*—even if that solitude is meant to be realized, in Schiller's "aesthetic state" for example, as an experience of oneness with the whole of humanity—and therefore tends to reduce the study of art to the study of individual psychology. It now becomes difficult to see how the work can be said to exist, as a work of art, beyond the solitary receptive experience, how it can exist for the community or in history. The work's communally available existence, it appears, must now be based on a kind of ad hoc verbal *contract*, a contract represented by our talking with one another, and especially by our writing, *about* the work. This contract recalls, as it were nostalgically, the broad cultural matrix of pre-autonomous art, but can never replace it. For there is now too deep a category difference between the contract and its content. Is the contract valid for me if I have never seen or heard or read the work? Suppose my private experience of the work conflicts with the terms in which it is discussed publicly. Am I contractually committed to feel joy or sorrow or wonder at some specific point in my personal life?

The form of the ironic novel, however—that genre from which no conceivable type of discourse is excluded, not even the extreme case of the empty page in *Tristram Shandy*—is capable of complicating these problems still further by including them in its content. And in *Wilhelm Meisters Wanderjahre*, the idea of the contract appears in the heightened form of the *constitution*, the contract that constitutes and regulates the very community of its subscribers. The rules of the Tower Society, which is now the Association of Renunciants, and the system of the Pedagogical Province are such constitutions, as are the founding precepts of a new American society and the plan to reinvigorate the tacit constitution of present European society. And I suggested earlier that the novel itself must be regarded as the constitution of the scattered community of its readers—on the model of the Association of Renunciants, who live widely separated from one another, whose only duty is to live in accordance with their true individual needs, and who conduct the Association's business only sporadically, in their correspondence and often merely accidental meetings, as people might occasionally talk together about a book they have read and taken seriously. We saw that the presumed serial quality of the experience of reading, the convention of romance reading, is thoroughly disrupted in the *Wanderjahre*, especially by the two collections of aphorisms, which compel us to recognize in our reading a procedure that I compared to the manner in which we read the Bible. I now compare it to the manner in which we read a legal document or contract. The two comparisons are not widely separated, especially in German, where the terms "alter Bund" and "neuer Bund," the "old covenant" and the "new covenant," refer not merely to the content of the Old and New Testaments but also, often, to those books themselves.

The idea of the novel as the constitution of the community of its readers, however, opens the whole problematics of autonomous art. Critical discourse considered as the contractual establishment of a work's existence as art, for example, is enacted in the description of the nonexistent watercolors that we discussed in Chapter 1 (*WMW*, pp. 505–7), where Goethe uses the word "fraglich" for the concept "in question" ("the watercolors in question"), and leaves it to us to recall that the word more commonly means "questionable." Also, a strong preference for *non*-autonomous art is suggested in the description of the galleries in the Pedagogical Province and in the singing of the gathered Associates, the preference for an art whose existence is anchored by its function in a regulated community. Or we think of the first novella-figure in the novel, St. Joseph the Second, whose whole life represents an answer to the question: how can the immediate experience of a work of art—in this case a series of paintings, a form that defies Lessing by being situated between painting and narrative—extend beyond the solitude of the "aesthetic state"? The answer St. Joseph hits on reduces this question to the absurd; one must *live* the work of art, transform one's entire existence into an imitation of what it depicts. And the gallery of the Oheim, who tries to preserve, beyond the experienced instant, tangible manifestations of human individuality, and expresses especially a deep distrust of "written tradition" (p. 341), belongs to this thematic complex as well.

But in the *Wanderjahre*, the question of the novel is paramount. The artist Wilhelm meets in Italy is interested in Mignon's early surroundings, and so turns out to be a reader of the earlier *Wilhelm Meisters Lehrjahre*. The trouble is that *as* a reader he is still living with Wilhelm *in* the fictional world of that earlier novel (namely, in its sequel), like St. Joseph, who is both viewer and participant with respect to his frescoes. And we, in reading this passage, are maneuvered into an exactly parallel situation; our imaginative dwelling inside the fiction must now also include our self-recognition as readers of the book. This device in itself, the confusion of imagination's inside with criticism's outside, had of course been part of the novel's artistic arsenal at least since Cervantes. But when it is employed in connection with the idea of the artistic contract—which is emphasized in the same section of the *Wanderjahre*, in the discussion of the watercolors—it suggests to us the possibility of regarding the novel as the contractual establishment of its *own* existence. The conversations between Wilhelm and the artist on Mignon are a contract establishing the availability as imagined experience of the content of the *Lehrjahre*; but they also belong to the extended fictional content of that same book.

We are thus asked to consider as a possibility the idea that the content of the novel is *nothing but* our subscription to the establishment by contract of the novel's own existence. This idea is outlandish, but also obviously significant, for it would provide a solution to the problem of autonomous art. The problem is that the work of art is realized, as art, only "aesthetically," only in our strictly private experience of it, which means that the public existence of the work as an artistic object (without which it could not be a "work," available for aesthetic experience, in the first place) must be established separately, by critical discourse considered as a kind of contract; but the validity of such contracts—which is inherently questionable, since criticism *is* a questioning—is decidable only by way of exactly the private experience they had apparently circumvented. And how shall this problem be solved except by eliminating the gap between private experience and public contract, by reducing what we "experience" in reading to *nothing but* the act of contracting?

This whole state of affairs is allegorized in the mysterious casket found by young Felix, which is compared to a book in size and shape (*WMW*, p. 302), and evidently represents the book we are now reading. (We recall the similar function of the skull in the poem "Im ernsten Beinhaus war's . . .") For if we ask about the contents of Felix's casket, at least a partial answer is suggested by the parallel with the magical casket in the novella "Die neue Melusine," which contains a *life*, a whole real world, in which the casket's possessor can participate if he but wishes to—just as the novel's fiction is a world we can supposedly experience as real by reading. But the content of Felix's casket, which is the governing mystery of *our* novel, is never revealed to us. The key by which it can be opened is in our possession—it is offered us, in fact, almost physically, in the form of an iconic sign, in Hersilie's letter (*WMW*, p. 599)—but as soon as we try to use it (as Hersilie does) it fails us. That is to say, as soon as we try to identify the novel's content as life, as immediate experience, the very act of trying detaches us from that immediacy, and our efforts prove futile. Or more precisely, as soon as we attempt to achieve the novel's central content in language, our language assumes the character of critical discussion with respect to its utterly solitary, incommunicable object, and so fails to reach the center. The text talks literally "about," or around, its content, in concentric circles; and that content, the contents of the casket, is never revealed directly, which means in effect that it is not there for us, that the text is *nothing but* a public, contractual determination of itself. We are caught in a double bind. Precisely to the extent that we succeed in submerging ourselves imaginatively in the fiction, we are obliged to accept the inaccessibility of the casket's content; only when we detach ourselves to the level of contract or critical discussion are we in a position to identify the casket's contents as that radically solitary experience we might *otherwise* be undergoing.

The first main action in the story is another allegory of this situation. Wilhelm and Felix attempt to enter the domain of the Oheim by a kind of back door, in the same way that the novel reader attempts to enter the fiction, to realize it for himself as an experienced world, but without making his own personal presence felt in it, as it were without knocking. Like Wilhelm and Felix, however, we are trapped by a double gate at the very boundary of the fiction (*WMW*, p. 304), thus at once both inside and outside with respect to it. And when we are then permitted to enter after all, we find ourselves in a house filled with books and bookishness, all hung about with biographical signs and aphorisms and allusions and quotations and cross-references, a house in which living, like reading, is a constant skipping around, a constant manipulation and balancing of various traditional stipulations. We find ourselves, that is, in the domain of the text as a public contract.

Finally, let us suppose for a moment that the text of a novel *can* operate as the contractual establishment of its own existence as a work of art. The contract in question would then be strictly self-grounding or self-sanctioning, thus in effect an aboriginal contract, a contract by which the very possibility of contracting is established. And this possibility is equivalent to the existence of an incorporated society whose constitution the novel now represents. Thus at least the association of *ideas* suggested above, by which the novel is related to Rousseau's "social pact," is not irrelevant to the understanding of the *Wanderjahre*.

The Two Contracts of Reading: Goethe and Thomas Mann

This argument appears to suggest, however, that the convention of romance reading can be completely and permanently circumvented, which we saw in Chapter 1 is not the case. In fact, that convention is itself a form of contract, as becomes especially clear in a later novel that still moves in Goethe's orbit, Thomas Mann's *Doktor Faustus*.

I have more than one reason for introducing *Doktor Faustus* into the discussion. But for the time being, what is important is the obvious quality of a humanistic or critical contract in the reader's relation to the narrator Zeitblom. Precisely our recognition of Zeitblom's many foolishnesses reminds us that by accepting his word—as we must, since his are the only words—we are making concessions, as it were negotiating for ourselves a critical position in relation to the fictional content.

And once we have come this far, it becomes equally clear—under the influence of the fiction—that our reading is also governed by a *second* contract, which is not humanistic but demonistic, a pact with the devil. Zeitblom's emphasis on his ambivalence, his humanistic skepticism, toward the documentary evidence of his friend's unholy association, reflects a corresponding ambivalence in our own position. For we, the readers, are not even strictly obliged to accept the devil as a "real" element in the *fiction*. Why should Zeitblom regard the interview with the devil (written, we recall, on music paper, and not datable as to its composition [*DF*, pp. 295–96]) as anything more than a kind of initial program-sketch for the "Weheklag"? Has Leverkühn himself never read *The Brothers Karamazov*? How does Zeitblom even *know* that Leverkühn had followed his hetaera to Pressburg, or that he really has syphilis? He never makes clear when Leverkühn had told him about these things (*DF*, pp. 204–6). Why should that story, like the story of the American Capercailzie—which Zeitblom dismisses! (*DF*, p. 354)—not be an artistic self-mythologizing on Leverkühn's part, after the model of Nietzsche? But on the other hand, our situation as novel readers includes our *assent* to the fiction as an entirety; even if we disbelieve, therefore, we nevertheless assent to the devil's existence, we assent at least to the quasi-referential use of his name, which is to say, we make a kind of pact with him. (The devil himself dismisses our quibble about the difference between what is "real," "wirklich," and "what operates," "was wirkt" [*DF*, p. 323].) And like Leverkühn's, ours is a pact that had been sealed, in the history of the novel as a genre—in the convention of romance reading—long before it is spelled out for us.

As readers, therefore, we actually subscribe to two different contracts, a demonistic contract and a humanistic contract. In the first, we share with others, or pretend to share, the solitary experience of submergence in the fiction; in the second, we engage with other readers in a latent rational discourse by which we are detached from the fiction, fully aware of its gaps and inconsistencies. And the involvement of these two contracts with one another, especially the complicity of the humanistic contract (critical discussion) in the demonistic contract (the required *object* of discussion), evidently reflects the disastrously interinvolved relation of fascism and liberalism, which makes it possible for human beings to become Nazis, the situation of fascism and liberalism on opposite sides of an uncomfortably permeable border, like that membrane, the pia mater, that fails to exclude the spirochetes from Leverkühn's brain. Mann thus presents Nazism as a phase in the history of the novel, or in that larger movement of which the novel is a crucial element, the development of the idea of autonomous art. It is clear in both *Doktor Faustus* and the *Wanderjahre* that a humanistic contract, in the form of critical discourse, is needed in order that the work of autonomous art exist in the first place and be available for our solitary reception; but the humanistic contract is then inevitably implicated *in* this reception, in the demonistic assumption that with respect to the work of art we communicate, we achieve community, not in the medium of rational discourse, but by way of our feelings, our radical solitude—our "Seele," not "Geist," as the pre-Nazi thought of Ludwig Klages has it. The situation in what Schleppfuß calls the "classical" age of faith is parallel (*DF*, p. 137); and Leverkühn's career is a direct enactment of the dynamics involved. Leverkühn's goal is precisely to put an end to autonomous art, but in the process he produces an esoteric music that the *humanist* Zeitblom must interpret in terms of feeling and so transforms into a demonistic contract—a contract to which *our* subscription is the more significant, and in a sense more shameful, since we lack the actual experienced music on which to base it.

The *Wanderjahre* as Social Contract

The history of the novel as a genre is also the main concern of the *Wanderjahre*. And in Goethe's book the idea of the constitution in a sense straddles the distinction between the humanistic and the demonistic contracts by authorizing critical discussion, thus participating in it, while also being prior to it, as the never fully accountable foundation of the community in which it occurs. But once the discourse is underway, it attempts unambiguously to suppress the demonistic contract in favor of the humanistic one. The structure of the *Wanderjahre* repeatedly defeats the process of serial or romance reading; and Felix's casket, which presumably contains the core of the novel as solitary experience, is never opened. (Actually it is opened for a moment, by the goldsmith who knows the key's secret, and is then immediately clapped shut again, because "it is not well to touch or disturb such secrets" [*WMW*, p. 743]. Perhaps what the goldsmith sees is the possibility of demonistic reading, hence of something like Nazism.)

There are plenty of shady characters in the *Wanderjahre*, smugglers, thieves, poachers, suspicious vagrants employed as messengers and guides, people of no fixed abode about whom we are made curious but never receive definite information, and even one gentleman of science who has on his conscience a certain complicity in murder for the obtaining of anatomical specimens. This shady element, which threatens constantly the social goals of the novel's more enlightened figures, is readily associated with a silent, dangerously introverted element in the community of readers, whose insistence on imaginative solitude threatens the quality of the book as a humanistic contract. We have already seen that types of character in the *Wanderjahre* stand allegorically for types of reader; and the enormous amount of written material that is passed back and forth for reading in the fictional action keeps us in mind of this allegorical move. Moreover, the conflict of demonistic and humanistic appears directly in that anatomist whose conscience has transformed him from a "Prosektor" into a "Proplastiker" (*WMW*, p. 612). He now manufactures artificial anatomical specimens that enable the student to learn by *constructing* a body, not by dissecting. The solitary reading of what most European languages call a "romance," we infer allegorically, is in truth not an expansion of our experienced world, not an instance of life, but only the morbidly minute examination of fragments of dead experience, a kind of dissection. We must learn, rather, to take the novel as a set of manufactured building blocks for experience, which receives the quality of immediacy or life only by way of our own social actions in fulfillment of the humanistic contract we subscribe to as readers.

We think also of Makarie, whose relation to the human world is recognizable as that of a novel reader, in that she is privy, mainly by way of written documents, to other people's true and secret thoughts. But she does not merely know about other people, she also takes a direct hand in their lives, and so reduces to an ethical absurdity the passive, "aesthetic" attitude of the reader of romance. How can a human being endure the situation (even the merely feigned situation) of knowing about other people without doing something for them? There is a radically solitary side to Makarie, when she withdraws from all human contact. At such times, however, she undergoes a sympathetic submergence not in human experience but in the dynamics of the solar system, of which she is an "integrating part" (*WMW*, p. 391); and in this she is paralleled with the geologically sensitive girl discovered by Montan. The structure of this parallel, including the correspondence of Montan to Makarie's astronomer friend, in fact suggests that the proper function of the ego, of the solitary component of our existence, is *scientific*. To reformulate our discussion of Goethe's science in Chapter 1: the ego, considered as the individual human sensorium in combination with the power of discourse, is a scientific instrument, nature's own principal self-observing and self-integrating *organ*. (We recall the aphorism about the experiencing human being as a scientific "apparatus" [*WMW*, p. 760].) In all our contact with human beings, by contrast, including the practice of literature, our solitary or aesthetic being must be suppressed in favor of the actively social.

But what are we left with if we succeed in suppressing the demonistic or brooding aspect of the *novel*? The content of a novel, without which, *as* a novel, it has no content, is the reader's solitary imaginative participation in a world of fictional experience. Suppose the *Wanderjahre* succeeds in suppressing this content, enclosing it in a locked casket. What does this book become? The answer is suggested by the echoes of Rousseau in the story's various community-constitutions. The novel becomes nothing but its own humanistic contract, hence a contract that has no specific content whatever except the belonging together, as the community of its subscribers, of those who read it. It becomes an exact structural equivalent of the original social contract of Rousseau.

In Rousseau the social pact is not an actuality so much as an inference from the consideration that every contract with any actual content presupposes the corporate quality of its body of subscribers, hence an earlier contract, hence ultimately an "original" contract that we can have no knowledge of except by such inference. Even the popular assemblies upon which Rousseau lays so much stress cannot approach the actuality of originary conditions; as Derrida points out, those assemblies are still an institution dependent on the institution of writing. But Goethe, in the *Wanderjahre*, suggests a circumvention of this problem of non-actuality. For the novel as a genre is the culmination in practice of the idea of autonomous art; it is that form of writing in which the imaginative solitude of the reader becomes maximal, that form in which the reader's "supplying" of meaning becomes the *whole* content. And if the content of the novel can be suppressed, locked away out of sight, then the reader is left with *nothing but* his or her solitude, an aesthetic solitude which, although in real life it is a social danger, is also the only conceivable condition in which the individual can subscribe to the social contract in its original form; without radical solitude as a starting point, there can be no reenactment or resubscription of the original contract. What is suppressed in the *Wanderjahre*, to be precise, is not the reader's ego itself, which would be impossible, but rather the brooding demonistic contract by way of which the ego can flatter itself that it is really the "subject," a "soul" in some direct mystical contact with other souls. And the suppression of this potentially fascist delusion liberates the signifying power of the ego, which in turn interprets the humanistic contract of reading as a sign of the communal, of the social pact, as such.

This argument—which, by way of the *Wanderjahre* and an intertext that involves especially Sterne, claims applicability to the eighteenth-century ironic novel in general—loses much of its theoretical tenuousness if it is regarded as a response to the problem of autonomous art, which it deals with by using the problem itself (the aesthetic solitude of the ego) as its own solution (the ego mobilized as signifier). Drama, correspondingly, in its inevitable de-subjectification of the social, signifies precisely the thinking subject, on a sufficiently preterpersonal level to suggest the possibility of a locus of irony.

Is There a Social Contract?

The questions to which we were led by our discussion of drama have thus in some measure been answered. We have found points, in Rousseau and Goethe, where the signification of the communal by the ego is built into eighteenth-century social and literary or novelistic thought. And the structural relation between this signification and the signifying process in drama supports our treatment of the theater's materiality as a literary fact by suggesting the possibility of its anchoring in a form of community. But by using the comparison with Thomas Mann, we can be a great deal more specific about the rôle of the communal in constituting a locus of irony.

In particular, *can* the content of the novel—the demonistic content, as we have learned from *Doktor Faustus* to call it—be suppressed in the manner required by our argument? If *Doktor Faustus* is a "taking back" of Goethe's *Faust* (like Leverkühn's taking back of Beethoven's Choral Symphony [*DF*, pp. 634, 639]), is it not even more directly a taking back of *Wilhelm Meisters Wanderjahre*, a historical demonstration, with the reality of the Nazi period as its overwhelming evidence, that the demonistic contract cannot be abrogated, that the content of the novel for the reader's "soul" cannot be suppressed? Does Mann not in fact go his friend Adorno one better, by suggesting not only that poetic literature must find itself henceforward in the shadow of Auschwitz, but that (at least in the history of the novel) it always *has* stood anticipatorily in that shadow?[17]

Thus we perhaps at last gain some leverage with respect to the question of the politics of irony, which we discussed but did not settle in earlier chapters. Is irony really subversive, or always covertly conservative? If Goethe's *Wanderjahre* makes a capstone to the whole eighteenth-century poetics of irony by appropriating even science and social-contract theory, not to mention the history of the novel, for the production of a discourse that turns out to be nothing but the quasi-contractual enactment of its own origin; and if the *Wanderjahre* then turns out to be merely an irresponsible juggling with tradition, the pretended suppression of an ineluctable literary-discursive reality (the novel as demonistic contract) that later comes back to haunt not Goethe, but us, in the form of Nazism, perhaps precisely *because* it had not been faced as a reality: does it not follow that the whole idea of irony, as we have developed it, is discredited?

I think the happening of Nazism, and especially of the concentration camps, does in fact clarify matters, but in exactly the opposite sense. To whom, namely, and for whom (or in whose name) is Adorno speaking when he worries about the difficulty or barbarity of continuing to write poetry in the shadow of Auschwitz? (That he later changes his mind changes nothing; that he worries about the question is what matters.) At least one thing is clear about the audience presupposed by his discourse: it is emptied of, and in effect blind to, precisely the Jews; it sees only dead Jews, Jews not even available for the Goethean *gesture* of exclusion that we have discussed. And is it not exactly the shadow of Auschwitz that erases the difference between being blind to the Jews and exterminating the Jews? The discourse that makes Auschwitz into a German or European *problem*, a problem that concerns all literature or civilization, but does not concern Jews—no matter how deep that problem cuts, no matter how much it hurts—is a continuation of exactly the discourse that

[17]See KuG, pp. 7–31, esp. p. 31.

achieved its real correlative *in* Auschwitz. Adorno and Mann both in effect proclaim the inescapability of that discourse. Otherwise, why worry about whether it is permissible to write poems? That they proclaim it in the posture of reproach and (within limits) self-reproach does not change matters.[18]

Most of *Doktor Faustus*, in fact, was written or planned before the shadow of Auschwitz actually fell on European consciousness. That that novel ignores the single major *achievement* of the Nazis—the elimination from Germany, and to a lesser extent from all Europe, of the Jews—that in effect, like Adorno, it does not really even quarrel with that achievement, is therefore perhaps excusable. But when Mann himself later makes excuses after all—by chewing on the question of whether *Doktor Faustus* can be regarded as "anti-Semitic," in the figures of Chaim Breisacher and Saul Fitelberg, which is *not* the issue—he does so in a text, *Die Entstehung des Doktor Faustus*, that consists mainly of name-dropping (including, of course, Jewish names) and so wraps itself defensively in a culture of precisely the type that needs discrediting, a culture whose exclusion of the Nazis, for all Mann's inventiveness in expressions of contempt, does not balance or nullify the blindness to the Jews, the complicity in their extermination, from which it begins.[19]

[18]See Theodor W. Adorno, "Commitment," in *A&P*, pp. 188–89, where, in responding to Brecht, Adorno unfolds in detail his sense of the problematics of literature after Auschwitz. Lyric poetry after Auschwitz is still "barbaric"; but "literature must resist this verdict . . . [must] be such that its mere existence after Auschwitz is not a surrender to cynicism. . . . The abundance of real suffering tolerates no forgetting. . . . Yet this suffering . . . also demands the continued existence of art while it prohibits it." The trouble with this agonized meditation is that it raises all over again "the Jewish question," the question: what shall "we" do with the Jews?—which now, thanks to the Nazis, refers only to the memory of the Jews. The question by which a European "we" is blinded to precisely the Jews. Even more insidious, however, is that in insisting on the double bind in which the Jewish question places "us," Adorno is himself *playing at being a Jew*, reproducing the double bind (the necessary and impossible silence) that had characterized precisely the situation of European Jews for centuries. (See Sander L. Gilman, *Jewish Self-Hatred: Anti-Semitism and the Hidden Language of the Jews* [Baltimore, 1986].) And he is *only* playing, as he also only plays, throughout the passages I have mentioned, in his scrupulous avoidance of the *word* "we"—mainly by using abstract concepts as grammatical subjects—which is a device for concealing the consequences of his thought. My point about Goethe and Lessing and the German eighteenth century, by contrast, is that the culture of irony *discredits in advance* any such European or German "us"—however much Goethe and Lessing may use that word. In this culture of irony, the situation of the European individual is *already* homeless, exiled, the situation of speaking a foreign language as one's own and one's own language as foreign; the gesture of identifying the reader with the Jews is here more than a form of playing.

[19]See Thomas Mann, *Die Entstehung des Doktor Faustus: Roman eines Romans* (Frankfurt am Main, 1960), pp. 142–43, for the worry about anti-Semitism. The very end of the

I take Adorno and Mann, then, to represent the view that European literature and civilization (especially the German version) are seriously discredited by the concentration camps. This view is very common. But Mann takes on Goethe directly, by suggesting a "retraction" of *Faust*, and by actually retracting the attempt to suppress the demonistic contract in the *Wanderjahre*; and Adorno insists theoretically on the "slow" (*A&P*, p. 184) and "irrevocable" (KuG, p. 30) historical process that, having revealed itself in Nazism, makes necessary the retraction not only of "poetry" but even of the stance of the "committed" artist. My point, on the contrary, is, first, that this search for things to retract in effect *rebuilds* Auschwitz by losing sight of the Jews while still staring at "the victims" (as Adorno calls them) and, second, that these retractions are not necessary, that what is necessary is positive remembrance, not of Auschwitz, but of the ironic force in eighteenth-century European literature and civilization, especially in Germany. For that literature is neither suddenly discredited by Nazism nor slowly discredited by a process that ends in Nazism. On the contrary, it *starts out* by being discredited; it is, in its radical irony, *nothing but* the condition of being discredited; and Auschwitz, cognate with an uncriticized European "us," is precisely the extreme form of a typical and repeated (but by no means inevitable) *forgetting* of that condition of originary lack of credit.

A cardinal instance of this forgetting is found in Otto Weininger, who describes the typical Jew as an individual with no "center" in existence, no self-belief, no ability to assert a place for himself in reality, an individual, in effect, with no individuality, who lives in a world that has no stable unity.[20] What is interesting about this catalogue is that it unloads onto the Jews a set of characteristics that describe quite exactly the situation of the individual, the discredited Cartesian individual, in the communicative culture of irony in late eighteenth-century Germany. When Herder presents "himself" in his writings, he presents the exact opposite of an individual with a secure center, with a place in the grid of discourses and languages from which that grid might offer the illusion of stability. And if we agree that a certain amount of what Weininger says does actually apply—not to an essential Jewish psychology but to the evolved

---

book (p. 163) is still marked by this worry, in the self-satisfied recounting of a Zürich audience's favorable reaction to a reading of the Fitelberg scene.

[20]Otto Weininger, *Geschlecht und Charakter: Eine prinzipielle Untersuchung* (Munich, 1980; orig. 1903), especially chap. 13, "Das Judentum."

problematic situation of Jews in Europe—then it follows that the culture of irony is inherently anti-fascist, in that it holds open the possibility of keeping the Jews *in sight*, without either insisting on their assimilation (assimilation to what?—given the disruptive force of radical irony) or setting them apart as the despised negative of some supposed European or German wholeness. This possibility is mainly unrealized in actual eighteenth-century thought. Herder's personal view of the Jews, for example, is no model. Only Goethe and Lessing appear to have thought the matter all the way through and understood exactly the disruptive and disrupted situation of the Jews as a uniquely advanced and prophetic version of the European situation at large. But even without Goethe and Lessing, the inherently problematic cultural *type* arising from radical irony is anti-fascist—in a manner that had to be scribbled into oblivion by the nineteenth century before Germany could become, for itself and its Jews, what it became in the twentieth.

Hegel can refute Kant all he likes on the matter of boundaries and their inevitable transgression (KuG, p. 25).[21] Precisely Hegel's systematic mastery of the dynamics in question is a forgetting of the problem *as* a problem—as the European Jewish problem, for instance, of how to *have* boundaries, how to be what one is—a forgetting of the problem of ironic conscience that still existed for Kant in *Der Streit der Facultäten*. And this forgetting, while unquestionably a fact, is merely (in a double sense) romanticized when it is given the status of an inexorable "dialectical" process. Even in this century there have been strong and accurate literary responses to fascism, among them a work of Thomas Mann himself, "Mario und der Zauberer."[22] And if Brecht's *Arturo Ui*, as Adorno insists, is a trivializing of fascism, a "conjuring away" of its "true horror" (A&P, p. 184)—again we hear the pathos that rebuilds Auschwitz—then so much the better. Fascism in a strong sense *is* trivial, the final and extreme symptom not of a problem in European literature, but precisely of the trivializing of a problem, the repeated and itself repeatedly trivial and entirely "resistible" trivializing of the complex of

[21]As far as I can tell, Adorno is referring to the "Vorrede" and "Einleitung" to Hegel's *Wissenschaft der Logik* in the 1812–13 version. See Georg Wilhelm Friedrich Hegel, *Wissenschaft der Logik*, ed. Friedrich Hogemann and Walter Jaeschke, = *Gesammelte Werke*, vol. 11 (Hamburg, 1978), pp. 5–6, 17–19.

[22]See my *Theater As Problem: Modern Drama and Its Place in Literature* (Ithaca, 1990), pp. 164–68.

problems we have found in the eighteenth century, especially in Germany.

The failure (and the manner of failure) of the Auschwitz-minded retraction of such texts as the *Wanderjahre* thus suggests that perhaps Goethe's suppression of the demonistic contract is neither a futile nor a politically or historically refutable strategy after all. In any case, I see no reason to retract my assertion that eighteenth-century German poetics is infused with a radically subversive irony, a far more thorough political and cultural anti-fascism than is found in most of what the present century considers a response to the Nazis. Of course none of this answers the question of whether the novel's demonistic contract *can* be suppressed. But this question is undecidable in the abstract; its answer depends on the whole cultural context in which the novel is read. If, in European culture as experienced by Thomas Mann, the demonistic contract is irrevocable, this implies only that the culture envisaged by Goethe's project—the project of reducing the novel to nothing but its humanistic contract, to a new secular social scripture with no aesthetic component whatever—is a type of culture that the modern West, especially the Nazis, has made a point of forgetting. Perhaps it is too late for Goethe's project; perhaps the eighteenth-century cultural type it presupposes is no longer retrievable except in an antiquarian sense. But this "perhaps" is not grounds for simply *dismissing* that project.

The Jews as a Reader

If *Wilhelm Meisters Wanderjahre* were written today, in the shadow of Auschwitz, the exclusion of the Jews at the end would immediately be marked "anti-Semitic." We have forgotten how to read in that dialogical eighteenth-century manner—the manner in which Lessing and Herder read each other—which might give us time to recognize that precisely our condition as reader is reflected in those excluded Jews, and reflected *by* exactly that gesture of exclusion, which corresponds to the book's pervasive ironizing of the reader's position. The reader's relation to the Jews approaches one of identity; and the result—if a book like Goethe's could be written today—would be a response to Auschwitz, not a rebuilding of it.

But let us turn back to the theory of the novel, and to the peculiarity of the situation here. The reader (singular—singular*ized*, if need be, by the convention of romance reading) is reflected in the Jews (plural), but without *belonging* to the community of the Jews. The reader, even if he or she happens actually to be a Jew, is kept from belonging by precisely the gesture of exclusion that creates the reflecting structure. Thus the idea of "the Jews (plural) as *a* reader" arises, and gives substance the idea of "the community as a reader" as worked out above.

This notion of "the Jews," moreover, is referential. It means the real Jews, not merely Jewry as the sign for a *self*-distancing in "our" community, by which a subcommunity is envisioned that can fill a rôle, like that of reader, while also being sufficiently separated to stand over against the actual individual reader as his or her paradoxical reflection. Such a deliberate, experimental self-distancing of the community is in fact carried out by the Association of Renunciants, in their sending of a contingent to America. But this move is not sufficient; for it is still only a replication of individual readerly self-consciousness. A group is needed that will be excluded even from this deliberate self-exclusion—as the Jews are excluded even from the group of emigrants—yet a group whose radical exclusion is still sufficiently a *relation* with the community (not merely a blind spot) to be interpreted as a communally significant rôle, if now perforce a profoundly disruptive rôle. Which adds up to the Jews, with a specificity that makes the *Wanderjahre* literally illegible in any cultural situation in which the Jews are not an actual positive intellectual force.

Or to develop the matter more theoretically: the operation of the novel as social contract, as the community's enactment of its origin (which includes the idea of the novel as a new developing holy scripture), hinges on the signifying relation of the ego to the communal that is suggested in Rousseau's *Social Contract*. But how is this signification articulated, how is it made socially effective? The reader-as-ego can be shown, by abstract argument, to signify the communal. But the ego-as-reader (the empirical person doing the reading) actually sees or apprehends, in this signifying relation, only the signifier, the reader-as-ego, whose function is precisely to stand for (and so to stand in the way of) its signified, the communal. The ego-as-reader, the actual person upon whom the novel must have an effect, is not in a position to see itself directly mirrored in the communal as such.

This is the kind of situation C. S. Peirce talks about. In order that the signification of the communal by the ego be articulated, in order that it even exist semiotically for the ego-as-reader, a third element is needed, an additional signifier as "interpretant."[23] And this new signifier must have a number of specific qualities. First, it must have a *referential* component strong enough at least to open the semiosis without immediately requiring yet another interpretant; it must be and mean an entity sufficiently concrete for the ego-as-reader to "see" itself reflected in. Second, it must possess intrinsic qualities that are strongly referable to the signified, to the difficult idea of the communal; it must therefore have the quality of a *community*, and as far as possible that of an aboriginal or ancient community, a community definitely antedating what we experience immediately as "our" community. And, third, since its function as interpretant or co-signifier is to set itself and the reader-as-ego *over against* the actual reader (ego-as-reader) as articulated signifiers, this new signifying communal entity may not yet have the quality of the *social* for us, to which we belong by conversation, but must be subject to the gesture of exclusion from the social. All this, again, adds up to the Jews. And again, Goethe's novel becomes literally illegible in any cultural situation in which the Jews are not an actual positive intellectual factor.

The correspondence here to the idea of the theater, considered as interpretant in the signifying relation of the social to the subject, is fairly clear. And the manner in which the Jews make concrete—if precariously so—the ultimately speculative interpretive concept of the community as a reader is paralleled by the manner in which the materiality of the theater might be said to concretize the (so to speak)

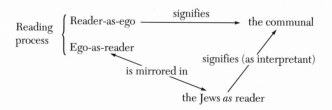

[23]See the *Collected Papers of Charles Sanders Peirce*, ed. Charles Hartshorne and Paul Weiss, 8 vols. (Cambridge, Mass., 1931–58), vol. 2, pars. 92 and 227–42.

speculative materiality of what we have called the "body" in Herder.[24] Just as the body, which is *in* the realm of discourse, but not yet ego, is thereby a constitutive and revelatory rupture in discourse-as-monologue, so the community as a reader (in the person of the Jews), which is *in* the realm of European communal discourse, but not yet the social, is a constitutive and revelatory rupture in discourse-as-conversation.

The achievement of the Nazis, in relation to this expanded semiotic mechanics, is the *literal* exclusion or elimination of the Jews, a simple crossing out of their position in it, which prevents the Jews' needful function in what the eighteenth century understood as its inherently disrupted or ironic literature and civilization. And we, to the extent that we submerge ourselves in uncriticized sensibilities that require us to reject the *Wanderjahre* as anti-Semitic, or to see it as definitively retracted by *Doktor Faustus*, simply carry on the Nazis' work for them.

Lessing and Goethe: Subversiveness and the Real Jews

The Nazis, by practically emptying Europe of its Jews, therefore also practically emptied Europe of its eighteenth century and of the possibility of retrieving its constitutive irony *as* Europe. I say "practically," in the hope that this qualification means something. For although the reestablishment of the Jews in Europe, not as mere numbers but as European Jews in a culturally active and crucial sense (not painted over, and crossed out, with the "victims" myth) is not something that can be achieved in historical-interpretive discussion, and although the corresponding retrieval *for* Jews (including American Jews) of lost historical possibilities may in this case be questionable even as an aim, perhaps we can still at least do our part in restoring to Europe its (especially German) eighteenth century,

---

[24]This idea of the "body," of a special version of the self that intrudes into discourse but is radically nondiscursive in nature, can be paralleled in writers besides Herder. Avital Ronell, *Dictations: On Haunted Writing* (Bloomington, Ind., 1986), p. 66, for example, analyzes the relation with Eckermann as signifying a "double desire in Goethe, the desire for completion [as 'oeuvre' or writing] that divides and denies itself," thus a form of Herderian quasi-bodily ambivalence toward the discursive realm. Or we recall the kinetic, performing "Lessing" of *Laokoon*, especially as developed in Carol Jacobs's argument in her article "The Critical Performance of Lessing's *Laokoon*," *MLN* 102 (1987), 483–521.

which is to say, its principal subversive tradition, its only defense, perhaps, against the danger of an ultimate, media-driven quasi-fascism.

The Jews, in any event, are the final and definitive form of the community as a reader, which is a crucial move in the ego's signification of the communal. And since this signification, in turn, is crucial in establishing the materiality of the theater, hence the theater's quality as the locus of irony, the actual organ of ironic thinking, it follows that in a strong sense the Jews also occupy precisely that locus of irony, that point of subversive leverage, in eighteenth-century Germany.

Nor is this conclusion merely speculative. I argued a long time ago that Lessing's *Nathan der Weise* is the definitive establishment of an eighteenth-century German ironic theater, and that it accomplishes this establishment by recognizing in Jewish thought the shape of an ironically self-relativizing religion, a religion that cannot even be recognized as "religion" by contemporary Christians, yet reveals precisely the inevitable future and the subversive intellectual obligation of Christianity.[25] (Nathan at the end, incidentally, like the Jews at the end of the *Wanderjahre*, is excluded, the only character on the stage unrelated by blood to any of the others.) And as in the *Wanderjahre*, we are talking here about the real Jews, about the Jews not merely as representing a Gentile problem, but as the vessel of a disruptive self-conception that is otherwise inaccessible to European Gentile Christians, yet is also the necessary medium in which these Gentiles *are* Europeans.

Thus the Jews are present and operative in both the founding dramatic work (*Nathan*) and the concluding novel (*Wanderjahre*) of the German eighteenth century. And is it merely an accident, or what kind of accident is it, that whereas Milton's seventeenth-century Old Testament epic is militantly Christian, Klopstock's eighteenth-century New Testament epic is titled not "The Savior" but "The Messiah"?

[25]See my *Modern Drama and German Classicism*, chap. 3, "Breakthrough in Practice." Also see my "Reason, Error, and the Shape of History."

Conclusion:
The Use and Abuse of
the Eighteenth Century

I began this book by suggesting that the usefulness of a reinvented Renaissance for literary thought in the late nineteenth and early twentieth centuries might be paralleled by the usefulness of a new eighteenth century for literary thought in the late twentieth and early twenty-first. This parallel cannot be pushed too far without verging on the delusion of total historical self-reflection that eighteenth-century ironic literary discourse, as I understand it, is designed to prevent. But still, I cannot unsay what I have said, any more than Herder, for example, can divorce writing from system in presenting his "ideas" on history.

Germany

The unification of "Germany" in 1990 brings to the surface what seems to me a significant anomaly in our view of the Nazi period. On the one hand, Nazism is regarded as having fundamentally discredited large segments of German cultural history (German "thought," as we say) since the eighteenth century, or at least as having unmasked dangerous tendencies in that history. On the other hand, the legitimacy of a relatively recent phenomenon that is more directly connected with the genesis of Nazism, the German *state* as fashioned in the last decades of the nineteenth century, is not subjected to serious discussion.

This division of attitudes has to do with the distinction between *culture* and *politics*, between a deep mechanism by which history shapes itself and a relatively superficial mechanism. When confronted with historical events that we find (or pretend to find) humanly and politically incomprehensible—events such as the dogged mechanical reduction of Jews to things, and ultimately to dead things, in the Third Reich—we tend to imagine the root causes of these events in the domain of culture, beyond our immediate political control. But the distinction between culture and politics, in our normal sense of these ideas, brings with it the distinction between the national and the international. Culture is what belongs to each nation or people as its unique historical identity; politics consists of practical systems that can be reproduced reasonably well in different cultural situations. Of course this distinction is unsound. A national culture is not a kind of organism that forms a clear boundary between its "own" substance and its "environment"; and political practice never even approaches systematic control or knowledge with respect to itself. Precisely the failure of the distinction, however, sharpens the question of why it apparently operates in our view of Nazi Germany.

One reason suggests itself immediately. By thinking of Nazism in cultural terms, we mark it as a *German* national phenomenon, as a sickness specific to the imaginary German historical organism. We therefore never even entertain the question of whether Nazism is perhaps merely the extreme form of a normal tendency in the *politics* of Europe and North America. Walter Jens says that "Germany, unlike England and France, did not organize itself [in 1871] as a nation that represented a universal idea—freedom or reason—but . . . came onto the scene as an authoritarian state that displayed nothing but naked power, national hybris, and an arrogant self-awareness that was countered by no regulatory ethical idea, no supra-national moral commitment, no social Magna Carta."[1] But even this extreme liberal-democratic profession of faith peters out in the word "countered" ("konterkariert"), which suggests, unwittingly, that what is entirely flagrant in the history of the recent German Empire is only kept precariously at bay, or concealed, by the more complicated traditional situation of the other Euro-American states.

---

[1] Walter Jens, *Juden und Christen in Deutschland: Drei Reden* (Stuttgart, 1989), pp. 46–47.

The unification of Germany, in any case—which Jens is opposed to, on the grounds that a country without a powerful Jewish element is not "Germany" to begin with (Jens, p. 33)—has been characterized by a compulsive recollection of the Nazi period (the Wall is breached on an anniversary of the "Kristallnacht") combined with a resolute refusal to ask any of the questions prompted either by that recollection or by the whole idea of unification: questions about Germany's supposed "right" to unity; about the cause, nature, and justification of its status as two nations; about the applicability of the principle of "self-determination" (shades of Kant and Fichte); and about the practical aspects of that principle's application—e.g., the phrasing of the electoral question, the time required for clarifying issues, the size and structure of a decisive electoral majority. The recollection of Nazism has in fact served only to muddy the situation by foregrounding nonissues—will Germany become a military aggressor? should the present generation of Germans be "penalized" for the past?—and so favors an atmosphere of politics by supposed acclamation and undoubted fait accompli that reminds one precisely of the Nazi period.

One of the most significant casualties of this refusal to ask questions is the German eighteenth century. As long as our attention is focused on Nazism as a *cultural* phenomenon, the eighteenth century, in which we have been taught to place the origin of modern German culture, is automatically implicated. The force of this hidden complex of preconceptions can be felt even in arguments aimed at defending the eighteenth century against the confusion of issues that arises in connection with German unification. Jens, to quote him one more time, faces up to the question of whether Lessing's *Nathan* is really only "a sop to the conscience" of anti-Semitism (p. 110), in its advocating a simplistic idea of Jewish assimilation; but then he misses the historical point completely by himself dreaming of assimilation, in the form of what he claims might have been a Jewish "rapprochement with the progressive intellectual element of the liberal German bourgeoisie . . . on the basis of reason" (p. 113). As if precisely *Nathan* did not demonstrate that the practice of Enlightenment reason, for the individual (like Nathan) who insists on all its consequences, is inevitably a form of *exile*, and that the importance of the Jews for Germany is therefore precisely their resistance to assimilation, hence their *interference* with the dangerous and delusive project of a rationally unified social or even intellectual order.

The Abuse of the Eighteenth Century

In order to see how the extermination of the eighteenth century continues to work, even in the post-Nazi period, let us consider two books that are as different as possible in method and outlook: J. P. Stern, *Hitler: The Führer and the People*, and Max Horkheimer and Theodor Adorno, *Dialektik der Aufklärung*.

Stern's book is distinguished mainly by its clarity and good sense, both in the theories it advances and in the limits it observes with respect to theorizing as a procedure. And it barely mentions the eighteenth century. But precisely by minimizing theoretical complexity it permits a number of uncriticized historical prejudices to infect its argument and the view of the eighteenth century it implies.

As a rule, Stern carefully avoids the idea that a national historical organism is at work, or at fault, in the shaping of the German twentieth century. That this is an act of avoidance—the avoidance specifically of an intellectual resonance with Nazi thought—becomes clear on the few occasions when it falters, when the guard is let down: when Stern compares Jaspers with Jung-Stilling, for example (JPS, p. 105); or when he speaks of "the characteristically German situation in which the craven belief in historical inevitability is rationalized in a theory" (p. 121). But more important is Stern's discussion of "The Language of Nature," in which we read "even today we are not clear enough to what extent the language, the thinking and the practice of fascist movements generally and of National Socialism in particular were determined by the 'Nature' vocabulary that has its roots in nineteenth-century Romanticism, and that had once been the repository of the most poignant and beautiful lyric poetry in European literature" (p. 49). This passage does everything it possibly can to avoid saying that Nazism is rooted in the eighteenth century. It speaks of fascism "generally" and divides it into aspects (language, thinking, practice, which add up pretty much to the whole); it keeps the dangerous organic metaphor of "roots" at one remove from Nazism itself; it focuses on the relatively broad and diffuse phenomenon of Romanticism—avoiding the further historical step back that is obviously required by a discussion of nature rhetoric—in the hope of leaving enough room for a positive aesthetic judgment and a negative political-moral judgment to coexist, so that the Nazis might be convicted of at least some arbitrariness in their use of history. But these gestures of avoidance avoid not only the assertion but also the *question* of eighteenth-century "roots," and so leave open the possibility of regarding Nazism as the result of a quasi-organic necessity after all.

Exactly this possibility in fact then makes itself felt in what I think is probably a slip of Stern's pen. He continues the passage just quoted by speaking of Romanticism's suggestion of "an alternative to the Christian moral tradition," a dangerous alternative which, embedded in "the idea of Nature," "comes to dominate the philosophical and ideological writings of intellectuals on the fringes of the Wilhelminian political establishment"—intellectuals like Spengler, who provide at least a partial transition to Nazi thought. And then he says that "however doubtful the compliment, Goethe and Nietzsche are the two modern writers most frequently acknowledged by Spengler; and it is no accident that Spengler builds his entire world-historical megacycle on an analogy with plant-life taken from Goethe's botanical and morphological studies" (JPS, p. 49). If Spengler mentions Goethe repeatedly, how can it occur to us to suspect an "accident" in his using Goethe as a structural model? The words "it is no accident that . . ." thus suggest involuntarily that there may be more to the matter, a deeper-running, quasi-organic connection between the two thinkers.

I am dealing not with Stern's actual argument but with the fringes of his writing, where he is no longer in control of what happens. And the fact that even as lucid and circumspect a writer as Stern loses control at the points I have noted is a sign of our need for a new eighteenth century. A badly grasped eighteenth century, which, being situated supposedly on the other side of a strong Foucauldian shift, can be granted a kind of innocence with respect to its consequences—and especially a badly grasped German eighteenth century, disarticulated into an expectant intellectual humus—must inevitably tempt forth that habit of organic historical thinking, that digging for roots, which ignores and eventually buries altogether even those possibilities for resistance to a repressive political systematics that history actually provides.

In fact, the discussion of modern politics in terms of a historical development of the idea of system-as-such, the idea of sheer efficiency, has a tendency to be blinded to the eighteenth century by its *own* systematics. If Stern, in the course of an argument on the self-destructiveness of the Nazi program, mentions "the German Enlightenment" only as "a high-minded and noble experiment" in assimilating the Jews (JPS, pp. 207, 208), Horkheimer and Adorno endow the *concept* of "Enlightenment" with a dialectical life that verges on the demonic and so appears to bypass altogether any question of responsibility for fascism. But at the same time, the vocabulary of their argument, the *word* "Enlightenment," suggests inescapably that it was in the eighteenth century that a special overt act of complicity, a pact with the devil, was carried out.

And as in Stern, this suggestion is nourished by the absence of any attempt at a clear view of eighteenth-century intellectual conditions. Horkheimer and Adorno set forth with great precision the inherently "totalitarian" quality (H/A, p. 12) of the concept of Enlightenment considered as an operator in public discourse. Their discussion of the dynamics of the concept in Homer is, in its way, brilliant. And their analysis of modern anti-Semitism as a violent reaction of the masses provoked by the apparent violation of a repression that characterizes painfully their own situation (H/A, p. 181) not only compromises Stern's impatience with analytic subtlety (see JPS, p. 208), but anticipates and overshadows even Hannah Arendt's careful development of a similar perception, that "the Jews [in Germany] . . . grew prominent and conspicuous in inverse proportion to their real influence and position of power."[2] The eighteenth century, however, the actual

[2]Hannah Arendt, *The Origins of Totalitarianism*, 2d ed. (New York, 1958), p. 354. Note that I have not enlisted in support of my argument on the German eighteenth century and the Jews Arendt's celebration of the Jewish salons in Berlin in the first years of the nineteenth century, especially Rahel Varnhagen's, with their "genuinely mixed [not assimilated] society," their moment of "innocence and splendor" in a subversive position "on the fringe of society" (pp. 59, 60). There may be a connection between this phenomenon and the culture of irony I am concerned with, but it is not one that can be pinned down. My point, again, is not that the implications of irony with respect to the Jews (as recognized, perhaps exclusively, by Goethe and Lessing) were manifest in actual society or in Germans' specific *ideas* of the Jews, but rather that those implications (recognized or not) reflect an inherent and historically valuable anti-fascist tendency in the culture as such. Both Arendt and Sander Gilman, incidentally, are unfair to the very young Goethe who wrote a review of the poems of Isaschar Falkensohn Behr (WA, 37:221–25). Arendt associates Goethe with views expressed about thirty years later by Herder (SW, 24:71–75), which appear to oblige the Jews of Europe to be "more intensely human individuals" and "exceptional specimens of humanity" (Arendt, pp. 57, 58). And Gilman sees in Goethe's review merely a masking of the "old canard" that "Jews, especially those who come from the barbaric East, perceive the world differently" (Sander L. Gilman, *Jewish Self-Hatred: Anti-Semitism and the Hidden Language of the Jews* [Baltimore, 1986], p. 136). In fact, Goethe only takes his cue from Behr's own puzzling self-description; and if Gilman's very subtle interpretation of Behr's stance (pp. 134–35) is correct, as I think it is, then Goethe can be excused for being puzzled. But the main body of the review, which Gilman dismisses as "the ideal of romantic love set in bourgeois terms" (p. 136), shows that what Goethe had actually hoped for from Behr was not a different (natural or "naïve") way of experiencing, but rather *a clearer critical grasp* than that demonstrated by most Germans of the inherent imaginative tendency of rococo or Anacreontic poetry. The little narrative

historical matrix of the concept on which Horkheimer and Adorno make everything depend, is absent in their thinking, shouldered aside by a discussion of Sade that is penetrating, but also misleading. For the remnant of characteristically eighteenth-century thought that still appears at the beginning of the Sade chapter is Kant, mainly the Kant of the *Critiques* (H/A, pp. 88–94). As in Foucault, precisely history's attempt to escape from the difficult, ironic eighteenth century—an escape, we have seen, that Kant himself did not fully achieve—is permitted to represent the eighteenth century itself.

And eventually that escape is successful, especially in nineteenth-century German literary historiography, where even people operating in the liberal-to-subversive range of the political spectrum (e.g., Georg Gottfried Gervinus, Friedrich Theodor Vischer) help rewrite the eighteenth century into a relatively unproblematic shape that conceals what might otherwise have been its political usefulness. There is a certain amount of scattered resistance to this tendency in writers as different as Nietzsche and Hermann Hettner; but the process of escaping, or forgetting, once under way, proves irreversible, and eventually makes possible not only the notorious intellectual support enjoyed by the Nazis but also a continuing postwar vagueness about what the German intellectual past actually looks like.

Even Fritz Stern's universally respected study of "Germanic ideology" does not escape this charge. Supposing, for the sake of argument, that a "curiously idealistic, unpolitical discontent constitutes the main link between all that is venerable and great in the German past and the triumph of national socialism": what does it mean to say that this idealistic attitude is derived "intellectually" (how else?) from Goethe, Kant, and Schiller, or that the nineteenth century retains only a "residue" or "recollection" of these figures' thinking?[3] Evidently Stern wants to rescue a "venerable and great" eighteenth century, and wants even to rescue, in the process, a certain amount of

---

Goethe puts together here, which reads like a version of *Werther* with all the obstacles to a happy ending removed, is presented as a *logical result* of tendencies in Behr's poems. Even if neither rococo poetry nor, later, *Werther* itself is able to establish that little story in textual tradition, still the story is operative on some level nonetheless. And that Goethe here associates it with a Jewish poet suggests that he was perhaps already developing that sense of the Jews as critical readers (readers of what is *behind* the text) that we have seen in the *Wanderjahre*, the Jews as an indispensable esoteric critical conscience in the German literary situation.

[3]Fritz Stern, *The Politics of Cultural Despair: A Study in the Rise of the Germanic Ideology* (Berkeley and Los Angeles, 1974; orig. 1961), pp. xxiii–xxiv.

Lagarde, Langbehn, Moeller, and the "conservative revolution" (pp. 296–98). But the eighteenth century he wants to rescue is the wrong eighteenth century. His final judgment on Lagarde, Langbehn, and Moeller is that "they were artists without talents of creative expression, prophets without a god" (p. 269), which only repeats the German myth of an epigonal nineteenth century, hence the idea of an eighteenth century in which artistic talent and philosophical certainty were still available in a measure that raised their possessors not only above actual politics, but also above whatever unfortunate political consequences might later appear in the tradition they established. The eighteenth century that needs to be replaced is precisely this hallucination of a serene, epistemically undeveloped eighteenth century that has no direct relevance to our own continuing political and cultural difficulties.

The Culture of Irony

My aim has been mainly to suggest a reasonable alternative to that damaged and damaging view of the eighteenth century; and at various points I have attempted to summarize my argument by diagramming the conceptual relations that make up the poetics of the age in late eighteenth-century Germany. I will now attempt to complete that diagram.

The form of the diagram is especially useful in representing an argument that involves the notion of radical irony, for it suggests a plurality of possible formulations that all stand in something resembling an ironic relation to itself. In the present case, however, the diagram needs to be used with special care, for a number of reasons:

1. It does not represent *thought* in the sense that thought might be attributed to an individual mind. One of its implications is that the individual thinking mind is itself an illusion. But the operation of *thinking* is not denied. The enclosed area labeled "locus of irony" marks what seems to me the most fully developed eighteenth-century answer to the question of *where* thinking happens. In practical terms, the diagram is a guide for the coordination of interpretations that involve the notion of radical irony.

2. The quality of the diagram as a plane figure is misleading, since the concepts around which it is formed are categorically disparate, belonging, so to speak, in different dimensions. Two of the concepts,

the theater and the Jews, are historically referential, and do not operate except in their referentiality; if one treats them as abstractions, they lose their interpretive force. The concepts of the ego and the social, by contrast, arise only as the result of a theoretical *analysis* of either experience or discourse into opposed aspects (self-awareness vs. awareness of others, monologue or self-expression vs. conversation, text vs. intertext); they therefore presuppose an argument on the historical appropriateness of that analysis as a basis for interpretation. And the concepts "Community as Reader" and "Herderian 'Body'" require an analysis of the *content* of specific interpretations. The former can be associated most easily with Goethe and Hölderlin, the latter not only with Herder but also, clearly enough, with Lessing as the wanderer from his own path, with Hamann as Magus, even with Ronell's Goethe as "effect."

3. The most difficult concepts, since they have no referential component at all, are those of the subject and the communal. In the argument of Chapters 4 and 6, these concepts were introduced as heuristic notions and then fleshed out. But in the logical structure that supports the finished diagram, they are arrived at by a kind of conceptual triangulation. If we agree, first, that the ego and the social may be regarded as signifiers (rather than the bearers of substantial identities), and especially if we agree (in accordance with interpretive arguments in Chapter 6) that the Jews and the theater may in some important cases be regarded as co-signifiers or interpretants of the signifying relations thus suggested, then the question of an appropriate designation for the *signified*, in each instance, arises. And if we agree, further, that discourse has an inherent referential component, that discursive entities by their nature make the gesture of referring to substantial, extralinguistic entities, then it becomes possible to ask after the implied *referent* (whether or not, or however, it exists) of the ego and of the social. This is where triangulation enters. For my argument on radical irony has as a principal consequence that the signified of the ego and the referent of the social (that which supposedly appears in discourse, or enters discourse, as the social) coincide, as do the signified of the social and the referent of the ego. And these two coincidences—which are strictly coincidences, locations, *not* referable to substantial entities—I have named the "communal" and the "subject."

4. This interplay of intellectual locations, however, does not claim general validity even within the realm of the literary; it is indissolu-

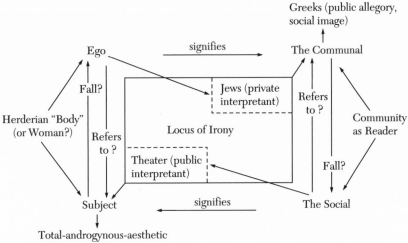

bly bound up with the interpretive arguments from which it arises. In a sense it supports those arguments (on Goethe, Hölderlin, Lessing, Herder, Rousseau, and Kant) by sketching a historical background in terms of which they can be made to support one another. But its historical specificity is such that it also stands or falls with the interpretive arguments. In any case, I have added to the final diagram two historically specific elements that seem to me to function as allegories of the two triangulated locations on which everything depends: the eighteenth-century German vision of the Greeks, especially Winckelmann's Greeks, considered as an allegory of the communal; and Schiller's vision of an aesthetically completed self, considered as an allegory of the subject.

5. The diagram, it is true, still asks as many questions as it answers. The relation between the Jews and "Community as Reader," for example, which I think evidently operates in the *Wanderjahre*, is hard to categorize by type. Are the Jews a sufficiently developed textual figure in Goethe's novel to have the function, say, of signifier, or of allegory, in any reasonable sense? And the question of the materiality or quasi-materiality of the authorial "body," and of its relation to the material theater, is by no means closed. But then closure, in any sense, is not the point. The diagram and the arguments it recollects are focused (in defiance of the paradox involved) precisely upon possibilities of nonclosure, possibilities of resistance to the sys-

tematic historical closure of meaning. The concepts are related dy-namically—in requiring structurally that they be supported by the very interpretations whose ground they form—and constantly pre-sent new aspects of themselves that threaten even the structure from which they arise. In the final diagram, for instance, I have associated the concept of the feminine with that of the authorial body, an idea whose development I reserve for another study. And I have replaced the idea of "entry into discourse," to describe the relation of the implied referent to either the ego or the social, with the idea of the Fall of Man, the idea of the ego and the social as "fallen" forms of the subject and the communal, which I will go into shortly.

6. The discussion of the Jews in the preceding chapter also has loose ends. For there is no adequate answer to the question: Is the use of the Jews in Lessing's and Goethe's thought not exactly that, a *use* of the Jews, having little to do with the actual situation or experi-ence of German Jews? It remains true that there is a definite reso-nance between the silence of radical irony and the silent or "hidden" significance ascribed to the Jews' speaking, that the discourse insta-bility arising from general linguistic conditions in eighteenth-century Germany (as discussed in Chapter 5) places the sensitive literary thinker in a position that has clear correspondences, via the problem of a native or natural language, with that of a German Yiddish-speaker, and that these resonances and correspondences are understood (in Lessing and Goethe) not as a cultural danger but as the confirmation of a valuable, if highly problematic, cultural identity. It is true, above all, that the culture of radical irony is inherently anti-fascist and cannot operate, except negatively, in the historical background of Nazism. But none of this answers the initial question. Perhaps the unanswerability of that question reflects precisely the disruptive quality, the enforcement of nonclosure, that makes the Jews a valu-able cultural presence in relation to radical irony. But this does not answer the question either.

In any event, I have argued that if we avoid compartmentalizing literary discourse according to genres, that if we simply follow the ramifications of the literary wherever they lead, into literary criti-cism, philosophy, history, theology, and even (with Goethe) natural science, then in the eighteenth century, especially in Germany, we can observe the increasingly purposeful growth of a literary discourse that is focused not on its content or purport, nor on its inner system-atic cohesion, nor on anything reasonably termed "style" or "spirit," but solely on the development of its own ironic discourse-*type*, hence on a particular type of communicative culture, which is regarded as an enactment of cultural origination, and which is radically subversive with respect to any determination of the content of any specific text. And it follows in principle that this eighteenth-century discourse must be *politically* subversive in any conceivable situation, which is what makes it interesting from a late twentieth-century perspective.

One has only to read at random in recent literary and philosophical criticism. Texts attract interest, as a rule, by how they "undermine" or "subvert" the assumptions imposed in this or that tradition, or by their quality as "performance," rather than as a repository or conduit of meaning, which suggests a subversive relation to hermeneutic culture as a whole. And it is clear that this interest in the subversive has to do with our sense of entrapment in the inexorably co-optive mechanics of a culture characterized and dominated by mass media. But the question, explicit or not, that haunts all this speculation, is whether any literary discourse—however indisputable in theory its subversive aspect may be—can ever in this sense be *effective* in the political realm.

It seems to me that the study of late eighteenth-century literary culture in Germany suggests the possibility of a positive answer to this question. For the Jews, in a form of existence that combines the metaphorical and the actual, are the anchor, the point of transparency, of an ironic literary discourse in that culture, a discourse whose structure implies its radically subversive operation; and those same Jews then become, for a radically countersubversive Nazi government, the ultimate nightmare, to be dealt with only by extermination. It is tempting to infer that the force of that eighteenth-century discourse, the ironic discourse of Lessing and Goethe, still belonged inherently to the object of the Nazis' phobia, which would imply its *effective* subversiveness. This sort of speculation does not prove anything. But it suggests lines of inquiry that may at least help protect the notion of the subversive from the effects of overuse.[4]

---

[4]I borrow the notion of the "countersubversive"—referring to a government or system, a practical politics, that (despite its public pronouncements) has no constant or continuous positive content whatever and operates only in response to what its rhetoric of the moment enables it to read as internal subversive tendencies—from Michael Paul Rogin, *"Ronald Reagan," the Movie, and Other Episodes in Political Demonology* (Berkeley and Los Angeles, 1987). That the strictly or exclusively countersubversive is an actual possibility in

The History of Consciousness

One further way of summarizing my argument on an eighteenth-century culture of irony is suggested by the tradition of the Fall of Man. For the effect of radical irony is to *revoke* that myth, and to revoke, with it, the whole idea of a history of consciousness. That the eighteenth century, even before Kant, exhibits a critical attitude toward the Cartesian cogito, will probably not be disputed. And it is clear enough that this attitude includes a rejection of the type of history of consciousness that is implied by the cumulative and self-perfecting attributes of Wolffian symbolic knowledge. My claim, however, is that eighteenth-century irony attacks the possibility of the history of consciousness at a much deeper level, a level at which even the notion of a "phenomenology of mind" is undercut. There is no phenomenology of mind, because the myth of a characteristic structuring event in the operation of mind—no matter whether this event is viewed as original or pivotal or repeating or an asymptote or a result of analysis—is no longer valid even *as* a myth; it is no longer even a convincing story.

We must be careful to underestimate neither the importance nor the difficulty of the problem of literary origination in the eighteenth century, especially in Germany. If there is such a thing as the history of consciousness in the sense of a history structured by the dynamics arising from its being, in various aspects, itself precisely the content of consciousness, and if there is a corresponding history of texts, whether its ordering principle be thought of as Bloomian "influence," or as an intertextuality in which every understanding of what a text "does with" or "makes of" other texts must itself be figured in other texts, then literary origination, in anything approaching the eigh-

---

politics, is one of the things we have been taught by the Nazis. This diagnosis of fascism—that it operates by having no locatable content whatever, no content that ever continues to be what is meant by a serious attack on it—is made very early on, for example, by Thomas Mann in "Mario und der Zauberer" (see my *Theater As Problem: Modern Drama and Its Place in Literature* [Ithaca, 1990], pp. 164–69). And it is confirmed—if at the same time romanticized, and combined with a very narrow interpretation of exactly that Thomas Mann story (JPS, pp. 66–68)—in J. P. Stern's argument that Hitler had no positive goal, but was "lured by the prospect of a universal annihilation which included his enemies, his victims, his people and himself," and which "emerges as the secret that bound his followers to him" (JPS, pp. 221, 224). On the diagram as a critical technique—not only for our purposes but (Gaier shows) in the eighteenth century as well—see Chapter 4, note 32.

teenth-century sense of the term "genius," is out of the question. There is a parallel here to the problem of the subversive. For literary or textual tradition—unless we water down the concept by making it refer to only one force among others in some vaguely conceived world of free mental activity—is universally co-optive; even the most radical or violent gesture of opposition, precisely by asserting the relation of opposition, entangles itself in a web of concentrically graduated relations that constitutes in the end its belonging to tradition after all.

And the importance of this problem, in turn, is not solely a function of the peculiar "disinherited" situation of Germany with respect to literary tradition. The whole question of the origin of the work of art, especially of poetry, becomes crucial and pressing in an age where the rational exactness of discourse is widely proclaimed as a value—the question of origin, not in Heidegger's sense, but on a thoroughly practical level: How do poems get written? Is the desire to do something new in the literary field merely a kind of atavism in the history of consciousness, conditional upon our being blind to the self-referred and co-optive structure of literary tradition? Goethe appears to worry about this question in connection with Kant's *Critique of Judgment*, about the type of "interest" that must motivate the creating artist. And I have argued elsewhere that the result of this worry is a revision of the whole idea of literary tradition, which Goethe now sees as requiring an "anti-poetic" element that repeatedly disrupts its cumulative order, hence any possible order of the history of consciousness, and opens fresh space for poetic initiative.[5]

Herder's concern with the same question is writ large in the structure of the third section of the revised *Fragmente*. This section opens with a narrative "The Ages of a Language" (*SW*, 1:151–55), which is really a history of consciousness, an explanation of how the reflection *upon* language *in* language must inevitably unfold in four major ages: primitive articulation (childhood), poetry (youth), prose (middle age), and finally "philosophy," which is the old age of language, where it has relinquished all its "beauty" in favor of "accuracy" (1:155). But the fragments that follow, which are supposed to "explain" this "philosophical language romance" (2:60), actually tend more and more to undermine it, especially by showing a component of natural experi-

[5]See my *Goethe's Theory of Poetry: "Faust" and the Regeneration of Language* (Ithaca, 1986), especially the last four chapters.

ence even in what had been described as the rigid system of "philosophical" language (2:97–102). And then the collection is closed, after a short discussion of translation (2:105–8), by a long commentary on Thomas Abbt's speculations about an ideal language, a commentary which arrives at no firm conclusion beyond the idea that German has much to learn from other languages, and which concludes with the words: "But one also sees that in any genre of writing, no genius should be ashamed of his mother tongue, or complain about it, since in general, for every excellent writer, thoughts are the sons of heaven, words the daughters of earth" (1:240). Whence this sudden insistence upon a detached level of thought somehow prior to language, which might conceivably imagine itself the actual creator of its language (2:100)? How can this idea arise in an essay that begins by placing consciousness itself within an inexorable history of its language?

The context is all-important here, and includes prominently the idea of a comparison or translation of different languages. As in our discussion of Herder in Chapter 5, the existence of a *plurality* of languages is crucial. Each language still reflects and enforces a history of consciousness for its speakers; but the possibility of knowing different languages, in the international civilization of modern Europe, also provides consciousness with a point of view from which something that at least has the effect of a free, creative, poetic initiative can be undertaken. This is Herder's strategy for accommodating both elements of the contradiction that arises between the unavoidable development, in philosophical thought, of a history of consciousness and the necessary idea of an originary creative force, without which that history's actual repeated *carrying out* of its inherent structural possibilities for self-reflection could not be accounted for.

The effects of this contradiction, and of attempts to deal with it, can be followed further in late eighteenth-century German thought, into *Die Erziehung des Menschengeschlechts* and *Über naive und sentimentalische Dichtung*, perhaps even into a new view of the whole idea of "Bildung" and human totality. Perhaps the supposed ideal of totality, and of the well-formed individual, is never really an object of belief or striving or desire, but rather a *critical move*, a deliberate shaping of literary rhetoric in order to set limits to what is already recognized as the threatening hegemony of history of consciousness in something like the form later given it by Hegel. In any case, such a critical move is to be expected in a culture of irony, since irony requires a locus (a place where thinking happens) that can perhaps be defined in concrete terms—as the theater, for instance, or the Jews—but can never be incorporated into the history of consciousness, where, by definition, all thinking is eventually articulable as meaning.

The whole question of history of consciousness, however, would lead us afield. I wish now to recall only the manner in which the argument of this book suggests the idea of an attack on history of consciousness by way of the dismantling of its founding event, the Fall of Man. The discussion of Goethe and Harold Bloom in Chapter 1 belongs here, Goethe's sense of the Fall as a hypochondriac myth, which, *as* a myth, marks its tellers not as the degenerate people that the myth actually describes but as a myth-making people, a people of the origin, on the model (publicly) of the Greeks or (esoterically) of the Jews. And Chapters 2 and 3 both focus largely on a typical eighteenth-century poetic logic that begins with exactly the idea of self-reflection that is later developed into a history of consciousness (the poem as a conscious "process," in both Hölderlin and Lessing), but then arrives at a *refutation* of the idea that the tradition and culture of writing represent a fallen state of either individual experience or social integrity.

The most important argument in this connection, however, is the one on the subject as signified of the social in Chapter 4. That argument must not be watered down; it must stand or fall, as an interpretation of eighteenth-century literary culture, on the basis of a strict understanding of the notion of the semiotic signified (as distinct from the referent), the signified in the sense that it can receive no attributes whatever except by way of the signifier. My use of the name "subject" for that signified is already an inherently unstable interpretive act, based on what I have called a triangulation with respect to the inescapable referential gesture of the ego considered as a discursive mode. (Again, it is only the *gesture* that operates here, the implied analogy, for example, to the relation between a word and some physical thing it is recognized as naming; no actual referent of the ego is presupposed.) And I contend that this act, unstable as it may be, does still encompass any notion of a "subject" as the vessel of consciousness. Therefore consciousness can be an attribute of the "subject" only to the extent that it is already modeled in the social signifier, which makes nonsense of the Fall of Man considered as the story of how consciousness constitutes an individual self

that is strictly alone and abandoned in its mortality. The crucial signifying feature of the social for the eighteenth century, I argued, is
misunderstanding. And the signified of misunderstanding is not consciousness or reflection—not even Lacanian *méconnaissance*, which
still requires too substantial a subject—but *irony*, in a sense that no
longer admits individual consciousness as its locus.

Beyond Theory: The New Mythology

The argument in this form tends to become speculative, to lose sight
of its own quality as interpretation. Let us conclude, therefore, by
looking at two relatively late texts in which an eighteenth-century
view of the Fall of Man is summarized: Friedrich Schlegel's "Rede
über die Mythologie" and Kleist's "Über das Marionettentheater."
   The content of Schlegel's "Rede" is the typical three-part progression of history of consciousness. An age of mythologically grounded
poetry is succeeded by an age of fragmented or alienated consciousness in which mythology is no longer possible, in which the poet
must "work everything out from within himself" (FS, p. 312), until
that same alienated consciousness finally arrives at the stage of "ide-
alism," which establishes "a firm point whence human power can
expand and increase in all directions, without fear of losing itself or
its return path" (pp. 313–14). And this idea of literature as the outward form of a historicized consciousness is reinforced, in the context
of the "Gespräch über die Poesie," by the preceding section,
"Epochen der Dichtkunst," which emphasizes the manner in which
natural poetic power is constantly used up by reflection in the form
of imitation or parody.
   But why does Schlegel insist on the idea of a new *mythology*, a
renewal of "the beautiful confusion of fantasy," of an essentially poly-
theistic "chaos" (FS, pp. 315, 319)? Why is the "new realism" not
enough by itself, realism in the form not of a philosophical "system"
but of a "redoubled vitality" arising from the "recognition," in ideal-
ism, of the self-legislating power of mind ("Selbstgesetz") and cou-
pled with intimations of solid objective validity provided by "physical
science" (pp. 314–15)? The establishment of the idealistic worldview
already guarantees "unlimited abundance of new invention, general
communicability, and vital effectiveness." And even if "this phenomenon takes a different form in each individual," does the phenome-

non itself not constitute a new "central point" (p. 312) for poetry? Why must this burning focus of knowledge, of philosophical revelation, be dissolved into the fantastic and chaotic variety of a mythology?

It is clear in any case, if we turn to the context again, that the new mythology in a sense does already exist, in the realm of the *novel*, which the "Brief über den Roman," following closely upon the "Rede," refuses to set off as a separate "genre," but defines simply as "a Romantic book," a book that "presents a sentimental matter in a fantastic form" (FS, pp. 335, 333). Like mythology in the "Rede," the novel is described as a kind of literary "arabesque" (pp. 319, 331); and only "the Romantic" (the matrix of the "Roman" or novel) produces "these eternally fresh blossoms of fantasy" that are "worthy to garland the ancient images of the gods" (p. 335). Like Goethe later, with the idea of a new secular scripture, Schlegel thus views the eccentric and idiosyncratic literature of the novel (in which he makes a point of including personal "confessions" [p. 338]) as an impending but not yet complete historical revelation, as a mythology *in potentia*, requiring only to be recognized and used as such.

Exactly this hovering, moreover, on the edge between the potential and the actual, is then made explicit in Schlegel's idea of a "theory of the novel" which "would itself have to *be* a novel" in its chaotic fantasy, while also being *not yet* a novel, but "an intellectual viewing of its object, in a calm, cheerful, balanced state of mind" (FS, p. 337). And to what type of text does this paradoxical description refer, if not to the type represented by the "Rede über die Mythologie" that we had read only a few pages earlier? For in insisting on the vision of a new mythology (not just, say, a new idealistic nature poetry), in thus going one step beyond where its expository logic actually takes it, the "Rede" becomes a kind of fantasy. And yet, at the same time, this leap into fantasy, into a condition just barely short of being what it talks about (a piece of mythology, a "novel"), also *validates* precisely the text's "calm" expository logic, since any less ambitious vision, any vision fully implied and determined by that logic, would by definition not represent the move to another level in the history of consciousness. And thence, by yet another turn of the paradox, it follows that the history of consciousness has no standing whatever as a description of how things actually are in time, since it is validated only by taking on the fantastic, eccentric, idiosyncratic quality of myth.

Mythology, as far as we can tell, is therefore *always* (at best) on the brink of being itself. The fall of humanity into an alienated consciousness incapable of mythology is something that has never happened;[6] or at least we have no way of knowing it has happened, since our renewed mythical mode of being appropriates even the history of consciousness *as a myth*. (We think of Lessing's *Erziehung des Menschengeschlechts*, in which the goal of God's education of us, the morality of the good strictly for its own sake, is the state of not requiring a God to be educated by—or for that matter, to have been educated by.) Even the rigid system of Spinoza's *Ethics*—which is precisely (one would think) the combination of "system" and "realism" that Schlegel denies has a future (FS, p. 315)—turns out to be merely "martial adornment," a suit of armor concealing a profound spirit who promotes mythology by himself *being* a concealed chthonic myth, a new "Saturn" (pp. 316–17). Even the practice of arguing from first principles on a level of maximum generality—even, that is, "the procedure and laws of rationally thinking reason," whose *suspension* is "the beginning of all poetry" (p. 319)—somehow becomes in Spinoza "the beginning and end of all fantasy" (p. 317) and "the general basis and anchor for every individual form of mysticism" (p. 321)—as if the "individual," only one paragraph earlier, had not been associated with a strict "originality" beyond all generalizing (p. 320).

The Garden of Eden

This appropriative tendency of mythology, its transformation into myth of even the historical logic of consciousness from which it itself is supposed to have emerged as a possibility, is also evident in Kleist's "Über das Marionettentheater." The repeated emphasis on whether the various stories told in this dialogue are believable raises, for the reader, the question of the believability of the whole text (HvK, 2:341, 342, 344, 345). If the text is regarded as an essay in the historical theory of consciousness, then its argument rests upon several assumptions that are formulated in a manner that foregrounds their most questionable aspects. "Affectation occurs, as you know[!], when the soul (vis motrix) is located in some point other than the center of

---

[6]On the *persistence* of mythology in modern Romantic consciousness, see chapter 6 of my *Goethe's Theory of Poetry*.

gravity of the movement" (2:341). Why, then, does the (intended?) movement not simply become a *different* movement? "I said that I knew perfectly well[!] what disorders consciousness causes in a person's natural grace" (2:343). How can "natural grace" be known to exist in the first place, if it is always already interfered with by the consciousness that must know of it? Even the mathematical analogies are sloppy (2:343). The logarithmic curve has no asymptote in a positive direction; and a first-order equation produces exactly the straight line from which Herr C. differentiates it.

What we have here, then, is not an essay or a theory but a story, which, like the stories told within the dialogue, requires a specific act of belief on our part. But if there is such a thing as consciousness, then this act of belief will make a substantial difference in it, hence a difference in the truth or falsehood of precisely the story that is to be believed. It is essentially this structure of feedback or self-reference that Paul de Man, in his reading of Kleist, correctly associates with "aesthetic education" more or less in Schiller's sense, which turns out now to be not an extended historical process, but a tight focus of paradox. For a belief in the Fall, in consciousness as the product of an original disintegration, will now tend precisely to *integrate* our consciousness, to produce in it the fallen or alienated state that makes it congruent with its own content (so that its self-knowledge becomes true). And yet, this move of integration also contains an element of ultimately reflexive *violence* by which it is marked not as a refuge for us, not as a paradise, but as a trap, an entrapment in exactly the fallen state it had apparently transcended.[7] It is at this point that de Man's own text, like practically all his writing, becomes self-reflexive. For surely this text's critical mastery of its object— which includes not only Kleist's text, but also "the trap which is the ultimate textual model of this and of all texts" (PdM, p. 290)—is yet again that hopeless move of self-integration by which the Fall, yet again, is enacted and confirmed.

But this whole structure of paradox presupposes the attribution to consciousness of a substantiality sufficient to support structuring, sufficient to support, for example, a judgment concerning its integrated or disintegrated state. De Man insists, "One should avoid the pathos of an imagery of bodily mutilation and not forget that we are dealing

---

[7]Paul de Man, "Aesthetic Formalization: Kleist's *Über das Marionettentheater*," in PdM, pp. 279–81, 288–90.

with textual models, not with the historical or political systems that are their correlate" (p. 289). But his last paragraph, in its entirety, reads:

> But *Fälle* [*sic*], of course, also means in German "trap," the trap which is the ultimate textual model of this and of all texts, the trap of an aesthetic education which inevitably confuses dismemberment of language by the power of the letter with the gracefulness of a dance. This dance, regardless of whether it occurs as mirror, as imitation, as history, as the fencing match of interpretation, or as the anamorphic transformations of tropes, is the ultimate trap, as unavoidable as it is deadly. [P. 290]

This may not be a historical or a political pathos, but it is definitely the pathos of fallen consciousness that Goethe called "hypochondria," the pathos of a self-seemingly tough-minded acceptance of the consequences of critical thought, an acceptance that actually only sustains by sheer insistence the substantial ("unavoidable" and "deadly") consciousness from which it suffers.

Is de Man right to agree, by implication, with Goethe, in attributing a pathos of this type to Kleist? It seems to me that once we recognize this pathos in de Man—the pathos of the *problem*, which finds problems everywhere: in reading, mimesis, education, interpretation, the aesthetic, the use of examples in philosophy, even in driving a car—we must be struck precisely by the contrast with Kleist's text, which, we have seen, treats its complex presuppositions as if they were simple facts, and which closes with its narrator in a state of mind he describes not as consternation or critical stimulation or even concentrated attention, but as *distraction* (HvK, 2:345). De Man of course recognizes that there is a problem here; but his aroused "suspicion" (PdM, p. 269) leads him only as far as the "ambiguity of the word ['zerstreut,' 'distracted']," which he claims "then disrupts the fluid continuity of each of the preceding narratives" (p. 289).

Kleist's narrator responds enthusiastically to the story of the bear, and then becomes distracted during Herr C.'s drawing of general conclusions from that story. Indeed, the question he now asks could be understood as an ironic dismissal of those conclusions: "Therefore we would have to eat of the Tree of Knowledge again in order to fall back into the state of innocence?" (HvK, 2:345). (The mocking[?] incongruity of "falling" into a "state" or "standing" is even clearer in the German.) Perhaps the narrator has begun to understand that it is only the story that matters, the story as a narrative act, more or less in the sense of Schlegel's new mythology. His remark, in any case, does develop Herr C.'s abstract speculations in a historical direction.

What actually distracts him, however, what the back of his mind is busy with while he asks his last question, is probably the *form* of the two main metaphors in Herr C.'s elucidation of the bear story. For in both of these metaphors, the actual extent of the history of consciousness, the space between original and renewed innocence, is represented as a dimensionless *point*, the point beyond which the angle between two intersecting lines reappears, or beyond which the image, now reversed, reappears in a concave mirror. The metaphor of a laborious trip around the world to seek a back door to Paradise (HvK, 2:342), or of the meeting of the extreme ends of the "ring-shaped world" (2:343), is now superseded. The problem has now been reduced to a *point*, to a focus of paradox: which is to say, to the question of why on earth we bother to fence with the bear in the first place; why we insist consciously on the problem of consciousness and so only repeatedly reestablish the infinitely self-reflexive, hence insoluble problem that torments us; why we thus actually create that huge imperturbable mythical bear, that *Ursa major*, which can "read our soul" (2:345) only because it is the very substance of which our "soul" is incessantly reconstructed.

And once this question is asked, the answer is obvious. That punctual instant of infinitely problematic consciousness is nothing but the needful irritant, the splinter in our foot (HvK, 2:343), by which the integrity of our being is made accessible in the domain of representation—*our* being, in the sense of the Goethean nos, not "my" being. It is the ground that we marionettes brush against only in order to reenergize our mobility (2:342)—we little maries, we irreversibly virginal spirits whose very seriousness is always also "a rejection of the seriousness" we insist on (PdM, p. 286). Even if we use that ground for resting, even if we make a huge philosophical-historical system of it, a "phenomenology of mind," it is still really only a part of the game. And if, eventually, the army of readers in the manner of de Man does find a back door to the Garden of Eden, even they shall be welcomed there by Kleist and the rest of us, and given to drink equally from the Big Dipper of the new eighteenth century.

Index

352 Index

Library of Congress Cataloging-in-Publication Data

Bennett, Benjamin, b. 1939
    Beyond theory : eighteenth-century German literature and the
poetics of irony / Benjamin Bennett.
      p. cm.
    Includes bibliographical references and index.
    ISBN 0-8014-2841-6 (alk. paper)
    1. German literature—18th century—History and criticism.
2. Irony in literature. I. Title.
PT289.B38 1993
830.9'006—dc20   92-46530